Dear Miye

Mary Tomita

ASIAN AMERICA

A series edited by Gordon H. Chang

The increasing size and diversity of the Asian American population, its growing significance in American society and culture, and the expanded appreciation, both popular and scholarly, of the importance of Asian Americans in the country's present and past—all these developments have converged to stimulate wide interest in scholarly work on topics related to the Asian American experience. The general recognition of the pivotal role that race and ethnicity have played in American life, and in relations between the United States and other countries, has also fostered this heightened attention.

Although Asian Americans were a subject of serious inquiry in the late nineteenth and early twentieth centuries, they were subsequently ignored by the mainstream scholarly community for several decades. In recent years, however, this neglect has ended, with an increasing number of writers examining a good many aspects of Asian American life and culture. Moreover, many students of American society are recognizing that the study of issues related to Asian America speaks to, and may be essential for, many current discussions on the part of the informed public and various scholarly communities.

The Stanford series on Asian America seeks to address these interests. The series will include work from the humanities and social sciences, including history, anthropology, political science, American studies, law, literary criticism, sociology, and interdisciplinary and policy studies.

Dear Miye

Letters Home from Japan, 1939–1946

Mary Kimoto Tomita

Edited, with an Introduction and Notes, by Robert G. Lee

STANFORD UNIVERSITY PRESS
STANFORD, CALIFORNIA

The costs of publishing this book have been supported in part by an award from the Hiromi Arisawa Memorial Fund (named in honor of the renowned economist and the first chairman of the Board of the University of Tokyo Press) and financed by the generosity of Japanese citizens and Japanese corporations to recognize excellence in scholarship on Japan.

Stanford University Press
Stanford, California

Printed in the United States of America

CIP data are at the end of the book

To Miye, whose free spirit is now soaring among the constellations she loved

and

To Ira Condit Lee and Mickey Fong Lee

Author's Preface

"I want to live fully, and to taste life to its fullest heights and depths," I wrote on April 5, 1946. Looking back over this series of letters from 1939 to 1947, I see how close I came to realizing this goal I had set for myself. My heights were achieved most of all in relationships with close friends such as Miye and Kay, but also in those times when I was elated by the beauty of nature or had won some small victory for justice. On the other hand, the depths were when Pearl Harbor left me stranded in Japan, lonely, hungry, and ready, in my despair, to enter into an arranged and loveless marriage.

How fortunate I was to have close friends who inspired me to write my innermost thoughts and feelings, especially during times of change and stress. Writing was a form of therapy that has stood me in good stead all these years. I hope that readers will be encouraged to write and keep journals and letters. There is much satisfaction and revelation in reading them in later years.

While working on this book, I realize that my pen seemed to flow when I wrote in anticipation of events to come and when I reflected on these events. I never wrote when events were actually happening. Also, I find it very easy to write to intimate friends, for the words pour out without any effort.

As a young Japanese American woman I was faced with so many problems. What was the meaning of life and how did I fit in? One big problem was identity—just who was I? Was I Japanese? Was I American? Before going to Japan I had dealt mostly with people in schools, sheltered by and large from discrimination and racism. In Japan I was surprised to find that I was so different from the Japanese, and not accepted by them. Gradually I came to realize that my upbringing and environment had made me more American than Japanese.

But when I read my letters now, I realize I had never resolved this question of identity because I was always looking down not just on the Japanese but even on the Nisei, with whom I shared very little sense of community. Is this a manifestation of self-hate? I cringe now to see how arrogant and self-righteous I used to be toward others of my race. Only through these letters did it become clear to me how much a product of this sexist and racist society I was. It never occurred to me, for example, to question how minorities such as Koreans, Burakumin, and Ainu were treated in Japan. I was so naive that I felt no identity with other oppressed minorities there or in the United States. Nor did I see the dangerous implications of emperor worship. Incredibly, I even called only white Americans "Americans," as if we people of color born in the United States were not Americans as well.

Yet in these letters I can also see my growth and development from the unworldly young provincial who arrived in Japan in 1939. At first envious of the rich Japanese and their possessions, especially their beautiful art objects, I came to see how transient these things were, that what really mattered were inner resources and close relationships. At first prone to make snap judgments about people I met, I came to see that outward appearances could be deceiving, that what really counted were shared interests and values.

As a stranger in a foreign country, away from home for the first time in my life and with only a passing acquaintance with the Japanese language, I often felt as though I would burst if I could not express myself. So writing letters was a means of assuaging my loneliness and lack of close friends. My joy and salvation was above all in writing letters to Miye, my dear friend from childhood days. And she valued them enough to save them.

The war put an end to our correspondence; it was impossible to write to anyone back home. Though I could and did write to friends in Japan, what copies I kept were burned in the Tokyo air raids, along with my journals. For the sake of continuity, I have drawn on memory to reconstruct them here as best I could.

After the war, when I went to work for the occupation forces pending my repatriation, I returned to letter writing with a vengeance, overjoyed at being able to communicate with Miye and my family after the long endless years when I did not know whether they were dead or alive. Repressed for so long in Japan, I needed to tell my close friends all the feelings and thoughts that had been pent up inside me for years. Besides, I had to relieve the boredom of sitting in an office with nothing to do. I kept carbon copies of most of these letters.

It is my hope that the letters presented here will strike some universal chord with those who have had to adjust to different cultures, and specifically, with those who, like me and my fellow Nisei in Japan, had no choice but to do so. I will feel rewarded if they bring some understanding to those who have never been in similar situations. Perhaps these letters will show also that people are fundamentally the same, regardless of culture and place, that everyone deserves to be treated with dignity and respect, and that tragedies and adversities strengthen a person as long as they are met with a positive attitude. Finally, my hope is that these letters will commemorate my long precious friendship with Miye and others.

So many friends and relatives have helped and encouraged me in writing this book that I am afraid if I name some, I will overlook others. However, I do want to thank those who have been so supportive over the years in so many different ways.

First of all, I owe a great debt to my dear friend of over sixty years, the late Miye Yamasaki Nishita, who valued my letters from Japan so much that she saved them even though she had been forced to leave home and live in a concentration camp, like other Japanese Americans, during the war years. I do regret that this book was not published while she was still alive.

I am indebted to Robert Lee, who first saw the possibility of a book in my box of old letters. He and his wife, Jennifer, visited me many times and hosted me twice in Providence, Rhode Island. Besides making crucial and creative decisions, Bob has put much time, money, and work into the project, for which I am very grateful.

The following people have helped me fill in the history of our family: my siblings Emma Himeno, George Kimoto, and Blanche Baler; my nieces Emma Lee Yu, Laura Baler, Claudia Baler, and Diana Kimoto; and my old-time Modesto friends Masako Kiyoi, Ada Haratani, and Thelma Couchman. Among those who have helped to do the same for the years in Japan are Yuki Crider, Clara Seko, Ann Hashimoto, Kimi Sugamura, Tomi Okada, and Michiko Nagumo. I am indebted also to Izaya Nagata and Kiyoko Kurosawa for sending me old photographs for inclusion in the book.

Karen Perkins, Roger and Julia Estrella, Charlotte Fonrobert, and Gloria Morita have patiently taught me the fine art of word processing and generously let me use their computers. Masako Hamada, David Coates, Hisayuki Ishimatsu, and Noriko Kato, with their expertise in Japanese language, history, and culture, have been invaluable sources.

Toyoji Tomita, my son, and Marianne McDonald, my daughter-in-law, have done work for me on computers and printed out the manuscript. They have always been present to listen and give advice.

My precious friends Lucy Ijichi, Miya Okawara, and Julianna Rousseau have given me continuing moral support and acted as sounding boards for many years. Others who have been supportive in various ways are Lloyd Nebres, Dorothy Wong, Choi-sing Louie, Donna Kato, Stephen W. Foster, Yoshio Fukuyama, and Ronald Fujiyoshi.

I can never thank Judy Yung enough for sharing her time and advice as an experienced librarian, professor, and author. She has always been wise and encouraging, from the beginning all the way to publication.

Finally, I would like to thank the knowledgeable and patient editors at Stanford University Press who have shepherded this project to completion: Muriel Bell, Amy Klatzkin, and Barbara Mnookin.

M.K.T.

Editor's Preface

Mary Kimoto's letters are reprinted here with minimal editing. Where long passages were repeated in letters to her two principal correspondents, Miye and Kay, I have deleted the less informative passage. The capitalization of institutions and the like has been standardized to some extent; obvious typographical and spelling errors have been corrected; and in the few places where the syntax created confusion, it has been changed. Inevitably in correspondence that takes place over an extended period of time and often under stressful circumstances dates of letters are sometimes in error. In addition, not all the original letters survived intact; on occasion pages are missing or a misinserted carbon failed to record parts of pages. In such cases we have tried to reconstruct letters as best we could from both the logic of the text and memory.

Unfortunately, the journal and other materials Mary wrote during the war were destroyed in the Tokyo air raids. In their absence, I have used several "letters" from the collection that she submitted as an English term paper in 1947 to cover the war years. Based as they are on Mary's memories and imagination, they are as authentically her voice, it seems to me, as the letters that survived. All are clearly designated by an asterisk on the dateline. In the postwar letters I have included a few letters from Mary to her sisters Emma and Blanche where they provided context.

A few notes on style: Mary herself almost always gave Japanese names in the Western manner. In my Introduction, Epilogue, and footnotes, I have preferred to use the conventional Japanese form, with the surname first. The exception is Japanese authors of works published in English, whose names are given as they appear in print. Many of the names of private individuals have been changed for the sake of anonymity. I follow Mary's practice of omitting macrons on these and other Japanese words. Italics are generally used for Japanese terms except when those terms have entered into English usage.

Since she wrote almost daily to Miye and then to Kay, Mary necessarily filled her letters with the minutest details of her days, telling them that she washed her hair or ironed that morning and the like. Some of this kind of material has been retained to preserve the flavor of the correspondence, but much has been pared out. I chose not to show these cuts with the conventional ellipses, which promised to be both a needless distraction and an aesthetic disaster.

I would like to thank the following people for their help in various ways: Mari Jo Buhle, Joanne Melish, Susan Smulyan, and Dana Takagi for their helpful comments on the Introduction; Kathy Franz and Yuko Matsukawa for their help in research; and Nan Boyd, Stephanie Fujii, Emily Houh, Jennifer Ting, and Bonnie Youn in preparing the manuscript. A special note of appreciation goes to Gordon Chang, Editor of the Asian America series, and Muriel Bell, Executive Editor of Stanford University Press, who early on saw the value of this project and stayed with us to the finish.

R.G.L.

Contents

Dear Miye

Introduction

On December 2, 1941, Mary Kimoto and over a hundred other Americans boarded the SS *Tatsuta Maru* in Yokohama and set sail for California.[1] Six days later, while the ship was still steaming across the North Pacific, the Japanese Imperial Navy launched its attack on Pearl Harbor. Notified of the attack, the *Tatsuta Maru* immediately reversed course and returned to port. As the passengers disembarked, the *kempeitai*, or military police, carefully registered and interned all Americans of European descent as enemy civilians. But they virtually ignored Mary. She, along with twenty thousand other Americans of Japanese ancestry, was stranded. It would be a long five years before Mary Kimoto would again be able to leave Japan and make her way home to her family in the United States.

In the seven years from her first arrival in Japan in the late summer of 1939 until her departure in the early days of 1947, Mary's life and her worlds in the United States and Japan would be irrevocably transformed. Mary recorded those transformations in hundreds of letters to her family and to her two best friends, Miye Yamasaki, her dearest friend in California, and Kay Oka, another young Japanese American stranded by the war in Japan. With a few exceptions, this book is a selection of Mary's letters to Miye and Kay. The letters tell the story of one Japanese American woman's courageous struggle

1. The *Tatsuta Maru* was at the time one of the largest civilian passenger ships afloat. Another American of Japanese ancestry who tried desperately to return home on it was Iva Toguri, who after the war was prosecuted for her radio broadcasts to U.S. troops as "Tokyo Rose." See Masayo Duus, *Tokyo Rose: Orphan of the Pacific* (Tokyo, 1979) for a detailed account of Toguri's persecution by the postwar press and judicial system in search of traitors.

to survive, physically and psychologically, in the storm of two countries at war with each other. Mary's letters provide a vivid view of Japan on the eve of war with the United States and a moving account of the years of hardship during that war and the first years of the Allied occupation. Her letters to Miye and to Kay not only chronicle the struggles that these women faced in surviving in a world of upheaval and often bewildering change, but also celebrate the friendships that made survival possible.

As soon as Mary returned to the States, she sat down to write a memoir of her experiences. In the decade immediately following the war, however, Americans sought to weave a single story of the conflict, a nostalgic epic of unity and heroic sacrifice. Alternative stories that might have disturbed this master narrative were unwelcome. The notable exception was John Hersey's report *Hiroshima*, which appeared in 1946. The Japanese American (Nikkei) community tried to fit its own experience into this orthodox vision of the wartime experience. In 1957, when John Okada published his now-classic novel, *No-No Boy*, which explored and attempted to heal the still-open wounds within the Nikkei community, the book met such a cold rejection that it was quickly withdrawn by its publisher, Charles Tuttle.[2]

When Mary Kimoto put her letters and her memoir away in 1947, they became quite literally part of the hidden transcript of Japanese American history. Had they been published at the time, they would have been the first English-language account of a Nisei woman's experience.[3] It had predecessors of a sort, to be sure. In 1928, Etsu Sugimoto, the daughter of a Japanese aristocrat who emigrated to New York as the wife of a Japanese merchant, wrote her autobiography, *Daughter of the Samurai*. And a half dozen years later, in 1935, Shidzue Ishimoto, the daughter of a peer and the wife of a baron, published *Facing Two Ways: The Story of My Life*, which included an account of her travels in the United States and her work as a progressive feminist in Japan.[4]

But neither writer could of course speak to the Nisei experience. And when Mary left for Japan in 1939, those who could speak to that experience were just beginning to find a literary voice. Their principal outlets even then were limited to the English-language sections of Nikkei community newspapers. Among the notable works of the time was Taro Katayama's short story "Haru," which appeared in the journal *Reimei* in the spring of 1933; it por-

2. Reprinted Seattle, Wash., 1979.

3. Nisei (lit., second generation) refers to the sons and daughters born to Japanese immigrants (Issei, first generation). Although these terms are used for overseas Japanese generally, here they refer to Japanese Americans. The term Nikkei refers to all Japanese residing in America, regardless of generation or citizenship.

4. Republished Stanford, Calif., 1984.

trays the bleak dilemmas of a young Nisei woman coming of age on a poor family farm in central California and facing an arranged marriage to a man she cannot stand.[5] The advice columns of Mary Oyama Mittwer, who counseled young Nisei on ways to negotiate the difficult shoals of dating and interracial relations, also found a wide and enthusiastic audience in this period.[6]

The war and internment ruptured any chance that Nisei writers might have had to gain access to an audience outside the Japanese American community. Although internment camp newspapers continued to publish an occasional short story, few accounts of Nisei life aimed at a wide non-Nikkei audience appeared in print before the end of the Second World War. Toshio Mori's short stories depicting life in the Nikkei communities, which had begun to appear in magazines such as *Common Ground* in 1940, would have to wait until 1949 to be collected and published.[7] In the same year, "Seventeen Syllables," Hisaye Yamamoto's poignant short story of a woman's bitter life on a family farm in central California, appeared in *Partisan Review*.

It was not until Monica Sone published her autobiography, *Nisei Daughter*, in 1953 that we had a book-length account of a Nisei woman's life.[8] Like Mary, Sone was in her early twenties when the war broke out. Sone's account of her life and struggle for acceptance in American society is sharply marked by the traumatic experience of being uprooted and interned. For her, the racial shadow of being Japanese was "a problem of blood," and acceptance in American society required a rejection of her family and heritage. She remembered a childhood trip to Japan as marking the sharp difference between her American self and the Japanese Other.

Another young Nisei, Charles Kikuchi, a graduate student in social work when the war broke out, kept an extensive diary of his experiences during internment, an edited version of which was published in 1973 as *The Kikuchi Diary*.[9] The entries in Kikuchi's diaries, written at the behest of the Japanese American Evacuation and Resettlement Study, the social research arm of the War Relocation Agency, are a detailed, if somewhat detached and restrained, observation of life in the early days of the internment. The distance that is apparent in Kikuchi's account is perhaps a measure of his self-consciousness

5. Reprinted in Janice Miritikani, ed., *Ayumi: A Japanese American Anthology* (San Francisco, 1980), pp. 120–29.

6. See Valerie Matsumoto, "Desperately Seeking 'Deirdre': Gender Roles, Multicultural Relations, and Nisei Women Writers of the 1930's," *Frontiers*, 12.1 (1991): 19–32.

7. Toshio Mori, *Yokohama, California* (Caldwell, Idaho, 1949).

8. Monica Sone, *Nisei Daughter* (New York, 1953).

9. *The Kikuchi Diary: Chronicle from an American Concentration Camp*, ed., with an Introduction, by John Modell (Urbana, Ill., 1973).

as a young social scientist writing for a quasi-official readership and may also reflect his prior estrangement from his own family and the Nikkei community at large.

Mary was roughly the same age as Sone and Kikuchi when she began writing home to California from Japan. Although their backgrounds were wholly different—Sone's parents ran a hotel in Seattle, Kikuchi's father was a barber in Vallejo, California, and Mary was from a farm in the Central Valley—they had all shared, to varying degrees, the ambivalence of being Nisei in America. They faced rigid racial discrimination by American society on the one hand and cultural marginalization by the Japanese Issei generation on the other. Despite this shared ambivalence, these three narratives, when read against one another, reveal the wide range of the Nisei's wartime experience and the vastly different ways in which they responded to it. Mary's narrative details a quite different, though equally traumatic, experience from that of either Sone or Kikuchi. Her letters, written for a private audience, without the self-consciousness of publication or official review, reveal a greater range of raw emotion, from ambivalence and confusion to anguish and anger, than either the self-denying Sone or the distanced Kikuchi.

In the face of the erasure of the Nikkei experience from the American historical record, Mary's correspondence and memoir constitute what Michel Foucault has called a countermemory, which is to say, a trace of the resistant strain that ruptures the continuity of official history. Mary's letters tell, on the one hand, the unique story of a young Japanese American woman from rural California defining herself against the demands of both American and Japanese cultures, at the very moment these two societies went to war with each other. From moment to moment, between the summer of 1939 in prewar Imperial Japan and the winter of 1946 in American-occupied Japan, Mary's marginal status in both societies demanded that she constantly adapt to both freedom and constraint, comparative luxury and extreme hardship, insider privilege and alien status. Against the canvas of global politics, Mary's letters record very personal struggles. It is precisely in her specific and particular experience of these years that Mary's letters gain their power as countermemory. Mary's letters challenge "the omissions, exclusions, generalizations, and abstractions of history,"[10] reminding us that millions of ordinary people, unable to control the events that shaped their lives, experienced those events in ways not often echoed in our public histories of war.

Letters from one friend to another operate in fundamentally different ways from the kinds of media—news stories, official reports, and diplomatic

10. Natalie Zemon Davis and Randolph Starn, "Introduction," *Representations*, 26 (Spring 1989): 5.

correspondence—that produce the public record. Unlike historical narrative or journalism, which hold fact and objectivity at a premium, Mary's letters make no pretense of distance from an event. Furthermore, since like most letters they are written as part of an assumed dialogue, there is an open-ended quality to their rhetorical strategy. In anticipation of a reply, historical judgment is never fully foreclosed. In the context of the established relationship, the letter writer invites her reader to share her experiences as an emotional participant in the event. Where official history sees the event as an explosion of meaning into social space, personal letters document the event as implosions upon an individual who is always at their center. Unlike the public record, which encodes events in terms of social importance, private transcripts document them as the emotional catalysts of subjectivity and relationship, as contextual elements in experiencing the self. The letter writer is called forward not as a witness, but as the narrator of her own history.

Reading letters written as private communication demands a reorientation to the particular use of language. Letters script a relationship. They contain subtexts of cues whose intention is to elicit a specific emotional response. Familiarity between correspondents allows written language to drift closer to spoken language as the writer imagines the presence of her reader and imagines the letter itself as a performance. In this sense, letters have a ritualistic quality that is not immediately accessible to the public reader. Often, the letter writer deploys a personal vocabulary, words whose encoded meanings are shared by the correspondents and whose use underlines the relationship between them. In order to decode this language, the public reader is compelled to enter into that relationship.

Such private vocabulary need not be esoteric to encode personal meanings. For example, in Mary's letters to Kay and Miye after the war, she frequently uses the word "Jap" in reference to the Japanese. Her use of this term, its public meaning so encrusted with racism and freighted with the uprooting, incarceration, and dispossession of Japanese Americans from the West Coast, including Miye and Mary's own family, seems, from our vantage point, jarring and out of place. Yet within the safety of their friendship, Mary is free to use the pejorative to signify her anger at the maltreatment of Nisei in Japan during the war and to distinguish herself as an American of Japanese ancestry in a situation (the American occupation) where the choice of Japanese or American identity is always presented to her as binary and exclusive.

Preparing such a private correspondence for publication is therefore a somewhat daunting task, especially when the letters tell the story of great personal strength and courage. Reading someone else's letters is an inherently illicit experience. The public reader is an unanticipated reader—an interloper, an eavesdropper, a voyeur—and, moreover, is aware of it. This knowledge introduces moral uncertainty and a necessary contingency into the reading. This is felt all the more acutely in the process of transforming a previously private conversation into a public text. However, in the initial process of reading hundreds of letters, a number of themes immediately revealed themselves as principles for shaping this collection. Of course, Mary's experience as a Japanese American in Japan in these turbulent years tells a unique story. Just as significant is the way in which her letters demolish the stereotype of Japanese American women, particularly those of her generation—particularly those brought up in isolated rural settings—as mute, almost uncomprehending. Mary's letters demonstrate an intellectual liveliness and a love of literature and culture that is broad and well articulated. Her letters abound with references to poetry, fiction and philosophy, the movies, and especially the Bible. Religion played an important role in Mary's life. Brought up under the strong influence of the Holiness church, an evangelical strain of Protestantism that flourished in her community, she rebelled against the narrow and more provincial of the denomination's teachings and strictures as she was exposed to new ideas and experiences. Even so, a more internalized if less prohibitive Christian faith sustained Mary through her most difficult years during the war. The letters also reveal the extent to which Mary not only had close and intimate relations with Miye and Kay, but also enjoyed a wide range of friends, both Japanese and non-Japanese, in California and Japan. The occupation brought new hazards for a young woman who spoke English, working mainly with white American soldiers. Many of the letters in the last part detail the day-to-day joys and trials of having to negotiate through the thicket of sexual politics with little but her own dignity for protection.

California Days

Mary Kimoto was born in 1918 on her family's twenty-acre farm in Ceres, California, a sleepy town of about four hundred people in the fertile Central Valley seven miles south of Modesto. Her father, Kimoto Kusutaro, had left Wakayama Prefecture to come to America just before the turn of the century. Though not one of the four main "emigrant prefectures" that supplied immigrants to the United States, Wakayama had seen a dramatic rise in the proportion of farmers driven into tenancy, from 18 percent in 1873 to 47 percent in 1892, and had sent a steady stream of agricultural workers to Hawaii and the West Coast in the late nineteenth century.[11] The eighteen-year-old Kusu-

11. See Alan Moriyama, "The Causes of Emigration: The Background of Japanese Immigration to Hawaii, 1885 to 1894," in Lucie Cheng and Edna Bonacich, eds., *Labor Immigration Under Capitalism: Asian Workers in the United States Before World War II* (Berkeley, Calif., 1984), pp. 258–62.

taro joined their number after the crops on his family's farm failed two years running. He arrived in San Francisco in 1895. Like hundreds of other young Japanese men he found work in the city as a houseboy, began to study English, and then moved on to a new job, in this case, as a cook in a lumber camp in Nevada.[12] There he saved enough to buy a small parcel of land in Ceres.

In 1898, as he was arranging to buy his farm, Kusutaro met the Rev. Shimanuki Hyodayu, who was traveling up and down the West Coast observing the conditions of Japanese immigrants in the United States. Shimanuki was the founder and principal of Nippon Rikko Kai, a Christian academy that prepared young Japanese for emigration to the United States, Brazil, Peru, and other parts of the world.[13] The young farmer asked Shimanuki to help select a wife for him from among the young women who hoped to come to the United States.

That process led to Kusutaro's marriage to young Kanazawa Toku, six years his junior. Toku's mother had died when she was very young, and her father worked as a baggage clerk at the train station in Yonezawa, an inland city in northeastern Japan. From her father, an educated man, and others, Toku had heard much about America, and after her conversion to Christianity by a missionary in Yonezawa, she decided to emigrate to the States. Hardly anyone ever left that remote mountain village, and for someone, especially a young woman, to go to faraway America was virtually unheard of. But Toku was determined to go and could not be moved. She traveled to Tokyo to enroll at Rikko Kai in order to prepare for the journey. When Kimoto Kusutaro returned to Japan in 1910, he met and married Toku. Shortly thereafter, they returned to his farm in California.

The Kimotos had five children in Ceres. Their first child, a son, died in infancy. A daughter, Emma, was the next, followed three years later by George. Mary was born in 1918, when Emma was five and George two. Six years later, their baby sister, Blanche, was born.

Although Kusutaro had little formal education, he built his own house and successfully managed his farm, trying out many different crops. The whole family worked on the small plot, where they grew mostly grapes, asparagus, watermelons, lettuce, green onions, tomatoes, and strawberries. In some seasons, to supplement his own crops, Kusutaro would buy another farmer's crop, often grapes, and the family, perhaps with the help of some hired workers, would harvest and sell it. From time to time, especially when they had grown strawberries, Toku would hire four or five pickers to help

12. Evelyn Nakano Glenn, *Issei, Nisei, Warbride: Three Generations of Japanese American Women in Domestic Service* (Philadelphia, 1986), pp. 28–31, 107–8.

13. See Yuji Ichioka, *The Issei: The World of First-Generation Japanese Immigrants* (New York, 1988), p. 13.

with the harvest. In addition to working in the fields, weeding and picking, the girls helped their mother with the household chores and laundry. When hard times hit in the Depression years, George, then in high school, worked as a hired hand at a nearby large fruit orchard during summer vacations, and after he graduated from college, he went to work at the orchard year-round.

The Kimotos had six Nikkei families as neighbors in Ceres, the Ishidas, the Sumidas, the Matsushiges, the Kimuras, the Kiyois, and the Suzukis. About a dozen children from these families attended the local elementary and high schools with the Kimoto children. In addition, there were dozens of Japanese families in the nearby towns in the 1920's, as well as substantial Nikkei communities in both Modesto to the north and Turlock to the south. Often Kusutaro would go by horse and buggy to the Yamato colony in Livingston, fifteen miles away, where he had Wakayama kinsmen and friends. Established in 1906 as a cooperative Christian community, the colony could count over a hundred residents by 1915.[14] Mary's father maintained these ties as the children grew up, frequently piling the whole family into the car to visit his Yamato friends to discuss problems and get advice.

The Central Valley had been the site of considerable anti-Japanese agitation since the late 1880's, when Japanese agricultural workers were first employed in the area. In 1913, only three years after the Kimotos purchased their farm, California passed the first Alien Land Law, prohibiting immigrants who were ineligible to become naturalized American citizens—which at the time meant Japanese and Chinese immigrants—from purchasing farmland. Then, as the agitation against Japanese immigrants continued unabated, a series of even stiffer federal, state, and local laws and ordinances was enacted, sharply restricting Japanese immigration and the ability of Japanese immigrants to make a living in America. By 1920, California had amended its Alien Land Law with the intent of driving Japanese immigrants off their farms. In July of the following year, armed gangs attacked and drove Japanese farmworkers from the towns of Hopland in Mendocino County and from Turlock, only a few miles from Ceres. Though anti-Japanese sentiment was widespread throughout the Pacific Coast and discrimination against the Nikkei was commonplace, the most intense violence was focused on Japanese farmworkers. Outbreaks of violence against Japanese laborers were not rare in the early 1920's; night-riding attacks similar to the one at Turlock occurred in 1922 in Delano, Los Angeles, and Porterville.[15]

Although under intense legal and economic pressure, Japanese families like the Kimotos who owned their own farms went largely unharmed. Day-

14. See ibid., p. 149; and Kesa Noda, *Yamato Colony* (Livingston, Calif., 1981).
15. For details on the Turlock incident and similar attacks, see Ichioka, *Issei*, p. 251.

to-day relations between the Japanese families in Ceres and their white neighbors were cordial, if not intimate. Blanche recalls that their close neighbors the Baltazars, an immigrant family from Portugal, would sometimes keep an eye on the Kimoto children when Kusutaro and Toku were both out working in the fields or called away. When the Kimotos were sent into internment during the war, Robert Baker, a local fruit broker, watched over their farm.

Apart from casual visits among the Nikkei families from time to time, the Kimotos' social life was organized around the church they helped to found—the Holiness congregation in Modesto. In addition to the Kimotos, the Yamasaki, Kawamura, Kiyoi, and Yamate families attended regularly, as did several single Japanese men. Most of these churchgoers did not live in Modesto either, but unlike the Kimotos, they did not own their own farms.

For Mary and her friend Miye, church was an all-Sunday affair. The Holiness denomination, which developed a following in the Japanese immigrant community in the 1920's and 1930's, had sprung up in the rural American South, a product of a schism that fragmented the Methodist church in the 1870's. At the turn of the century, Nakata Juji, a former Methodist evangelist who had studied at the Moody Bible Institute in Los Angeles, returned to Japan to establish a branch of the Holiness church. In 1917, Nakata founded the Oriental Mission Society Holiness Church in Japan and became its first bishop. His son, Nakata Ugo, held prayer meetings in Hollywood, and in 1921 the Japanese Holiness Church was established in Los Angeles. By the mid-1920's, Holiness congregations could be found in the California Nikkei communities of Los Angeles, Modesto, Baldwin Park, Centerville, and San Lorenzo, as well as in Hawaii and Washington state. The church preached an evangelical gospel that included a belief in the imminent Second Coming of Christ and demanded the discipline of a plain and unworldly life, coupled with loudly demonstrative prayer, personal testament, and hymn singing.[16]

It was at these services that Mary and Miye as boisterous nine-year-olds began the intimate friendship that would last a lifetime. One of the early Holiness ministers who had come from Japan tried to reform the girls into quiet and obedient Japanese maidens. The attempt backfired: the two friends, finding comfort in each other, became still more rebellious and noisy, even though their mothers scolded them and reminded them that when Jesus appeared in the clouds for his Second Coming, they would not be taken up with him. Their mothers, too, were great friends, "Bible-toting mamas" who visited all the nearby Japanese and tried to convert them.

The girls were required to sit through long Sunday services, including

16. See *Nihon Kirisuto-kyo rekishi dai jiden* (Historical Encyclopedia of Japanese Christianity; Tokyo, 1988), pp. 560, 939, 990.

hour-long sermons in Japanese. To alleviate their boredom, they read the only book permitted in church, the Bible. In this way, both girls became well versed in both the Old and the New Testament, and the holy book had a major influence on their thinking.

Although the elder Kimotos had come to the United States with relatively little formal education, they were both determined that all their children, including the girls, should receive a college education and not have to spend a lifetime in back-breaking labor on the farm. After Mary finished high school in Ceres, she enrolled at the two-year Modesto Junior College. Mary's sister Emma had gone there for a year, and a dozen or so Nisei from Livingston and Modesto were attending. Miye graduated from high school in Modesto and joined Mary at MJC. They both worked as "school girls" in homes about a mile away from campus, earning their room and board by cleaning house and preparing the meals.[17] It was in these two years that Mary and Miye's friendship really blossomed. They walked to school together nearly every day, and often in the evenings, when they had finished the dishes at their respective houses, they would get together and talk endlessly about everything under the sun: religion, philosophy, and people. They found in each other a kindred spirit with a love of reading and poetry and great curiosity about the world around them. In the years that they were separated, it was easy for them to open their hearts to each other in letters.

When Mary started at MJC, she was not sure what she wanted to study. She liked science and loved nature, so the idea of becoming a botanist appealed to her. Her studies ran mostly to science; chemistry and bacteriology were her favorites. But she also enjoyed philosophy and the two literature courses she took. It was at college that Mary began to have doubts about the Holiness theology. Whenever she had asked questions at church, the answer would be, "Have faith—don't question anything." Mary thought that it did not make sense that God gave people brains but did not want them to use them.

Like thousands of other young Japanese Americans graduating from college in the late 1930's, Mary faced the dilemma of having a degree with little prospect of suitable employment. She could go on to the University of California to pursue her passion for botany, but the prospects after that were bleak. She could continue to work as a housekeeper, get a job in a Japanese-owned shop, or go back to the farm; few other employment opportunities existed.

17. In a labor market where employment opportunities were limited to working on a farm or in domestic service, hiring out as a "school girl" housekeeper for room, board, and spending money while studying in college or completing high school was a common practice among young Nisei women. Indeed, in San Francisco over 60 percent of Nikkei women were employed as domestics before the Second World War. See Glenn, *Issei, Nisei, Warbride*, pp. 122–28.

Spending some time in Japan, learning the language, renewing ties with relatives she had heard of but never met, and becoming acquainted with the culture of her parents seemed like a natural way to avoid this problem, at least temporarily. Mary's mother was particularly eager to have her widowed father meet his grandchildren. Mary's older sister, Emma, had already spent a year at the Japanese mother church of the little Holiness congregation in Modesto; and their brother George had studied for two years at Waseda Kokusai Gakuin, the international institute later affiliated with Waseda University. He had come back to Ceres full of enthusiasm for the bachelor life in Japan.

In June 1938, Mary graduated from MJC and moved to Tiburon, a small, affluent community near San Francisco, to earn money for her passage to Japan by working as a full-time maid for a young well-to-do couple. Full-time work as a domestic turned out to be far different from earning one's way through school as a housekeeper, and Mary found it not at all satisfying. Like many other well-educated Nisei women in her position, she rankled at being treated like a servant. After a year, when she had saved enough for the trip, Mary set off for Japan.

Japan Under the Clouds of War

In June 1939, Mary left San Francisco bound for Yokohama. At the dock to see her off were her family (except for Emma, who was studying at Drew University in New Jersey) and her best friend, Miye. When she arrived three weeks later in Yokohama, Mary was met by a Rikko Kai teacher, who took her to the house of Mr. Nagata, the academy's principal. The Nagatas were a large family with seven children, five of whom still lived at home. A daughter, Miyoko, and two of the sons, Yoshiya and Izaya, were about Mary's age.

At the time Mary arrived, there were many thousands of Nisei in Japan, including by the estimate of Yamashita Soen, about fifty thousand from the United States and Hawaii.[18] Some had come there hoping to find careers in which they could use their education; others were looking for spouses; still others wanted to spend a year or two studying the language and taking in the culture of their forebears. But most had come just to visit relatives they had long heard about and never met.

The large number of American-born Nisei in Japan, as well as the numerous Nisei from Brazil, Peru, Korea, Manchuria, the Dutch East Indies, and Indochina, generated considerable interest and curiosity among the Japanese.

18. Yamashita Soen, *Nichibei o Tsunagu Mono* (Those Who Link Japan and America; Tokyo, 1938), pp. 173–74. Yamashita does not seem to have counted as Nisei the many Kibei, U.S.-born Japanese Americans who had been sent to Japan at an early age to be raised by grandparents or other relatives while their parents worked in America.

Many of the young people had enrolled in Japanese universities and colleges. Waseda and Meiji universities had the largest contingents, with about sixty and fifty, respectively, but Hosei, Rikkyo, Keio, Toyo, Doshisha, and Ryukoku universities all had some foreign-born Japanese students. In fact, there was a whole industry of preparing the Nisei for university study in Japan. Among the institutions offering such programs were the Aoyama, Waseda Kokusai, and Nichigo Bunka academies and the Aoyama, Kyoto Heian, Hiroshima-Sanyo, Sutoku, and Koryo middle schools. Young Nisei women had their choice of several programs, too, at such institutions as Nippon Joshi Dai (Japan Women's College), Tokyo Joshi Dai, Surugadai Jogakuin (the YWCA), and Chiyoda Josen.[19]

The interaction among the young Nisei and their Japanese hosts, however, was fraught with ambivalence. In his sympathetic account of the American Nisei experience in Japan written in 1938, Yamashita attempted to dispel the widely held perception among the Japanese that their U.S. cousins were materialistic, ignorant, and ill-mannered. These young people, Yamashita pleaded, needed to be better understood, since they faced not only a barrier of racial discrimination at home in America, but the barriers of custom, education, and culture in Japan.[20]

Mary's letters to Miye on her arrival in Japan express the full range of her reaction to a foreign land, from wonderment at the sophisticated metropolitanism of Tokyo, with its crowded Ginza shopping district, theaters, and parks, to revulsion at the "primitiveness" and "dirt" of the rural villages, to awe at the tranquil beauty of the landscape. Mary was excited to be in this altogether different environment, whose culture and language she did not understand, for even though she might look Japanese, her background and ideas were indelibly American.

The U.S. Nisei were expected to "chew gum on the streets, to speak a loud mix of Japanese and English . . . and to wear their hats cocked."[21] Though it cannot be said that Mary did such things, she did behave in ways that surprised and sometimes dismayed her hosts, the Nagatas. As soon as she enrolled at the Waseda Kokusai Gakuin (Waseda International Institute), she became the first woman to sign up for the kendo class. Kendo, Japanese fencing, was a fierce sport and a male preserve; proper young ladies were not expected to consider kendo an appropriate extracurricular activity. It was with considerable delight that Mary could report to Miye on the notoriety that accrued to her for crossing this boundary.

Though Mary arrived in a country that had been at war with China

19. Ibid., p. 157.
20. Ibid., p. 3.
21. Ibid., p. 146.

for two years, life in Tokyo, even as shortages were already being felt, was certainly more exciting than anything Mary had experienced in Ceres or Modesto. In 1932, through the incorporation of outlying suburbs and villages, Tokyo had become the seventh largest city in the world in area and the second largest in population. In cosmopolitan sophistication, Tokyo was the equal of any other national capital. Despite the war, the coffee shops and cafes of the Ginza remained open late, the movie houses, cabaret revues, and kabuki theater drew crowds, and the symphony still performed, although its programs now reflected a particularly strong taste for German composers like Beethoven and Wagner. Although Tokyo had lost out on its bid to host the 1940 Olympic games, Japan's new professional baseball league (stripped of its Americanisms) competed with sumo wrestling for sports fans.[22]

Immersed for the first time in a whirlwind of entertainment and culture, Mary often stayed out until eleven or midnight with friends from school, exploring the Ginza, attending concerts, going to the movies, and talking about everything. The Nagatas were scandalized by this behavior; the more so since their son Izaya happily acted as Mary's guide to the great city of Tokyo. For her part, Mary was chagrined when she was admonished by Mrs. Nagata and hurt by the accusation that she had led Izaya astray. The Nagatas' traditional expectations rankled her. She and Miye had always prided themselves on their identification as *otemba*, or tomboys, with independent and free spirits. The freedom, openness, and adventurousness that Mary and Miye sought for themselves was indeed the template against which Mary measured all her relationships. Her letters to Miye are replete with disparaging comments about the "oyome-sans," the young traditional brides, and the "ojo-sans," the filial daughters whose obsequiousness Mary disdained. In the 1930's, under the hegemony of successive conservative military-dominated governments, the public role of women was increasingly circumscribed. To meet the demands for labor and conscription, the military governments made a high birthrate a national priority. The roles of dutiful daughter and mother were elevated above all others for women. Even the noted feminist Yamada Waka, long an advocate of legal protection for mothers and children, was induced to proclaim the sanctity of the family and the special duties of motherhood.[23] This form of Japanese womanhood, at least as it was traditionally and customarily practiced, held no attraction whatever for Mary.

On her arrival in Japan, Mary had defined herself as a distinctly Japanese American woman by her dress, behavior, and attitudes. As speculation and

22. See Edward Seidensticker, *Tokyo Rising: The City Since the Great Earthquake* (New York, 1990).

23. See Tomoko Yamazaki, *The Story of Yamada Waka: From Prostitute to Feminist Pioneer* (Tokyo, 1985).

rumors of war between Japan and the United States spread, she confronted the potential of conflicting political values and loyalties. Both in her private conversations with her friend Izaya and in her discussions with students at school and the senior Nagatas, Mary tested her ideas about the differences between Japan and the United States. In both countries, the political loyalties of the Nisei were a matter of open speculation. Yamashita's study of the American Nisei had found, despite disappointment and frustrations about racial discrimination, an overwhelming loyalty to the United States. When pressed, although they dreaded the idea of a war between the two countries, the Nisei he interviewed were virtually unanimous in their willingness to fight for the United States against Japan. It was for this reason, when a rapprochement between Japan and the United States still seemed possible in 1938, that Yamashita optimistically referred to the American Nisei living in Japan as "those who can bridge the gap" and called upon them to return to the United States to help bring about an understanding with Japan.

The Trauma of War

George's cable sending money for her trip home in September 1941 was the last Mary heard from her family in the States until the end of the war. Her correspondence with Miye was suddenly broken off as well. For the first time in her life, with no money from home and no more of the letters that had buoyed her spirits over the past two years, she was thrown completely on her own resources in a foreign land. Even if regular mail between Japan and the United States had not been halted, paper and ink were hard to come by. Besides, Mary had to attend to the matter of survival.

Once the *Tatsuta Maru* returned to port, Mary called again on the Nagatas. But the Nagatas, with a large family to support, were quite poor, and with the strict restrictions on food supplies, they were in no position to take her in. Mrs. Nagata advised her to continue her enrollment at Joshi Dai and to place her name on the family register in her father's village so that she could be issued a rice ration. Even early in 1941, Mary had written that food in Tokyo and other consumer goods were hard to come by. She did not want to burden anyone else as an extra mouth to feed, and since she had not received any instructions or information from the U.S. consulate or the neutral Portuguese government, which represented American diplomatic interests in Japan, she registered.

That was to prove her undoing, for registry in one's family records was later held to imply application for Japanese citizenship, and, for thousands of Nisei, this act alone put their American citizenship in jeopardy. Moreover, because, under the principle of *jus sanguinus*, the Japanese government deemed any person of Japanese descent a national and did not recognize the Nisei's American citizenship, it refused to consider them eligible for repatriation to the United States or for the protection of the neutral Portuguese government or the Red Cross. Japanese Americans stranded in Japan thus lost all contact with their own government for the duration of the war. Although the police had always kept track of the Nisei in Japan through the system of family and neighborhood registries, after the outbreak of war with the United States, the military police also took an interest in their surveillance. While seemingly allowed a freedom not open to their compatriots, American citizens of Japanese ancestry were placed in "double jeopardy," first with the Japanese government and later with their own government.

When Mary reenrolled in Joshi Dai in January 1942, she took a job once again as a "school girl" domestic, in the employ of Mrs. Sakai, a doctor who ran a small private hospital in Tokyo. In return for room and board, Mary worked essentially as a scullery maid in the kitchen, scrubbing the floors and washing vegetables outdoors in ice-cold water. In addition, Mary was expected to teach English to Mrs. Sakai's young son. Mrs. Sakai treated her American housekeeper with utter contempt, lording it over Mary at each report of a Japanese victory over American forces. Luckily for Mary, this arrangement ended after two months, when one of Mary's teachers noticed her distress and distraction in class and arranged for Mary to live in a Joshi Dai dormitory, where her only duties were to tutor Japanese students in conversational English.

By 1943, the civilian economy in Japan was in shambles. Fresh vegetables were a rarity, and even rice, rationed by the end of 1940, was in short supply. Scrap metal drives stripped the school rooms and dormitories of iron stoves and radiators. Mary's classrooms were so cold that it became impossible to take notes. As early as 1941, the government had begun periodically mobilizing students to do manual labor. Initially, they had been put to such tasks as policing the grounds of their campuses, but by 1943, classes had become sporadic as students were recruited to work in munition plants, factories, and fields. Students on their own planted sweet potatoes to supplement their meager rations. It began to be whispered that Japan was losing the war.[24]

During these difficult times, Mary supplemented her teaching income by translating a Japanese history textbook into English for a professor at her former school, Waseda Kokusai. Although every family was by now working desperately to keep body and soul together, a few Japanese families continued to befriend her. For her part, Mary helped her friends at times by traveling

24. Thomas R. Havens, *Valley of Darkness: The Japanese People and World War II* (New York, 1978), pp. 114–32.

on the overcrowded trains to outlying districts to buy food from the farmers or barter clothing and family treasures for precious food.

As the war dragged on and day-to-day hardships worsened, hatred of America became more intense and widespread. Being seen reading an English-language book on the streetcar could bring an angry rebuke or even assault. The American Nisei struggled to remain inconspicuous. Nisei students gravitated to the families of their Nisei friends who had come to Japan before the war. Only here were they able to speak English and express their feelings openly. It was at this time that Mary became close friends with Kay Oka, a casual friend before the war and now a classmate at Joshi Dai. Kay's father had moved the family from Seattle to Tokyo in the late 1930's to further his business interests in Japan and Korea. The Oka home became a haven for Mary as she and Kay discovered that they had much in common. They both hoped to reclaim a freedom of spirit, and increasingly they shared a disdain for the suffocating insularity and arrogance they felt around them.

Mary was graduated from Joshi Dai in September 1944. By that time, the chronic lack of nourishment had taken its toll on her, and she fell ill with jaundice. Other students had been able to supplement their diets with food packages sent from local kinfolk, but Mary's relatives in the countryside were unable to spare anything. While she was still at the college, Mary was invited to stay with the family of a Holiness church minister in Hokkaido. Though the Reverend Ito Kaoru, whom Mary had visited before Pearl Harbor, had been arrested and imprisoned because, like many Holiness ministers, he had refused to recognize the divinity of the emperor, his family welcomed Mary into their midst. Gradually in the relative peace and quiet of Hokkaido, Mary regained her health.

To Mary in October 1944, the future seemed hopeless, and the war appeared to have no end in sight. With no employment prospects in the now completely devastated economy, Mary faced a grim struggle for survival. At that moment a ray of hope appeared in a proposal of marriage by the brother of a Joshi Dai schoolmate who had been friendly with the Nisei students. For Mary this was a chance to become part of the well-to-do and presumably enlightened Kinoshita family. The father of the prospective groom had, after all, studied in the United States and sent his three daughters to the exclusive and progressive Joshi Dai. Mary would have preferred a marriage to Izaya Nagata, who had been her closest friend in Japan. She was quite sure that Izaya, then serving in the Japanese navy, cared for her, but she felt that Izaya's mother would object to their marriage. In fact, Mrs. Nagata seemed relieved that Mary would be taken care of by the Kinoshitas and encouraged her to accept the offer.

After the traditional marriage interview with Kinoshita, arranged by a go-between, Mary consulted with her friends, who with only one exception advised her to go through with the arrangement. In the end, despite some misgivings, Mary gave in to the lure of security and married Kinoshita.

The marriage was a disaster for Mary from the first. Even in the relative tranquility of the late 1930's, Yamashita Soen had observed that among Nisei "who came to Japan after they were fifteen years or older and married Japanese, 90 percent [of the marriages] ended in failure." Indeed, the differences of ideas, customs, lifestyle, and background were so great, he said, that it would take another book to explain the reasons for this dismal record.[25]

During their short honeymoon, Mary's new husband ignored her completely, preferring to read. The couple lived with his family, where the young husband spoke only to his parents and sisters and never to Mary; he preferred to communicate with his bride through his mother. Although this was common practice in traditionally arranged marriages in Japan, it was a devastating blow to Mary. During the few months that they lived together under the same roof, Mary, in desperation, would even write letters and notes to him. None ever brought a reply.

Worse still, her new husband soon returned to Shanghai, where he worked for a trading company, leaving Mary in Tokyo to live with her in-laws. Her mother-in-law was an upper-class woman from Kyoto, the most conservative and traditional of all Japan's important cities. Mrs. Kinoshita attempted to make Mary into a traditional oyome-san, completely subservient to her husband's mother. Once again, Mary was cast into the role of servant.

Even sharing the hardship of the last years of the war was not enough to bridge the huge chasm of expectation and behavior between Mary and her in-laws. After the devastating firebombing raids on Tokyo and other cities in March 1945, Mrs. Kinoshita brusquely reported to Mary that her son had told her not to add Mary's name to the family register and to dismiss her with 500 yen. Mary was dumbfounded, hurt, and insulted, but since she was penniless, she accepted the money and, joining the stream of women and children whom the government order evacuated from the cities as the air raids became systematic, she sought refuge with her aunt in Wakayama.

The Aftermath of War

In Wakayama, Mary shared the abject poverty of her aunt's family, who welcomed her despite their own miserable circumstances. Kay and her mother had also fled from Tokyo to Wakayama. Although they were shocked to see

25. Yamashita, *Nichibei*, p. 171.

the conditions in which Mary was living, the three nevertheless shared a joyous reunion.

For Mary and Kay, the end of the war truly arrived when together they watched American GIs come ashore at Wakayama harbor. In a memorable outing, two GIs gave them rides all around the Wakayama countryside in their troop carriers, singing and laughing. Even the C rations tasted wonderful after years of chronic hunger. The GIs urged Mary and Kay to get jobs with the occupation government, which was just then being set up.

Mary and Kay moved to Osaka, where they rented a room from a Japanese family and found their first jobs with the occupation forces. Mary worked in the American Red Cross canteen, and Kay in the ARC office. But for Mary, Kay, and thousands of other Nisei who had been stranded in wartime Japan, the most important job was getting back home.

Few had anticipated how difficult this would be. For a start, with the collapse of the Japanese empire, the victorious Allies, embodied in the Supreme Commander for the Allied Powers (SCAP), the occupation government, faced the massive problem of dealing with millions of uprooted and displaced people. The U.S. State Department estimated that there were over twelve million such people in various parts of Japan, including millions of Korean, Taiwanese, and Chinese workers and thousands of others from Southeast Asia, Okinawa, and the Pacific Islands. At the same time, some three million Japanese citizens in Manchuria, Taiwan, China, Korea, and Southeast Asia were pressing to return home to Japan.[26] SCAP was given the task of facilitating this massive relocation. One stipulation imposed on Gen. Douglas MacArthur by the State-War-Navy Department Coordinating Committee in Washington was this ominous directive: "Persons of the Japanese race claiming citizenship in any United Nation should be repatriated only upon concurrence of the government of such nation."[27]

We do not know exactly how many Japanese Americans were in Japan at the outbreak of war or how many survived. Though Yamashita estimated that there were as many as fifty thousand U.S. Nisei working, studying, or visiting in Japan in 1938, many had managed to return home before Pearl Harbor. Even so, some twenty thousand are thought to have been stranded there. Of these, hundreds, if not thousands, were almost certainly killed in the atomic bombing of Hiroshima, since it was the home prefecture of many emigrants to the United States, and many of the Nisei would have sought refuge with relatives there late in the war. Roger Baldwin, reporting on his mission on

26. Jane Perry Clark Carey, "Displaced Populations in Japan at the End of the War," *Department of State Bulletin*, 13 (Oct. 7, 1954): 530–37.

27. "Draft Directive to the General of the Army Douglas MacArthur Regarding Aliens," U.S. State Department, *Foreign Relations of the United States, 1946* (Washington, D.C., 1947), 7: 242.

behalf of the Japanese American Citizens League in 1946, put the number of U.S. Nisei then living in Japan at ten thousand, whereas the occupation authorities estimated the number to be fifteen thousand in late November 1948.[28] The considerable discrepancy between these two estimates can be explained, at least in part, by the return of some eight thousand Nikkei to Japan in 1946. Among these Nikkei who, under the extreme duress of internment, had chosen to be repatriated were not just first-generation (Issei) immigrants, but American-born (Nisei) "renunciants" and their Sansei (third-generation) children.[29] The SCAP directive that persons of Japanese ancestry would be allowed to return to their country of citizenship only on its concurrence repeated the racial logic that had led to the internment of Japanese Americans during the war. For thousands of Japanese Americans who had been stranded in Japan, the battle to have their citizenship reinstated and to regain their right to return home would be long and arduous.

The U.S. Immigration and Naturalization law of 1907 stipulated that people could lose their U.S. citizenship if they became naturalized citizens of another country. However, what constituted "naturalization" differed from country to country. In the case of Japan, the simple act of entering one's name in a family register, or what was called the "recovery" of nationality, was interpreted as naturalization. Nevertheless, the 1907 U.S. law had also allowed all Nisei who registered to claim dual citizenship. That option was eliminated under the Immigration Act of 1940, which went into effect at the end of January 1941. Under that act, the recovery of Japanese nationality was defined as naturalization, and Nisei who were entered in their family register after January 1941 automatically lost their U.S. citizenship.

There was, of course, a cruel irony in this state of affairs. The very Nisei who had not claimed dual nationality and had most carefully preserved their U.S. citizenship as their sole nationality came under the greatest pressure and hardship, once hostilities broke out between the United States and Japan. These Nisei suffered the loss of their American citizenship when they were finally forced by the need to survive to register on family rolls. For the thousands among them who could not recover their citizenship through the American consular offices in Japan, the journey home was often circuitous. Hundreds had to sue in Japanese courts to have their family registrations nullified; hundreds more had to sue for relief in American courts.

28. Roger Baldwin, "The Nisei in Japan," *Common Ground*, 8 (1947–48): 24–29; General Headquarters Supreme Commander for the Allied Powers, *History of the Non-military Activities of the Occupation of Japan, 1945 through 1950*, 6: *Legal Reform, Public Safety and Freedom of Expression*, part 4: 67.

29. For the tragic story of these so-called "renunciants," see Michi Weglyn, *Years of Infamy* (New York, 1976).

Mary was extraordinarily lucky in dealing with the seemingly arbitrary bureaucracy that controlled her right to return home. For her, the most difficult aspect of recovering her citizenship was the confusion surrounding the procedures for accomplishing this task. Rumors abounded in the dispersed and still relatively isolated community of stranded Nisei. Mary and Kay would ask officers and GIs alike, but no one seemed to know what procedures were being set up. From time to time, the *Pacific Stars and Stripes*, the American military newspaper published in Tokyo, printed articles and letters discussing the issue, but no official notices appeared. Finally, Mary received word through the grapevine that the U.S. consulate at Yokohama was taking applications for the restoration of citizenship. She immediately went there. At the consulate, she filled out a lengthy form, which chronicled her residence in Japan during the war years. Consular officials asked Mary whether she had served in the Japanese military, whether she had voted in Japanese elections, and whether she had worked in a job reserved for Japanese nationals only. Able to answer "no" to each of these questions, Mary found her application for the reinstatement of her American citizenship routinely approved.

In 1948, SCAP officials reported that over 3,000 of the 15,000 Japanese Americans had already reestablished a valid U.S. citizenship and departed for the States; that 2,923 others who had recovered their citizenship had decided to remain in Japan, many working for the occupation administration; and that about 1,800 would ultimately be able to recover their citizenship. Therefore, a combined total of 7,700 or about half the Japanese Americans in Japan, had had or were about to have their U.S. citizenship restored.

Working for the Occupation

Mary and Kay stayed together in Osaka until Kay returned to school in Tokyo. After a short stint as an interpreter-typist for the Signal Corps in Osaka, Mary moved to Kyoto to work first for the Inspector General's office and then with the Chaplains' Office, where she found congenial military and civilian co-workers.

Mary's separation from Kay, with whom she had shared both the despair of the war years and the heady jubilation of the first year of peace, together with the relative luxury of paper, typewriter, and time, brought a flood of letters to Kay from Kyoto. At the same time, through the Red Cross, she was able at long last to contact her family and then, thanks to her sister Blanche, to renew her correspondence with Miye. It was through these letters from the States that she learned what had befallen her family and her best friend on America's home front.

On May 12, 1942, the Kimotos, along with all the other Nikkei families in the Modesto area, were rounded up and taken to an "assembly center," hastily constructed on the Merced County fairgrounds. They stayed there until the end of August, when they were taken to the Amache Relocation Camp in Colorado. Amache (along with Jerome in Arkansas) was one of the smallest internment camps, each with about seven and a half thousand internees. Located near Granada, a tiny town of about two hundred people in the southeastern part of the state overlooking the Arkansas River, the camp was desolate, the land barren and beaten by sun in the summer and whipped by icy winds in the winter. Sand storms were frequent, and the place provided a hospitable home for only snakes, scorpions, and desert tortoises.

In the fall of 1943, the War Relocation Authority began a program to relocate internees to Midwest and East Coast cities. Eager to get out of Amache as soon as possible, the Kimoto family soon scattered across the country. Emma and her husband took jobs teaching Japanese at a navy civil affairs training school at Harvard University. George and his family left Amache to work on a farm outside of Chicago. Blanche left camp to enroll in South Dakota Wesleyan College. Eventually, George decided not to try to return to California and arranged with Robert Baker, the broker at the fruit orchard where he had worked, to sell the farm. After Hilo, Emma's husband, found an apartment in Cambridge, Massachusetts, Emma brought the elder Kimotos, Kusutaro and Toku (by now living in Chicago), to join them.

Miye too had left Amache as soon as she could. By the time she and Mary were finally back in touch again, she was married and living in Maryland, completing work on an M.A. degree in agricultural sciences at the University of Maryland. Her husband, Nick Nishita, was then nearing the end of his tour of duty with the U.S. Army.

Mary's letters from this period provide a revealing picture of daily life in the first years of the occupation. Her bitterness toward the Japanese is moderated by her sympathy toward the victims of the war and the poverty that surrounded her. Her own position as a Nisei, foreign to both the Japanese and her fellow Americans, was a particularly marginalized one at this time.

Mary lost her first occupation job at the American Red Cross because her supervisor, a white woman from the States, took her independent attitude and outspokenness to be "uppity." In addition to the racism demonstrated by some of her "liberators," there was considerable tension among the Nisei working for the occupation forces. Nisei who had come to Japan with the Military Government often looked down on those who had been stranded during the war.

After Kay's departure for Tokyo, Mary filled the void of loneliness by spending much of her time with her GI co-workers. Her letters to Kay and Miye reveal a good deal about the everyday sexual politics of the occupation. Mary and Kay both dated a number of GIs, looking for companionship and genuine affection, only to find that many of their dates had less-than-honorable intentions. Yet if Mary often complained to Kay of the behavior of GIs and their unscrupulous exploitation of Japanese women, she could also be critical of Japanese women whose morals she believed had been compromised. Nevertheless, she understood the power relationships that created such situations. In one letter to Kay, Mary writes that she thinks it might be fun to take the part of a native Japanese woman, feigning an inability to understand English, to see how GIs would treat her. Putting a sudden halt to this line of thought, she acknowledges that she knows full well how the GIs would treat her. Indeed, even as an American Japanese, she has her hands full keeping the wolves at bay. Mary's letters chronicle her constant negotiation of her tenuous position as an American woman confronting GIs' sexual expectations of Japanese women.

Mary's letters to Miye and Kay cover the full gamut of life in Japan during the first year of the occupation. In addition to her observations about the daily drudgery, cameraderie, and tensions of army life, she reports on the responses of the Japanese to their American conquerors. Still angry over her own treatment during the war, she sometimes seems less than charitable in describing Japanese behavior. But her letters also reveal a healing process well under way. Mary's devotion to the Japanese friends who had stayed with her and helped her weather the war years eventually enabled her to make peace with Japan.

On January 1, 1947, seven and a half years after she had first set foot in Japan and five years after the *Tatsuta Maru* had marooned her in Yokohama, Mary boarded the S.S. *Livingston* for the long trip home. Soon after she was reunited with her parents in Boston, Mary wrote "Dear Kay," a memoir that condensed, reconstructed, and recombined some of her letters to Miye and Kay, and added remembered details. Selections from "Dear Kay" are reprinted here to cover the war years. This moving and imaginative account was written as an assignment for an English course at Boston University. The final sad irony of Mary's wartime odyssey is that her literature instructor, not looking for the unexpected and unable to see its significance, casually dismissed her work. Mary put her writing away. It would be forty-three years before she took her story out again.

The Prewar Letters

1939–1941

HOKKAIDO
Sapporo
Hakodate
Aomori
L. Towada
Akita
SEA OF
JAPAN
Sendai
Yonezawa
Fukushima
HONSHU
Toyama
Tokyo
Yokohama
PACIFIC
OCEAN
Kyoto
Nagoya
Kobe
Osaka
Odawara
Hiroshima
Shimonoseki
Wakayama
Fukuoka
Beppu
SHIKOKU
Nagasaki
Kumamoto
KYUSHU
0
200 km
0
200 mi

Tokyo, August 6, 1939

Dear Miye,

Just read your two wonderful letters and am just shaking with fervor and excitement and gladness for having had the extreme and supreme pleasure of having some of my unadulterated Miye again. Gosh, but it was swell of you to write two letters. And they sounded so much like you! You surely do flatter me but I think that you are the only one who really knows and understands me. You tell me such sweet things.

Life is so different now. What is it, I ask myself, that is so different? Is it that I'm in the leisure class now? I never had so much time to fool around before in all my life. Until now I've always been working or studying. Now I have absolutely nothing I have to do. It is a strange sensation. I can't even read because there's nothing available in English. Life goes along so smoothly and timelessly at my auntie's.[1] She has two maids, and all we do is just sit and talk and lie around. It is heavenly to sit at a set table, eat, and not have to lift a finger to clean up. And not have to clean house.

Rice tastes so good. I've never enjoyed meals so much in all my life. Yesterday I weighed myself and got the shock of my life—I weigh 127.6 pounds with my iron shoes on.[2] Toshi looked at my iron shoes and said boys

1. Ito Yae. The "auntie" is a courtesy title, translating *obasan*. She was actually the sister-in-law of Mary's 28-year-old maternal cousin, Tomi-san. Mrs. Ito, about 40 years old, owned a four-story house in the downtown district of Kanda, and with her husband, ran a business renting out kimonos for traditional dances.

2. Sport shoes that were rugged and heavy.

wore that kind in Japan and I was an *otemba* [tomboy]. He probably thought he was insulting me and didn't realize I was proud of it. How many times have we been scolded by our mother for being tomboys?

They sure have a crude sewer system! My aunt's place in Tokyo is exceptional in having flush toilets, but at the Nagatas' it is all accumulated. In Toyama,[3] I saw a farmer come to collect the night soil in "honey buckets." No wonder the country smells to heaven. In the small towns little streams run in front of the homes, and all the garbage is thrown into it. It is filthy and a good breeding place for mosquitoes. Also, children use it for their bathrooms. Did I tell you I counted 227 mosquito and flea bites on my arms and legs when at my cousin's place? I was scratching all the time, and it was driving me crazy!

You can observe feet at your leisure here. Everyone goes barefooted in the homes. Japanese have fine hands, well shaped with long fingers. I haven't seen a clumsy big hand yet—even among workmen.

The cicada is crying or chirping as you might say. It is getting toward sunset already. Miye, I am proud of you. So you like music now. I long for music. They have some swell records here—classical and it's such a relief to hear old music again in a foreign country. I love Beethoven. Ito-san played the koto[4] for me and I had a hard time trying to keep from going to sleep. Don't you think the samisen sounds sad? I do. But the Japanese say that it is gay. I want to learn ikebana and kendo and judo. O boy—wouldn't I love to know judo and be afraid of no man! There is a satisfaction of being physically superior. It feels so good when you win from a boy—even if he is small.

Tokyo, August 28, 1939

Dearest and only Miye,

Well, Miye, your old friend has seen, done, and absorbed more than at any time in her twenty-two years of existence. You see, I'm twenty-two according to the Japanese way of figuring age,[5] and proud of it. I'm so happy that I can't even write straight. And such nice long fat juicy letters you wrote too. Miye, my *Reader's Digest* has not come, much to my sorrow, but you might as well tell them to cancel the order because Japan and the USA are on bad terms now and they let in nothing from the USA. I'd been hoping that they'd let in private subscriptions but it doesn't look like it. They have no reading matter at all from America here, and I miss it too! So please tell me what's going

3. Toyama Prefecture, in northwestern Japan.

4. A Japanese horizontal harp, somewhat like a zither, with a wooden frame, a curved wooden sounding-board, and thirteen silk strings mounted on ivory bridges.

5. That is, a person is one year old at birth and becomes another year older every New Year. Mary was 20 by Western count.

on—what old FDR is doing, who's going to run for president? I sure miss the funnies, *Blondie*—even more than church on Sundays. Aren't I degenerated!

I've been visiting my relatives in the country. I was at my cousin's place in Toyama from July 30 to August 19, then at my grandfather's[6] in Yonezawa until the twenty-sixth. After returning to Tokyo, I have been at my aunt's place in Kanda. It's been interesting and different, and I don't know where to begin. I'll just write thoughts at random and if you can't understand, think of me as being scatter-brained as usual.

I had a swell time yesterday. (The immediate past blots out most of the remote past.) I went with my cousins to Ueno Park and to the emperor's gardens (but they wouldn't let us enter) and Meiji shrine and another shrine. My aunt's name is Mrs. Ito. She had to stay home, but her little brother and her fourteen-year-old daughter came. She had a guest from Toyama—a man about forty-eight and quiet and reserved and seemingly nice (I don't look under the surface like you) with an enormous nose for a Japanese. Her brother's name is Toshi-san.

Toshi-san was fun. Just a kid, and that's the good part of it—going to Meiji University. We went to the zoo and stared at the animals. That Toshi-san says all the Japanese animals are quiet and pretty while American animals, such as the bison they had, are all clumsy and ugly. We sure get along good. He's full of lies and tall stories. He actually reminds me of you sometimes. But I can't understand hardly anything he says; he has to explain very simply. It's terrible how I can't get the drift of what these people say. It's all right if they only talk, but when they ask questions I can't do anything but show my ignorance. But I don't mind. I like being different. But I got awfully tired of it in the country. I've never been so stared at in all my life. Now maybe I understand how all those animals in the zoo feel. It's kind of fun at first because I flatter myself that I am so lovely and individualistic that they all gaze at me with awe.

But it's more like they glare at me as on some poor ignorant animal which is different. I can't understand it. I don't mind the women staring. I can always look down on them and stare back. Besides, the women are usually picturesque and it's fun to look at them—but the men are not handsome and not so small, so I cannot look down on them so much.

The girls I met on the boat are out in the country and they just hate Japan. One is a kid yet—only a sophomore in high school. She is from Stockton. She surely was cute. So full of pep. We used to play games. The other girl is out of high school and from Salt Lake City. She was kind-hearted and sympathetic. We had a little group. The latter girl and another girl who was Blanche's[7] age

6. Mary's 78-year-old maternal grandfather, Kanazawa Manjiro. He was a widower.
7. Mary's sister, six years younger than she.

but didn't look it. She had two little kid sisters who always tagged around. Those girls got along swell with the sailors and used to always go up front and talk to them. I used to go too sometimes. The sailors were so young. They weren't fresh like American sailors. They were so boyish and funny. We used to play keep away and talk and stuff. There were two brothers from Stockton with us too. One was sixteen and the other about fourteen and they were lots of fun. That Blanche-like girl and I used to fight with the boys and cut up. I had big black and blue marks where they hit me. The boat is fun because it is so temporary I didn't care what other people thought—I did anything I pleased, from talking to Buddhist priests and a young Hawaiian sissy-like preacher to chasing little boys and playing with sailors.

My cousin Tomi-san's husband[8] was at war in China for three years and just came back last month. Tomi said he looks like Mussolini but he hasn't that tremendous jaw. He looks like Charles Boyer, only not as good looking—if CB is good looking. Toshi-chan worships Myrna Loy. Deanna Durbin surely is popular here. Nine-tenths of the movie stars' pictures on sale are of her. They all think she is so cute.

Tomi-san's husband said that when you chop off a Chinaman's head, the blood spurts in two spots for a yard in the air. He used to scare me because he wasn't ever home much, and all he ever said when he was home was "*baka*" [stupid]. Around the time I left I finally was able to talk to him a little. He said that Issa is a better poet than Basho because any one can understand Basho.[9] In order to appreciate a Japanese brush painting one is supposed to sit and look at it for hours, imagining the colors. First time I heard that. He brought back a painting from China of a sage who sits for weeks on a stump of a tree without moving. His fingernails grew three inches long, his whiskers grew, while he meditated on "It is not *yes* and it is not *no*." The idea I think is that there is no affirmative or negative—there is no "yes" or no "no." When I saw that picture I thought, suppose that stump he was sitting on is still alive—would the leaves make a bower around him? Or would the shoots grow through his legs? Isn't that a gory thought? But living plants break rocks, so if a man sat without moving, the plants might grow right through him.

Tomi-san said Americans are Yankees who swallow live goldfish and go crazy over the Dionne quintuplets.[10] In Japan, they look down on multiple

8. Mr. Okada, brother of "Auntie" Ito. Tomi-san had met him while he was a student in Yonezawa.

9. Kobayashi Issa (1763–1827), a Haiku poet whose work is marked by satire and cynicism. His verse is written in a colloquial style and expresses sympathy for the poor and downtrodden. Matsuo Basho (1644–94), one of the most renowned Haiku poets of all time, is credited with transforming Haiku from a popular verse-form based on playfulness into a mature aesthetic.

10. The five daughters born to Oliva and Elzire Dionne on May 28, 1934, in Ontario, Canada. As the first known quintuplets to survive, the Dionnes were instantly world famous.

births and liken them to dogs. They show such handsome pictures of Hitler in their newspapers. Tomi-san thinks he is wonderful and the savior of the German people. She said all the women are crazy about him. Her everyday life consists of reading the newspaper from the beginning to the last page, preparing three meals, and lying around all day. What an existence! She has two girls, aged nine and four.[11] [The nine-year-old is] an *otemba*, the younger one is a bawling baby and stubborn. I bet I was like that when I was a kid. She said Blanche was just like that when she visited Japan with Mama. Every morning I used to get up at six and take radio exercises with the kids at school. All the girls look alike and all the boys are like so many duplicates of the same pattern. Black round heads with hair cut one inch at the most. Skinny, browned limbs, white shirt and black shorts. The girls wear dresses and have their hair cut (in a bowl cut).

We had to go to public baths there, and it is the first time I ever saw so many nudes. You surely can tell how old women are by their skin and shapes. It was dirty and crowded. You see women nursing children everywhere. Lots of women go bare to the waist when cleaning house. The men wear skimpy G-strings. It's all very shocking at first, but maybe it is a healthier attitude towards the body than Americans have.

On the train from Toyama to Yonezawa I came across three men travelling. My mother told me not to talk to anyone on trains, so I didn't say anything until they started talking to me. They had been fighting in China. They said that they camped at night and got water from a pond to drink, and found dead Chinese men floating on it the next morning. One of them talked to me a lot, raving about how great and glorious Japan is, the emperor, the people, Noguchi.[12] I couldn't understand much of what he said, and said "*ah, so desuka*" [is that so?] during the pauses.

In Yonezawa my grandfather lives with his sister. His sister-in-law lives nearby. She was so ignorant and asked the stupidest questions, such as: Do we have a moon in America? Do we have stars? Or thunder? It's so funny how you can trace heredity by our noses—my grandpa, my mother, and me. We all have the same small stubby noses. Grandpa hardly ever says a word, but they said he was very happy to see me.

My aforementioned ignoramus *obaasan*'s[13] cousin was rather interesting. He was of solid build and round-faced, and spoke fast and energetically. I really marvelled at him because *he*—a *Japanese*—said that maybe Japan was

11. Michiko and Eiko, respectively.

12. Noguchi Hideyo (1876–1928), a prominent bacteriologist responsible for several important discoveries in his field, including the fact that malaria is transmitted by the mosquito.

13. "Grandmother" or, loosely, an old woman. Not to be confused with *obasan*, (spelled with one a), which means aunt.

wrong in the Sino-Japanese War. He asked intelligent questions about the U.S. and he spoke slowly so that I could understand him. He said, among other things, that in Japan it is terribly immoral for a boy and girl to shake hands. His 26-year-old daughter seems Americanized because she is not always looking at the floor. She offered to take me skiing if I came in the winter. They love skiing here. In Yonezawa even old ladies ride bikes. I went bicycle riding lots of times.

At Yonezawa they eat from morning to night. They have tea and sweets before breakfast, then whenever they have guests they bring on the food. Oh, but it is torture to have to sit on the tatami! My legs go to sleep, my knees ache, my back aches and I am in such misery. Thank goodness they have a table and chair in my room at the Nagatas' in Tokyo.

Maybe I've only seen the surface of Things as They Seem but they don't treat women bad at all. And I don't see why they say Japan is a man's country, etc. I think it even feels better not to have men opening doors for you and letting you go first. It makes you feel more equal. The girls are not demure little things either, that I've seen. They surely look pretty in their kimonos. Tokyo is not so busy. San Francisco is much busier because Japan has few cars now on account of gasoline is scarce because of the war. This morning I saw a whole streetcar full of soldiers in white kimonos (wounded men). You see soldiers once in a while. Most of the men from twenty-one to thirty-five years of age have gone or come back, except for those attending universities. That girl I met on the train, Chieko, said that during high school a girl can't be seen even talking or walking with a boy without being questioned. She said they can't play at all, so they study awfully hard and wreck their bodies. One of her classmates died from TB because she worked so hard.

I'm so hungry for news from America. Give me all the gossip you can dig up. And anything in the newspapers, *Reader's Digest* or *Life*. Gosh, I miss *Life*. They're not supposed to turn on short-wave here either. I'm tempted to use my charming persuasive powers(?) on Izaya and make him turn on short wave—he's a radio fan. I am going to move when school starts, I think, because it takes one hour to get to school. I ought to make girlfriends because they are more lasting. And you can go every place with them. I don't know if you are right about men and women being the same. You know what Alexis Carrel[14] said about it—that sexes are fundamentally different. Anyway it is a relief not to see all those silly love birds around here like in America. Out in the country (every place is "country" except for Tokyo), you never see a man and woman together except if they are married.

14. Alexis Carrel (1873–1944), surgeon and author of many well-known books, including *Man the Unknown* (1935) and *Reflections on Life* (1952).

On the train when we stopped at a station I saw a soldier carrying a white box containing the ashes of another soldier. He had a sad little group following him—a young woman and some old people. It was a pitiful sight. All the people were hushed and quiet. It surely was sad. The people seem so patient and willing to accept the inevitable. Tomi-san said that in her village there were lots of them killed in the war. One woman in her village saw her son in a dream bowing to her the very night that he was killed. I can't understand it. I wish I knew what they were thinking. When they think of the war they look—I don't know—I haven't seen that look in America. These people seem to have something deep down that I can't reach. Is it fancy or is it real? Especially the country people.

The rice fields are so very neat. There is not one weed. The plants stand in water. The farmers work barefooted in the patches. They look like turtles with straw backs and peasants' straw hats. I have to go to Wakayama next. There I'll see the real country life. I haven't seen the poverty-stricken millions of Japan that I read about in *Reader's Digest.*

They had *Obon* this month from the thirteenth to the sixteenth. In case you don't know, that is when the spirits of the dead return to their living relatives. I was at my cousin's, and they had something like a carnival come to the school grounds. There was one big tent in which they had a marionette show. Then they had a tent in which you could see a ten-legged baby and a baby with fur like a bear and also embryos (human) showing the development until birth. There were various booths selling toys, candies, pencils, etc. The kids loved to go. It was quite gay with the lights and crowds and phonograph records blaring.

Japan was just what I needed. I wanted a change and surely am getting it. I am glad that you did not go to [the] Korbs'.[15] It was such a hard place to stay. I don't see how I stood it for a year.

Harry Tonai's stepfather's girl was just here. I was thinking, another Japanese girl when she suddenly burst out talking English. She's been here two years. The man she came with said that she was going to school preparing to be a *yome-san* [bride]. The girls now in Japan don't have much choice because all the men have gone off and got killed and only the scum are left. The soldiers look so romantic in their uniforms and swords. They have a band of red on their caps and red epaulets on their shoulders; the uniforms are khaki color. I saw some fresh ones at the zoo yesterday (on this side of the cage). They looked so weak and skinny as though they'd blow away.

I surely do miss you. Lots of times I feel so alone and friendless and I

15. The Tiburon couple for whom Mary worked as a maid to earn her fare to Japan. (See the Introduction.) Miye was considering working for them.

think "Miye—on the other side of the world." How I wish you were here! But maybe it's better that you're not because we'd raise the roof. Remember—even on the streetcars in Oakland people used to stare at us, so what would it be like here? I saw a chameleon yesterday. It was a yellow green color and was on brown bark. The fickle creature. Yet I am just like that. You are right—I was very quiet with Elma. In fact—I am quiet with almost every one except you. Miye—do people really bore you? I thought they never. They surely do bore me. But now everything is interesting (for a while) and "to bore" is now a verb of the past.

You are so cute, Miye—I just love to read your letters over and over. I just sit and grin and am happy all the day. School starts September 11 and I can hardly wait. One month went by awfully fast already. (I can't get over how everyone is Japanese here.) It seems so funny that all the people are Japanese. And they are not as Japanese-looking as I expected. I mean—they have quite large noses and eyes too. It's fascinating to sit and observe all the different types of faces. Don't you find men's faces more interesting to study? They seem to have more character than women. The girls are pretty to glance at and nothing more. But men are more varied. Farmer women too. They surely work hard—the farmers. Manpower is the moving force here. Bicycles [are] omnipresent. They carry carts in back of bicycles, and big packs on their backs. You wonder how people can work so hard.

The name of my school is Waseda Kokusai Gakuin. It is a school for those of foreign birth who wish to study Japanese. They teach reading, writing, history and in the second year, Chinese. There are about ten teachers and fifty students. I'm going tomorrow to see if they'll let me in. If George got in I surely can.

I went to Holiness church in Yonezawa with an *obaasan*. They were full of pep and sang and prayed and testified with vigor. That's the way I like to see a church. About fifteen women and two men attended. We had to sit on tatami that was so hard, and I got sleepy. I'm going to go to church in Tokyo because I like the atmosphere and it's good for me to have to suffer a couple of hours a week. I really used to do some deep meditating while *sensei*[16] was preaching long long ago (when I wasn't sleeping).

Gee, it feels swell to be twenty-two. I'm older than you now [counting our ages in the Japanese style]. At twenty-two you have the whole world ahead of you. You have just enough experience and knowledge not to be too dumb. And you're not old, conservative and stolid. I'm a very moody person, yet there is a joy in feeling sad and alone and philosophical. I'd love to go for a

16. "Teacher" or "minister," often used as a term of respect. Here Mary refers to the Rev. George Yahiro of the Modesto Holiness church.

long, long walk tonight and gaze at the stars and think and think. I wish you were here. We used to do that when we were going to JC.[17] Really, though, aren't you glad that you are you and I am I? With all my faults I'd hate to be anyone else. Don't you feel the same?

Now Miye, be sure to write me a book—I'll be looking forward to it.

[P.S.] I'm surprised that you didn't write "Mary, the Kimo" on my letter.[18] I hope we don't have another war.

Tokyo, September 17, 1939

Dear Miye,

I just received your most welcome letter. Now I feel so sad and homesick. Miye, don't ever say things like that, "what if I never see you again." Can't you see that I am trying to be brave and courageously sticking it out these *long* two years. And you don't even help me. You give me a phrase like that to be ringing in my mind. I have thought of it too! I know I'd just die if anything happened. I've thought that "if anything happened to Miye I would be utterly lost." The hope and background of my very being is you.

O, Mary—cut out this kind of stuff! Anyway, Miye, I had a hard time trying to keep from bawling my eyes out when I read your letter and then [as] I looked at your picture, such a feeling of sadness and longing came over me. I have your favorite—maybe you don't remember it—it is of you in typical farmer's clothes—pants—leather belt—shirt—straw hat. You have the cutest expression. That really makes me feel good all over again as though you were laughing at me. And the background of weeds and trees surely is becoming. "Hi! Mon Amie, From the Tomboy Miye" is written in the corner. That is my most treasured picture.

Enough of such sentimentality. And yet, Miye, I'm having quite a time getting adjusted. When I come home from school I feel so lost, my life feels aimless and I ask myself why I ever came to Japan and I feel very moody. I wish you were here. I'd be having the time of my life then. There are so many funny things here if only you were here to giggle at them with me. But I am alone, and I take myself so seriously, and become so introverted. Gosh, Miye, I just cannot stop pouring out all my pent-up feelings to you, so I'll just keep on.

I still haven't got *Reader's Digest* but I got a letter from them same time as yours stating that I was soon to receive it. I hope and hope that it will come. I

17. Modesto Junior College (also referred to as MJC).

18. The Korbs nicknamed Mary "Kimo" (short for Kimoto) because they thought she should have a Japanese name to fit her appearance.

wonder if [the Japanese] censor letters? When I'd read that you'd not received mine yet, I thought maybe they threw it out cause I spoke my mind in the letter. You surely are faithful to write back before even receiving mine. I was thinking the same thing about you, "why doesn't Miye write?"

I've been going to school for one week. (I'm not crazy over it.) There are about fifty boys and nine girls in the whole school, divided into three classes. I'm in the beginning class. (Ah—music! From the next room—he's playing records. I love music and am starved for it now—it just fits my moods now—heck! He shut it off.) As I was saying—that school doesn't seem to be so much. There is one girl who came over on the boat with me from Oakland. Her name is Fumi. Just graduated from high school. She is a nice girl—really. She is in the same class as I and sits with me and we stick around together. But all the girls stick around together. One is from Deutsch and talks like it. Another is about forty years old and a Korean and she's been in America about ten years, graduated from Oberlin and Michigan and was in Hawaii nine years and she is a physical ed teacher. She is kind of funny but rather boring because she takes a long time to say anything and she always tells us to speak in Japanese. One is a Canadian and something like Elsie Noguchi—so dainty. The others are Nisei from Idaho and another from I forgot where. The one I forgot where from is the best I think. There is a girl also from Siam and one from Java. None of them are beautiful but the I forgot where from (Yuki) is cute and so is Fumi, and Tosh is attractive because she paints up and is well groomed. I don't know any of the boys (yet) and only talked to one who rode home on the same trains as I. He is from Siam and is not a twin. He is black—no, not black—a sort of orange-brown-black mixture in the proportions 1-1-3. Mix well and you get his color. He is small and his name is Si or something and is in the same class. I asked him questions and he answered but I don't know what he said, but I tried to act knowing.

And I'm going to take kendo! I tried to persuade some girls to take it with me but they wouldn't except that girl from Siam and she's going to quit. Fumi says she'll lose her dignity. None of these girls look like they'd take it anyway, except for the Korean woman, who said she's already taken it. But I think it's going to be fun. I am as big as the average boy here. So I don't think I'll be too much of a weakling for them. Those girls must want to act like the weak clinging female, but that stuff is not for the likes of me, the big Amazonian! I wanted to take judo too but was too bashful. I'd love to be able to knock down anybody with judo.

One boy in our class was absent Friday because he was home in bed sick from homesickness. His name is Baba. There are two of them: brothers. Most of the kids just graduated from high school. My class is the beginners and is so easy that it is an insult to my intellect. Therefore, I want to get into the first year. I took the test to try to get in to first year and not preparatory but I got the grade of 43%. They said if I study hard they'd give the test to me over again. So I've been cramming and learned all the *kanji* [Chinese ideograms] in [elementary school] Books Three and Four, and now I'm tackling Book Five. If you cracked open my skull now you'd find a lot of jumbled up parts of *kanji* all messed up together. I feel almost as crazy and studious as I did before a chemistry exam.

I got a letter from my ma, and she said not to write so much but to write a lot of letters and then send them all together. That's what I'll do to you. I have to go pretty soon—I have a date! No, not with a male (I'm not that fast—besides they don't do such things in Japan, I think) but with that girl I met on the train coming back from Yonezawa. My mom told me to be sure to go to Holiness church on Sunday and today being Sunday it hurts my conscience a bit to be galloping off. But I read the Bible faithfully when I feel like it.

Got back about six. I had a pretty good time. I met the girl at the train station. (Eki, they call it, and it sounds like Ikky.) She had a girlfriend with her. Chieko is eighteen and her friend is nineteen. They are pretty. We went to the Ginza and walked around and I bought a parasol. It was windy and threatening rain. We walked through a park and then to the Imperial Palace grounds. Only up to the bridge. Everyone bows, so I did too. You can spot a Nisei by the stiff bowing and awkwardness. (Such English.) My head aches and so do my eyes. I've had a cold for over a week now. I have awfully crazy dreams. A psychoanalyst might say I am verging on insanity if he analyzed my dream life. I've dreamt about you but can't remember what it was. I've dreamt about all my friends. That's one sure sign of homesickness.

As I was saying, we walked around Tokyo. Just crowds—you can hardly walk. All the students have on black uniforms. The Waseda cap looks like the cap they wear for graduation minus the tassel. All the university caps are square, more or less. The Koto are round. Koto is equivalent to high school, although this Izaya here insists on calling it college. He's kind of funny. He helps me out a lot in my lessons because he's taken English eight years now. You ought to see the complicated essays he has to read—"Discourse on Roast Pig" and I forgot what else. Anyway they are dry and use mile-long words. A man staying in Rikko Kai dormitory[19] came to have me help him with his English, and boy, did I feel ignorant. There was a sentence five lines long and full of phrases. I couldn't make out what it was. Language like they use in legal papers. Full of whereas, to wit, etc. Something about metaphysical poets. He knew more about it than I did. These people can read a lot of English but they can't even start a conversation. When Izaya said "works," I thought he

19. Mr. Shoji (generally referred to as Shoji-san), about 25 years old.

said "wax." I laugh at them because they pronounce English so funny. They laugh and make fun of my Japanese and the way I write.

Again—I've wandered. We had dinner at a swell place and I paid fifty sen for a hamburger dinner and twenty-five sen for a scoop of ice cream. American food surely tasted good, for a change. Later we went in again to a dining place and they played records and even had an orchestra of four pieces. We sat there for an hour. Chieko was expecting a friend and he finally came. He wore thick glasses almost like my ma's and was kind of stooped and looked like a poor student. He tried out his English on me, but I couldn't understand a word, nor could he understand me. The other girl and I and he went to another eating place and [Chieko's girlfriend] said she forgot her handkerchief at the other place, so I was left stranded with that poor bespectacled guy. Chieko didn't like him so she told that girlfriend that she had to go to her sister's and so we went back. Later I learned that Chieko had met him on the train and asked him to bring some friends but he didn't have any friends. Her brother was sitting with her, and I thought he was someone else that she'd picked up. He was handsome. Such beautiful teeth. All the women and men shave their eyebrows. They look neat. The girls are not so breathtakingly beautiful. I think on the whole that Nisei are better looking than the Japanese young people here. The girls here don't paint up, or fix their hair like mine. Miye—I am disappointed in you—So you've fallen and are worldly now with your frizzed short hair.[20] Send me a picture of you to look at when I feel gloomy. I'm scribbling something awful and my sentences are terrible, but I don't care. I'm so tired. It's only eight yet but I'm going to sleep pretty soon. Tomorrow after school is Kendo! That is going to be fun, I think and hope. Emma[21] said she's going to send me some tennis balls. And I am happy because they don't have tennis balls here. They play with rubber balls. I bragged that I'm a good tennis player—to Izaya and I want to beat him before he gets too good. He's taking it at school. That guy and my mind surely run in the same direction. Sometimes he reminds me of you and then I like him. But he's conceited. And he doesn't tell funny stories like you or get excited. In fact no one gets excited here. They talk softly and accept things calmly. I walk to the station with those brothers when I don't go with the girl. I wish I had you to walk with again. But we might scare those little shopkeepers out of their browned skins by our loud talk and argument and laughter. We surely used to have fun in Modesto, huh? I wonder if we'll ever be together like that again?

I broke a glass out of their window already. The wind is blowing right on

20. Miye had gotten a permanent wave, even though the Holiness church forbade what was seen as a worldly practice. In 1939 the Japanese government discouraged women from getting machine waves as too wasteful of electricity.

21. Mary's sister, five years her senior, the oldest of the siblings.

me now as I sit at the table. Gee, I hope I get the *Reader's Digest*. It's Sept. 17 now, but maybe it will come. Do you remember a Harriet Rose who was in MJC? Emma said you said her head was too big for her. I got a letter from her, and she sent me a picture out of the paper of Mary Jane Klinke and her dozens of attendants. It surely must have been a magnificent affair. How about sending me some clippings in your next letter—my one and only? Anything—any newspaper comments on Japan or America or Europe—or a "Grin and Bear It" [cartoon] or anything at all. I'd surely appreciate it. How I miss the funnies! Their papers seem so empty without them. They were pretty sore about Hitler and Russia. They're glad Europe's at war because then [the Europeans] can't help China. Everyone wants this war to end. Everyone except the munitions makers, I suspect. Because munitions makers headed the list for income taxes. I wish I could read Japanese newspapers. By the end of two years I can, they say. Say, Miye, be sure to come to Japan! And while I'm here. I'll take you around and we can have a grand time.

Think I'll go to sleep now, I'll write later. We only have baths three times a week. You feel so sticky and oily here. I've never been so uncomfortable before. I bet that's the way a doughnut feels when it is fried (me—the cook forever). Anyway, I sure felt good when Izaya was impressed because I took calculus and he said there weren't any girls in all of Japan who took something like that. They don't believe in educating girls here. Their education consists of teaching them to become good obedient *yo-me-sans*. You must think I am crazy about Izaya, but I'm not. It's just that I know so few people here and these people are like my family. I like to fight with Yoshiya. Miyoko, the girl, is handsome; she has wavy hair.[22]

Good night

Tokyo, September 18, 1939

Dear Miye,

Here I am in the first-period class at school. The teacher is very boring and I get so sleepy. He looks like a walrus. He wears glasses, has grey hair, pauses five minutes between every sentence, and is so tiresome. Most of this stuff they teach us is simple and easy. I would much rather be in the regular class, not in the preparatory class. At least that would be hard enough so that I couldn't get bored and sleepy. It's like botany and chemistry. Botany was too easy, but the latter was so hard when he lectured I didn't have time to get sleepy.

22. Mary shared a room with the Nagatas' daughter, Miyoko. Yoshiya was another of the sons at home who was close to her own age.

The trains are so packed! There is no space left at all. Everyone pushes in and you just about get crushed. I'm glad I'm big here for that reason. If you're weak or small, there won't be anything left by the time you get to school.

It rained last night and this morning. The road to the station was unpaved and muddy. I walked to the station this morning with Miyoko—the boys were still sleeping. We have rice, miso soup and pickles every morning. My belt was actually loose this morning. Such a triumph! I do hope I don't get any fatter.

It's so gloomy outside (and in) today. No sun. Every morning there are millions of students in uniform walking along the street. Waseda students and Waseda Koto Gakuin. The people's unpainted little shops look so shabby. They open early in the morning and are open until late at night. Everything is all out. There is no glass. It's all in one room which opens into the street. Things hang from the ceiling. It's rather pathetic how small everything is—people eking out a living on little patches of land. Even on the mountains. Such neat and small patches. In Wakayama my uncle's[23] home surely was poor. At night the mice used to eat the roof and dirty pieces would fall on to our mosquito net. My uncle has two girls. One of them is pretty, and the other has funny eyes. Like my father's one eye except it's both of them. My father's sister has rotten eyes too. Like a dead fish's—blue and runny and it looks so dirty I could not look at them at first.

The pretty sister kind of reminded me of your mother. She works in a cloth-making factory for one yen. And works twelve hours. It is so dirty in that factory. It's nearby and I visited it. It is terribly noisy. Some women work in there bare to the waist.

Hurray! This hour is just about up! I want after school to come so I can do kendo. I want noon to come too. I bring an *obento* [box lunch] of rice and a little *okazu*.[24] All the girls eat down in the basement with the teachers and some of the boys. Everyone is quiet and I feel so funny. They told the girls not to go out to eat because there are too many men students around and besides girls are not supposed to eat out with men.

There is a Chinese boy sitting right in back of us. He surely can write *kanji* well. He is loud and sings popular songs—especially when we have the woman teacher. The old man Benioff was just talking about something onomatopoetic. I'll have to get it from Fumi later. Last night I dreamt I got the *Reader's Digest*.

Now that Japan is not going to fight Russia, the war with China may end.[25]

23. Mr. Teramoto, Mary's father's brother-in-law. Uncle Terry, as Mary called him, had lived for a while at the Kimoto farm before returning to Wakayama.

24. A side dish, usually of fish or meat and vegetables.

25. Japan and the Soviet Union signed a ceasefire agreement September 15, 1939, after the Japanese Guandong (Kwantung) army was defeated in the Nomonhan Incident. This was a setback for advocates of military confrontation with the Soviet Union and allowed those who favored invading southward to gain the upper hand.

I certainly hope so, and so does everyone else. They have no sugar, eggs, butter, cotton or woolen fabrics, or iron. Food is high and so is everything else. The other class is out now—I wish that we could go too. Why do stale teachers always take up more than their time? There's the bell. An old man clangs it. They have a shortage of electricity too now, and they can't get permanents and their electric clocks run way behind.

Tokyo, September 20, 1939

Dear Miye,

Before school—It's raining. Just drizzle, drizzle. It sounded sweet when I got up, but it's not going to be sweet walking through the mud to the train. The sidewalks are so dirty when it rains. I bought an umbrella.

Gee, my arms are sore from practicing kendo. There are 12 in the class, and I am the only girl. It's fun. You think of the stick as a sword and hit your opponent on the head, trying to split him in two. I've even had my name in the paper already. They think it is unusual that a girl would take kendo.

In school—gosh I'm sleepy. This Shimada sensei is a woman and so darned slow and her voice is lulling. She acts to us as though we were little children. I just found out that a Johnny Nakayama is in the next class. He asked if I was from Modesto. He's the guy that used to go around with Mako, isn't he? Well I thought you said he went back to the USA. Fumi talked to him before and said he said Japan is no place for girls. So he must be the same person.

We go sightseeing today. We are going to the Navy building. Good, there's the bell.

Just got back from the Navy building. They had some interesting exhibits, but I couldn't read what they were about or understand the lecturer either. Fumi said that she went to the zoo and saw an American turkey all caged up and exhibited. The people she went with thought she was so funny when she told them that she ate turkey for Christmas.

There are quite a few students from around the [San Francisco] Bay region. Two Babas—one "Porky" Yamada and that Johnny. That's all I know of now. There's one from San Francisco but I forgot his name. He looks like a Chinaman. Fumi is tall and slender, like Tai Tanji. She has round eyes and is cute. She is talkative too and grins all the time and is good company. But no one will ever compare with you. Some boys kind of remind me of you, but boys aren't much help. You can't stick around them. Besides, girls are more social.

Tokyo, October 6, 1939

Dearest Miye,

Thanks a lot for the letter and it surely felt good to hear from you. The letter dated September 14, I mean. I only got it about a week ago. I was surprised that you hadn't received mine yet. Hope they don't censor letters because I surely let myself go and express all my innermost thoughts to *you.*

I am so sleepy (as usual). It is only eight pm yet, too. You know what—I think I'm beginning to get used to Japan and liking it a little. For one thing, I like the family I'm staying with. And school isn't so bad. I have one good friend, her name is Fumi Taira, and she is from Oakland. She surely is lively and fun and talkative. Everyone likes her.

Miye, I'm so happy about receiving the *Reader's Digest*! I've received two all ready. I read every word in them from cover to cover. The old one I let Fumi read and it is still going around the kids at school. I let Fumi have the new one and I've only glanced through it as yet. Even Iza-san reads them. So Miye, you surely have done your good deed and your life has been worthwhile and may God add another room to your heavenly mansion. (Gosh, I'm sleepy.) Did I really used to say "good night" to you at the Wickings[26] to make you go home? I'm so sorry. I wish that you were here now and I swear I'll never be so mean again. Every time I get a letter from you I feel so sad and far away.

Last night I actually went out! I had a really good time, too. I went to the Tokyo Symphony with Iza-chan. Got home at 12. The music was pretty good, considering it's Japan. They played Bach and somebody else and Sibelius. Miye—I think you'd like Sibelius. They played his second symphony last night. I love *Finlandia* by him. If you ever get a chance, listen to it. I'll never forget the first time I heard it. It is so big and grand and impressive. Sibelius is from Finland, and those mighty blasts are like those big icebergs and beautiful frozen blocks like mountains. Anyway, he loves to use contrast in volume. Very soft and very loud. Last night I was so sleepy, this work was the last on the program, and when they played the soft parts, it was so lulling and made me feel so good inside that I practically snoozed off, and then when the music would become blaringly loud, I would wake up with a jolt. It's terrible. I'm paying for having gotten into the habit of sleeping in church and it is so embarrassing. I went to sleep when the professor was speaking in assembly at school.

As I was saying—the symphony. It started at 7:30 and we got out at 9:30. There were thousands of students there. Not so many girls. And all young people because the old Japanese don't like foreign music. They all listened

26. The family for whom Mary worked as a "school girl" while she attended Modesto Junior College. (See the Introduction.)

so attentively, too. It felt good to get into a music-loving audience. Well, the thing was over at 9:30 and it was raining but we walked up the Ginza.[27] Japanese towns are transformed at night—and especially in the rain. For there are bright lights and the reflections in the streets. You see only the clean parts at night. All the little stores are open until ten pm, too. The typical store is one room opening out into the street. People live in the back of that room. We had some icky sweet Japanese stuff to eat and tea. Then I said I wanted to drink some coffee, so we walked about a half mile up to where [Iza-chan] said they have superb coffee but when we got there the place was shut and we were disappointed and got on the train and came home. It was fun because we get along pretty good together. He surely is like you in some ways and I holler at him like at you, only I have to talk slow because I can't talk enough Japanese to go fast. Anyway, it's good practice and I'm learning a lot. I talk to the boys here and learn their slang instead of the polite ladylike flowery language an *ojo-san*[28] like me ought to learn.

I'm still taking kendo. We have it on Mondays and Tuesdays for an hour after school. The beginners haven't put on masks yet, and we haven't done any serious fighting. They holler so loud when they fight and they get exhausted. Sometimes I feel like quitting because I'll never be able to compete with those boys in the class. And it is a waste of time and energy, but I don't care. Every day I play ping-pong with the German girl for ten minutes in between classes. I'm getting to be kind of good for a beginner. I'm crazy about it. It's fun if you hit the ball hard instead of just patting the ball gently over the net. Last Saturday I had a date to study with the girl from Java after noon, but I got there late and she went home. I was to meet her at school, so I was just sitting there when a bunch of University students came along and one asked me to play ping-pong, so I played with them and got beat every time. There was one American boy (who comes to our school) among them and they talked English with him. I was surprised at how well they spoke. They don't all speak broken English like my little mama (I sendo my mele fo somu egusu).[29] Remember?

Last night was the first night we slept without the mosquito net. The mosquitoes are practically gone now. It seems so funny to just pull out a blanket and sleep on the floor.

I guess I haven't told you that I'm in the first-year class now. When I entered I was in preparatory. That was too easy and slow and boring, so I'm in the upper class now and the dumbest one in there. We have books, 11 and 12 grammar school and 1 and 2 of middle school. They are so difficult it takes

27. The Ginza is the premier thoroughfare in Tokyo, not unlike the Champs Elysées in Paris or Fifth Avenue in New York.

28. Daughter or single young lady.

29. Mary was recalling how her mother used to say to their neighbor, "I'll send my Mary for some eggs."

me an hour to get one page. Therefore, I do not get it. But I'm feeling studious this weekend. Last weekend I didn't study at all. I don't study so much at night either. It's so hard, it seems useless to study. And you know how I love to memorize. That everyday routine of memorizing just gets me and I hate languages anyway. But I have some good teachers and then those classes are interesting. One teacher is Masuda and he's so cute! He's like a little boy, so eager and still wondering about this world. His sleeves are too short and his pants are high water. There is one lady teacher and they call her "grandma." She is awful. So *teinei* [polite] and soft voiced and lulling. She is so slow and too talkative and boring. In preparatory class we had her most of the time, but thank goodness we don't have her in 1st year so much anymore. Then there's Natori-sensei,[30] who is like the principal. He is dark and wears glasses and looks like some kind of an animal, but I'm too lazy to think up which one he looks like. He likes to imitate people and to talk about them and he is very energetic. But I don't like him so much. He's not cute.

There is an 18-year-old girl in the family, Miyoko, and she shares her room with me. But she is not the clinging-vine dainty Japanese *ojo-san* type. As Yoshiya told me, "There are two kinds of girls—the ones who are like girls and the ones who are like boys. Well, Miyoko is the latter type." End of translation. She uses unladylike slang and she is not what I thought Japanese girls were. You'd be surprised, Miye. Why should I learn to obey and honor the mighty male? It's not like you think. Maybe I've only seen the surface and don't know their real life yet, but I'm sincerely not seeing the Sakuma-sensei and *okusan*[31] type of married life here.

The trains are so packed in the morning. The other day my pencil in my purse was broken because we were so crushed. That girl from Korea had her watch smashed.

Fumi is in preparatory [class], and she says they have a swell time in there. There is a Ma-san, a Chinese in there. He is loud and rich and has been around. He's a graduate of Rollins College in Florida. He was raised in China. Fumi was telling me about some things he says. They had a French teacher in college who wore short dresses and sat on her desk and crossed her legs. The attendance in that class grew tremendously. Ma and his friend took her out on a date and got her so drunk that she couldn't walk. Then they never took the finals, but they passed her course. Those kids throw spit balls and chalk in class and cut up and shoot firecrackers and have one grand time. They're not

30. Natori Junichi, founder and president of Waseda International Institute. Mary worked for him during the war translating books.

31. The Reverend Sakuma had preceded the Rev. George Yahiro as minister of the Modesto Holiness church. The congregation used the honorary term *okusan* exclusively for a minister's wife. Mrs. Sakuma was the epitome of the subservient Japanese wife.

supposed to smoke, but they do and throw the stubs on the floor. That class is small and crazy and sometimes I wish I'd stayed there for the fun of it. In first year they don't cut up so much and the class is larger. That Nakayama got his hair shaved off and he looks so funny. He never studies and he makes a lot of noise and eats peanuts in class.

Last Sunday I went to my second cousin's[32] place. We just sat and talked. She was alone. She is small and about 50 and seems intelligent.

October 8, morning. I've got about ten minutes to write now. It's Sunday morning and I'm going to church at school with Fumi. Last night we went to song practice at a girl's place. She lives in an international house. It felt almost like America in her room, with furniture and *Life* magazines and popular music the kids played on the piano and Nisei. I got home about eleven. Fumi surely is nice and I'm lucky to have her for a friend. She is tall and slender and has round black eyes, and she is so cute. I like to look at her. Looking at *Life* magazines I realized how really beautiful American women are. Japanese girls don't begin to compare with them. Japanese girls, when they are loud, are terrible. They wear lipstick and try to make their mouths smaller, so they paint their lips white and then put a little bit of lipstick on and you can see the shape of their lips where it is white, and it looks sickly. Their hair is not pretty either, most of them. They either have permanents or don't. The ones with have their hair all kinky and out. The ones without wear their hair [long and straight] like me, and you know how attractive that is. Besides, they don't have any shape. If they are slender they are just straight and if fat they are like a barrel. What criticism!

Today I am going to play tennis with Iza-chan with those precious tennis balls Emma sent me. He says he's just beginning—they're hollering at me to beat it, so here goes. Think I'll send this now so that it will make the *Asama*, which is sailing on the twelfth. Be sure to write and give me lots of gossip and stuff. Good-bye—love and lots of it.

[P.S.] I just love *Ferdinand*[33] and I've read it to the boys and Miyoko, and they like it too.

October 8, night. Reading this over I discovered this blank page, so I'll fill it up. I had a very pleasant time today. Went to the church at school in the morning with Fumi. It was in Japanese but it felt good to hear hymns again—

32. Mrs. Suzuki, daughter of Grandfather Manjiro's older adopted sister. She lived in the exclusive Denenchofu district. Her husband lived with his mistress.

33. *The Story of Ferdinand* (1936), a popular children's story by Munro Leaf about a bull bred for fighting that preferred to sit beneath his favorite cork tree and smell the flowers.

although different from our church. I got home about one. I was to play tennis with Iza-san but all the courts were full, so we went boating instead. It felt good out on the water. He is very interesting and my best friend next to Fumi. But Fumi is feminine, you know, and I don't talk to her like to you. Every subject under the sun like we used to—especially religion, sex, people. We just talk people and everyday superficial subjects. But Iza-chan is very brainy. And now I pour out some of my theories at him, whereas before it was you always. Not that anyone could ever take your place. But a poor substitute is better than none.

Our school is going on a nine-day trip down south starting next Sunday.[34] There are about 50 going. Hope it will be worth going. We speak English to each other at school. It's bad for us, but it feels so good to be able to talk without hesitating for words.

I think I'm practically over my homesickness now. But I still miss the funnies. We have one real nice teacher. His name is Mukotani-sensei and he surely acts like a real Christian. He always has a smile on his face and not a stupid grin. But he is one of those people who just shine out with goodness and purity. As though his soul were shining through. He is so kind and considerate. Such people are inspiring. Really the salt of the earth.

This morning we had an earthquake. That's the second I've felt so far. Just little shakes and it's all over with. I'm hardly aware that there is a war going on in Europe. I'm so shut up in my own little world of school, Fumi, and this family. Besides I can't read their newspapers anyway and English papers are too expensive.

Tokyo, October 13, 1939

Dear Miye,

It is five o'clock in the morning now. I don't know what's come over me, but since coming to Japan I haven't been able to sleep like a log as usual. Last night I went to bed early (9) for a change. Practically all of last week I'd been going to bed around midnight.

I saw Orion and Sirius this morning. They were so sparkling and bright against the dark blue sky. I thought of those days [in the] long gone past of my girlhood. Sounds like an old lady, huh? But I don't know if I do like getting old. Somewhere along the line, my dreams and ideals and ambitions were all crushed. And now I am content to be one of the masses. When and where is it that the rebellious me was lost and left me just flat and lazy? Now I wouldn't even think of studying astronomy or having religious experiences.

34. A field trip to Kyushu for the whole school.

So I thought I must be at the stage when girls want to get married. Just drifting along without aim. I used to wonder why many girls ever chose to get married. Some of the most brilliant girls in high school, too. And I used to think I'd never be one of them. But my barriers are gradually breaking down. It's awful because I don't even care.

Maybe I feel so disillusioned now because of Emma. She has her hair in curls now. Miye—can I trust you? I really should not tell anyone. But Emma has a boyfriend she found at school and they plan to get married as soon as she gets her M.A. You know, I always had Emma up on a pedestal. The first blow came when she talked of getting married. Well, she was that much lower in my opinion. Yesterday, in Blanche's letter she says Emma has her hair in curlers now. That surely left me dazed. Because straight and stern hair symbolized an apartness from the world. "Do not conform to the things of the world." I wonder if her religion is now that sissy and easy-going modern stuff—she said she was going to look into modernism to see what was in it. Miye, it's sad to be disillusioned.

Even you with a permanent. So I'm the only one left suffering long straight hair. Why should I keep it up?

And our Modesto church, too, is something that makes me sad. You hate to see decay going on right in front of your nose. And when you think of how earnest our parents used to be when we were small, it puts those sleepy-looking people sitting in church now to shame. Maybe what we learned is true and we are living in the last Age. Something else that makes me feel this way is that all the letters I get from the U.S.A. seem to be so *shikataganai* [resigned]. None of those kids seem inspired. And they said everyone talks about the European war now. It seems as though the people over there are living in the shadow of the great war in which the U.S. is to be fool enough to participate in. But when you hear about the international situation you feel like "what's the use?" We'll all be blown up anyway. What is it in people, anyway, Miye? Why should the masses go out to murder and be murdered just because the heads of the states say a few words? Wasn't the World War enough? Iza-san said that they spent enough money on the war in China to build ten universities. Yet the people just accept it with a look of resignation. Iza says events just come about so that Japan has only that course left to follow. And yet it gets me. And that article in *Reader's Digest* about German youth. You wonder if human life is really so cheap that even minds can be mechanized. With those methods of psychology you can move people around like animals. Maybe someday when man really is at the door of knowledge they'll be able to manufacture life. And if a Hitler wants soldiers he'll just order them out and they'll come out all uniformed and gunned—all in rows like cans of milk or something. Gee whiz, Miye—I haven't felt so philosophical for ages.

But once in a while it just gets me and I wonder why did I come to Japan? What am I to do after going back to the U.S.A.? What's the use of it all, anyway? Is there a reason in life—or should we just wander aimlessly about? I envy someone who has a definite goal and just works toward it. I do so wish I had you to talk to here. When I feel this way I haven't anyone to confide in. Therefore, I just poured some out in paper.

Dawn is breaking outside now. The roosters are crowing and there is that distant rumbling of the trains. Some insects are chirping and humming. Some horns are heard far off. This hour just before the sun rises is just enchanting. So quiet. The breathing space before the start of another day. The pause before the world wakens. I almost said "The pause that refreshes." I surely missed cokes in summer. Now I miss coffee. And dessert.

Yesterday it rained all day. I was so cold and soaked by the time I got home. I'd worn a print dress and light sweater, and Fumi and I and a girl from Hawaii went shopping. I got this stationery there. Isn't it pretty? This is the last sheet. And I only wrote to Thelma Christiansen and you. Everything is so expensive here. Food is so high. Apples five sen apiece. Some melons seven yen. Candy is ten sen for just a very small bar. They said rice has gone up (high) too. Of course it's not so expensive if you think in terms of the dollar, since one dollar makes four yen now. But to the people living here the yen is their dollar. And with a dollar in America you surely can buy more than you can with a yen in Japan. Their wages are low, too. Girls working in stores get about 20 yen. You wonder how they can live on it.

The sunrise is so beautiful! It just takes my breath away. When I see something perfectly beautiful, it makes a lump in my throat and tears come to my eyes. Sentimental, huh? But there were streaks of clouds all in that salmon shade and some brighter. I'll write on the back [of the sheet] now so you won't have to pay for postage. The sunrise reminded me of Tiburon. We had such beautiful sunrises there. And you could see the sun breaking out over the water. Or rather over San Francisco. Then you were near and I could look over to Berkeley and think Miye is sleeping now.[35] Whereas now, you are so far away. But the clouds were travelling fast. And it seemed like I could ride on them and go way over to America again.

Have any American ships been submarined? Do you really hear a lot about the war? Blanche said the radio was full of it now. Over here I'm hardly aware that a war is going on. No one talks about it. Or if they do, I can't understand them. I just read the one or two articles in the English newspapers, but they're not really excited about it. It seems like they're not really fighting yet. You know how they said that in This Next War cities would be bombed and

35. Miye was attending the University of California at Berkeley.

vast destruction would start so quickly. But it looks like a slow long-drawn-out affair to me. Tell me what they say about it. But you are busy, seeing as how you are going to graduate next year. Gosh—and I won't be able to see you graduate either.

I ought to study. But it is so hard. Too hard and I'm the most ignorant one in the class. Starting next Sunday we are going on an eight-day trip to Kyushu. First day we ride twenty-two hours on the train. There are about 50 going, 13 girls.

Did I tell you about the German girl? She was in preparatory class. Her name is Marie Grünow. Well, I was going to go to the Tokyo Symphony concert with her and planned to meet her in front of the Imperial Hotel. She drove up with her chauffeur and said she was so sorry but she wasn't allowed to go because the drum player is a Jewish refugee. They live (the Grünows) at the embassy and her father is an aviator. I play ping-pong with her. I can't hardly understand her English. But I like to look at her because she is so fair-skinned and blue-eyed and a blonde. It's a treat after looking at Japanese day in and day out.

I went to the second concert of the Tokyo Symphony with Iza-chan. I had a swell time too. I think I wrote to you about it already. And then, last Sunday I went boating with him but I think I told you that, too. The boys come home late almost every night. They teach. Yoshiya is taking up aviation and he likes it but says he gets bawled out every day.

The sun is up now and it is past six o'clock. I have to clean my room. And try to cram in a few *kanji* before school.

Now, life seems worth living again. The start of another day. I'm quite used to Japan now. Be sure to write.

[P.S.] I dreamt about my cute mom last night.

Tokyo, October 29, 1939

Dear Miye,

Just received your letter today and surely was happy to hear from you. And your letter was a masterpiece and sounded just like you. I felt so moody and far away when I read it. I never can get over the wonder that I rated such a good friend—a perfect friend—like you. Your letters surely inspire me and bring me back to my senses.

I've been in bed. It's 11:00 pm now. But the sirens rang for air raid practice and also I kept thinking about you, so here I am up again and writing. I'll be sorry tomorrow because I'll be so darned sleepy in class. And last night I stayed up until one. Stayed home, too. I ironed my clothes which I washed during the day. It was Saturday yesterday. It took me until about 11:30 to iron and then I determined not to go to bed until I'd written that dreaded composition about our trip to Kyushu. I'll write about that trip later. We had to write one English composition and one in Japanese, so I decided to write one in English and translate it, thereby killing two birds with one stone. (Don't you hate people who always use those stale phrases?) The lesson in composition was last Tuesday and I'd kept putting it off until the writing mood fell on me, but it didn't. So I had to discipline myself and not go to bed until I finally got it written. Now all I have to do is to translate it into Japanese. That takes hours upon hours because I try to impress the teacher by using whatever *kanji* that I've supposedly learned, but haven't, and therefore must laboriously look them up in the dictionary.

My head kind of aches already from not enough sleep and it's going to be awful tomorrow. I have to get up at least by quarter to seven as I leave at seven and it takes an hour to get to school.

What do you mean, showing my letters to people? But I know you won't show the special private parts meant only for you. Kids flatter me, though, and tell me I write such interesting letters. And they show them around, but I don't care with other people because I only write my heart out to you.

Today I went to my relative, Mrs. Ito's, place in Tokyo. She has two maids and one 15-year-old girl and one husband and one pipe, which she smokes continuously. But it is not a manly pipe like in the USA but a long, delicate, Chinese-like one, which she stuffs on one end with tobacco which looks like mice fur—or hair, or like brown roots of weeds. One puff, then she has to fill it up again. Not many women smoke here and especially in public—you never see women smoking. They say only geishas and old women smoke.

I could write a book on our trip and the kids who went and the kids at school. So here goes and if you get bored—well—I'll just give you another bedtime sleep producer. I'll give you the data first: We left Tokyo 10:20 a.m., October 15, on the train. There were about 70 students: 12 girls, four teachers, including one woman teacher, Mrs. Shimada. We rode 21 hours straight—had lunch, dinner, and slept on the train. Breakfast at Shimonoseki, then to Moji, Fukuoka, Nagasaki, Unzen, Kumamoto, and Beppu. Then to Osaka by boat (21 hours), then back to Tokyo by train and we reached Tokyo Monday, October 23, 5:30 in the morning.

That is that, and now I'll just scribble scattered impressions and stuff. My fingers are tired of writing already. It was altogether rather an interesting trip, but, oh, we were so dead tired. Every morning we had to get up at 5:30. Travel in Japan is so inconvenient and dirty. Nagasaki was the dirtiest place of all and not a bit romantic. Except we saw a very awe-inspiring stained-glass-windowed gothic architecture Catholic church there. But the Nagasaki hotel was the worst one of the whole trip. It smelled. It was dirty. There was no water. We could not take baths. In the morning we had to wash with rain water and wash our teeth with it too. We were glad to get out of there. At Fukuoka it was raining and we had to walk around with umbrellas and our feet and clothes got soaking wet. At night we had to wallow through mud to get to the (girls') high school, where we gave our "wonderful" program. And we really had to wallow through mud three inches deep and it was such an awful experience. I wore those white high-heeled toe-less shoes and could feel the mud squishing through my toes and up my ankles. That night I was so sleepy and nodded and slept through our teacher's speech. The kids laughed at me for it. In fact, I'm already famous for sleeping when I'm not supposed to. Just that old habit from dozing in Yahiro-sensei's dry lectures.[36] It's embarrassing at times.

At Shimonoseki we had the best breakfast I've had since coming to Japan. We actually had chairs and tables and American-style food. Ham and eggs, toast, coffee, cereal, fruit. It surely tasted good after all the breakfasts I'd had of rice, *misoshiru* [miso soup] and *umeboshi* [pickled plums]. Their coffee never tastes right, however. They make it out of soybeans. I'm getting a new attitude towards food now. As Naka (more of him later) said: Japanese are the hungriest people in the world. They eat for pleasure. Before, food to me was just work and I was tired of it before even eating. But now that I don't have to prepare it, I look forward to meals and eating between meals too. Now I can understand my relatives. I used to think they were trying to stuff me and I didn't feel like eating all day long. But after a steady diet of rice three times a day, you crave sweets and tea. And you get pleasure and look forward to in-between meal snacks hosts put out for you.

More of the trip: I never knew what we were seeing or what the statues were of or anything because I couldn't read or understand the guides. Their guides! We get on buses and there is a bus girl who is the guide. She stands and chants off in a monotone. No one knows what she is saying. It is all memorized and she stops only for breath to pour out more of that peculiar high-pitched chant at us again. We all laughed at the guides but they kept right on going strong. We surely had to walk all over, too. Miye—you have no idea what Japanese towns are until you actually see one. They are all the same. Narrow streets. No sidewalks. Small unpainted one-room shacks on either side of the street. Carts, bicycles and people—people swarming everywhere. Starving people—children. Dirty children with sores on their heads. Working men scantily dressed and browned and weather-beaten. Country girls with straight hair in a short pigtail with fat legs and thick ankles.

36. The Reverend Yahiro's sermons were in Japanese and at least an hour long.

Along the Ginza I know you would be just fascinated. Millions of people. But they are a different type from that of small towns. Here you see pretty girls—students—kimonoed *ojo-sans*, middle-class men. Girls in American dress with painted faces and permanents and short dresses. *Ojo-sans* with that fancy piled-up hairdress and kimonos, so colorful. Students—always students in black uniforms and caps. Students with glasses. University students in square caps. *Koto* (junior college)[37] students in round caps and *geta* [wooden sandals] and needing a haircut and shave. Staring people. Always looking at others and especially you. People just stream along every place. You wonder where they ever came from and where they are going.

Again I've wandered. We climbed a Mt. Aso, which is a live volcano. It was smoky. I climbed it with Ted Ozawa (more of him later). It was windy up at the top and sandy but felt good to look down on the valley. We didn't see any lava. We also went to hot springs. One girl said it looked like Yellowstone minus the grand scenery and geysers. All it was was bare grey rocks and bare grey sand with dirty water boiling up and steam all over. The smell of sulfur was omnipresent, and after a while you didn't notice it. At first it reminded me of chem lab. Gee, that was fun. Those awful unknowns, but I wouldn't have missed that chem lab for anything. Iza-chan took chem for six years and here I'd been feeling so superior just because I took one year in JC. They had hot baths but I didn't go in. The boys took pictures in them—they even took in a moving-picture camera. The boat from Beppu to Osaka was like a slave ship. Hundreds of people all crowded together down below. We had boards to sleep on—or rather, it was a floor and they gave you a blanket and you shifted for yourself in that stuffy humid room. We had fun on the boat, though. Talked and sang. It was cold and we took up blankets and sat together and sang. Those old songs like "Long, Long Ago," "Penny Serenade," "John Brown's Body," even Christmas songs. I got bit by bedbugs on that boat. Some of the scenery from the train was too beautiful for words! The train, in some places, was way up on top of the mountains. And you could look out down below into the valleys and see their neat rice fields—so small and golden yellow and their cottages. It looked so pastoral and like a picture. They cultivate even along the mountain sides—terrace it off. From far off they look like velvety steps of green and gold. And then there are little shrines and idols all over with trees around. Sometimes we could see the ocean—the water so blue—deep blue, and the beach so smooth. Japan really has some beautiful scenery, all right. But their towns are dirty enough to more than make up for it. They have no sewer system and you smell it all over and it is sickening. You know, they use it for fertilizer and oh, the smell—it's overpowering. I don't see how

37. Not precisely equivalent to an American junior college; in prewar Japan, high school graduates attended *koto* for two years before going on to university.

the farmers stand it. And yet—it seems so ridiculous—or out-of-place to see power lines, electric poles, so modern, along with these small paddy fields and humble shacks.

Think it's midnight now, but what do I care. I feel inspired and must write now or never.

But you know on a trip like that it's always the kids you go with that you're most interested in and all the shrines, buildings, scenery are pushed into the background.

At first I went with Fumi. Haven't I written about her? She is 18, cute, the popular type, and very talkative and girlish. You know—the type that fascinates you for the first few days and then you wonder—then you know—that they are shallow and all their talk is just pleasant jibber-jabber. The type it's fun to be with if you want light easy entertainment and feminine gossip. Well, I was crazy about her at first and tried to be like her but still the old stubborn Mary does not want to be catty, feminine, cute, and entertaining. We sat on the train to Shimonoseki together and she never slept a wink and I slept about two hours. It makes me feel so unpopular when I'm with her because the boys all crowd around her because she is so cute and knows all the answers and taps them so lightly. Here I am taking her to pieces when she really is a very nice girl. Well—the boys came down and visited us from all over the train and it made the time pass quickly. After a few days of the trip, she started going with Yuki who is another cutie pie, and it kind of made me feel sad and lonely but I went with a girl from Hawaii whose name is Natsuko. Now I like Natsuko. She is so pretty. And tall and slender, five-feet-four or so. And she observes people and thinks about them more than I. At Beppu we had a very pleasant time walking up and down the streets at night. The shops were open and gaily lit. At first we were with Fumi and Yuki and their respective boyfriends but they seemed not to want us along, so we went alone. On the way back we almost got lost and could hardly find our way back to the hotel.

Ask Yamamoto *no obasan*[38] if she remembers a Ted Ozawa. He said he used to go over to her place. He went to Armstrong after Sacramento JC. He surely is beautiful. He came over on the same boat as I, but I never talked to him. His looks used to scare me because he looked so handsome and upperclassy. I thought he was only a kid of 18, 19 or so and acted such to him, and was I surprised when I found out that he is 25! Well, he surely does giggle. Fumi says he giggles too much. Natsuko and I were together the latter half of the trip. We sat opposite different kids and talked practically all night. The rest of the kids slept. There is that before-mentioned Naka. He comes from Oregon and is rather stout—not fat, but he has eyes that kind of snap and

38. "Auntie" Yamamoto, who lived in Berkeley. Miye and other Nisei students at the University of California visited her quite often.

shine like yours. He is a brainstorm and a debater and interesting to pump. But he talks in a soft voice and I have to strain to catch what he says. He says Oregon is beautiful. He is the type who works crossword puzzles and is full of odd information. Something like my debate partner in high school—who looks like Ichabod Crane. There is a boy in our class who used to remind me of him. He is German—named Fritz Langer and he studied in Berlin and Paris and he's the smartest one in the class but he can't pronounce ra, ri, ru, re, ro and says instead wa, wi, wu, we, wo and sounds so childish. He wears thick glasses and looks something like Mr. Gordon of the Wickings only his eyes are not so tremendously large. He did not go on the trip. Another one who sat across from us is a Komuro, who is a graduate of University of Washington. He is ugly. Fumi said he reminds her of that actor who plays Frankenstein—I can't think of his name. But you get used to all kinds of ugly people. One time I was with a group that was like what I like—student types. Marie Grünow, Johnny Nakayama, Mori, and Yamanaka. Mori dominated the talk. He is going to graduate from Waseda University and is over 30 and very talkative and thinks he knows a lot. He said Nisei boys get to be just like the real Japanese-y students by the time they get in the university. They expect the professors to pick out wives for them. And he said that Nisei girls don't have a chance—if a Nisei girl wants a date, she has to run after the man. I don't know any Nisei girls in Tokyo and thus know nothing about them, except the girls coming to our school. Yuki is planning to enter a Christian Women's University. They don't believe in educating females here. I would like to be a boy student here. What Iza-chan said made me want to be one. He says that those who wear university caps are a special class and privileged. They get to go to rich homes and are looked up to more than the rich playboy who is too dumb to pass the exams to get into university. They brag that they are poor. If one gets some money, they all go out and drink and eat it up and have a grand time. They cut class and go boating or play ping-pong. But they study too—before exams. He surely has some [of the] same attitudes as you and I do. Does only enough to get by the skin of his teeth and yet he's got brains.

Miye—I think I'll go to bed. It's almost one now. Wonder if Orion is out?

Wednesday, November 1, 1939. I'm down in the dumps again. So I'll pour out my heart to you. Do you think that you will come to Japan in two years? I surely wish you'd come while I'm here. I miss you so much and it would be so too, too good if we were together again. No one can ever take your place.

Mrs. Yahiro sent me a letter, along with *The Echo of Calvary*.[39] *The Echo* is quite good and Andy seems to have a style, don't you think? Getting more

39. The newsletter of the Modesto Holiness church.

like the *L.A. Burning Bush.* I don't see how he fills the pages when there's really nothing much to say. *Okusan* said Mrs. Treebelly[40] is still in Japan. I'd surely love to see her and hear her chatter and laugh again.

This Friday is the Emperor Meiji's birthday so we don't have to go to school. I'm glad. I'm going to take ikebana from a teacher near our place this Friday. I'm also planning to go ice skating and to a movie with a girl from Alaska. She is my latest girlfriend. She wears glasses and is about five feet and doesn't stand straight and is a girl scout. She kind of reminds me of Esther Loose. She said she's gone camping and bear and deer hunting. She's going to show me how to ice skate. Everyone learns when they come to Japan.

Yesterday we broadcast over short wave. Did you hear me? A bunch of Nisei read off a story-like and they had the Japan Symphony Orchestra for the musical background. There were about 150 Nisei there—some from Keisen Jogakkuen and from Nichi-Bei Home[41] and some others. I'm glad I didn't go to the Keisen because I heard that the girls are very catty. The girls at Kokusai are not. Our girls are more the nice, studious type—but are they? They are the type that likes sports and mathematics. Not flirty.

I get so disgusted with the learning of Japanese. I feel like just giving up and quit trying. It seems like I haven't learned a thing since coming to Japan. I hate to memorize anyway. And I hate languages. But going down the street I get somewhat encouraged because now I can read about 1/20 of the words—or, at least recognize them.

Two more months and I'll be 23 years old! In Japan age. Growing old and what have I to show for it? Many times I wonder why I came to Japan at all. It is so crowded and you feel like you can't even breathe. Mori said that it's bad for Nisei girls to come to Japan. They change for the worse. After all, we are molded by our environment. But deep down, I don't believe it.

The trouble with me is I have no aim in life. No one goal for which I strive with all my might. Just aimless wandering. Once I thought that the object of my life was to experience everything possible—life in all its moods—in all its ups and downs. To know the highest happiness as well as the deepest sadness. But how?

Even now I feel as though I'm losing my grip of English. In writing or in talking, the right words do not come out easily. I'm beginning to even think some things in Japanese. I only hope I never talk in my sleep in Japanese because then they'll understand. Iza-chan is next door, and he says Miyoko and I talk in our sleep all the time.

40. The boys in the Holiness church facetiously called the Yanagihara family "Treebelly" because the characters of their surname could be literally translated that way. In fact it should be translated "the plain of willows." The Yanagiharas had returned to Japan in the late 1930's and Mary visited them in July 1941.

41. Keisen Girls School and the Japanese American Hostel.

It is Thursday morning now. I have such awful dreams at night. One night I dreamt I drowned and then that I was shot in the war. You probably hear a lot about the war. I don't. It seems so unimportant now. It's so funny how some people can be suffering at this very moment while other people are carefree and happy. But just as you said—there doesn't seem to be anything important anymore. I wonder how much is true that they say about Hitler? I'd love to pump that Langer and Grünow. But I'm afraid to. Langer is intellectual and he frowns when he talks. He said people are much more sincere and open in Europe, especially Paris, than here. Maybe that's it. These people just stare at you and you can't imagine what they are thinking. Gosh, I wish I could read and talk Japanese. And yet—it's so hard to study. I study once in a while when I'm in the mood. Besides, when I feel like studying I don't have time and when I have time I don't feel like studying.

Even the letters I get from the USA, in them there seems to be an undercurrent of dissatisfaction and "what's the use of living?" Or is it my imagination?

I'm overeating and I bet I'm getting fatter. Hope not. But I surely am hungry in between meals and I take practically no exercise. My dear old grandpappy sent me a box of some delicious fresh crispy apples and some persimmons and chestnuts. He is so thoughtful. My cousin also sent me a box of persimmons. Fruits take on an added glamor here because they are so scarce and expensive. Oh for the days when we used to go out and crack a watermelon in the ranch and dig in with dirty hands and eat only the nice center red juicy seedless section. Oh for some grapes and peaches—and green apples. I surely miss them. Rice, rice and more RICE. Three times a day. Every day of the week. I don't see how they live on it.

It's almost 6:30 and here I haven't studied at all this morning. Went to bed early last night with the idea of getting up early to study. It's not very pleasant to be the dumbest one in the class. Write loads again.

Tokyo, November 19, 1939

Dear Miye,

Just got your most down-in-the-dumps letter just now. But it was so good to hear from you and besides you never gloss over your real feelings, for which I love you with all my heart. I was wondering when I'd hear from you next. It seemed ages. That poem you sent me sent a chill all through me and I still feel dreamy over it.

Just now I have an awful headache and my feet are cold and my stomach is empty and I'm worried about the test coming up Monday. You are right, Miye, I'm attempting too much. We're having the test on Book Two, which is two books above book 12, which you warned me against. Woe is me—I studied hours upon hours on those darned lessons and still I feel so confused and blank and like a Know-nothing. Yesterday I studied all day. This morning I studied about one hour, then just gave up because there is a limit to my memorizing ability and my head aches and I feel lousy. It feels good to use that word! This afternoon I did not study but polished my shoes and darned my socks and talked to this Iza-chan of whom you are very curious.

Your last letter sounded so hopeless and not a bit like you. I read what was on the back of the poem too and it sounded so typically American. I was wondering why my long awaited and hoped for R.D. did not come. I'm sorry I've put you through so much trouble. But you know how I look forward to and enjoy them.

That was surely a shock about Fred['s death], and I can't believe it. Isn't it terrible? It's so unreal how some people can be suffering horribly while others at the same time are so unaffected and *heiki* [unbothered, oblivious]. (I'm getting Japanified.) But I wonder if I will be "Japanified"? Going to school seems just like going to school at home. Now my interest number one centers around a Fritz Langer. He sits at the desk to my right and I'm always jabbering with him in class. He's interesting to pump. He is an intellectual with spectacles and talks English-y. Been to Paris and England. He says French women have something that Americans lack—American women are too simple. French women are not beautiful but they have a certain something. English men don't pay much attention to women. Something he said which surely surprised me was that English towns are dirtier than Japan's. They dump all their garbage out onto the streets. When you are in the U.S.A. you just take it for granted that foreign countries are just like at home essentially. And it is such a shock to see the dirty parts in a different country. In America it seems like they are proud of the dirt and squalor in the slums and down South and in the "Little Oklahomas."[42] They have photographs of them so everyone can see the bad parts in the USA. But in Japan I've never seen photographs or even descriptions of the humble rickety shacks, unsanitary sewage system, and narrow streets. It must be that they take such things for granted, whereas in America the standard is high. I can just picture Modesto in my mind now. It was such a clean city with wide streets and lots of space. I love it now that I am away, the broad broad streets, the lawns, trees lining long avenues. You never see that here. Everything is on such a small, crowded scale.

Fritz says the average Chinese is much more intelligent than the Japanese. Maybe not for building armies, but for brains of another sort. Fritz doesn't

42. Settlements of poor people displaced by the Dust Bowl and the Great Depression of the 1930's. Such camps would have been a familiar sight to Mary since California was a notable promised land for thousands of these "Okies."

seem to like the Japanese much. He says there are too many people. He is rather talkative. But he also says that educated people are the same everywhere. Now I think that surely is true, as little as I've seen of the world. That education counts more than race. And yet, there must be characteristics typically Japanese. I'm a poor observer. Most of my life is spent at school and there I have an American environment. Talk in English all the time and it's bad for my Japanese speaking ability, which has improved little, if at all.

Gosh, Miye I wish you were here. Tell me if you really can come in a couple of years. I'd hate to stay more than two years. Two years stretches out so long before me now.

I'm just freezing. At school we have no stove and I freeze there too. And cold weather is just starting.

Japan's general population is just beginning to feel the pinch of war. Until this summer they said that everything was the same as before the war. But now rice is scarce and the price is the highest it has been since 1918. There is a scarcity of all materials. They send out all they can, so they can get gold to buy armaments. Everything is so expensive, I wonder how the poor people live. And there are so many children all over Japan.

I'm so pooped out. We finally had our test this morning and what a relief to have it over with! I was aiming at 50% so will be happy if I make around 60%, which I think I made. I have such a bum memory and it is taking me so long to learn this language! But I guess I have learned quite a bit, I say to myself, as I keep groping in this sea of unknown *kanji*s.

Alberta is right: you have a strong personality. The opposite of me because I am flat and colorless and therefore take on the color of whoever I'm with. Seems to me that there are two types of people—those who impress, and those who are impressed. Lots of times I've compared us to the sun and the moon. You shine of your own inner light while I only reflect. No, that's a little strong, and I hope I do more than feebly reflect others. Usually the oldest one in the family is the one with the outstanding character. And the second one in the family, of the same sex, is the genius or the complete failure. Some psychologist said that—I forgot who. Of course, he was the second son, so the implication was that he was the example of the genius. But I think there is some truth to that. One thing for sure, the second is really stubborn—just like me.

Today I stayed after school for an extra grammar lesson, but I still can't get it. I guess I'm attempting too much. More than half of the class has been there since last March, and here I'm trying to cram in all that when I started in September. Anyway, it's much more interesting in there than in the easy preparatory class.

Last Wednesday night I went to the Imperial Hotel auditorium to a lecture on Japanese history. It was a bore, and I slept nearly all the way through. But I'm glad I went because the audience was interesting to observe. Lots of Nisei. It was a sight for sore eyes to see so many well-dressed Nisei women. They are such a contrast to the droopy-looking native women in Western clothes. The beautiful Frank Lloyd Wright–designed room was actually heated, which is a rarity.

My *ojiisan* [grandfather] is so sweet. He's sent me two boxes of fruits already. I sure appreciate them too because fruits are a luxury here.

A couple of Sundays ago I went to my aunt's place and she took me to an *odori* [traditional dance] recital where she lends kimonos. The kimonos are so colorful. They wear four or five sets at a time and successively show one layer at a time. It is not a strip tease because they are always dressed. A man helps her quickly take off each outer kimono.

Merry Christmas!

Tokyo, December 21, 1939

Dear Miye,

Just got your letter yesterday and was I happy to get it! It was so funny and clever and just like you that you made me forget, for a while, all my worries. And that picture is the best I've ever seen of you. It surely caught that mischievous sparkle in your eyes, and it makes me feel good all over to look at it.

Only one more test to go now. That is tomorrow—in *shushin*, which is ethics. We have the darndest teacher for it. He is very earnest and his eyes are deep set and he scares me when he glares at me. He surely grades hard and I feel like not even going to the test because I'll flunk anyway.

I didn't think that I'd live through this week, but you'd be surprised at the "will to live" in even me. Last weekend I was really sick. The following parts of my anatomy ached: head, stomach, back. I tried to study Saturday and Sunday but couldn't. Took an aspirin Sunday night and lo! next morning (two am) my head did not ache, so I got up and studied. That was just when Iza-chan was going to bed. I studied steady until about seven in the morning. This last week I'd been going to bed around eight or nine and getting up early to study. Had about four tests in all. It's a good thing I didn't take the tests seriously because if I had, I'd be a nervous wreck now. It's terrible, though, to be aiming at 60%, which is barely passing. So I'm satisfied if I get a little more than half. I do so hope they won't put me back into that preparatory class.

Enough moaning. But that's all I can do. And my eyes ache now. We got one test back today and of all the mistakes I'd made! It made me feel so dumb and ignorant. Especially because Natsuko (my friend from Hawaii) missed only half as many as I.

Remember back in MJC how Jake said one time that we never cheated in tests because we never had to? I've been thinking about that lately—how true it is. And it's just natural for us to rationalize if we do cheat. In taking these tests Fritz, who sits across the aisle from me, always tells me and Natsuko the answers. At first I felt guilty but later I didn't even care. How low I have fallen! And that had always been a point of pride and self-righteousness with me—that I never got information from others during exams. But if you're dumb and still want to pass, you develop a different attitude and I can understand now why those kids cheated before in school.

We had a test on Book 12 on Tuesday and the teachers have their tests all mimeographed. This Book 12 teacher got mixed up and gave us the Book 11 test instead. After he found out his mistake, he hastily gathered the papers. We had our test on Book 11 today. Some kids grabbed the Book 11 tests and kept them to study from, so I copied it down. We had the same test today and it was easy for us. The teacher never knew some kids had copies of the tests. Johnny Nakayama, after he handed in his paper, said "I cheated like Hell, sister, but you don't know it."

Today Natsuko and I, Fritz, Hanisch and Naka went to the Ginza. I just got home now—about eight. Hanisch had to go home but the rest of us had dinner downtown—Fritz's treat. Roast beef and for dessert cake and ice cream, all fancy with whipped cream on top. It was delicious! For lunch Natsuko was going downtown and I wasn't planning to, so I brought my lunch. But I couldn't resist the temptation, so I went with her and Naka. We had steak and it surely was good.

I guess I never told you about the Chinese dinner we had. We had a good time then. It was a Saturday—two weeks ago. Natsuko and I and two other girls—from Alaska and Bakersfield—and Fritz, Hanisch, Naka went to a show [in the] afternoon, then to a Chinese dinner. We had a room to ourselves and sat on tatami. They kept bringing in the food for an hour and lastly they brought rice and *tsukemono* [pickles]. We sat around and talked until 11:30. It was expensive, too, something like 30 yen for seven of us and those poor three boys had to treat.

I've never gone out for dinners so much in all my life. As Naka said, the biggest places in Tokyo are the restaurants.

I got a letter from Miyoko Suzuki this morning and was I surprised to hear from her! She sent me her picture and she is so cute and looks different—more worldly and smart and slender. That chubby, cute and innocent child was not there anymore and instead there was a grown-up young lady. She said Tamiko got married and Hidee's husband died and Elsie and Harry were getting hooked. Her letter made me feel sad and so far away and getting old.

I was glad to hear about Elma getting a job at Turner's. That surely must have impressed me because I dreamed about it last night. I got a letter from her the other day. She sent me pictures of my ma and papa and of the 30-pound fish she caught. I bet she won't go to school anymore, do you think so?

I wonder if I'll go to school again after getting back. I surely don't feel like it 90% of the time and it's only that 10% when I get an unusually ambitious feeling that I think of school and career. But school is so much work and I love to go out and have a good time.

Tomorrow I'll be 21! And this January I'll be 23 in Japan age! How old! And I act like a 16-year-old or worse. When I and Hanisch get together, it's terrible. We fight and hit each other and act like kids. Did I ever tell you about him? He is about five-foot-ten, Czechoslovakian, and about 21, and very loud, and his face is all broken out with pimples. He sits right in back of me and talks all the time. But he's fun and I feel rather at home with him. Fritz is more intellectual and older and interested more in Natsuko than me. We form a kind of little world of our own—us five, including Naka.

Tomorrow is the last day of school. Our school all has lunch together, then I'm going to the Ginza with Natsuko. I have to buy a present for the Nagatas. And some food for my relatives up North whom I'm going to visit this vacation.

I feel so uninspired and not like writing and I'm probably boring you.

That surely is nice of you—a poor struggling student—to offer to send me the *Reader's Digest* every month. I feel sorry for you because it won't be easy for you—lots of bother. But I surely would appreciate it if you would send it. I'm sorry I made you cancel the subscription.

Golly, I'm sleepy. I overate because after dinner downtown I ate my lunch and then some sweets after that. But I'm no fatter—yet.

Now this is personal, Miye and you being my bestest friend, I'm pouring forth my heart to you. But I surely like Iza-chan. Sometimes I think I'm in love—but I'm not, really. It's just that I have to have some male to be goofy over. But he is so funny and brainy and absent-minded. And reminds me of you. His room is right next to Miyoko and mine, and the other night we were both supposed to be studying, but instead got to talking and we jabbered until 12 and his ma came up and bawled us out and told us to go to bed. He's interesting. He is my chief information bureau about Japan. He says his thinking is a lot different from mine and that all Japanese are different from Americans. And that it takes at least five years for a foreigner to begin to understand Japan. Well—and I thought our thinking was alike. He says Jesus' disciples were often jealous of him because he attracted women.

I get so irritated sometimes because it seems like I've learned so little since coming to Japan. Especially in conversation, I'm no better than before. This learning is so slow and I get disgusted and think I'll never learn. I want to be able to read as fast in Japanese as in English before going back.

I've been taking ikebana lessons but seem to be getting nowhere. But it's rather fascinating and really beautiful.

I showed the Nagatas your picture and Miyoko surely liked you. She says you look like an "*itazuramono*" [mischievous kid] and she likes that sparkle in your eyes. She said you look like the girl who draws those cartoons of monkeys and "kimo." Miyoko is quite clever. She surely is not the clinging-vine, simpering *ojo-san* of Japan.

It's funny how different people's views are. I talk to Naka and Fritz and hear all the bum side of Japan and when I ask Iza-chan I get entirely different views. And then I don't know what is what.

Something that is so different here from America is all the shrines and temples in Japan. Everywhere you go there's one. "Sightseeing" here means going to a shrine and bowing. Japanese history is interesting. I want to read up on it. But when I go to school I don't have time for anything. Those ancient legends are so fairy story-like. Like Yoshitsune,[43] who jumped over eight boats. Iza-chan told me to get a grammar school book on history and read it instead of English books. Fritz reads nothing but Japanese newspapers. So does Naka. Naka has been here only a year and a half but he says he thinks he knows enough about Japan now. He's got brains. But younger—just graduated high school.

December 22, 1939. I'll write smaller so that I won't have to pay 32 sen postage.

I'm 21 today. And it makes me feel sad and philosophical and dreamy. Miye—I want to see you. I want to go home for Christmas. I want to see that old sandy farm, the dried-up tomato vines and rotten tomatoes, the frost in the morning. I want to go home and see my old mom and pop look at me with affection—as though I really meant something to them. Gee—I'm glad I have parents. Even if I don't consciously love and adore them like some people say—still they're always there—solid and believing and steady. So like that good soil. There is a smell to the old place I love. Miye—I'm only a farmer too, and being away from the good earth leaves nothing to rely on. I smelled some leaves burning the other day and such fond memories it brought up. I used to go out and help Pop burn brush. There's something about a fire that makes me believe in something deep down and lasting. I know I'm indefinite. But it's just an emotion. And the sounds of the brush crackling. And oh—I loved the end of the day on the ranch. Sunsets. All is quiet. Hear sounds of milk cans in

43. Semilegendary samurai hero of the 13th-century epic *Heike Monogatari* (The Tale of the Heike). Yoshitsune, the perfect knight, masterminds the victory of the Genji (Minamoto clan) over the Taira (Heike) but is later betrayed by his half-brother and forced to commit suicide.

the distance. The last glows of sunset beyond the mountains. The birds winding their way toward the gum tree grove. Going home. I love Nature. I used to pull up a weed and just sit awed by the very beauty and harmony of even such a trifling plant. The balance between leaves and roots. The delicacy. O God—if for no other reason than Nature I believe in You. To sit in the dirt. To let the water run over my feet. I used to love to irrigate lettuce and strawberries. Just sit with a shovel and [feel] the clean and delicious crunchiness—no, the smoothness, of the sand underneath. The clear sky over head. Able to see from horizon to horizon. And then by noon it would get so hot. And lunch would taste so good. Grass—green grass—even the weeds of Japan are different. They don't seem carefree and happy to be alive like our weeds. The sweat running down my face. And hoeing—I used to think in those days. Philosophy—astronomy—O—Miye—I haven't had the ability to express my emotions.

Home—gee, I'm so glad I was raised in the country. Browned and tough. Boss of the world. Slave to no master.

And I still want to go home. But no—I'm way over on the other side of the world. In this crazy world. You're right, Miye—people bled to build ships which are built only to be sunk. What is wrong? The people don't want to fight. Then why must they? There's no reason in life—you just drift.

I'm cold. It's almost midnight. Went to the Ginza after school today with Natsuko and saw Japanese movies—went shopping and then had dinner. I felt in the discovering mood—so after I left Natsuko I looked around and then went into a cloisonné store. They had vases, boxes, and incense burners. There was a man there who spoke English like a regular American and he explained it to me how they make them. They have a copper shape first, then draw a design on it, then put wires on the design and dig and fill in the spaces, then bake and smooth it down. It was interesting. And oh, so beautiful! I love to look at them. Their shapes—colors—designs are so pleasing to the eyes. But how expensive. Cheapest about 15 yen and most of them up in the hundreds and thousands. I long to have nice expensive goods. I wonder if I'll ever be able to afford them? I wonder.

Gee, I'm in a fix. I'm broke. This morning I went to the Post Office to draw out 30 yen when she informed me that I only have 17 yen left. I was shocked because I thought that I had 80 yen more left at least to see me through January. And now I don't know what to do. The only thing, I guess, is to borrow from my grandpappy, but I hate to.

No more school for 2 weeks! I was getting bored of it, too. So was beginning to cut classes (like at JC). Tests and vacation bring in some variety.

My advice: don't be either Republican or Democratic. I would vote for the most interesting person. Saw the picture *War Clouds Over Europe*, did you? Well, there's a swell actor in there—the one who played Denny (?) in *The Citadel.*[44] Anyway, he's funny looking but a character. And independent and acts as he pleases. I surely like him.

I'm so glad I have a friend like you to write down all my feelings. Otherwise I'd burst. No one to really talk to like you. At first, I meet someone and think that they might possibly be a Miye—but no—the more I see of them they are just ordinary.

I bought a Japanese Bible and feel so proud of myself because I recognize a lot of words in there. All the *kanji* have *kana* [phonetic syllables] on them, so I can at least read it. And I know the meaning from English.

I'm down in the *kotatsu* now. Did I ever tell you? It is the Japanese poor equivalent of a stove. They dig a hole in the tatami, and put in a bowl of charcoal. On top of the hole they have a table. On top of the table are some blankets. You sit with your legs dangling down and your lower part gets warm while your back freezes. Like this: [sketch]. I bet you don't get the idea. My friend is sitting here too and he's cramming for the exam tomorrow and I'm not saying a word. He's going skiing next week. There's a boy in our class who is quite a skier—they say he's got medals. His name is Toda and [he's] 14 years old and cute. I told him I'm 35 and have a Ph.D. and he takes it all in. His aunt is champion tennis player of Japan. Gosh, I'm scribbling.

Naka said that on the Sumida River if you go in the morning, you find lots of babies floating around. That river runs through the slum section of Tokyo. I want to go there someday. And see the misery that Kagawa[45] fought against. Iza-chan said that wasn't true that kids are floating around dead like that in Japan.

Mrs. Nagata said that in Manchuria they throw kids that die out in the streets and the dogs come and eat them. There's a big Jew from Manchuria in the preparatory class who looks a little like Beatrice except that he doesn't look so crazy.

I want to talk to him some day and see if I could pump anything out of him.

Their dolls are beautiful here. But so expensive. If I only had the money—there are so many beautiful things here. And I don't see how the Japanese can be so artistic and yet so dirty. Their streets are so narrow and garbage all over. O, for the spacious lawns and neat highways of Modesto! When you get away from it, those things have a mist surrounding so that you see only the good and none of the bad. Even Tiburon—I look back on it with pleasure—even working for Mrs. Korb. I wrote her a letter but she never answered. Tamiko is

44. The British actor Ralph Richardson.

45. Kagawa Toyohiko (1888–1960), a prominent Christian social reformer, novelist, poet, and playwright.

married, huh? Masako[46] must have had her baby by now. How does it feel to be an aunt?

Gosh—I wish you were here to talk to. I feel like talking to someone but no one to talk to. So I'll write. But it's not so much fun to write because paper can't answer.

Phooey—I have to get out of this dreamy homesick mood. But I enjoy it. I love moods. Variety is the spice of life. Fritz surely is moody. I don't like moody people sometimes because they are too self-centered.

Good night, Miye, and write a lot, too.

[P.S.] Just got your two *Reader's Digests* this morning. Thank you so much. I'm so happy.

Yonezawa, January 1, 1940

Dear Miye,

Happy new year! Can you realize that another year is gone already? And now I'm 23. Gosh, I'm old and I hate to get much older. Maybe I'm beginning to get an old maid complex.

I'm at my cutie pie grandpappy's place. Came here last Thursday.

Oh, Miye, it snowed last night! Remember that article in *Reader's Digest* about the magical morning after the snow? It was every bit as good as that! You can't imagine the thrill—the sheer cold beauty—it's a world transformed. The snow is so pure and clean and soft and comforting. This morning I went out for a walk in it and certainly enjoyed it. O—how I'd love to ski! But I can't. I just sit around and write letters or try to talk to my old wrinkled grandpop or grand-aunt. For variety I visit my 75-year-old grandpop's sister. Such a life. What did I ride ten hours on the train to come up here for? I'm getting tired of it now. And counting the days until I get to go back to Tokyo. Only three more days.

And yet, I get something here that is missing in Tokyo. Is it someone who loves me? I think so. My dear old grandfather tries so hard to please me. So do my *obaasans*. They worry about me and try to do as much as possible. They buy me fruits and *gochiso* [delicacies] to eat and always urge me to eat more (imagine!) and ask me if I'm cold. They worry if I go out even for a short walk. It's a bother to have someone worrying about you—but yet, that fills a certain need in a person. Now I can understand such things as why the Spanish refugee children want someone to belong to. When you have parents near, you just take them for granted, and when you're away you surely miss it. A per-

46. Miye's younger sister. The first among Miye's siblings to get married, Mako (as she was familiarly known) had settled down in Modesto.

son has to have someone in the background—someone who roots him to the soil—someone you know loves you no matter how crazy you are. That's why I get such a comfort from writing to you and my ma and getting letters too.

When I'm in Tokyo no one seems to give a damn. I'm free. But freedom is always bought with a price. I can do what I please and stay out as late as I want without anyone worrying. And I'd hate to have to live with my grandpop. He would never let me go out at night or go out for dinner or spend any money at all. He is so tight with his money and always keeps it on his person. Imagine—Miye! An old 70-year-old like my grandpop had a mistress! I think it's so ridiculous. Who was it said "hope springs eternal in the human heart"? This is strictly personal—between you and me. I trust you because after all that's not such good advertising for my old grandpop.

Also everything I pour out to you about my Iza-chan and me is strictly personal. Because you understand, whereas someone else would just spread around gossip and think I was in love or something. Day after Christmas we went to the opera. I surely had a good time. He gave the ticket to me for Christmas. That was my one and only Christmas present. The opera was nothing wonderful with that Fujiwara in the main role and paper scenery. I detest Fujiwara. He is a conceited Romeo. They sang it in Japanese. The opera was *La Traviata* and I didn't know the story and Iza-chan wouldn't explain because he said I don't know enough Japanese to understand. I'd love to see a masculine Wagner opera—something weird and big and grand. That *La Traviata* was nothing but where that darned Fujiwara hugs his "Liebe" [Darling]. That's what Iza-chan calls it. After the opera we walked around the Ginza, then had coffee and bread and walked around again, then had "sushi" standing up. The latter was fun. It's an institution. You go in and there's a man behind a stand. In front of you are all sorts of raw and cooked fish and *ika* [squid] and eggs. You point out what [kind of topping] you want, then the man takes a hunk of rice and shapes it and places the fish on top. You dunk it in *shoyu* [soy sauce] and down it with one gulp. That sushi man took it for granted that I was Chinese and asked me the price of sushi in Shanghai.

I was also mistaken for a Korean by the man who fixed my suitcases. It's just that my Japanese accent is strange, so they have to take me for some Oriental besides a Japanese.

I stayed at my relative's place in Tokyo for a couple of days before coming up to my grandpop's. Talk about *nonki* [carefree]. I slept until noon one day there. She took me to Asakusa, which is the other bright spot in Tokyo besides the Ginza. But Ginza is more stuck up and people dress up to go there. Asakusa is more the student's hangout, and people are more carefree and happy. Food and shows are cheap there. We saw a Japanese show. In the theater there during recesses men come around with candies, drinks and fruits like at a football game or circus. And people throw bottles and peelings on the floor. Mrs. Ito (my relative) is going to make me a kimono. She is the brains of her family. Mr. Ito is more simple and not so cunning.

They're playing band music over the radio now and I recall how you used to like band music. They're celebrating the 2,600th year since the founding of the Japanese Empire. We can't conceive of a nation being 2,600 years old. And yet—I can't see what good all that history is to Japan. Look at the USA—only about $\frac{1}{20}$ that age but she's more advanced than Japan. Yo-chan (Iza's brother) says he can't understand why the U.S. has unemployment when she has most of the gold of the world. Well, I can't either.

I got exactly three Christmas postcards from kids at school. But I didn't give any. One was from a girl, Kay Haga. She came from Idaho. She surely is nice. But I don't see much of her because she is a second-year student. I only see the kids in our class. The other card was from Shimazu, who I told you about, I think. His mother goes to LA Holiness church. The other was from Eugene Hanisch. I must have told you about him. He is Czechoslovakian. Has to go next February to war. He was an exchange student.

January 2, 1940. Miye, I think you have so much stick to-it-ness (to use Popeye's language),[47] and I surely admire you more and more with every letter. I'm so proud of you for going to be a Cal graduate. Thanks a lot for the cutest Christmas card I ever got. The little blackie is so darned cute.

Your ramblings about death and your soul floating were so funny. You surely have queer ideas—just like me. I've thought the same thing. Only I haven't thought about death for a long time. Didn't you love that letter in *Reader's Digest* where a soldier said goodbye to his mother and said he wasn't afraid to die. And that life is measured more by quality than by quantity. If a person lives deeply and intensely for a few years, it is better than living for years and years in mediocrity. But I look at my old wrinkled *obaasans* and wonder if I'll ever be like that. But yet, old people just hang on to life and hate to die. Maybe it is better to die in the prime of life.

I've seen quite a few Japanese movies whose theme is that a girl loves a boy and he goes off to fight in China and then dies. They are so sad. I hate to admit it but I can't help the tears falling. Japanese movies are practically all sad. They are slow and thoughtful. Some beautiful photography—artistic scenery.

And next year Iza-chan has to go after he graduates. My cousin—Uncle Terry's grandson—will have to go this year. And Mrs. Ito's brother is graduat-

47. Popeye was one of Mary's and Miye's favorite cartoons, and they had fun using his unorthodox language in their correspondence.

ing next year, so he'll probably have to go—I told you about him, Toshi-chan. I can't imagine him a soldier—he is such a sissy. When I was going to get on the train at Tokyo, they had a lot of white boxes lined up in a room. Each contained the ashes of a soldier. The fourth year of war now. And no one knows when it will end. I do so wish it would end and so does everyone else. What's it all about? Why must the best men of a land go out for cannon fodder?

Later. I've written about ten letters during this vacation. Some I've owed for three and four months. Got a letter from Yahiro-sensei same time as yours. He didn't say anything. But he said he "trusted" I'd write for the *Echo of Calvary*. I hate that because now it will be on my conscience and I know that I'll be too lazy and stubborn to write.

Miye—be glad that you haven't tasted of vices, as you say. You know they say that only the saint understands the sinner. I wonder if that is true. I've had it [as] an ideal of mine to experience as much as possible. But I doubt if that is the wisest path. Because there is no turning back. Every sin leaves its mark and you aren't the same again.

Wasn't it you who said that it's just too bad for a girl to have boyfriends while going to school? You can't serve two masters. I'm so glad that I never had even a chance to go with boys while in JC. And it rather worries me now. Not that I go out with boys in the sense that we say back home. I rationalize by saying I want company, some one like you, and boys are the ones like you. I wonder what is the matter with me—why can't I get down to studying? Is it that I hate languages? I always have. I want something that I can lose myself in—something big and grand. I thought I found it in chemistry. But after the course was over, there was nothing left. Also calculus. And now I couldn't begin to tell you one thing about calculus. Was all that work and worry a waste of time?

Got my report card last week. I was so surprised! I expected to get just barely passing. But I only flunked one subject and that's because I never took the test. Shiojima-san [48] wrote my geography theme for me and I only got a C on it. I wrote my own history theme and got a B! I'm so proud of that. Because that was really tough. I can't understand it. Either the rest of the class is awfully dumb or the teachers grade very high. Next time I'm going to get a high average—without cheating. I cheated in some tests because I was desperate, but I could have got Cs without cheating.

Yes, it really does feel good to know a little Japanese. I think I know how my mother feels now. It's terrible and you feel so inferior when you can't read or understand people talking. Did I tell you—you said how one man said what a beauty New York neon signs would be for someone who couldn't read.

48. Shiojima Hifumi, a classmate of Emma's at Pasadena College who now lived in Tokyo with his wife and son and taught English at Meiji University.

Well, I experienced that in Tokyo and it was not a beauty. On the other hand, it made me mad because I couldn't read any of the signs. Ignorance may be bliss for some people but not for me.

I'm just beginning to realize how great my mother and father really are. And the rest of the Issei. My mother is really wonderful and I've been too self-centered and unthinking to realize it. When I think of my slaving, sacrificing parents, I know that I have to make good—I've got to not disappoint their trust in me. I hope there is a heaven for my mother's sake because she surely deserves a reward.

And maybe it is selfish for me to want a career. I ought to be a good obedient daughter and settle down like my ma wants me to. After all—I haven't got the brains or the perseverance to get anyplace. But yet—I'm still not cowed down enough to accept the beaten, uneventful path. It was so queer—but Fritz said the same thing as you: that he felt as though he were missing out on a vital part of life because he'd never been in love. I said I don't believe in love, and Naka was surprised and said it's serious stuff. Sometimes I wonder if Naka isn't just a puffed-up balloon? He talks so much and so knowingly and every other sentence starts with "back home." He reads the encyclopedia.

Fritz and Eugene said there was a European girl coming to school last year who was crazy. I asked Eugene if he liked her and he says no—she always argued. I wish she'd come again. Some crazy people are interesting.

January 4, 1940. Got back to Tokyo yesterday. It feels so good to get back. And now I'm looking forward to school starting again.

Emma sent me a lot of *New York Times* and *N.Y. Herald Tribunes*. It felt so good to see papers from home. I just sprawled out in the sun and read them all morning. Thelma had some *Modesto Bees* sent too. I liked the society page best. It had a picture of Mary Halley because she is Mrs. Bob Maxwell. It's a pity such a mathematical brain should be wasted on a girl who ends up by being a housewife. I'll never get over the wonder of how a girl who looks so pretty and feminine can be a whiz at calculus.

I wish that I were home to see those pictures now. I'd love to see Garbo—never have. And Virginia Fitzgerald and *Gone with the Wind*. Did you see *We Are Not Alone*? I loved that condensation of "Wind, Sand and Stars" in the *Reader's Digest*. That was really beautiful.

While in Yonezawa I bought a child's book, *Mountain and Soldiers*, written in Japanese. I read part of it at Grandpa's and then finished it on the train. All the *kanji* had *kana* on the side. I'm going to read more—because that's a good way to learn. Iza-chan said that when he was learning English he read such books as *Alice in Wonderland*, *The Covered Wagon*, and *Andersen's Fairy Tales*.

The Yonezawa people wear layers upon layers of clothes. I took pictures of my relatives and might send you some if they come out. The last night there I had dinner at my grandpapa's cousin's place. We had individual trays. It was so nice. I like to go there because they are quite well off and the dishes are pretty and their home is clean. The food is expensive and well prepared. I love luxury. I see those beautiful paintings, vases and boxes which cost hundreds of yen and how I long to have them! I am getting so worldly.

Some people here are so impressed when I tell them I'm going to go back to Cal to major in chemistry. They say all the girls here don't even think of higher education. I wonder if I'll have guts enough to go back to college after going back? It will be hard because my contemporaries will be out. Sometimes I envy you because you stuck to your major and it's really an accomplishment to graduate Cal. Are you going to buy a ranch in Modesto and start to work? Just think—Miye—you'll be on your own! How I wish I were making my own money instead of being a parasite on my old hard-working parents.

Tomorrow I'm going to Shiojima-san's place. I like the fashions now—bigger hips. And that is me. How I wish I could hear [the radio show] "Information Please." And the Metropolitan Opera broadcasts. And Charlie McCarthy and Bob Hope—even if they're not so funny at times.

Tokyo, January 29, 1940

Dearest Miye,

Thank you very, very much for the fruit cake. You surely were nice and thoughtful to send it to me. I repeat: I don't see how I ever had such a worthy friend like you. You are so faithful and considerate. It costs so much even for postage to send something over.

But I'm mad because I haven't got a letter from you this year yet. You're probably thinking the same thing about me, too. It's just that letters take so long, especially now. They take over a month. It seems so funny to get letters now that ask me about Christmas.

We had *gakugeikai* last night, which is a program something like open house back home. Students get up and sing or howl or talk. I didn't do anything. Miyoko went with me last night. It seemed so strange to talk in Japanese with my school friends but I had to for her sake.

Gee, it's cold now. It was sunny this morning but just now it's getting cloudy and gloomy.

Also I was sorry to hear that Senator Borah died.[49] I didn't know much

49. William Borah (1865–1940), Republican senator from Idaho and chairman of the Senate Foreign Relations Committee, 1925–33. Borah opposed restrictions on Japanese immigration to the United States and advocated a noninterventionist foreign policy.

about him but I rather liked him. Just the idea that there he was there—a stolid, stable thing that was an institution.

I'd love to read *Abraham Lincoln in the White House*, or something like that by Carl Sandburg. Also *Thoreau* by Canby. Did I tell you that I read *Grapes of Wrath*? Have you read it? It's good after you get over the shock of their immoralness [*sic*] and raw language.

We went last Wednesday to visit a *Hanayome Gakko*—Brides' School to you. It was rather interesting, and they treated us to tea and cakes afterwards (which was the best part). I guess that's the best thing for Japan, though, not to give the girls crazy ideas of independence and career. But it's hard on a girl who wants to rebel—much harder than in America. There are no real women's universities here. There are a few women students in Waseda. I heard that about four passed the entrance exam out of the 2,000 who took it. But the Japanese girls will have to do something—their ideas will have to change, or they'll be nervous wrecks. For here they prepare them to be brides and most of the eligible men go off to China for cannon fodder.

Couple of Saturdays ago the school went to see sumo. Now I know what Mr. Kiyoi meant when he said I looked like a *sumotori*. What a slam! Those Sumo men look like huge mountains of fat and blubber. They are stupid looking too. We went at eleven in the morning and didn't get out until seven at night. I was interested until four in the afternoon, after which I was bored and my head ached. We had to sit on tatami and it was so crowded and smoky and stuffy. It was a huge building—do you call it a coliseum? And we were on the second floor, so could see quite well. There is a house-like thing in the center and the two sumotori get in and try to throw each other out of the ring. Their actions are so slow and deliberate. I wish that they had Japanese news in America like they have American news here. Then the people of the USA could get a better idea of what Japan is like. Everyone is crazy about sumo here. Something like football back home. They broadcast it over the radio and have it in the news in the movies.

Iza said that the people here have a better idea of what America is like than the USA has of Japan. I wonder if that is true. I keep forgetting that these [folks I live with] are special because Mr. and Mrs. Nagata have been to America. Mr. Nagata surely is smart. He's been to Mexico and South America, too. I asked him the other night what's good about Japan in comparison to America and he said that everything is better. But he is broad-minded. He said that someone raised in this country is taught that Japan is the best country in the world. Even in Peru, the poorest country in the world, the kids are taught that it's the best country in the world. So you can't say what's good about one country or another. You can only say what is different. But I think it is true that Japanese are more broad-minded in that they don't have lynchings. And they don't persecute minorities. The Chinese in Japan are living in peace and he said that you wouldn't find a similar example in any other nation. Look at the Germans during the World War. However, I think that it is all propaganda that the Japanese are so artistic and clean and nature-loving. However, I can't judge yet for I'm only beginning to know Japan.

I've been studying quite hard this year. I've actually kept a New Year's resolution for one month! I made it a rule to study 15 hours per week or otherwise I can't go out on Saturday and Sunday. You feel good, though, when you begin to be able to understand the newspaper and movies and people talking. I like Japanese movies because they are different. Did you see *Mr. Smith Goes to Washington*?

This weekend I've a chance to go skiing. With Natsuko, Fritz, Hanisch, and some other people who are going with Fritz and Hanisch. I'm looking forward to it so much that I haven't gone out all week. I haven't got any clothes or equipment. My dear brother sent me some money day before yesterday, and was I happy. There isn't even any sarcasm in that "dear" anymore. However, I feel a little guilty in spending his money to go skiing. How I wish I had my own income! Maybe after I go back I could teach Japanese school and earn my way through college that way. But I'd hate to teach Japanese school for my life work.

Shiojima-san is quite smart, too. I like to go to their place because it is so nice and expensive stuff that they have. They gave me two fluffy silk blankets to sleep on. That was luxury after the thin dingy one I sleep on here.

It is Sunday today. Afternoon I am going to go to an art exhibit with a man who stays in the dormitory of Rikko Kai. He is trying to learn English. I talk English to him and he uses bigger words than I do. He is fat and studious and is a social worker. He said that he'll take me to see the slums of Tokyo. I hope so. His ambition is to read Thoreau and Emerson. I marvel at him because he studies by himself every night.

Hanako wrote me a letter. Didn't say anything and even her way of saying nothing was not interesting. What a contrast to you, Miye—you can say even nothing in such a funny way. Besides, you always have something to say. But it was sweet of her to write. She told me to pray and read the Bible and that hurt my hardened conscience. For my poor Bible is collecting dust, as usual. I got a Japanese Bible and meant to read it—but there's always something else to do. Hana sent me some pictures. Among them, one of you. She said that you were high class with a permanent. Your picture was so darned cute.

They say that there are no swear words in Japanese. Poor Georgine would surely be at a loss if she ever had to use this language, huh?[50]

50. Georgine was a mutual friend at Modesto Junior College who used to swear a lot.

The people here were all excited over the *Asama Maru* being stopped by the British.[51] The people take such incidents to heart. I think that they are more patriotic than Americans. Their country is something personal and deep.

One teacher said to us in class that a teacher of his was put in jail because he said the emperor and the people were the same: that the emperor was not divine. This teacher told us that he thought the same thing, too. So it seems that people really don't deep down think the emperor is a god.

And [their] God is funny too. It's just dawning on me how different it is from the Christian God. *Kami* originally came from *kami-sama*, which means "someone superior," or *meue* [lit., "above one's eyes"]. And anyone who dies and has done something great is worshipped. So that it's really their ancestors and no sublime aloof Absolute.

The other day I was feeling so sentimental. Maybe it's because I'd got through reading *Grapes of Wrath* and Walt Whitman—Naka loaned me an anthology of American poets. Walt Whitman kind of gets you. As I was saying—I was walking to school when I felt like not going at all. Instead, I got the crazy idea of walking, walking and walking—just to think and think. So I did. Just skipped school.

I'll have to send this letter off now or I'll never get it sent. It's so cold here. Japan is going to have a famine if it doesn't rain soon. She surely is a persecuted country.

And I'm still mad because I haven't got a letter from you yet. Maybe they censored it.

Tokyo, January 31, 1940

Dearest Miye,

Gosh, Miye, I love you! More than anyone else in all the world! I just got through reading your letter dated January 4 and it sounded so much like you that I've got a grin from ear to ear. No letters even begin to compare with yours.

And those cartoons were so darned cute! Especially that one about the "No more coffee—it keeps me awake." Woe is me! I still sleep during lectures and it is a triple embarrass[ment], when I think about it.

By all means, Miye—COME TO JAPAN! I've picked the poor country all to pieces and told all my troubles and complaints to you, but it really is not so bad. You surely can learn a lot here that you'd never get in the USA. It's good

51. The *Asama Maru* was stopped by a British naval vessel, which seized draft-age German males. Coincidentally, this was the very liner Mary had taken to Japan.

to get out of America just to be able to compare. I do so wish you'd come while I'm here. For me, a year is almost up now. One more year and then back to the Free and Open USA! Land of Space and Sunshine! Where you can shout and holler about anything you want—where you can get good food—where there are not millions of people at every step.

I admire you so much for graduating [from] Cal! Do buy a farm! That sounds so romantic. Just think, Miye—you'll be on your own! I don't realize, though, how much worry and hesitation there must be ahead of you.

Biggest disappointment I've had this year: I'm not going skiing this weekend. I'm almost compensated for it now, though. Natsuko cannot go. Neither can Fritz. And I don't want to go alone with Hanisch. Iza-chan said he'd take me if I found a girlfriend to go along too, but there's no one. He said he'd take me some day but I doubt it.

I've told you I have to beat it out of here, haven't I? Mrs. Nagata says she is too weak to have a boarder. But something tells me she doesn't like me being friends with Iza-chan. And maybe it is better for me to not see him anymore because I can't get to like him too much. But he's just a kid. And I learn so much from him. He's a brainstorm but he is so funny.

Japan—the land of rain—has not had rain for over a month! Such a thing has not happened for 60 years. A famine is feared. There is not much electricity so that the factories have to rest one day out of the week. Poor old Japan! She is so persecuted! There was a fire recently in Shizuoka which wiped out one-third of the city. And there was a train wreck on the line I take coming home from school. It happened on New Year's and the driver was drunk from New Year's sake. Just day before yesterday there was a train accident in Osaka and 50 or so people were burned to death. Prices are soaring. We never know when the government is going to crash. They just formed a new cabinet. The people are mad because a British warship stopped the *Asama Maru* and took off twenty-one Germans. They think it's an insult to their honor. There is no charcoal. There is no butter. No eggs. No water. Boy-oh-boy—what a depressing situation! And men coming back as ashes from China. Always talk about save this or save that—All their materials have staple fiber in them now. *Sufu*,[52] they call it.

Gosh, I'm glad I'm not one of these suffering people.

I'm reading *The Good Earth* by Pearl Buck in Japanese.[53] It is rather difficult but interesting. Since I read it in English, I get the meaning even if I have to skip half of the *kanjis*.

O, Miye! It feels so good to go down the street and be able to read the

52. An acronym for a synthetic fiber used as a substitute for cotton and wool during the war. It produced inferior cloth.

53. *The Good Earth* (1931) sympathetically describes the hardships of Chinese peasant life.

signs. And to begin to read the headlines of the newspaper. I get so discouraged at times but at other times I feel so optimistic and self-improved!

I think that you still have the idea that the females here are like Reverend Sakuma's wife. Well, they're not. And I'm surely far from learning to be a demure Japanese maiden. Quite the contrary. For at school I talk loud and cut up with the boys—and at home all I do is eat and sleep and study. I can't even sit on my legs correctly. And neither can Miyoko, the girl here.

But these Japanese girls in American dress give me a pain in the neck. Such loud, clashing colors they wear! And high heels—when they look like they'll topple over at every step. And paint—that's their worst point. American schoolgirls are conservative compared to their whitewashed faces with red blotches on cheeks and around their eyes.

I never realized until my mom told me—that I only write the bad points about Japan. So I must give you an awful impression of this country. But heck—I don't know any good points. But it's pleasant for me here because I'm in the more-than-middle-almost upper part of society. I mean, with my money I go where I couldn't go in America, by comparison. For instance, I never used to go to restaurants back home. But here, in Tokyo, only the better-off people eat at the places where we go. But the theaters are always packed. There are more students on the streets, in restaurants and theaters than all the other people combined.

You surely would laugh at me if you were here. In the mornings it's so cold when I walk to school so that my nose gets red. And really a bright, flaming red. It looks so funny. But people at school are too polite to laugh at it. Iza-chan said he could tell the temperature by the redness of my nose. Miyoko laughs at it too. It surely looks funny.

This morning I saw Fuji-san [Mt. Fuji]! It was so beautiful, all covered with snow. And I'm so absent-minded and unobservant. Yo-chan (Izaya's brother) rode part way to school with me on the train and pointed it out to me. And here, I'd been riding on the same train all this time and never even noticed the mountain in the distance.

Yo-chan is going to take me to the Ginza some day. He is fun. Altogether different from Iza. Iza looks more persecuted and he studies more. Whereas Yo-chan is more simple and loves to have a good time—but so does Iza.

February 12, 1940. Two weeks since I wrote the foregoing! I'm really slipping—this has never happened to me before. But I've just not been in the mood to write.

And before I forget—you needn't send *Reader's Digest*s because there is a boy at school subscribing [to] it and I borrow his. Thanks anyway. It's so much bother for you, and expensive, too.

I've been quite studious. Studied 15 hours per week up to last week. That's a record for me for a New Year's Resolution. But if I study so much I feel so machine-like and dull and unstimulated. Last week I rebelled—so I've got a little pep left in me. Had quite an interesting week. Saturday went ice skating up in the mountains. It was beautiful. They have a swimming pool outdoors all frozen over. About 15 kids from school went. At night we built a bonfire and had a wiener roast. I'm a terrible skater.

Then Sunday I was planning to go to Shiojima-san's to study, but since Iza was home, we went to the *Nichi Nichi* newspaper's planetarium. It was as nice as the one in LA only the room was not as large. And the speaking in Japanese, of course.

I certainly brag about you to him. Last night I dreamt that you came to Japan. Do dreams come true?

Last Friday I saw *Only Angels Have Wings* and enjoyed it.[54] Went with Natsuko and Fritz. And Wednesday our school went on a sightseeing trip to Yokosuka, which is an hour's ride from Yokohama. There is a battleship there, *Mikasa*, which was Admiral Togo's[55] flagship during the Russian-Japanese War. It was snowing that day and very cold.

Honestly, Miye, I'm not in the mood for writing (as you've undoubtedly observed). Therefore, I will just quit trying and write Thoughts at Random—Remember O. O. McIntyre?[56]

You surely have to know your English here if you want to teach anyone. That man who boards at the dormitory here asks me some English and I sweat blood trying to make out the English. It's just that in reading I take so much for granted, so that when I'm asked the precise meanings of words I'm sunk. And that *Webster's Collegiate Dictionary* is not detailed enough. If you come you ought to bring a big dictionary. Because it gets you when you find out how little of the English language you know. And I'm just beginning to realize how different the language of the English people is from Americans! They learn English here and not American. When I went skating there was an *ainoko*[57] of English mother and Japanese father, the sister of a boy coming to school. She didn't look at all Japanese-y. She says "cawn't" and other Englishy words. Tomorrow I'm going to a concert with you-know-who. Last night we met Natsuko on the Ginza. I hate to meet people when I'm with him [and] so does he because Japan is different. Well, Natsuko razzed me this morning and I burned and burned. How I wish I could not blush. Are you bored?

54. A 1939 movie starring Cary Grant and Jean Arthur.

55. Togo Heihachiro (1846–1934), commander of the combined squadron that destroyed the Russian Baltic squadron in the Russo-Japanese War of 1904–5.

56. A syndicated columnist carried in *The Modesto Bee*.

57. A person of mixed parentage.

not. I'm enjoying doing this.—Say, if you ever have a chance, read *Les Enfants Terribles* by a Frenchman, I forgot whom.[58] Wonder if there is an English translation? It's translated into Japanese. I'd love to see the following movies: *Grapes of Wrath*, *Of Mice and Men*, *Gone with the Wind*, *Abe Lincoln in the White House*. (Have you read the book?) Iza said *Les Enfants Terribles* is a queer book and about 18-year-olds who are sexually deformed and that it is a book old men should read. Maybe I'll get a one-sided view of everything in Japan because Iza is the only Japanese native I really talk to. I think you'd like him. He writes poetry and short stories and even composed some music—says he is a "boheme." Did you see the movie *La Boheme*? I didn't like it. Or *Tailspin*, either. We have one cute teacher I like more than any other. His name is Nagano and he wears high-water pants and he is like a little kid still wondering about this wonderful world. He's studied in Paris. Fritz said he knew an American student (girl) in Paris who spends $220 per day. He saw a bull fight in Spain and said it was terrible. If *Prison Without Bars* comes to San Francisco, see it. It is a French picture and worth seeing. I wish I'd studied French and German and history and literature. Of what use to me now are physics and calculus and chemistry? I've forgotten it all. Gee, I'm cold. It is eleven o'clock now.

Later. Oh boy, oh boy—now I do feel like writing! Mrs. Nagata just got through bawling me out. First time—And I never knew that she felt that way about it. She told me to go to bed at ten o'clock after this. And to quit running around. And not to talk to Iza at night. She said she worried so much about me that it made her sick! Mary—you fool—not to have seen it coming. I suspected that she didn't like it. But I didn't want to face the facts. She said no girl comes home at eleven at night in Japan. So that's really the reason why she wanted me to move! Well, Mary, I'm glad that you found out. She doesn't trust me. I guess hereafter I really will be a jailbird. And go to bed at ten. It's funny—we were just talking about it today—how I was free as the air. And Natsuko too. That girl from Alaska got clamped down on and she goes no place. And Naka said that Japanese girls can't go out and I didn't believe him. But I believe it now. But she makes me mad, too. She said that I go down to the *kotatsu* now because I wait for Iza and that is false—damn it! I go to get warm before going to bed. And what kind of a female does she think I am? Am I a child that I must go to bed at ten every night? And get up early in the morning. Phooey on her and all her tribe—well—the sooner I get out of here the better. And my crazy days are over. Really a jailbird. And Natsuko said just today that if I move I might be a jailbird. Well, well—so after all I am to

58. Jean Cocteau (1884–1963).

follow the path of the *nihon no ojo-san*.[59] Hell—O pardon my speech. But it gets me! It really does. She said she's been telling Iza the same thing for a long time. But I won't go to bed at ten. And she can't make me. Neither can anyone else. O America—I want to go back where a woman is a person and not a good-for-nothing female—one to be a mother of soldiers.

She said my ma would be surprised at my *darashino nai* [undisciplined or immoral] living. She said I shouldn't copy these boys and their manner of living. But rather, should be like Miyoko. Darn it. Miyoko doesn't go anyplace. It's all right for her. But I'm here to learn—I want to go places and see things.

Well—an unforeseen move in this jumble of my life. The only thing that bothers me now is should I go out with Him tomorrow night? Doggone it—who wants to take the well-beaten, mediocre dull path of existence that these Jap girls tread? They give me a pain in the neck. O, Miye—I'm so darned mad! I wish you were here so that I could just shout and holler to my heart's delight. But no—instead, I must bear it and wear the hypocritical smile omnipresent here.

Scarlett O'Hara wanted to be rich enough so that she could tell the world to go to hell—well—I want the same thing. Now. But that gets me when people don't trust me—my God—I can't help being a girl! Why can't I talk with another person who enjoys the same things I do and [who] has a brain—should sex make so much difference! Miyoko—she is no company. Her world is so limited. What does she know about science? Or care? Besides, she is so uncommunicative. I ask her what she's going to do after graduation and she changes the subject. O, she's all right for light change—like all girls. But Miye—there's no one like you. As I've repeatedly said—only the boys begin to remind me of you.

It still makes me rave! I want to go to bed whenever I want to go to bed and no one is going to boss me around like a child. Boy, I'm surely thankful that I'm not a girl here.

If I were home now I'd just walk and walk and walk this out of my system. But no—nice Japanese girls stay home—Oooh—I'm so mad—

But then, after all, she's only thinking of my welfare. And my dear mother would not approve of my life in Japan. I wish I could do something well so that I could be independent. I ought to live in an apartment. Some day I'm going to be my own boss and I won't give a damn what anyone says. Some day.

It's funny, though. It's ridiculous. Sometimes don't you find yourself laughing at you because you are so queer and stupid and blundering? I surely do. It's funny because I take it all so seriously. When and what does it mat-

59. Proper young Japanese lady.

ter—I am only a bundle of electricity. Only an infinitesimal portion of this universe. And no one would know the difference 100 years from now—what I do now will not matter. If I go to bed at ten every night or not sleep at all—what matters it?

But poor Mrs. Nagata! I must consider her side too. She has a crazy Nisei boarding at her place who runs after her smart next-to-the-eldest precious son. And this loony girl comes home at all hours of the night. She always tempts her darling Iza-chan and entices him out at night. Not only that—she waits until he comes home, all tired from work at eleven at night. And then she comes down to the *kotatsu* and weaves her spell about him. She goes to his room and brazenly talks to him or otherwise she entices him into her room. Such a wench!

Well—if she thinks so let her think so. The truth will out. Justice will prevail. O, these bland self-righteous phrases make me sick.

Of one thing am I certain: I have to make myself scarce and the sooner the better.

And maybe you believe Mrs. Nagata's side of the story. But no—you're one person I can trust. And that is why I write only to you.

Because I have my side of the story too. I don't wait up for him and I don't entice him—or even try to. Miye—can I help it if I have no friends in Japan and then someone is nice to me and is interesting and funny too? What should I do?

O, Mary—stop your rationalizing and feeling sorry for yourself, you know that you've been going out too much and you only got what you deserved.

Miye—were you bored by my outbursts? I don't think so because I love to read your letters when you're real mad or real poetic-feeling.

I feel better now. But I still want to walk.

Goodnight. Gee—I want to get back to the Land of the Free.

Tokyo, March 9, 1940

Dearest Miye,

It seems ages since I've written, but I bet you think so, too.

First of all, don't you love this paper? It is "*maki gami*"—you know, the kind they write on with *fude* [brush] and you unroll as you read? Anyway, it's light and you might get a kick out of the long mess of the page.

Tests are over and am I happy! Today is first day of vacation. I feel so "*nonbiri*" [relaxed]. You'll be getting mad at me for showing off my Japanese soon. But I'm proud of myself because now sometimes I actually think of the Japanese word before the English.

Gee, I surely studied for the exams, too. It's just cram, cram, cram in the *kanji*. Hundreds of them. Reading and rereading and then reading more. I get so disgusted with myself for being so slow about learning those darned characters. But it's really surprising how much you can learn here in contrast to studying Japanese in America. I went to school about five years and didn't get above Book 7. When I came to Japan even Book 3 was difficult for me to read. And now Book 8 or 12 [is] easy for me. And I wonder how I ever could have been so ignorant. But there's a long road ahead of me yet. I bet Elsie and Emma still can talk better than I. And I can't read the newspaper fluently yet. That is my ambition. But now I'm beginning to like the study of this language. The more you get in to it, the more interesting it becomes. And if you know a little history it becomes more interesting. Their history is just fascinating and I want to read lots of it. In Japanese. You know, Miye, I never realized before how different it is when you read a book in the original language and when you read it in a translated language. For instance, in reading *The Good Earth* in Japanese I get an altogether different feeling from reading it in [the original] English. So I think that you can't understand a people until you understand their language. And I want to be able to read Japanese novels and magazines. Iza-chan said the reason Nisei cannot understand Japan or the Japanese is because they don't read enough. I think that is true. And I haven't much more time here. I think I'll go back next March after I graduate. And then if my sister is in Hawaii, I'd love to stay there about a month. Then go home and work and make money to finish college. My plans are thus.

Have you heard about Emma's fiancé? She sent me his picture and he looks kind of sissy but good-looking, don't you think? Or have you seen him? I bet my mom likes him. She makes me laugh. Now all she has to worry about is her "*ojosan*" daughter when she comes back from Japan. O, Miye—I had a terrible dream that I came back to America and all those church women were saying how "*ojohin*" [refined] and quiet and demure and Japanese maidenly I had become! O—it got me! They said my movements were so slow and graceful! It makes me laugh now because it is so impossible and ridiculous. I'm just as stubborn and pig-headed as ever and Japan will never take it out of me—I hope.

Did you know that I'm taking ikebana lessons? I like it. It is so beautiful. But not when I do it. They had an exhibit of ikebana at one of the department stores and you should have seen it! That's really an art and it makes you feel good way down to your toes! You think you're in paradise! The color arrangement—the spacing—the harmony of vase and flowers—it's all so perfect!

Tonight I asked Miyoko if I could cook and she's going to let me. I have no idea of what to make. They don't have: eggs, milk, onion, bacon, butter, tomatoes. It's easier to list what they have. I like to cook, though, when I don't have to. I want to learn Japanese cooking. They have some tasty food here. I like their style of sukiyaki. That is, they have a hibachi in the middle with a pot of *okazu* and everyone sits around it with a bowl of rice in one hand and chopsticks in the other. And then they all fish out the stuff from the family pot. It's good on the cold days. You get the food boiling hot. My pop would like it.

It's raining today. Ever since morning. This light and tender rain. We had an essay on "rain" in our readers, and you know what—I'm beginning to see the beauty of Japanese writings. At first it was just a mess of hard words and *kanji* but now it's beginning to make sense.

We have one month of vacation. I'm going to move. And then going out to my cousin's in the country and get flea-bitten. Also, Shiojima-san said that he would take me to Kamakura.

Two Sundays ago I went to my relative's place. There was a boy there who boards there and goes to college. He wanted to try out his English on me, so we jabbered. You would die laughing if you heard him talk! But I'm so polite, you know (to strangers), so I only flattered him. He said that one of his sisters "is the bottom of my sisters"—meaning the youngest. And then he says "I am suffocating" and he said that so much I asked him what it was, and he said he saw it in a conversation dictionary thus: "suffocate: to be full of food." He's a shorty but rather nice looking. And young—only a kid. But he said that he would take me to a Noh Drama. I hope so. I learned a lot from him, too. I talk to so few natives here. Really talk, I mean—say what I think. Like my relatives—I only sit around and act dumb and talk only about the weather or food or something prosaic.

Mrs. Nagata is sick again. She is so weak that I feel sorry for her. I would hate to be like that.

Yoshiya (Iza-chan's brother) was feeling sad night before last because he got a special delivery letter informing him of the death of two of his friends while airplane practicing. He tells me "Play, play, for we haven't long to live." And that is very true of a boy here. It's very doubtful if they will live to be over 25. Especially now. Yoshiya said that 20% of those who go out for airplane[s] die during exercises. And that if foreign ships ever came to fight Japan that they would not drop bombs. Instead the airplane would hurl itself onto the warship. Such nerve! But as I begin to understand the essays in the readers, I begin to understand these people. These essays are full of patriotism and nationalism. Japan: the great and glorious country whose people are as one family with the emperor as its head.

The other night I had an argument such as I haven't had for ages. There is a man who stays in the dormitory here and he comes over sometimes to study English from me. He is one of those not-so-brilliant, but nevertheless slow and steady and dangerous people. Opposite to you and me. Well, he wants to learn English conversation so we talked about *Bushido* and then got off onto the war in China and then what is man?, etc. Well—he is one type of Japanese who believes all that propaganda about Japan's Holy Cause in the Orient. He said Japan has a mission and duty to help and teach and lead the Chinese. That it is a Holy Cause and that it is not aggression. O, such pig-headedness! And boy, did he blow up when I told him that Japan is an aggressor and that she is bombing Chinese women and children! And then Iza-chan in the next room trying to study—he pops in and sticks up for my side. But I was surprised because Iza is not fooled by this propaganda. Well—Miye, I hope they don't censor this. I'm afraid [to] rave on because they open letters. Emma's letter to me was opened.

Tuesday before last our school went to the House of Peers. I actually heard the premier Yonai[60] himself! He talks like he has mush in his mouth. I couldn't understand anything that was said there. But it was impressive with all those lords and barons, etc. with bald heads and frock coats on. And half of them absent.

Thanks a lot for the *Reader's Digest*s. They would have let those articles on Japan through because I saw them from a classmate's.

Did you hear about the Saito[61] case? He was one of the leaders of a powerful party and gave a speech [on] Sunday, March 10, [1940], questioning what the army was doing in China and how long they were staying there and where all the money was going to. No one knows exactly what he said because the newspapers were forbidden to print it. Well—he was expelled from the party. But the people sympathized with him and he was only voicing their sentiments. And hereafter there will be absolutely no questioning what the army does. But the people are dissatisfied. And the government doesn't know what to do. I often wonder how it will all end. And what will happen to Japan. Today I read what the head of our school said about Nisei. I read it in Japanese, too. He makes me sick because he hates America and loves Japan. He said the Nisei have materialistic ideals—that Americans are self-centered and money is their God. In contrast to Japan, whose people love their emperor and are so loyal and self-sacrificing. Maybe I'm dumb—or prejudiced—but it seems to me that these people are not so idealistic and self-sacrificing. My God—they only go to war because there is no way out—and they camouflage it with patriotic words. Phooey—I don't believe they want to fight any more than Americans. It's only that they bow to fate more humbly and quietly whereas Americans raise the roof when they have to do something that they

60. Adm. Yonai Mitsumasa (1880–1948), prime minister, January–June 1940. His cabinet was overthrown by the army.

61. Saito Takao (1870–1949), a leader of the Minseito party and harsh critic of Japanese militarism.

don't want to do. These passive Orientals! And yet, I am Oriental too—to a certain extent. It's so funny how people can talk about The Masses or The Common People and yet, the speaker always excludes himself as being superior. Have you noticed that? It's so vain. I do it all the time. When we must realize that we are only an infinite portion of these millions of people. Therefore, what you want for yourself, you must think of the rest of the people on the same level. I do that with girls all the time—that is, I say most girls are so silly and brainless and clumsy, when after all it's myself I'm talking about.

Today I went with Miyoko to the family I'm moving to. Darn! What a place. I hate to go there. The woman is such a chatterbox and she keeps repeating and repeating, like a record. The only difference is that you can turn off a phonograph and you can't turn her off. I hate to leave Nagatas'—I liked this family. They let me alone. And these people—Odajima's the name—they wanted me to quit Waseda Kokusai and go to a bride's school.

March 4 was Dolls' Festival.[62] It is so pretty. There is a step-like affair covered with red cloth. On the top sit the emperor and empress. Next come ladies-in-waiting, then the musicians, then the samurai and lastly, the drawers and chest of clothes for the women.

I'm sleepy. It's 10:20. And I have to write a term paper for Yoshiya on "morals." It's an icky book about all those moldy philosophers. Emma's fiancé graduated from the same school Yoshiya is going to.

Miye—your letters are the only interesting ones that I receive. All the others tell me they are doing nothing and that nothing interesting is happening. I don't have my new address yet, so keep on addressing the letters here and they'll forward it. I'm going to move next Sunday. Woe is me. But only one more year now.

Tokyo, April 19, 1940

Dearest Miye,

Have I neglected you? I can't remember if I wrote or if I'd only thought and planned it so much that it took the place of actually writing. Anyway, I surely enjoyed your two letters. You have such a free and gay style of writing—so off-hand and natural that I feel I've actually met you.

Please come to Japan if you possibly can. If you don't grab the chance now you might never be able to. And a foreign country is so different—you can read and hear all about it but you can never know the real thing until you actually get here.

62. Another name for Girls' Festival, *Hina matsuri*, celebrated on the third day of the third month. Mary was mistaken in the date here.

I've been quite busy lately. And feeling gloomy too because here I have to get adjusted all over again. Life was going on pleasantly before in comparison. Yes, I've left the abode of the "intellectual Iza-chan." Last Sunday I left the place and stayed at my relatives' until Tuesday, when I came here. Note my new address. I'll write it at the end of this letter if I don't forget. It is even worse than my last address.

There are three Nisei staying at this place. You know Harry Tonai of San Francisco—his half sister is here. Name's Fukiko. And then another girl who is quiet and homely and her hair is queer and sparse and kinky. A boy is here who acts like a country hick except that he is very quiet. We are all quiet except the two small girls (ages ten and eleven) and their mother. She runs on like a phonograph record. The only difference is that she needs no winding and she is always on the same tone of voice. But she's really smart because she used to teach at a bride's school before. She's expecting a kid in June and looks it.

Has Mako had her baby yet? It does seem sad for one so young to have the responsibilities and sorrows of a mother. Johnny Nakayama was asking about her. She's experiencing things that I'll probably never experience for I'll be a selfish old sour maid. It's funny when I picture myself old and wry—I wonder—will we still be cronies then?

These people made me laugh (to myself). For they said if I should ever come home late at night, such as 7:30 or eight that they would send someone to the station after me. And to think that before, at Nagatas' I used to come home at eleven and twelve at night! But Miye, I've reformed. I never go out at night any more. And besides, Miye, you have a mistaken idea. I have no beaus. I don't even have boyfriends like you. The boys I rave about—I never go out with any of the school kids alone. Natsuko and I have gone with some but they are only friends. I've been out with Iza-chan but he doesn't count—I'm almost older than he is and he never thinks of me as a girlfriend—only as a stubborn Nisei who likes to argue and eat. But heck, it was a lot of fun with him because he was so funny and brainy and skinny. Well, I won't see him anymore. I'll just stick around this darned place and be a good girl and learn to be a demure Japanese maiden. Mrs. Nagata said it would be much better for me here because at her place there were too many boys and they talked rough language. But I like Mr. Nagata. He was so simple and kind and funny. Iza-chan said his father is still dreaming dreams and I think it is true. Well, Miye, hereafter you will be spared the misery of hearing me rave about that Iza-chan.

Hanisch went back to Czechoslovakia on the eleventh. They had a big article about him in the paper and his picture. He is in the news on the screen but I haven't seen it. I miss him a lot. He said he hated to leave Japan. We went to the Tokyo station to see him off. Why must friends be separated? Like you and me? But it won't be long (I think). Next summer I think I'll go back. I can't make up my mind. Just now I feel like going back next year.

I saw *Grand Hotel* today, after school. It was very good. Garbo is so bewitching. It is true that European actresses have a certain something that American women lack.

I live right close to Keisen Girls' High School now and these people want me to go there. I might, but I hate to leave Kokusai after I got used to it. I wonder how I'll be able to get along at school after I get back? I'll be such an old maid. Maybe I should give up my ambitions and just get hitched and take life easy. But no—my rebellion is still in me even though it is being dulled every year more and more.

Fukiko says that she doesn't want to go back. Her case is hard because she'll have to meet her stepmother and half brothers and sister and live with them. She and I talk a lot. We are roommates. She went to a bride's school.

Isn't Europe a mess, though? I'm ashamed of myself because I don't know a thing about what's going on. I don't care. I'm too lazy to study it out. Fritz says he hates to even think about it and tries not to.

Iza-chan just made a short-wave radio. Darn him—just when I'm leaving the place! I heard news from America and some loud jazz but it felt good and as though I were in the good old USA again.

I went to my cousin's place in Toyama for almost two weeks during spring vacation. I meant to write all my letters up there but did not get bored as I'd expected, so did not write many. She just had a baby a month old and one day I even washed diapers and felt very self-righteous and martyr-like. The kids are not pretty but they are lively and fun. I played with them and carried them on my back. Boy, these farmers in this country really work! They get out in the rice fields and work in the mud bare-footed. From sunrise to sunset, too. They are tough! The women are so strong! They surely are the backbone of Japan. These sissies in Tokyo make me sick just to look at them. They use human manure and it smells terrible! Such dirty work, too.

The cherry blossoms are all gone now. I never saw the really pretty ones. Natsuko, Fritz and I went to Ueno Park to see them, but it was too late and most of the blossoms were gone. Natsuko and Fritz get along so well together—I feel as though I'm not wanted and so go by myself. So that again I have no friends.

They say that during the rainy season here even one's shoes get moldy in one day. May is the rainy season. I dread it. Did I tell you that one day I took a flop? It was so funny—I was walking along with galoshes on and the sidewalk was muddy and slippery. There were many people sitting and staring at me, so I took a big flop in front of them all. My raincoat was covered with mud and my stockings ruined.

Tomorrow I'm going to get a permanent—maybe. I'll send you a picture of beautiful(?) me if I get one. I am getting worldlier every year.

Last Sunday I went to Holiness church because my mom wrote a letter bawling me out for not going. Those people were really "quivering with religious fervor" (as you used to say). They prayed so loud and they clapped their hands and beat their heads upon the tatami. The preacher had a bell and he rang it after a certain time as a signal to quit praying. But I like to go there to observe them—to think that people really can be so earnest is quite interesting. I'm going this Sunday too. One lady talked to me and said she knew Emma and for me to have lunch there next Sunday. She was so nice. It's a fact that these religious people have a light on their faces which others do not have. Virtue shining through.

We have the cutest new teacher. Very young. First day that he came he blushed when he saw that there were girls in the class. Today he brought some sandals that we'd read about and he actually got barefooted and wore them to show us what they were like.

Darn it—I wish I were still at the Nagatas. I miss Iza-chan. He was my best friend in Japan. But I wasn't his best friend—far from it. And he probably doesn't miss me at all. I wish that you were here. This Mr. Odajima—I don't care much for him. He did the washing today. He is small and henpecked. Phooey on him. But he's really quite nice. It's going to cost me about 15 yen per month more to live here because the room and board is higher and they don't have an iron and I have to buy my lunch.

I wish I were rich and could do anything that I wanted.

Accomplishment: I finished reading *The Good Earth* in *Japanese*!

Your fruit cake had no worms in it. It was good—I divided it with the Nagatas.

Gee—I'm fat. I hate myself. I take myself so seriously and am so self-centered and egotistical that it is funny. But I love you and want you to come to Japan and you'd better—or else.

Tokyo, June 10, 1940

Dear long-neglected Miye,

How are you? I haven't heard from you for ages. Don't you love me any more?

As for me, I just haven't felt like writing. And still don't, for that matter. I'm supposed to go to church today—but am tempted to stay home and write letters. Because I feel the mood growing on me to write.

Lots has happened since I wrote to you.[63] I think that I'm in the second stage of my stay in Japan. I haven't written to anyone besides my ma for the last half year. But still I don't love Japan. They say that after about six months Nisei get to like Japan and hate to go home, but I'm not that way. I knew that I wouldn't be. But now everything is not new and exciting like at first. And I feel more settled because I'm getting the hang of the language. Now I can understand most conversations and can get the general meaning of newspapers, magazines, and radio. That helps.

Do you remember a Shizuko Fukuda? She knew you in Cortez. She said she used to be Mako's best friend. They moved to San Jose. Anyway, it felt so good to talk to someone who's known you and Frances Yuge. She is coming to school—entered in April. A first-year student.

Yesterday the school went on a trip to Kamakura. I didn't go because I'm broke. My dear brother has not sent me money for this month. So I met a girl in our class from French Indo-China. She is a Nisei. Her native language is French and she doesn't speak English although she can read it a little. Therefore, I speak Japanese with her. We went downtown and she bought French books. She couldn't find a book that she wanted and when she asked for it, they told her that the government had censored it. We went to two shows afterwards, *Merry Widow* [and] *Capriccio* (a German movie), and [then to] a Japanese movie. They were all good and we enjoyed them. I had a good time the whole day. Last month I only went to one movie—I was really ideal last month. And I went to church every Sunday, too. I didn't go out hardly at all. But gradually I'm slipping back into my old ways. But anyway, I don't feel like running around all over so much. Besides, now my friends are all girls. Naka and Hanisch have gone home. I never go with Iza anymore since his ma bawled me out. And yet, after all it's better for me. His mother is smart. Because I was getting to like him too much. He was the only one who was so nice to me. I had so much fun with him—but no more. Fritz is still here, but he and Natsuko go out together and I go with them sometimes. He surely is different. Sometimes I think that he is a genius. He knows so much Japanese. Besides he speaks German, English, French, Hungarian, and other languages too. Chinese, too. His mother let him do just as he wanted. His father was an artist and died in World War I.

I might go to another school. I hate to part with the kids of our class, but still, I want to learn what a Japanese school is like.

Miye—did you get into Civil Service?

The other day I did not feel like going to school, so instead, went to

63. Among other things, Mrs. Nagata had agreed to let Mary return to her home on the condition that she be in by ten every evening, that she and Miyoko change their room to one not adjacent to Izaya's, and that she not consort with him.

some book stores and browsed all day. There are two stores which have foreign books. There was a good book by a Stanford Professor on the Nisei.[64] What is going to happen to us Nisei, anyway? I've been in Japan almost a year and many of my ideas have changed, but I still love America as my country. I heard that there is a bill before the House whereby Nisei who stay in Japan over six months automatically lose their American citizenship. Do you know anything about it? I can't believe that such a thing is possible. I was fortunate in not encountering any experiences of being prejudiced against because of my race. So that is probably why I like the U.S.A. so much. One thing good about Japan is that they treat foreigners with respect. And Japan is a peace-loving country. Proof: there have been periods in Japanese history where they have not had war for hundreds of years. There is no parallel to that in American or European history. Another thing I'm beginning to see is that the Europeans are grasping and cruel. They call Japan the "Yellow Peril." And why? Because Japan is trying to build an Asia for the Asiatics. Is that any different from the Monroe Doctrine? And the European countries were cruel in ruling their possessions. They purposely kept the natives ignorant so that they would not declare their independence. For instance, whenever a movement starts in Indo-China to free that country, France immediately sends over soldiers and they shoot down the leaders. Our teacher said he had a photograph of that, and I think it is true. And look at India.

The trouble with us is that we were reared in America and saw only the Occidental viewpoint. Small countries in Europe rule most of the world. Is that fair? Even the U.S.A. practically runs Brazil—she owns their transportation facilities and coffee factories. And then when Japan sees this injustice and tries to wake up these countries, the Europeans are afraid that their valuable possessions will be taken away, so they shout "Yellow Peril."

It's a mess, isn't it?

It gets my goat, though—these Occidentals who are so self-righteous.

We can't realize what is going on in Europe. The sufferings and misery of the people. Until we had [a] black-out in Tokyo I never dreamt how unpleasant it is. Only for one week we had to suffer. And to think that London is always like that. But I can begin to understand how it is in Germany—on a ration system. And it being a misdemeanor to throw away materials. Because in Japan we have a little of that. Sugar and matches are on a ticket basis from this month. They say there is a shortage of this and shortage of that. You get tired of hearing it.

Maybe war between Japan and America is not so far off as we would like

64. *The Japanese in the United States: A Critical Study of the Problems of Japanese Immigrants and Their Children*, by Yamato Ichihashi (Stanford, Calif., 1932).

to think. One fellow said that it would be more comfortable for Nisei to be in Japan than in America in case of war. Because in World War I they segregated all Germans—even naturalized citizens.

They had Boys' Festival fifth of last month. The fish are so big that wave on top of the homes.[65] We didn't have any here.

June 9, 1940. A boat came in Saturday (day before yesterday) and I was wishing so much for a letter from you. But none. I don't get any letters any more. I got one today from Thelma Christiansen. She said she might teach at Ceres Grammar School. She also asked me if I'm going to school after I get home, and if I did that she would pity me.

Right now, I feel like not going to school after I get home. What I want to do next is go to Europe. Wonder if I'll ever get to? But my education is so general and I can't earn a living doing anything. Maybe I ought to stay longer in Japan, then I might do some translating. Japanese literature is interesting. Have you read *Tales Grotesque and Curious* by Ryunosuke Akutagawa?[66] It is an English translation of short stories by a modern author. I think that they come up to any short-story writer—like De Maupassant or Poe or Hawthorne. We had a lesson in our readers at school by this Akutagawa and our teacher told us about him. Some people consider him a literary genius. He committed suicide when 35. I think that you might like him. I wish that I understood enough Japanese to understand him. I bought his book because much of his writing has been censored recently. I got a copy of his original book and the censored one and copied down all that had been censored. He makes fun of the army and says they are childlike and puerile (remember the word?). They delight in swaggering about wearing swords. If I stay one more year I think that I'll be able to read such things easily—I hope so. He likes to make fun of traditions and religions. It's surprising how his ideas correspond to modern American writers.

Did you know that some tanks are run by wireless? And that aeroplanes can run by wireless—but they can't drop bombs—*as yet*. It looks as though Flash Gordon's[67] exploits are not such a dream after all. And the next war will really be a war between machines.

Mr. Nagata says the English government will have to flee to Canada. But

65. Boys' Festival, *Tango no Sekku*, the fifth of May, now celebrated as the national holiday, Children's Day. Families with boys traditionally fly banners representing red and black *koi* (carp) on their houses.

66. Akutagawa Ryunosuke (1892–1927), a novelist who wrote under the noms de plume Gaki and Chokodo. He is best known in the West as the author of *Rashomon*.

67. Science fiction hero popularized in a comic strip and the movies. His chief nemesis, Ming the Malevolent, had a decidedly Asian appearance.

signs indicate that Germany will win, don't you think. Our *kanbun*[68] teacher said that not even America could save the allies now. For Germany is fast.

Did you read *Three Comrades* by Remarque? I'm attempting to read it in Japanese. When I read in Japanese it is so slow that it gets me down. So I start another book. Right now, I've started four books. One is by Kagawa. Did I tell you that he spoke at our school? He is funny but inspiring. He is one of these people who know everything—about philosophy and science. He looks like a pig and shouts when he talks. I read his poetry while in JC and expected to see a frail poetic-looking greenish person but instead there he was—so energetic and pugnacious.

I'm so ashamed of myself because I took a science course but what do I know? Practically nothing. Often I regret that I never took more French and German—especially when there are people in our school who talk those languages. It isn't of much use to know English—everyone knows it. It is so common. It would be much easier to get a job teaching any other language than English.

June 18. Gosh, I feel so dead it's work even to hold this pen. I could just lay down and die now. My head aches—my eyes hurt—it's so hot and the sun is burning hot. We have a test day after tomorrow and I don't know anything. France surrendered. England won't last long now. Japan has a drought and if it doesn't rain they can't plant rice. That means no more food for the people. The country's economy is based on rice and if there will be no more rice they might have a revolution. Darn it—I've been here almost a year but what do I know? I can't hardly talk in Japanese yet. Or read, or write. It's so slow.

Got your letter yesterday and surely was happy to hear from you. I can't realize that your *Obaasan*[69] is dead. She was so peppy and full of life. I like to remember her that way. Isn't death strange? And what gets you is that no matter if a loved one dies, life still goes on. As usual. And at first it hurts but Nature always heals. It seems sinful that one can forget so quickly. I remember when that Mary Shizuru died. It was the first time I really felt someone's death. And wondered—where did she go? What happened? Life is really so short and transient.

Our teacher said today that two-thirds of the students here play around and one-third study seriously. That is, college and university students. Those are the two schools of thought. Number one: After we graduate, we have to go to war and probably die, so what's the use of studying? Eat, Drink and Be Merry for tomorrow we die. And even if we don't die in the war since there

68. Classical Chinese literature.

69. Probably referring to the Berkeley "house mother," Auntie Yamamoto, not Miye's actual grandmother.

is a shortage of men in Japan, we can get their pick of women and jobs. The number two idea is that since we might die we ought to study as much as possible until death.

Maybe I'll stay here four or five years. Gee, Miye, do you really think I could be a Cal professor of Japanese? That's my ambition now. But all that chemistry and math was wasted. Instead I should have taken literature and French and German. Next year I guess I'll enter college here. I have now given up the idea of going to school after I get back. So I ought to graduate from college here. I'll be such an *obaasan*, 23 now—in five years 28! For I am 23 in Japan age. So old—and fat. I hate myself for being so fat.

It is now cloudy. I feel so at a loss, I'd better not bore you any longer. And this time I do hope you write sooner. I feel so friendless now.

Tokyo, June 28, 1940

Dearest Miye,

Just received your letter dated June 8, and it was the funniest and peppiest thing I've read in ages.

I'm falling so down in the dumps now. But thank God, I'll just load all my troubles onto you. Exams begin next week. Two term papers are due then. One [is] on Japanese spirit and culture and one is on Japanese people—my opinion of them. Both in Japanese. O, Miye—I'm so dumb it's pitiful! I know I'll flunk the exams in geometry and algebra! It hurts my pride because I thought I was so educated and un-feminine just because I took a lot of math. And now I can't even do the elementary geometry and algebra we have. And then I'm getting so old and ancient. Today they made a mistake on one of my papers and put on my age as 24 instead of 23. Isn't that old, though? 24—soon 25-26-27-30! Such an old, old maid. And still going to school. How can one grow old gracefully?

Did I tell you that I expect to go to women's college here? That will mean three more long years before I see the good old USA and YOU. I've been here almost a year but it passed so quickly.

I just feel desperate when I think of the exams coming on. And oh—I do so want to pass the entrance exams for college. But high school graduates take the exams here and only one out of four of them pass. So how can I hope to pass? I'm trying to cram in eleven years of these natives' study into one-and-a-half years. But I do have an ambition now—thanks to you. Do you really think that I can be a Cal prof? Please keep on flattering me and fanning the faint embers of hope in me.

This summer I'm hoping to study very hard. I have to. I'm going to take the summer course of the college—in preparation for entrance exam. If I get in I might stay at the dorm. I wonder how it will be to live in a female world? Staying at the Odajima place almost drove me hysterical—those catty girls. And caged in—always had to be home by six.

I miss Naka a lot. He kind of reminded me of you, too. Maybe you might hear of him—I think he's going to enter Oregon State this year. Now I don't have anyone to make fun of me. His eyes were kind of like yours—always looking around and trying to find something to laugh at. He was one of those walking encyclopedias.

Often now I feel so friendless. Even thinking of you doesn't help much. I'm back to the abode of Iza-chan. But things are not like before. I never go anyplace with him. Why should I when his mother doesn't want us to? And I respect mothers. I talk to him once in a great while on the rare occasions when he is home. But he doesn't impress me as much as before. I go to school with the younger one—Yo-chan, now. He is fun but such an adolescent. Same age as I. His main interest is girls. He says when he goes with a girl she carries all his books and packages for him.

I admire you for knowing *Heian* [literature].[70] You really know a lot of Japanese and I admire and respect you for picking up so much from people. I want to take up Japanese literature in college and that is the most difficult section.

Just read a modern novel by a Kan Kikuchi. He is still living. It was something like the best-seller novel type in the US. I surely learned a lot from that trashy novel because I never knew that there were Japanese women like the heroine of the book. She was a Scarlett O'Hara type—selfish, beautiful, clever and heard (look at me—I can't even spell *hard*). She was rich but worked as private secretary and tried to make her boss marry her, but he wouldn't.

Tomorrow I was planning to stay home and study but Natsuko persuaded me to go swimming with her and Fritz Langer and two student friends. I didn't feel like going because I'm afraid I'll be dull company for her friends—but we'll see.

It is Thursday now and it's a wonder to me that I'm still living. My head feels so heavy and dull. My skin is sticky and dirty. O, this summer climate is terrible. It was so hot today—the hottest it's been for ten years, they say. It reminded me of Modesto.

We had three tests today. O, I am so dumb! My report card is going to be awful but I don't even care. It is just physically impossible for me to study. If I even open a book my eyes start aching. And I cannot cram one semester's

70. The Heian period (794–1185), which took its name from the new capital, Heian-kyo (now Kyoto), saw an unparalleled flowering of court culture and the production of such classical literary works as *Kokin wakashu*, one of the world's earliest and most important poetry collections.

work into my head in a couple of days. Honestly, I even see those Japanese characters in my dreams. Do you know what *kanbun* is? They teach it at Cal, I heard, as Classical Japanese. Is it hard! We had a test today on it and I didn't even get half.

A girl from Hawaii, Takahashi-san, and I went out for lunch. She was quite nice—we had tomato salad and egg sandwich. She graduated from junior high in Honolulu and has been in Japan one year. But does she know Japanese! I feel so ignorant beside her. Anything in the book that I do not know, we ask her and she always knows the answer. But her English is not so good. Afterwards I saw *Paths of Glory* but didn't care so much for it. There's that theater which shows all those old American pictures. It's a good chance for me to see all those I missed while I was tied to my ma.[71] *Stagedoor* is coming soon. I saw *Of Human Bondage* there.

Last Saturday I did not go swimming with Natsuko because it was raining, but she and Fritz and her Keio University friend went. They're going this Saturday and I might go.

Last Sunday Iza-chan and I took his kid brothers to Yasukuni Jinja[72] and the war museum there. He surely is funny, though. He says some of the most unexpected things. When we were leaving the museum, he looks around and says we ought to go in from there, then we wouldn't have to pay. I brought the two kids home and he browsed around for books. Did I ever tell you about the bookshops here? They take the place of the libraries at home. Books are cheap—20 or 40 cents buys a novel. Those books are about one-fourth the size of this paper, and they have paper covers. Since there are very few libraries here, students buy those cheap books. I bought a book, *Things Japanese*, for George and if you ever see him, get him to loan it to [you]. The book is rather encyclopaedic and is an authority on Japan. The author has a sense of humor, too. This summer I want to browse around for an old copy and read the parts which were cut from this new edition.

Did you ever hear of a Reverend Kaneko of San Francisco Reformed Church? He came to Japan a few months ago. He invited me to lunch. He's a fat bald-headed man. His wife reminded me of Mrs. Earle—pretty and social and "I'm trying so hard-to-hold-my-husband" type. Except that she was the quiet Japanese version. Kaneko said that Nisei were going to the dogs because they couldn't find good work and the boys did not want to be farmers and the girls did not want to have children. Really, I wonder what will happen to us Nisei.

Iza-chan said that if he went to America and had kids, he'd make them study Japanese at least until they could read Japanese newspapers. And if I

71. The Holiness church taught that going to the movies was a sin.
72. A national shrine in Tokyo for the war dead.

ever have kids, I'm going to make them learn the language. I often wonder, though, if I should blame my parents for not forcing me to learn. Because it is such drudgery to learn while in America and so much faster and interesting if one learns in Japan. But Iza-chan said that Nisei, most of them, think Americans are superior to them and when they come to Japan, they look down on the native Japanese and make fun of them. Naka was like that. But he was really Americanized. He had to learn Japanese from [scratch]. And when he went back he still had an American accent on his Japanese.

In our readers we have excerpts from those old tales, such as *Heike Monogatari.* The language is altogether different from the modern one. But I like those old stories of samurai and their wars and revenges.

We have a new young teacher who likes to give us literature concerning love. He gave us some poems from *Manyoshu.*[73] The man writes to his beloved (a poem), then she writes a reply. He gave us a Chinese poem and when I showed it to [the Nagatas], they said that girls shouldn't read such erotic poems. But we can't grasp all the meaning, so it isn't harmful.

Did you know that Japanese don't think stars and sunsets are beautiful? Therefore, no poems or paintings have been made on them. Japanese literature really is interesting. The more you learn, the more interesting it becomes.

My brother is really great to send me money like this. I have life so easy now.

My grandpappy kindly sent me a box of cherries but they went to the Odajima place first and I had to go after them and when I brought them home they [were] all rotten! My grandfather really thinks a lot of me—even if he says nothing.

Thanks a lot for the gossip about what's going on in the world. You tell me things I'd never find here. Tell me more about Empire near Modesto. Did you buy a farm?[74] I admire you for your independence. Don't let anyone fool you—always remain as you are. I'm afraid I'll be a withered out old school marm by the time I get back home.

[P.S.] I learned the word "*kimo*" [liver]—anyway it makes me laugh because I think of you. It is a rather interesting word. Together with "*ki*," it makes [characters] (*tanki*), which means quick-tempered. But if you say someone's "*kimo*" is big, it means he is courageous and unafraid of people. You see, I made a special study of the word since it was the Korbs' [name for me] and you laughed at me for being a piece of liver.

73. The earliest extant collection of Japanese poetry, compiled in the 8th century.

74. On her graduation from the University of California, Miye leased a ranch near Empire, about five miles east of Modesto. Several Holiness church families rented farms around there.

Tokyo, August 3, 1940

Dear Miye,

Thank you very, very much for the picture. As soon as I return to the Nagatas', I'll make it a permanent desk decoration to cheer me up.

I am at my auntie's now. She and her husband went to the mountains to escape the awful heat of Tokyo. I am here with the maid and my cousin. I like it because it is so close to downtown.

Right now I am attending summer session at Women's College in preparation for entrance exams, which will be next January. I get rather tired of studying but anything is better than stagnating at home. I met the cutest girl there named Ann. She is suntanned, talkative and full of pep. She recently graduated from American High School in Japan. Their whole family came here from Vancouver, Canada. Her kid brother was attending our school last year and I used to play ping-pong with him. She invited Keiko (a classmate and a Nisei from Seattle) and me over for lunch yesterday. They have a lovely Western-style home. The father is a Stanford graduate and speaks English with the kids. They must be rich to be able to live foreign style. They are ski-crazy and the kids used to win tournaments back in Vancouver. Their older sister is attending the University of Washington.

Keiko, Ann and I sit together in class and make more noise. Ann doesn't know hardly any Japanese, although she's been here two years. It feels good to be with her because she is so typically American and you get sick of these sweet Japanese girls.

We went swimming at the Meiji Jingu pool twice. The last time we went with Natsuko, took lunches and ate on the lawn with the ants. Ann's friend, a lifeguard, taught us how to dive and I took belly-flops as usual. Afterwards Ann climbed over a gate and snooped around. She got caught and was really bawled out. The old guy said she must be from America because a Japanese girl would never climb fences like a boy.

I went to a puppet show, *Chushingura*, with Natsuko at Meiji-za [Meiji Theater].[75] It was just wonderful. Sometimes I feel like staying in Japan forever. I'm afraid that someday I will not want to go because the longer I stay, the better I like it.

I had Ann and Natsuko over for lunch, then we went boating. It was lots of fun. Ann talks so loud and climbs fences and runs around so that these natives are dumbfounded. But it doesn't bother her at all. Her sister is going to Smith next year. Lucky, huh? I wish we were rich, too.

Did you know that there is a Japanese grammar? It sure is hard and complicated. Who are you going to vote for?

75. *Chushingura* (Treasury of Loyal Retainers), the most renowned of all kabuki dramas, is about 47 *ronin*, or masterless samurai, who avenge their lord's death. The puppet show (*bunraku*) is one of Japan's classical performing arts.

Mary Kimoto's father, Kusutaro, early 1900's. With a farm of his own, the young emigrant was eager to start a family and gave intermediaries this picture to show to prospective brides in Japan.

Mary's mother, Kanazawa Toku, ca. 1906. Toku, from the remote mountain village of Yonezawa in northeastern Japan, was determined to move to the United States and went on her own to Tokyo to enroll at Nippon Rikko Kai, a Christian academy that prepared young Japanese for emigration. She was about 23 years old when this picture was taken at that institution.

Kusutaro, age 33, and his new bride, Toku, 27, on their arrival at San Francisco, 1910. This photo was on a postcard announcing: "Celebration of Safe Arrival. SF Photo Club."

The proud Kusutaro standing next to his wife and infant daughter Emma in front of the house he built on his Ceres property, ca. 1913. All the Kimoto children were raised there.

Toku with Emma, her second child (her first-born died in infancy), ca. 1914.

Rural life in California's Great Central Valley, early 1920's. From the tenderest age, Mary and other children of the Japanese American community helped out on the family farm.

Mary, far right, with her sisters Emma (left) and Blanche and her brother, George, ca. 1927. The Kimoto children wore traditional dress only for special occasions, as in this formal family portrait.

Mary and her dear friend Miye Yamasaki having fun out on a farm during their student days at Modesto Junior College, 1937 or 1938.

The Modesto Holiness church's Young People's Group, ca. 1936. Miye's sister Masako is the first girl (from the left), and Emma the third in; Mary and Miye are seated side by side at the right end of the row.

The Modesto Holiness church. The small Japanese congregation, which had been meeting in rented houses since its founding, managed to build its own church in 1937. The pastor lived on the upper floor; meetings and services were held in the large room below.

Mary at the Korbs' residence in Tiburon, outside San Francisco, 1938. Newly graduated from junior college, Mary took the only job available at that time—working as a maid for an affluent couple—to earn her fare to Japan.

Tokyo, August 10, 1940

Dear Miye,

So you are a farmer now. Oftentimes I long to get in a day of good, hard and honest toil out on God's earth. This lazy town life makes me feel so useless.

Yes, those Japanese books translated into so-called English are really stilted. Although recently there have been some decent ones. Translating is awfully hard work, though. I wish I'd taken more English.

Iza is president of his student body. Isn't that something? I was so disappointed because after I came home from my aunt's, he told me that he had tickets to an outdoor concert, a Beethoven program by Japan's best symphony orchestra. He was going to take me but I was at my aunt's place. What a chance I missed!

I'm beginning to think that the place for Nisei is in Japan. There are many opportunities here. Any girl with typing and stenography experience can get a job for at least 100 yen per month. So why should Nisei stay in America and take menial positions when they can get good positions and self-respect in Japan?

I'm reading *Kokoro* by Natsume Soseki, a famous author.[76] It is a kind of psychological novel. Nothing much happens except that two students boarding in a home fall in love with the daughter of the house. One asks the mother for her hand and wins her, then the other student commits suicide. I'm just reading where he commits suicide.

I really marvel at the way these kids learn English. In high schools they learn an awful lot. And can you conceive American high school kids studying Japanese for four years? By the time a boy graduates from university he has had 11 years of English.

Do you read any Japanese books that have been translated into English? If you can get it, read *The Composition Class* by Masako Toyoda.[77] It is short but quite amusing. She was a poor grammar school student and her teacher collected her compositions into a book. It gives a realistic picture of Japanese everyday life. But I wonder if I would be able to appreciate it if I hadn't come to Japan. It was made into a movie, which I saw the other night. Did you ever see Japanese movies? I used to be enthusiastic about them when I first came but don't care much for them anymore. It's too bad how the glamour wears off a subject when you begin to understand it. When I first came, these

76. Natsume Soseki (1867–1916), a literary giant of his time, is best known for his humorous novel *Wagahai wa neko de aru* (I Am a Cat), published in 1905. Akutagawa Ryunosuke was one of his disciples.

77. *Tsuzurikata kyoshitsu* (Tokyo, 1937), by Toyoda Masako (1922–), was a huge success, with sales of more than 700,000 copies by 1963. The movie adaptation, to which Mary refers below, starred the well-known actress Takamine Hideko.

shows were so new and I couldn't understand the language. Maybe it proves that there was not much in those movies. For in a really worthwhile movie, the more one understands, the more interesting it ought to be, don't you think? I hope that will be the way with Japanese literature, which is a limitless subject.

You must have read the article on Ambassador Grew in *Life*. He has one hilarious sentence that I can't forget in there: "The Japanese women follow timidly after their husbands, who swagger like rolling dreadnoughts."[78] What an apt description! I feel like punching those men, or sticking a pin in them to watch all their inflated hot gas ooze out. They give me a pain in the neck.

Last night I was invited to a Canadian Nisei's home for dinner. She is small, chubby and full of life. It's such a relief to be with girls who talk loud and laugh openly after being with these quiet dainty Japanese females. Esther is a secretary in a Mitsui firm and gets 100 yen a month. Not bad, is it?

I came back to Nagatas' night before last. It felt so good to be back here where I don't have to *enryo* [be deferential] and where I could act as free as I want and not strive to use honorifics every time I talk. When I was at my aunt's place, her daughter was shocked when I said that we have classes with the boys at Kokusai. She asked isn't it awful? She is very thoughtful, *kigakiku*. Just the opposite of me. She is self-effacing and is always thinking about how to serve others. As you know, the schools are segregated by sex above elementary school.

Natsuko and I went to Ann's place the last day of school. We planned to go swimming but it was too cold. Her family is quite unique. Her father's two brothers are in New York. One is wealthy and married to an Englishwoman. The other is the black sheep of the family. He married an American and is now lost in the slums. Another brother, in Denver, is poor and publishes a Japanese newspaper. Ann's father speaks English like the Keio University[79] boys here, who are the glamour boys and the idols of the high school girls. Natsuko has a Keio boyfriend who takes her to kabuki plays.

Iza-chan was looking at this letter, and he got sore because I said I wrote all about him to you. He said I didn't know or understand him. Therefore, I was showing you the wrong picture of him. And now, I rather regret that I unburdened myself on you.

Tell me all about your farm, Miye. What are you going to raise? I wish

78. Joseph Clark Grew (1880–1965) was U.S. ambassador to Japan between 1932 and 1941. Until the military grabbed power in 1940, Grew had cordial relations with Japanese leaders and had advised against economic sanctions. Interestingly, as early as January 1941, he specifically warned Washington of a possible attack on Pearl Harbor. The dreadnought was a large class of battleship, so named after the first of its kind, launched in 1906.

79. A large private university in Tokyo that had a reputation as a haven for the sons of the rich who were unable to pass the entrance examinations for the prestigious public schools.

you could see the countryside in Japan. Green and fresh and neat as a pin. They raise enormous tomatoes here. And very good daikon that is not bitter like ours used to be.

Sapporo, September 4, 1940

Dear Miye,

I've sure had a good time traveling up North. Left Tokyo by train August 18 at ten p.m., and arrived at Towada National Park the next day at five p.m. I never saw such a magnificent lake in all my life. Near the shore the water is crystal clear and you can see the bottom. Farther out it becomes a beautiful deep blue. When I hunted around for a room, there were none available. So there I was—a lone girl with no place to stay. There were students who were in the same fix but they could fit in anyplace, being male. I was looking lost and bewildered when out came a woman I had talked to on the bus. She kindly offered to let me share a room with her family, so I was saved. The family consisted of: her 24-year-old son who looked neat in his well-fitting army uniform, two daughters, aged 21 and eleven, and a nine-year-old boy who was very talkative. I liked the mother, who laughed and talked a lot and was curious about everything.

I felt very self-conscious at first. I had to tell them that I was a Nisei because otherwise they would think me very rude and stupid the way I acted and talked. I don't know the fancy feminine language and how to be polite. After a year, I thought I'd be able to say anything, but unfortunately, I can't.

We had dinner at the hotel. I hadn't had delicious Japanese rice for months because in the large cities we have to eat the imported tasteless rice. We went boating out on the lake. I rowed the boat and the older daughter sat and talked to me. She was really quite intelligent, and said she wants to go to America more than anything else.

Next morning I got up at 5:30 and went exploring. It was so refreshing to get up early and breathe the fresh mountain air. The stones and trees of Japan are all moss-covered. I went to a shrine and then climbed up to another one higher up. Then down the other side of the mountain to the edge of the lake. I felt like taking off my clothes and going swimming in that pure water, but resisted the temptation.

After breakfast I barely caught the sightseeing boat that goes across the lake. It was so scenic. We passed by many tree-covered little islands. The guide chanted in her high peculiar voice but I couldn't understand a word.

So I reached the other side just in time to catch the bus for Aomori.[80] It

80. A port city in northern Honshu facing Hokkaido.

was packed, so I had to stand. Oh, such scenery! I'd like to live there forever. It was somewhat like Yosemite. There was a brook running along the side of the road. It gushed over rocks and it's undescribable how spectacular it all was.

We reached Aomori about one o'clock and I was starved. It was raining, so I ran down the street to a department store and ate there. Again, I had the delicious real Japanese rice. In Tokyo we have the long-grained *gaimai* [foreign rice]. And if I, a foreigner, hate that stuff, how much more must these natives who have never eaten anything except Japanese rice all their lives. I can't understand why we have a shortage of rice. What I think is that Japan is exporting her good rice in order to get foreign gold and importing cheap, low-grade rice to feed the people. Oh, boy, and how these natives can complain about it! Don't ever believe all that bunk about Japanese patriotism. If you could hear these people complain about the *gaimai*, the staple fiber, and the high cost of goods, you'd think they never knew their country was engaged in a life-or-death struggle.

I had about four hours in Aomori, so I walked around the town. I took the bus out to Gappo Park, then walked back to the station. I got a favorable impression of the city. The pine trees are so picturesque. They still have horse carriages. The people have honest, open faces. The girls are so pretty—they have lovely complexions and a clean, wholesome attitude altogether different from the painted dolls of Tokyo.

I left Aomori by ship at six p.m. I had a third-class ticket, so I had to be below where there was no ventilation. A woman asked me about planning her trip, so I looked up all the train timetables and made out her schedule. I hated to do it because the sunset promised to be gorgeous, and I missed it. However, she was an ignorant but kind country woman of Hokkaido and I was glad to help her. After that, I went up on deck where many students were standing around.

I arrived in Hakodate, Hokkaido, at ten p.m. and transferred to the train for Sapporo, arriving there at seven the next morning. Hokkaido is altogether different from the mainland. It has been settled more recently, and there is a free atmosphere there. The sky seems higher and more blue. The flowers are brightly colored. The cities have been planned, so they have straight, wide streets. The buildings are new. There is a continental, open feeling in contrast to the hemmed-in, oppressed feeling of Tokyo and the mainland. Everything seems to grow bigger here—trees, vegetables, even people. The people look more like Nisei.

I didn't recognize Reverend Ito,[81] who had come to the station to wel-

81. The Rev. Ito Kaoru, minister of the Holiness church in Sapporo, who had preached at various Holiness churches on visits to California. He, along with a number of other Holiness clergymen, was imprisoned during the war for refusing to acknowledge the divinity of the emperor.

come me, because he had on a white suit and white hat. He had brought his bicycle and accompanied me to his home. He called "*Tsuma*" ["Wife"] to his wife when we reached his home. They had prepared a big six-mat room upstairs for me. They live in back of their church. I was so fatigued from the journey that I slept like a log all day.

The next day two preachers came up from Osaka. They had planned a series of special meetings in Hokkaido and Karafuto. I wanted to go along for sightseeing, so had to endure the meetings.

One preacher's name is Hamada. He is quiet, considerate and kind-hearted. The other, named Amatsu, is skinny and has large eyes. I get sick of his never-ending chatter and his holier-than-thou attitude. He has a habit of closing his eyelids that is most annoying.

I have discovered a new friend, Rev. Ito's oldest son, Atsushi. On Sunday everyone left the house except him, so we made lunch and talked all afternoon, then went for a walk in the park. He is interested in everything. One day he took me sightseeing in Sapporo. He went to school in Tokyo and used to sneak out of the window when the people he was staying with forbade him to go out. He has served some time in the army and is waiting to be called again.

Mrs. Ito is so nice. She seems to have come from a good family. She works hard and is very thoughtful. She is tall, has naturally wavy hair, very fair skin, and a good sense of humor.

I tagged along with the three preachers when they went to Karafuto, another island up north. The Nisei there are about the same age as we are in the US. At Toyohara, a quiet town without streetcars, I stayed with the Miyashima family. Mr. Miyashima is a forester and graduate of the Imperial University at Sapporo. They have two boys, aged three and five, who are so chubby and cute. Before breakfast the father recites a Bible verse in Japanese and English and I couldn't believe that five-year-old could repeat it.

Karafuto is noted for its fox farms. We saw a small one yesterday and the owner looked like a fox himself. The preachers all talked at a special meeting last night. I unashamedly slept and nodded even though I was sitting in the front row. I'm afraid my habit of sleeping during sermons in our church will be with me forever!

At one village where Rev. Ito has a church, they had a funeral service for a ten-year-old boy who had drowned. The crude coffin looked home-made. I felt guilty because I couldn't share their deep grief.

We went to an Ainu village.[82] It is the custom for an Ainu girl to cut a black border all around her mouth. It is a long, painful process which starts

82. The Ainu are an ethnically and physically distinct aboriginal people who live in the northern islands of Hokkaido, Sakhalin, and the Kuriles. They were traditionally discriminated against by the Japanese, and still are.

when she is nine, and is completed by the time she is eighteen. The Ainu are better looking than most Japanese. They have long eyelashes and prominent noses. The children attend Japanese schools and some are even able to enter the prestigious university at Sapporo.

We returned to Sapporo on the third. I am leaving for Grandfather's place tomorrow, then back to school on the tenth. This is the best summer vacation I have had yet. Life is exciting and new when you travel and also when you discover a friend. I don't mind getting old because every year gets better as the years go by. I am so lucky to be able to travel. Soon I'll have a reaction and I'll be in the depths of gloom again. But variety is the spice of life, as they say.

Tokyo, September 26, 1940

Dear Miye,

I am crazy about ping-pong now. We're having a tournament at school and I am seeded second. After school I practiced with Omura-san. He is Korean and was named "Son" until this summer, when all Koreans had to change their names to Japanese ones. He was studying medicine in China until his school was bombed by the Japanese, so he is attending Kokusai in preparation for entering a university in Japan. He knows so many languages—Korean, Chinese, Japanese and some German.

There are thirty girls in our school this year, and six in our class. Momoko, from San Francisco, just entered our class. She is a graduate of the University of California. Four of us pal around now—Natsuko, Chiyo, Momoko and I.

Darn that Atsushi—I wrote to him but he hasn't answered. That's the trouble with boys. You can think a lot of them, but they don't care a fig for me. I really ought to make girlfriends because they are more reliable.

Do you think you'll ever come to Japan? When I go back to America I want to go to New York. Even now I'm tempted to quit school and find a job teaching English here. But as I see it now, the only path for me is to become an expert in Japanese. Then I can earn money and travel. While I am here in Asia I do so want to see Korea and China. I want too much. That Hokkaido trip has spoiled me. I want to go places and have fun.

My hair is a mess. I hate it. No one is supposed to get permanents now. I wish I were beautiful and knew how to dance. Such wicked ideas! I hate to get into this trend of thinking because it does me no good. I still refuse to wear make-up. Maybe if I get a job I'll start taking care of myself. Or when I am thirty.

I wish I could write. I'd make money and not have to be parasitic on my family. It's a disgrace that at 23 years of age, I am still dependent. But they say working girls are lonely. I guess we have to pay for freedom with the price of loneliness. Marie Grünow is so lucky because she is going to visit Peking. She wears such chic clothes. Rev. Obara[83] told me I don't look like a Nisei because I'm so shabby, and not well-dressed like most Nisei.

If Japan and America fight, my plans will all be shattered. But what are individuals in this modern world? They are insignificant. And what if a girl is beautiful? That doesn't guarantee that she will be happier than a homely girl. It's personality that counts—but I don't have that either. I exist day by day here—and finally the grave.

Enough of such morbid talk. Think I'll stop before you go nutty reading my nonsense.

Tokyo, October 6, 1940

Dear Miye,

Just received your most delightful letter. It was the most cheerful and peppy thing I've read or heard for a long time. I'll send this letter to my ma, too. The only thing is, I write out my soul to you. Therefore, my letters are even too personal for my Blanche to see. I don't think she would understand.

It felt so good to hear all that everyday small gossip, because things are so unstable now. This war in Europe—London half in ashes, the Japan-German-Italy pact. War with America! Anti America. Anti Britain. What will happen to us Nisei? What will happen to us Nisei in Japan? Some say Japan will fight America this year and others say within five years.

And then my personal troubles—I can't find a job teaching English—will George send money for this month? Natsuko going with Fritz and leaving me by myself. My Hokkaido friend seemingly forgot my existence. Mr. Nagata had an operation. And school! Oh—so difficult. We have mostly exercises in preparation for entrance exams for higher schools here. So difficult it makes our heads ache.

David and Miye—Miye and Dave. That's a new idea. Has Dave really fallen for you? How cute! I envy you—how does it feel to have someone fall for you? All these girls at home and their love affairs. As for me—I've just given up hope.

Today Uncle Terry's grandson came to Tokyo. I was all excited and went to meet him at eight o'clock this morning. He is twenty-one and reminds me so much of my pop. His face is the same shape and the curve of his nose (or rather, hook). He walks the same, too. And talks like him—swallowing the ends of sentences and blurring words. Well, he is a wrestler (sumo-tori). He came up with thirty others from Osaka. They are going to compete in sumo,

83. The minister of a large Holiness church in Tokyo.

baseball, and tennis with others of the same company from all over the country. First, they all went to the Imperial Palace to pay homage, then to the hotel. Then I took him to see *Olympia*, and had lunch on the Ginza. He had to be back by three to practice. This Wednesday I said I'd skip school to take him sightseeing. I hate to because we have geometry [for] two hours and then we [were to go] to a temple for a sightseeing trip. I looked forward to that so much because I'm interested in Buddhism. But he doesn't know anyone in Tokyo and he is going to war this year or next—so why not show him a good time while he can enjoy it?

I suppose you won't get a chance to see *Olympia*. That is really a superb film. A German woman was the director.[84] It is about the Olympics held in Berlin. At first, it shows the ruins and statues of olden Greece, where the Olympics originated. The photography and music [were] wonderful! Then they showed the competition—discus throwing, relays, dashes, hurdles. Say, that picture—I don't see how it could be improved. Because it held your interest all the way through. Sometimes it showed the athletes in slow motion. An athlete's body is really beautiful. And their motions are so soft and graceful. Owens[85] looked like a black panther. Fritz said this and I really think so, namely: an animal's movements are beautiful. Much more beautiful than a human's. Well, those athletes were animalistic and beautiful. Such grace. And harmony. And balance. They showed Hitler, too. He surely puts his soul into the sport. When Germans win he looks so happy—and vice versa. There is really something grand about sport. When Japan's Son [Kitei] won the marathon everyone clapped. That's one thing I admire. It was so funny how when the others finally finished on the marathon, they just collapsed. But Son came in standing up and *genki* [full of pep].

Have you read *Mein Kampf*? When I came home today I met Shoji-san with a bicycle. So I went bicycling with him. It felt so good. We went out in the country. I have told you about him—he only graduated from middle school but he studied hard and now is equal to a university graduate in knowledge—if not more. He is not so brilliant or brainy, but how he studies! He surely has stick-to-it-ness. He comes over and talks to me in English for practice. He knows much more about English and American literature than I—Carlyle, Thoreau, Emerson. Well, he read *Mein Kampf* in Japanese. He said Hitler is a genius about psychology. Japanese practically all like Hitler. And he really is a great man, I think, in the sense that he is a great leader—one who is inspired with an Ideal.

Yesterday I had a lovely day. I met Hirata-san (Nisei girl from Java) and

84. The famous 1936 German film directed by Leni Riefenstahl (1902–).

85. The runner Jesse Owens (1913–80) who, to the chagrin of Adolf Hitler, won four gold medals for the U.S. in the 1936 games.

we went to the sumo amphitheatre where they had a chrysanthemum show. It was supposed to start from yesterday but when we went they were still working on it. They told us to go in, so we did. It was beautiful—what was half-finished. So much work, though. They make dolls of famous people of Japanese history and place chrysanthemums on their "clothes." Then they duplicate the scene, such as a room, or a garden or temple. Japanese history is so fascinating. Really, there's so much I want to learn yet.

And then we walked along the Sumida River, the famous river of Tokyo. We went to a park, then took a steamboat to Sumida Park. The park was disappointing—only lawn on the bank. So we went to Shinjuku and had lunch there; then we got the bright idea of going out to the country to pick pears. We went way out to the Tamagawa. You'd be surprised with their method of pear-raising. They train the branches along like this [sketch]. The man said the trees were thirty years old. And one tree bears about three hundred pears! They wrap each pear in paper so that the bugs do not get at it. What do you call it—an arbor? They raise apples and grapes like that, too. The branches are trained to go along parallel to the ground. The pears are round and hard and brown-skinned. We picked some and paid 12¢ for every "me." A "me" is about a pound? Anyway, they were about 10¢ apiece. He gave us one each with *kizu* [blemishes] on it. It was so juicy and good. We had to cross the Tamagawa on a raft-like boat. A man with a long pole towed us across. The water was very clear. It felt so good to get out in the country. Around Tokyo there are lots of scenic spots. I want to go. It costs so much, though, and I really ought to stay home and study. But when I have a chance to go someplace—study is forgotten.

I was so mad because Iza-chan said he'd take me boating today and then my cousin came! Iza-chan was mad because I write to you about him. I was rather mad at him because he says he doesn't like the following things about me: (1) the way I walk—very awkward and not straight, (2) my dresses—their color, (3) my hair—so sloppy, (4) the way I talk—too rough and masculine, (5) myself because I use no make-up. Well, all this didn't come at once but one at a time. So I came to the conclusion that a girl must be well-groomed and beautiful for men to love her. So I wished I were beautiful. Therefore I was blue. Because something in me still rebels from trying to look glamorous.

That is wrong what you said about the government forbidding fancy hairdress. There is a drive against permanents—but you know the eternal feminine. And women of Japan, especially Tokyo, are as well-groomed now as ever.

Did you know that Japanese schools are forbidden in Canada? So, with this friction between the US and Japan—maybe Japanese will be forbidden in America. Then what am I studying the language for?

Tonight Shoji-san came over. He helped me with my lessons. He is a big help, too. I learn a lot from him. I like him better the more I know him. He said Konoye[86] is very popular in Japan now. Being a prince is his greatest asset.

Did you know that foreign minister Matsuoka,[87] of Konoye's cabinet, is a Christian? There are quite a few Christians in the present cabinet.

School tomorrow. We're going on a trip the fifteenth and [I'm] wondering if I'll be able to afford to go. I hate this being so parasitic and waiting and wondering every month if the money will come.

Iza-chan saw the *Echo of Calvary*'s "Christ Above All" and said, "Power above All." That is true, though, isn't it? It's no use looking at the world thru rose-colored glasses. A country has to be strong to survive now. The fight is to the strong.

Please write soon. Lots of love from your Kimo.

Thanks for the flowers!

Tokyo, November 1, 1940

Dear Miye,

Recently I've had an attack of homesickness. When I think of staying in this crowded Japan for four dark years it casts such a pessimistic shadow on my future. So I have decided to go back next year. Don't tell anyone, because I'm so fickle anyway. I'll enter Joshi Dai[88] for three months and if it is too boring I'll hop on a boat and beat it back to the good ole U.S. I'm getting fed up with Japan. I have never done a thorough job in my life—I never stick to anything long—so why should I start now? And yet, if I go back now my Japanese is still poor, especially my conversation. But I do want a university degree. All I do in Japan is get fat and old and feel both. I want to see you, too, Miye. Friends can grow so far apart when distance separates them.

Only a few more days until [the] election now. But really, one stagnates in Japan. No new stimuli. I don't know or care what is going on in the world. And recently I have not been studying at all. That preparation for entrance exams that we are doing at school is so difficult I just give up. It really is hard to study when one is older.

86. Prince Konoye Fumimaro (1891–1945), elder statesman and three-time prime minister. He was the man the militarists installed when they ousted Yonai.

87. Matsuoka Yosuke (1880–1946), Japanese-born graduate of the University of Oregon and foreign minister from July 1940 to July 1941. He was tried as a war criminal after the war but died before the trial ended.

88. Tokyo Joshi Daigaku (Tokyo Women's College, now called Tokyo Woman's Christian University), founded in 1917 by the Presbyterian missionary August Karl Reischauer, Nagao Hampei, and others. Mary was accepted in the school's Tokusetsu-ka (special division), which was established for Japanese who had studied abroad and for foreigners. It was headed by Maruyama Kiyoko. Tokyo Joshi Dai should not be confused with Nihon Joshi Dai (Japan Women's College).

We have a new volleyball court at school. Today the principal could not come to lecture us. And was everyone happy! We all dread his lectures, which are so dull. And we are expected to attend. So instead of listening to his lecture we played volleyball. It is fun the way they play it in Japan, where they have a different way of rotation.

I've almost finished Kagawa's *Over the Death Line* in Japanese. I think I read too much. I've been bothered with persistent headaches for the first time in my life. Being sick for the first time, I realize how lucky I am to be healthy. But don't say anything to my parents because they will worry.

Last Saturday our class went on a picnic. We studied in the morning and went boating in the afternoon. Most of the girls pair off with boys, but I don't; therefore I feel unpopular and lonely. I rationalize that I don't care for any of them anyway.

I sure change friends a lot. My life now is altogether different from when I first came. Now I am in a rut and I stay home and don't study. Whenever I go someplace I go by myself. Sometimes I feel so lonely and sad. Now I have a new friend—a girl from Java named Hiroko. All the other girls I have been friends with are transient but I believe that finally I've really found a good friend. We are going to attend the *Dobo-kai.*[89] We are going to skip school one week to attend the festivities. The climax is a treat to Kabuki. I can hardly wait.

I miss you so much! I guess I'm trying hard to find a friend like you, but no luck so far.

Tokyo, November 11, 1940

Dearest Miye,

Just received your letter of October 28 and surely was happy to hear from you. Just as you said, I feel now as though life is worth living. I've been having a swell time.

To start out with today. Yesterday and today were special days in celebration of the 2,600th founding of the Japanese Empire. Today (Monday) we had school only two hours. Then I helped Fumi Taira do some translating. Went downtown afterwards to see an exhibition at a department store (Takashimaya) then suddenly remembered that all department stores are closed on Mondays. So went on the streetcar to Asakusa[90] and walked around. Today I was especially interested in the stores. They are all such small, shabby shops. There are: restaurants, selling coffee, cake and sandwiches and also small stores selling sushi and *dango* and *shiruko* [rice dumplings and sweet

89. The celebration of the 2,600th anniversary of the founding of the empire, for overseas Japanese.

90. A Tokyo district then considered a center of Bohemian life.

bean soup]. Then there are the hardware stores with all their goods hanging down, and then bright toy stores with their red and shining dolls and toys. Then the tailors, fruit stores, barbers, funeral wreath stores. I love to walk the streets and read the signs. I feel so accomplished because now I can read most of them.

In Asakusa I went into a small, dirty stand along with all the country people and had some fried *soba* [noodles] for ten cents. I'd always wanted to do it but never had the nerve before. There are many theaters in Asakusa but all of them had lines of people waiting to go in. So did not go to a movie. No—I don't enjoy movies so much now and hardly ever go. I like the news theaters but the Japanese pictures are boring. They are really so foolish and a waste of time and money. I did see a good Japanese film, *Moyuru Ozora* (*Burning Sky*, or something).[91] It was a picture concerning airplanes in the China war. Some of the photography was superb—even better than foreign. The story was not so much but it was sad and everyone (including your Kimo) cried when the pilots died. It is heartbreaking and yet big and wonderful how they say, "*Tenno heika banzai*!" ["Long live the Emperor!"] with their last breath. I saw that picture with Iza on Sunday and skipped church. I felt guilty because we left home at different times so that his ma would not catch on.

To get back to today. From Asakusa I went to the Ginza and saw a new movie. Oh all the people! The theater was really packed and I had to stand through half of it. They had a good travelogue about French Indo-China. And Popeye and Betty Boop. Then I met Iza at six. We went through the Ginza and Hibiya[92] and then to the front of the [imperial] palace. There were lantern parades and millions of people. I never saw so many people in all my life! Iza-chan said to write and tell you about it. In front of the palace we could see three lanterns way off and then the middle one would move up and down as a greeting from the emperor to his subjects. There was something very touching about seeing all these millions of people faithfully bowing before their *Tenno*, and this *Tenno*, a descendant of one who founded the Empire 2,600 years ago. We can't even imagine that long, can we?

Back to the Ginza and had dinner, then "*Gin-bura*" [Ginza-strolling]. Many drunk people. But all very gay and a holiday spirit. Because of the war, people did not dress up or spend much money. We got home about ten-thirty and I had lots of letters and was so happy. Yours—best of all, of course. And also Miyo Suzuki with her cute picture. She looks grown up and more slender.

Guess what—I have a new friend! Went out with him quite a lot last week.

91. Better translated as *Flaming Sky*, 1940. A propaganda spectacular about the heroism of Japanese pilots in the war against China, produced by Toho Films and directed by Abe Yutaka. It was the first Japanese film to show actual aviation footage.

92. A large park adjacent to the Imperial Palace.

He is from Java—a Java Nisei. Has been in Japan five years. Was in Kokusai same time as George. I can't decide whether he is brainy or not. Anyway—he's a lot of fun and I get along swell with him. He loves to eat, so we have one big thing in common. And he does not like to study—but loves to talk and is interested in everything about Japan. He really has the soul of a traveller. Very "*nonki*" and "hail fellow, well met" type. Last summer he bought a bicycle and went on a tour of southern Japan for forty days. I envy him—I'd love to do the same. He took me to a tea house, which I'd always wondered about but was afraid to enter because only boys patronize them. They play jazz music and the girls paint up and wear clothes with sex-appeal plus. They are the recreational haunts of students. There are easy chairs and the lights are dim and soft.

His name is Yabe-san. He also took me to have tempura and *ton-katsu* [breaded pork cutlet]. The *ton-katsu* is what Ginza is famous for and it surely was delicious!

I skipped school nearly all last week. Reason: Dobo Kai. Don't know how to translate it—it's a celebration of the 2,600th anniversary and the government called lots of the Issei from all over the world—America, South America, South Seas, Philippines, China, etc. And they had a program all made out for them. My friend Hiroko from Java persuaded me to join, so I did. It was very educational and lots of fun. Many Nisei were there, too.

On the first day, Monday, we all got Japan flags and marched from Hibiya Park to the palace to pay our respects. The streets were lined with grammar school students who waved flags and shouted "*banzai*" to welcome us. There were about 1,200 of us. We shouted "*banzai*" too and fluttered our flags and felt gay and carefree. Then we gathered at Hibiya Public Hall and heard addresses by Prince Konoye and members of his cabinet. They all read their speeches, so it was not impressive. Konoye is tall and handsome—best looking of the whole bunch. His assets are his title and his handsomeness. Otherwise they say he is not much—only a kind of robot. But I like Matsuoka. He looks insignificant but he is a good speaker. And he's almost a Nisei because he went to America when fourteen years old. O—we are lucky to be able to see all these great men! They gave us [a] delicious lunch. Then afterwards I took Yabe-san to see an *odori* [traditional dance]. We stayed so long that we were late for the dinner, so ate out ourselves. Then we walked around Ueno Park. In the park there were many lovers. It is really beautiful and quiet there. The pond is still and reflects the lights of the city. It is strange how there are lovely quiet spots right in the center of busy Tokyo.

Next day I went to school. Then at night we were invited to a banquet for Nisei. About fifty went from our school. There were six hundred Nisei all together there. The program was dull, so Natsuko and I left in the middle of it. So many well-dressed and good-looking Nisei girls were there!

Wednesday we went to a military school and saw planes fight and bomb another plane and do fancy stuff. It was very interesting. They had a loudspeaker explaining everything. Then the students exhibited exercises and kendo. The lunch was terrible—dry bread. It's a wonder the army can live on that kind of food. After that there was a discussion here at Rikko Kai, so we brought back about twenty-five people and had dinner here. I brought Yabe-san. They talked about the Nisei problem and [it was] very interesting. People from all over the world took part in the discussion. In Brazil they are not allowed to teach Japanese. Isn't that terrible? And then the question came up of what will Nisei do in case of America fighting Japan. Mr. Nagata—I admire him the more I know him. As president of Rikko Kai, he led the discussion. He surely is a dreamer. And very good speaker. He said that Japan must lead the world. Where Japanese are, there is peace. The Japanese of America must arise and lead the nation. Everyone laughed and cheered at his speech.

Next day we went to Yokosuka and saw the [battleship] *Mikasa*. It was raining and I got soaked and caught a cold. We saw the navy planes being constructed. The navy officers are handsome. I like to go with Yabe because he is my "walking dictionary." During speeches I always ask him words that I do not know. After that sightseeing, went with Yabe to Shinjuku[93] and saw news. Then came home just barely in time to teach Waseda students. First time I taught them. There are five who come over. We are studying Stevenson's *Suicide Club*. I get two yen an hour. Not bad, huh? It is good experience too.

Friday was the closing day. We had closing ceremonies at *Kabuki-za* [The Kabuki Theater]. Then saw kabuki [in the] afternoon. We saw the famous Kikugoro.[94] But it was not as wonderful as I had expected. Then to the biggest temple in Tokyo—Hongwanji. It was beautiful. But I now hate the way the priests read that Buddhist stuff—that awful dreary chanting gives me the creeps. Again had dinner with Yabe.

Saturday went to school in morning, then afternoon visited the beautiful garden of the emperor's. The men had to wear mourning or frock coats.

Sunday went to church, then had lunch at Obara-sensei's. I talked to Taeko. She did not impress me. It rather gets me the way bubbles come in her mouth when she talks a lot.

So there is my diary of a busy week. I am lucky to be able to do and see so much. I really enjoyed it.

I have not had enough sleep for a long time. It is past eleven now, so I'd better beat it. I have to write to my mom, too. My school grades are ter-

93. One of the major business and entertainment centers of Tokyo. It was known (then as now) as a center for young people.

94. Onoe Kikugoro is one of the most distinguished names among the traditional acting families in the Kabuki Theater. Kikugoro VI (1885–1949) assumed the name in 1904. He was an actor of extremely broad scope and an expert dancer.

rible. In one test I got 68% and in another 30%. But nearly everyone else does bad—or worse. That old literary style is just impossible for me to get.

It is twelve o'clock now. Woe is me—don't see how I'll get up at six-thirty tomorrow!

Was shocked that Roosevelt got in again.[95] They might as well leave him in for life. Dictator Roosevelt. Maybe that is not such a dream, after all.

Good-night, Miye. I'm always thinking about you. Maybe I'll go home pretty soon.

Tokyo, December 19, 1940

Dear Miye—

Thanks very much for your letter of November 25. Just received it the other night. And such a sweet flower!

Just got through writing to my family, so will have to write small if this is to all fit in one envelope and save me twenty sen.

Oh, I wish I were home so I could listen to you rave about David. I'm missing out on all the love affairs and marriages of my contemporaries. Really—I'm no judge but I think Dave is ideal for you. I used to think he was wonderful, but he's so young and short that I never thought of him other than a cute, clever kid. Just like you. Only of course you are much more than that.

Don't believe all the melancholy outpourings of my soul. No one here even suspects I have such blue moods. It's only to you that I can empty my soul of its labors and trials and so I do a thorough job of it.

Just now I am quite happy and content. Imagine such a state in the middle of final exams! But in our school hardly anyone flunks—you can even graduate by taking only two-thirds of the stuff. So we are *nonki*.

Last night I had a very good time. The Waseda students gave me a Christmas party. We had dinner and then games and stuff later. It is the group which is studying Stevenson's *Suicide Club*, so we call it that. They are first- and second-year students, so younger than I. Really only kids yet. Now that I don't have to teach them anymore, I look back with pleasure on it. It was good experience anyway. Miye—why do I attract ugly boys? One of the members of Suicide Club likes me and he's kinda pesty at times. He is a squirt and wears glasses, is nervous and skinny. But quite good sense of humor and he can speak English quite well, although I can understand his Japanese better than his English. But it's rather interesting to talk with him because he reads a lot—about philosophy and politics, etc. He says sometimes he stays home, cutting classes and reads in bed all day. However, the mystery of him lies in

95. Franklin Delano Roosevelt had just been elected to his third term as president.

that he eats and eats and yet he is skinny. He says he eats five bowls of rice for dinner. The lady of his place does not leave the rice by him for he eats it all up clean. I eat a lot but you can see where it goes to.

I learned a lot from those Suicide Club-ers. One is that these Japanese students surely can boast. If you believed one of them you'd think he was the greatest person in the world. I talked to Yo-chan about that (he's a boaster too) and he said that was what a student was for. Such a difference between the men and women of Japan! Especially among students. I've particularly noticed it since I have been going to Shiojima-sensei's cousin's place.[96] They are of very good family. I think that they are the real Japan type of ideal young womanhood. So thoughtful! And really gentle-hearted. They surely have class. And yet, it is a deep-rooted fineness. I admire them for it. Mrs. Ishida was something like that. I like Japanese girls if they are that type. There is that modern girl type which is awful. *Zabbekko*—a slang for them. Flirts who mimic American actresses. Can they paint up! Most waitresses are of that type. Bold and shameless. They really disgust me. The rich ones are the girlfriends of the smart Keio University boys.

Our principal said there was a position—office work—for 150 a month and asked if the girls of our class wanted it. I am the only one (girl) in our class who aspires to higher education. Just now I have a very ambitious streak in me, which comes about once in half a year. I will learn Japanese and do a thorough job of it! I will not be one of those good-for-nothing Nisei just wandering around!

And yet, I know that if I were popular and got along well with people like the other girls of our class I would not care to go to school anymore. Haven't you noticed that it is the not-so-pretty people who think and are discontented and strive for mental things? That is Osozawa, my Suicide Club "friend." He knows all about Kant, Nietzsche, and the rest of those philosophers. Of course he is young and at that stage. Some people never pass that stage—like Kagawa. Then they are inspired and can do something.

Really, Nisei are unambitious, don't you think? That Iza-chan is conceited but I have to admit he's got more brains than any young fellow I've met yet. He asked me—why do Nisei want to go back to America? Only in Japan can they get freedom. In America we are bound on all sides because of our parentage. Can a Nisei go into politics? Can he really become anything outstanding? No. Therefore he has no freedom. According to Izaya. But that is true, don't you think? Also, he said that Nisei are *baka* [dumb]. And it seems like it. Even at our school, there are no brilliant people—well—and so what!

96. Shiojima Hifumi introduced Mary to his distant relative, Dr. Shiojima Atae, a widower with two daughters at home, Yoshiko and Kiyoko. Mary went to their house to teach English conversation. They were students at Japan Women's College and became very good friends.

Haven't gone out with Iza-chan for ages. Last Sunday was planning to but I was a good girl and went to church instead.

Golly, it's cold. My fingers are numb. Last year Mrs. Nagata gave me charcoal all the time but this year there is a scarcity of it—besides, it is on a ticket system anyway.

Sometimes it gets me how the Americans are so smug. They ridicule Germans, Italians and Japanese because they have a scarcity of goods. I can remember when I was in America, how I used to love to read about how the Germans had to be thrifty and think it served them right for being under Hitler. But now I have a different angle on such problems. Who made Germany like that? Why should Americans be so smug? They like to look on and see others suffer. Now they won't sell Japan this or that. No matter who tries to stop Japan, I believe that Japan will continue until she realizes her dream of a New Order in the Far East. She has to for her very existence. If America were friendly and traded with her and quit persecuting her she would not be forced to do as she is doing now. O—it makes me boil! Americans are so prejudiced and one-sided. However, I was like that too—once upon a time before I knew Japan. Now I can surely sympathize with the have-nots. Like that joke about substitute food stuffs in Germany. Say—if Americans had to eat some of the substitute grub of Japan they might realize that it wasn't a joke. And thousands of fine young men dying. Yes, peace is all right for a rich country like America but when you begin to starve, you fight for life.

Well—so Mary has turned pro-Japan. I am afraid so. Did you know that 70,000 Italian and German Americans are fighting for the land of their ancestors? Is it true that they don't take Nisei for military training in America? I believe that we Nisei must be more Japanified. Believe me, if I ever have kids I'll teach them the language and culture of Japan. They say that the Nisei parents of Hawaii are more strict that way than their parents, and I can see why now.

But then it's so easy to be content in America. So much food and clothing and entertainment. The fight for life! You surely see it in Japan.

Well, I think that I have raved enough. And I feel better for it.

Good-bye—

Tokyo, January 8, 1941

Dearest Miye,

Just received your letter of December 15. And was so happy to hear from you! I feel so literary now—I want to write and write and write, so here goes.

Today was the first day of school after winter vacation. Last night I stayed over at Ito-san's (my Tokyo relative). This morning I left the place at ten and then went downtown to Nihonbashi Mitsukoshi Department Store. They had an exhibit on about Prince Saionji,[97] which did not impress me since I had the prejudiced opinions of Mrs. Nagata and Iza about him. Mrs. Nagata said he had a lousy face, and Iza said that he was the dumbest (*ichiban baka*) of that group of Meiji Ishin [Meiji Restoration] leaders and therefore he lived the longest. There was a lot of writing by him in *fude,* but I was not interested. *Fude* writing is an art that is incomprehensible to me. Then I looked at their English. They have one of the largest collections of foreign books there. But did not buy anything. Had lunch in the restaurant there, then went to Takashimaya Department Store. I was going to go to school but just did not get into the mood. I don't care to go to school at all now.

Saw a movie (Japanese) at Takashimaya. Rather enjoyed it. Felt so sorry for the sweet old lady. Japanese photography is beautiful, and I really enjoy their sweet sentimental movies when in the mood. Then to Kanda [district] and haunted the second-hand book stores. I love to do that. There are so many books on Japan that I want but can't afford. Bought one book on Japanese Fairy Tales and one other story book with both Japanese and English. Darn, this pen does not write well on here. Then came home to your letter.

The Nagata brothers (Iza and Yo-chan) went skiing. I've fallen for the former all over again. Sometimes I just hate him and sometimes I like him so much. Last Sunday we went out and I surely enjoyed it. Walked about two hours at first. Once we stopped and watched kids flying toy airplanes. He said he set a record for plane flying while in middle school. Had dinner on the Ginza, then went to Asakusa. All the movies were packed, so we went to a news theater. Then walked around and turned in an alley. The back streets of the Ginza and Asakusa look so wicked. Narrow streets and dim lights. Even brave I never venture back there when by myself. He started talking about *machiai*[98] and geishas and stuff. I was surprised to hear him. I must bore you by raving about him. But I do wish you were here, and we could talk about Japan and love and life. Really—I've never had a good gabfest since coming to Japan. Iza says he cannot understand how one can get married and see the same girl day in and day out. Miye—is your affair with David over? So soon? I really did not mean anything when I said I was "shocked." But I know I am wrong because I keep thinking you are superhuman.

Darn my hair! It looks like a wild woman's—all flying and thick and fuzzy. How I hate it! Think I'll cut it off.

Really, I'm afraid of going back home. Besides—it seems too far off and

97. Prince Saionji Kimmochi (1849–1940), last of the Meiji *genro,* or elder statesmen. Saionji played a significant role in the reforms of the Meiji Restoration, the nationalist political movement that began in 1868–69 and brought constitutional monarchy to Japan. Twice prime minister (1906–8, 1911–12), he founded a newspaper to disseminate Western ideas and helped draft the country's first constitution.

98. Inns used as places of assignation, now called "love hotels."

in the dim future. I won't fit in with anybody—maybe not even you. And Americans—I am beginning to dislike them. Maybe it would be better for me in Japan.

Was sick for a week just as soon as winter vacation started. Had quite high fever and felt like dying. Only a cold. Read Sinclair Lewis' *Babbitt.* He surely makes fun of Americans. So smug and ignorant and conceited. And America is noted for its lynchings. There has never been a lynching in Japan.

O, Miye—I am so confused and dissatisfied. Roosevelt's fireside chat made quite a sensation.[99] Of course the Japanese newspapers attacked it vigorously. Sometimes I wonder if America really will last much longer. It is such a mixture of races. And there are so many inherent evils in the American system. It seems as though France is having a hard time of it now, too. One editorial called America the greatest hypocrite on earth. And it is true that only one man profited (American) from the World War—i.e., the munitions magnate Morgan![100] There is so much that I do not know.

Was reading some children's books about Japanese heroes. It is so romantic to think that these samurai in beautiful armor once [rode] this very land I'm in now.

Hooray—I've finished that awful paper. Isn't this pretty [referring to the stationery with a border illustration of a maple branch heavy with autumn leaves]?

I had so much that I wanted to write but have forgotten it now. I feel like ditching school for a couple of weeks. I have no friends at school. There is no one I really care for, and I can get much more by reading myself.

Did I tell you about my Java Nisei friend? She found a Japanese boyfriend and within two months they were engaged. Now they're inseparable. It must be wonderful to be in love and stay there. I'm afraid I'll never know such bliss. She does not come to school anymore. When she used to come, she talked only about Him until I got disgusted.

Remember a Lillian Buoy? Or did she come to MJC? I guess not. Anyway, she is my Ceres High friend and I got a letter from her today. She said that she does not feel sorry for Japan or Italy or Germany, but she feels "sorry for the innocent people." A typical American attitude, isn't it? I'm afraid I'm getting very pro-Japan and anti-American. She also said Betty Fine died. Did you know her? I feel sorry because she was quite beautiful—lovely white skin and

99. In the very significant Fireside Chat on Dec. 29, 1940, President Roosevelt denounced the Axis powers' September agreement and stated that the United States must become the "arsenal of democracy," sending arms to Britain and other democratic countries.

100. John Pierpont Morgan, Jr. (1867–1943), head of the noted U.S. banking house. In calling him a "munitions magnate," Mary seems to have been influenced by Japanese propaganda. Morgan was connected to the munitions industry only in the sense that the firm helped finance the Allied efforts in the First World War.

dark curly hair. And Mrs. Kiyoi is dead—she was like a living corpse before, though, wasn't she? Yes—the place and people will be quite different when I go back.

My Joshi Dai *ojo-sans* (the women's college students that I give conversation lessons to) gave me fifteen yen [bonus] for teaching them last year. Now I feel so rich. I want to spend all the money I earn teaching on travelling. I went to Sugadaira for skiing [for] four days. It was lots of fun. I got so black. Remember Ann Toda who I said climbed fences? Her family was there, and Natsuko and I and two Russians (white) went up and stayed in the same hotel. Can Ann ski! I surely admire and envy her. Everyone comments on and praises her because she, a female, can make Christies and go like the men. She jabbers a lot. But she is efficient and thoughtful and very tanned. Something like Blanche.

Emma sent me some Food! Was I happy! However, it was too precious to waste on myself, so I gave the coffee and sugar to the Shiojimas, milk to the Nagatas, raisins to Ito-sensei, pineapple and cheese and candy to Iza—leaving only peanut butter and one bar of candy for myself. I felt very self-sacrificing and virtuous. And yet, I wonder if you can imagine what American food means? Food takes on so much importance in underfed Japan. Just to look around in a streetcar, one can readily see how true it is that Japan is an undernourished nation! And about half of the people have stomach trouble. Their everyday food is so frugal, so when they get a treat they soon overeat and "*onaka o kowasu*" [get indigestion]. How I'd love to bring over some of the abundance of California!

My mom said for me to enter Obara-sensei's Bible school. It hurts me because I cannot be unfeeling enough to frankly tell my mom that I do not believe any of that religion. And now I've even quit trying to go to church on Sunday. They are so stupid at that church. Never say anything worthwhile. Yes—I am a heathen.

Received a postcard from Ito-sensei saying to meet him this morning at nine. I am mad because I [only] received the card tonight, and I did want to meet him. I wonder why I like him? When I meet him we don't talk much, and yet I like to be with him. He has sparkling eyes and pep. Maybe he reminds me of my mama.

I envy you every time I receive your letters because you seem to be so content and happy. You must send me pictures of yourself and your tomatoes. You've got guts to be independent and farm and I am proud of you.

If I were a boy! Do you still think that? If I were a boy I could have gone skiing with Him—and mountain climbing. And I could go investigate back alleys and really know Japan. As it is—I must be conventional and not go to dangerous places and must see only the bright and sunny side of Tokyo. Iza said that before the war, girls made it a business to accompany boys on the Ginza, for which they received one yen. They winked at the boys and went to tea rooms and chatted and got one yen when they parted.

Shiojima-sensei has a very nice wife. She is small and slender and rather talkative. Very thoughtful. I marvel at the thoughtfulness of Japanese women.

My relative, Mrs. Ito, is an interesting person. She is more of the American type. I like her. She does not bow and mutter polite nothings. She has a brain. Mrs. Nagata does not like her because she is not polite and *reigi tadashii* [well mannered] like the typical Japanese woman. Her husband is ideal. He takes care of her and lets her do as she pleases.

It snowed today. The streets are muddy and I hate it. It is not beautiful at all because there is only about an inch of snow, and that is dirty.

I got an 81 average this quarter on my report card. That was not half as bad as I'd expected.

January 12. Sunday already. Lots has happened since I started writing. Last Friday (day before yesterday) I skipped school afternoon and went to Kabuki with Miyoko-san and Suzuki-san (man staying at the dormitory—from Canada). It started at noon and ended about five. We had dinner at an interesting place on the Ginza. Real Japanese food and lots of the dishes I'd never even seen before.

January 13. I'm afraid I'll never get this finished. I've had a spell of wanting to read. Today skipped school and went to library and read Baroness Ishimoto's *Facing Two Ways*.[101] I think that woman really has brains. She is pretty, also. Almost finished *Autobiography of Yukichi Fukuzawa*.[102] He was a prominent educator and liberalist [*sic*] of Meiji Era. I like him. He hated conventionalism and hypocrisy. Also am reading *Japan's Feet of Clay*.[103] That book has me scared. Here I was just beginning to think that Japan is wonderful when this book destroys my illusions. Of course it is prejudiced and very English—but it has many quotations and charts which show only the facts. Today as I walked downtown and saw all the bustle and people intent on doing their work, I thought, "Will Japan really go bankrupt? And what are all these people going to do?" That book proved how impossible it would be for Japan to carry on a prolonged war—and yet, she is doing it. How will it

101. See Introduction at n. 4.

102. *Autobiography of Yukichi Fukuzawa*, tr. Eiichi Kiyooka (New York, 1966). Fukuzawa (1835–1901) spent time in the United States before returning to introduce Western-style education to Japan.

103. Freda Utley, *Japan's Feet of Clay* (New York, 1937), a book highly critical of Japan and its militarism.

end? And then, as every anti-Japan book does, it brought out the women-of-Japan-are-slaves stuff and prostitution of the Yoshiwara[104] and geisha life.

I've certainly gone out with Iza a lot recently. Just yesterday went to a show, *Sea Hawk*, with him. Bum show. We had an interesting talk. About beauty—women—prostitution. Imagine. He is the only one, besides Natsuko, whom I talk to about such delicate matters. Natsuko is rather ignorant, though—so not profitable to talk to. Every time I read about Japan, I always think, "I must ask Iza about this." He is my one source of information on pro-Japan thinking. He said he read that no American college girls are virgins. Well, American morals are nothing to brag about.

I skip school about half the time now. It gets boring to read those middle school books. Now that I can read Japanese a little, I want to read about what's going on now. And biographies. And important things. Not old stuffy classical things we have at school.

This Shiojima's cousin has a friend who wants me to teach [her] English conversation. I'm glad. I like to teach girls. And more—I love to get paid.

Just now I'm quite self-satisfied. I love to read about Japan. The thing is, however, I ought to be reading in Japanese, not English.

Another thing Iza keeps telling me and I think it is true is that we Nisei are less sensitive than the native Japanese. We do not dress for and think about seasons like they do here. We are not careful about details. Look at the peoples down South near the equator—how they wear bright flashing colors and like hot foods. Why is that? It is because their climate is always the same and they become dulled, so they need very strong stimuli. On the other hand, Japan likes "*shibumi*." (This is hard to translate—it involves subtlety, delicacy, etc.).[105] Often I wonder—I'd hate to have children in America. But also in Japan.

This is a long letter and if you take out the ingredient Iza, nothing is left. I'm ashamed to write so much about him, and he'd be mad if he knew. Goodbye my farmer and don't work too hard.

Tokyo, February 18, 1941

Dear Miye,

Thank you very much for your long-awaited letter. Imagine getting your letter of January 13 on February 18! Over one month. It seems so out of place to hear you say "Happy New Year" now. That letter was so good—a real masterpiece and sounded just like you. Also, Sensei sent me the *Echo of*

104. Tokyo's notorious licensed quarter.

105. More precisely, a sensibility that reveres the natural, the understated, and the minimal.

Calvary and your editorial really was a masterpiece. In it you said the Jews say that beauty is in the faces of their old men rather than in their young, inexperienced women. Do you know that there is a corresponding Japanese idea? Our teacher said that it is typically Japanese—the classical, traditional Japanese standard of beauty is in "*sabi*" (rust).[106] Thus, for example, a teapot becomes beautiful only after it has been used and reused. The shrines are beautiful when they become old and weather-beaten. And also, old men are beautiful. And the objects of beauty must be beheld in dark places—and not in the glaring sun. He said that the beautiful women of long ago used to sit in dark rooms—and their being in the musty rooms was a large part of their charm. I saw the exhibition of rare art treasures of Shosoin,[107] but was not very impressed. Now I can see the reason why. Japanese beauty must be lived with, in the dark. It is directly opposite to the glaring, skin-deep beauty of the Occident. And one cannot grasp their loveliness at first sight. Did I tell you about that Shosoin exhibit? It was at the Ueno Imperial Museum. No one is ever allowed to see those old treasures, but by special Imperial permit in celebration of the 2,600th founding of the Empire, they were brought to Tokyo and opened to the public. We happened to go there at three-thirty (it closes at four), so the crowd was not so bad. However, Ito-san (my aunt) went to see them, and she had to stand in line for *three hours* before getting to go in. That is how much everyone wanted to see them. They are from the Nara and Heian Periods—many hundreds of years ago.

It is ten o'clock in the morning now. If I go now, I'll just have time to make the eleven o'clock class of *Bushido* translation—English to Japanese.[108] Guess I'll go—

I'm writing at the station now. I just missed the train. A friend of mine, Chiyo Takahashi, is going back to Hawaii tomorrow. I want to finish this letter by then. I'm having her take over a slide rule and book for Karl Naka, who is now in Oregon, but used to be in our class. He asked me to get a slide rule for him. He sent $12.50, which is 53 yen. The slide rules cost only 22 yen. He said to spend the rest on the Ginza. Iza got the slide rules for me from his school with a 10% discount, so we went to the Ginza and had dinner. Today we are spending the remainder on a farewell dinner for Chiyo. Five of us—

106. But *sabi* also, as here, can mean elegant simplicity or patina.

107. A treasury built in 756 that contains art and cultural artifacts from the height of the Nara period (710–84). That short period, in which Nara was the seat of imperial power, was marked by Chinese influence on Japanese culture and saw the rise of Buddhism under the auspices of the Emperor Shomu. Thanks to the continuous protection of successive rulers, the Shosoin collection has reached the present day virtually intact.

108. Nitobe Inazo, *Bushido: The Soul of Japan: An Exposition of Japanese Thought* (New York, 1905). Nitobe (1862–1933) wrote his book in an attempt to explain Japanese to the world through an exposition of its "chivalric code."

Natsuko, Fritz and Mizutani (girl from French Indo-China). When Karl was here, he and Fritz and I and Natsuko used to go out.

I am now at school. I came late ten minutes and found out they're having assembly. The speaker is already talking so I'm up in the library now—I hate to butt in there now.

Washed my hair last night and today it is flying all over creation.

We are having a farewell meeting for Chiyo at noon. We chip in twenty cents and get sweets and then everybody takes turns singing. They pick on localities, for example, they make Canada sing or Brazil or something. These meetings are patterned after Japanese get-togethers. In them everybody eats and then brings on their own entertainment. Usually singing. It's fun until your turn.

Emma is going to have a baby in July. The nerve! She said I could go there and wash diapers for my keep! I can't imagine her a mother. Now—can I imagine my mom with a permanent? Your letters are so informative and interesting.

Iza passed the exam to be an army engineer. He didn't want to pass because he wanted to get into the naval department. Probably going to the front by the end of this year. It must be awful for someone you love to go to the front. I'll probably never experience that. But I do like him and I'll feel so sorry when he goes. But Mrs. Nagata will have two of her sons go at once. Poor mother!

I feel so good because my hands are actually *clean*! Reason: I had a bath last night. Usually they get dirty and stay that way—I can't rub them clean. And they get so chapped and rough. Also washed my hair and underwear.

I wonder if I will continue to like Japan after I get out of Kokusai. Graduation is March 15. We're having a farewell dinner Friday after next. I'm going to wear a kimono! Mrs. Ito made a beautiful one for me. I've never worn it yet. I'm only worried because kimonos make fat girls look even fatter.

I stayed over at these Joshi Dai students (Shiojima's cousins) Monday night. They surely treat me royally. Even shined my shoes for me! First time in my life someone shined my shoes for me. They are rich and have a big home and two maids.

Teaching English keeps me busy and out of mischief.

I have to hurry and take this letter to the main post office.

Write soon.

Tokyo, February 25, 1941

Dear Miye,

Thank you very much for your letters. Just received one last night. Just met Masako Yamada of San Fernando tonight.[109] She looks very nice, gentle and pretty. I'm going to take her to church Sunday after next. She is the Japanese type of quiet girl and I feel big and boorish and wicked compared to her. Maybe I shouldn't tell you this, but since you are the friend of my heart, I will tell you all, as usual. I don't know how much everyone knows about this, but if they don't know please keep it to yourself. They wanted Masako to marry George.[110] George told me that he did not want to get married yet and that people said Masako Yamada is good-looking, so for me to go take a good look at her because he's afraid people will pull a fast one on him. And Mom told me her address and told me not to tell her what George said. In the next letter she said that she found out Masako is weak and can't marry for three years, so drop it all. Such a nuisance this go-between business must be!

Miye, what is the secret of all your pep and energy? And when did Margaret Shimizu get married and to whom? I never knew anything about it. She was the type to get married, though. Frankly, I think that Masako Yamada was not the girl for George. She is too passive and goody good. He needs someone more peppy and "bossy." Of course, she would make the ideal quiet sweet helpmate—but is that what George needs? I think someone more of your type would be better—he needs someone with brains and vigor.

It is a beautiful morning. The sun is shining. The birds are singing. I can see the smoke from our neighbor's home. So peaceful on the surface.

February 27, night. Oh, Miye—I'm worried again. What shall I do after graduating from Kokusai? I feel like going home. Last night I dreamt so realistically of those Ceres friends of mine. The only thing that keeps me here is that I'm ashamed to go back with my poor speaking ability—and what shall I do after I do go back? I'll be so dissatisfied to stay home. And yet—I want to put in some days of clean, honest labor on the ranch. Oh—and I hate to think of the presents I'll have to buy before going back—I'm writing this in bed. I'm beginning to catch a cold and feel rotten. Finished *Escape*[111] last night. Have you read it? Not so good as I'd expected. But I do admire the Countess. Tomorrow is our class party.

March 3. Tests are on now. A whole week of them but I'm not taking them seriously. Just received a notice tonight from Joshi Dai saying I can't enter the

109. The Yamada family had come back to live in Odawara. Masako (Masa), the oldest child, and her sister Youkiye had been members of the Holiness church in Southern California.

110. Mary's brother, two years older than she.

111. Unidentified.

school. Now what shall I do? Maybe I'll enter Waseda [University]. Kokusai kids have pull to get in there. But among all those boys—If I do get in, I'm going to study like the devil at *first.* I studied when I first entered Kokusai.

Saturday I went with Yabe. Remember—he's the funny-looking Java Nisei. Enjoyed seeing him because [I] didn't meet him for about four months. He's interesting if you don't see him too often. He gives me self-confidence. He is attending Waseda and he urged me to enter. I'm afraid George wouldn't like it. We saw *First Love* starring Deanna Durbin. Had lunch together. He always treats me. He is quite well off. His father is some big shot. He works at JDAK[112] every day now.

Last Friday was our class party and I wore a kimono! It is beautiful and I love it. It is not miserable at all to wear, either. But I had a hard time walking in *geta*. Everyone flattered me and said it was becoming to me. It is warm.

Got a letter from Thelma Christiansen and she said she met you in town. Gosh—Miye, I have a wave of homesickness now. But if I go home I'll be so useless now. I must master Japanese first!

Sunday a teacher at Rikko Kai got married. I helped make sandwiches. The bride was all painted and even wore a wig of Shimada hairdress.[113] She looked like a doll.

Really, my brother is so kind to let me live in leisure like this. He really is doing a lot for [me]. Please be kind to him for my sake. I think it's unfair to make him get married when he doesn't really want to.

Please write soon. Gee—I want to see you! I do, in my dreams.

[P.S.] It hurts me every time you ask me to write for the *Echo*. My religion isn't. And I cannot write hypocritical nothings. So please forgive me.

Tokyo, March 21, 1941

Dear Miye,

Please excuse the long silence. But that doesn't mean I ever have you out of my thoughts. Especially recently, since I've graduated I've been thinking so much of home and friends. My mother really was wonderful to go way out to America long ago. Those Issei were brave—they've got guts which we Nisei lack. I wish I had a talent for writing. I think my mother's life would make a fascinating story. People in Japan tell me that I am like my mother. When she came to this Rikko Kai she couldn't read a word, but by diligent and persevering study, she could write and read as well as she can now. She is much greater than I am. It is just beginning to dawn on me how much people respect her. When I think of her, I must study and work hard and never do anything to

112. The Tokyo Central Radio Station.

113. An old-style wig and headdress worn in the traditional Japanese wedding.

shame her. I wish I could remember that always, but I am but poor weak flesh and as such choose the easier road.

Today is the first day of Spring! It is warm today. The sun is shining—the birds are twittering—in the distance I hear the sound of the streetcars but otherwise the world is peaceful and content. I love Spring. More than any other season. Soon the cherry blossoms will be out. You don't know how one can look forward to them! However, the sky in Tokyo is usually hazy. I miss the clearness of the sky of California. They say that Osaka is worse—very smoky and grey. I want to go to Osaka.

Ito-sensei is in Tokyo now. Last Sunday after the meeting we went out to dinner. Had an eel "*donburi*" [rice and eel]. He said there were rumors that Kuzuhara-sensei[114] might quit. Who then?

I graduated on the fifteenth. Why are graduation speeches so long? The Joshi Dai student that I help with her English came with her friend. Afterwards a group of us went out to dinner, then to a Japanese show which was so boring we left right after it started. I've never seen an American movie which can be as slow and boring as some of these Japanese movies.

Tonight I am going to attend the *Merchant of Venice* given by Nihon Joshi Dai. My student gave me two tickets, so I asked Masako Yamada to come. I think that we will live together. Next week I am planning to move from the Nagata home to a place nearer to school. Did I tell you? I'm planning to attend Tokyo Joshi Dai. Masako and I are going to room together and cook for ourselves. I think it will be fun. We'll have freedom, and that's a very important ingredient in my happiness.

I am going to visit my grandfather out in the country also. He gave me a letter telling me to be sure to come, so I'd better go. I think of myself as a poor substitute for my mom.

Yo-chan, the Nagata boy next to Iza-chan, got appendicitis and was operated on last Friday. It was all very sudden. He went to Atami with friends and came back on Friday. He ate at a restaurant Friday night—then his side started aching. Soon he couldn't move, and they phoned home, and so Miyoko and Iza-chan rushed there and put him on a stretcher and hunted around for a hospital. All the hospitals are full now. They finally found one and he was operated on at one o'clock in the morning. Iza said he saw the operation and it was interesting. He has to stay in the hospital a month. Bet he's disappointed because he just graduated from Aoyama Gakuin (Emma's husband's school) and was planning to enter the navy. Now he has to wait another year. Mrs. Nagata is staying at the hospital nursing him. I am staying home and keeping house with Miyoko. Have to make lunch today and guess I'd better do it now—

114. Bishop of the Holiness church in the United States.

It is 1:10 now. I cooked some "daikon" for lunch. The two little kids, Mr. Nagata, and I were the only ones home. I'm so stuffed now. This afternoon I'm going to my relative's and then to second-hand bookstores to sell some *Reader's Digests* and books. They buy them very cheap but I hate to have a lot of unnecessary junk.

Since I am stuffed, I feel sleepy and stupid. Consequently, I can think of nothing to write. I'll just write at random anything which comes into my head. There was a beauty of a book on Japan and China written in English which I discovered while browsing around second-hand bookstores. But it cost 30 yen! I want to get a really good history of Japan written in English. There are some but they are so expensive! (Somebody is hollering down in the kitchen but I'm upstairs and too lazy to go down.) The cook for the Rikko Kai dorm is very religious. She said that her child wandered away and she prayed to *Kami-sama* [a god], and he showed her where her child was. So she goes to temples and worships faithfully. When Miyoko hurt her finger that cook told her to go to a certain shrine and pray, then it would be sure to get well. Many people believe that here—So many shrines in Japan. Everywhere one goes—even in fields and mountain. But I hate the way the Japanese sneeze as loud as possible—it gets on my nerves. Another pet hate is their spitting. Ugh—it makes me sick. If you walk along any road if you have your eyes on the ground you can see sputum. Sometimes I think Japanese are so dirty. And they make so much noise while eating. It is not so bad while they have a bowl and chopsticks, but give them a plate and knife and fork! They don't believe in carrying food to their mouth: their theory is take the food (loaded on the back of the fork) about an inch from the mouth, then, by suction power suck it in with appropriate noise. And their politeness is all forgotten on streetcars. Their motto is "Me first and Hell to the rest." Can they shove and push! They call it "*kotsu jigoku*" [traffic hell]. Of course, I am big here so I can take it (and give too) but the poor women and children! A little while ago a popular Manchurian actress appeared on the stage in a popular movie theater. The Waseda students crowded and jammed in front of the theater and some people were injured as a result. Waseda students are rough, anyway. They wear peculiar pointed university caps, and you see those caps all over.

Miyoko just came home (she went to the hospital.) I got my hair set for graduation. It felt so good. I felt beautiful. But my messy hair gets on my nerves and it feels so good to think you are neat. I met Yabe-san that day, and he was all upset because he flunked from Waseda. And I thought that they never flunked anyone! He said he might go back to Java. He said the Nisei from *nan-yo* [the South Seas] are good-for-nothing. I contradicted him, but I really think so too. And I would hate to live in a place even like Hawaii. The Hawaii Nisei generally speak poor Japanese and their coloring is different and dark. I don't see how Emma stands it there. Japan is preferable to Hawaii. I like the seasons and think it would be boring to live in one season all the year around.

I think I will be going. Please write soon.

Tokyo, March 22, 1941

Dear Miye,

Just received your letter of Feb. 28. Your nice long letter sounded so much like you that it made me homesick.

Last night I saw *The Merchant of Venice* at Japan Women's College and was never so disappointed with a play in all my life. I wonder if Westerners look as ridiculous when they try to put on Japanese dramas. I couldn't understand most of their English, only such well-known passages as "The quality of mercy is not strained." Their acting was stiff and unnatural, especially the love scenes. There was one Nisei that you could spot immediately because her English was understandable. Then I got to thinking—I bet our school play was just as ridiculous when we tried to put on a classical Japanese drama.

Mr. Nagata told me the other night that I am still "wild." According to him, I should have lived in a strict Japanese home so that I would have been molded into a humble, sweet Japanese woman. His home was not good for me because Iza uses "coolie" language;[115] consequently I am not exposed to feminine speech. However if I had been imprisoned in such a home I would have hated Japan and might have gone back by now. Fumi was in a strict home and couldn't ever go out, so she can't wait to return home next month.

I am amazed at the transformation of Hiroko since she fell in love. She was not good-looking at all, but after she met her Japanese boyfriend she has become radiant. I never saw anyone change so much. They are getting married in May, and she is leaving for his home in Osaka in April.

Yesterday on the streetcar I was watching some modern Japanese girls in Western clothes. How they bob their heads when they talk! Did you ever notice how a hen bobs its head every step it takes? These girls wiggle their heads with every sentence they utter. It is so funny that I was laughing all by myself.

How I wish you were here and we could talk about everything under the sun like we used to. I'll try to get some of my thoughts on paper, but it is a poor substitute for talking to you. I wish I were an artist or musician. Such wonderful music I would create tonight. How I envy you when you write that

115. Japanese speech is marked by strong gender and class differences. "Coolie" language here means masculine working-class speech.

you are listening to music over the radio. We can hear good music only in tea houses or at concerts. Nice girls don't go to tea houses, and concerts are very expensive. Or if I were a poet, such soulful poetry I would write while in this mood.

Now I yearn for a man. I want to love and be loved and forget the world and all its problems. I want someone who will appreciate and admire me just as I am, regardless of what I look like. O, I am the eternal feminine! "Study hard and become something"—such empty words for a woman!

Tokyo, April 2, 1941

Dear Miye,

I've been so busy and occupied recently. On the twenty-third I left for my grandfather's place in Yonezawa and returned on the twenty-seventh. I took the Joshi Dai exam the next day. I moved on the twenty-ninth and have been getting settled here.[116] Tonight I am leaving for Kyoto, Nara and Wakayama. My cousin, Uncle Terry's grandson, is going to enter the barracks, so asked me to come down to Wakayama. The cherry blossoms are at their height of beauty now. I've always wanted to see the historical sights at Nara and Kyoto. I'm going with Natsuko.

I am beginning to understand my grandpop and the elderly women up in Yonezawa. After all, he is my mother's father, and there are similarities. They stuff me full of food and put me to sleep. Three days of that was enough. It's a good thing I had the entrance exams as an excuse to escape from there.

It is so frustrating to go grocery shopping now because there is such a scarcity of food. But it's fun to cook for ourselves and to entertain. The other night Hiroko's fiancé came over with a friend, and we had a sukiyaki feast. Last night Natsuko came over with some bread, and we had *oden* [daikon-seafood stew] and toast. Rev. Ito had given me some butter, which is non-existent in the stores.

I've realized that I don't feel like writing when I am relatively satisfied with my life. Are writers misfits? I am afraid I am a misfit but no writer. You are a writer but not a misfit. So it doesn't make sense.

The sun is shining benignly this morning and spring is just around the corner.

116. Mary and Masako moved to a room in a Japanese home in the Otsuka district. Masako's sister Youkiye and their Nisei friend Clara Iwamoto joined them.

Tokyo, April 15, 1941

Dear Miye,

I'm going home in July—I think. Gee—what will it be like to go back? I am afraid—everyone will be so changed. I won't fit in anymore. I'll have only you—afraid of the future—what shall I do? I'll be a good-for-nothing. But I can't believe that I'm going home. After two years. It makes me feel so old.

Received a letter from Elsa and two pictures. Whew! Was I surprised! She is a fashion plate now.

O, Miye—I am so disgusted! Shall I pour forth my heart to you in its anguish? Last night I went out with Iza-chan. Had dinner, then he had a ticket to a piano recital and I went with him. It was all Beethoven and very beautiful and impressive. Only one I knew was "Moonlight Sonata" and [the pianist] put so much expression in it. Some of the pieces made me want to cry. There is such yearning. [Iza] met a girlfriend at the concert. She was with her girlfriend and we all had tea afterwards. O—he made me mad though—the way he paid attention to her. And she is so darn cute! And he says the very same things to her that he says to me. Fool that I am but I *do* care and I hate to admit it.

April 22. I'm going to Manchuria! Ito-san, my relative, is going to go with a group who are going to do *odori* for the soldiers. She lends the dancing costumes and she said I could come along and help. The army pays for all our expenses! This is a chance of a lifetime—just think—I'll really see that soldier life and Manchuria—so romantic. I'm so busy now my head is going around in circles. Going this afternoon to the embassy to get my passport changed. I quit school. Going to take the July 10 boat back home, I think.

Iza-chan successfully passed the naval exam so he enters the navy on the sixth of next month. I guess I'll see no more of him. My cousin of Wakayama entered the barracks this month on the tenth. Did I tell you that I went to Kyoto, Nara and Wakayama? My cousin is so nice.

Sunday, Natsuko and Fritz Langer came over for a sukiyaki dinner. It was lots of fun. Last night my Joshi Dai student came over for dinner. There were seven of us all together. We're having so much fun living here—I wish it could continue.

But I'm looking forward to going home—two years pass so quickly—

I'm so busy I'll have to stop now—

Osaka, April 28, 1941

Dear Miye,

Gosh, Miye—just four more months, then I'll be seeing you! I hate to leave Japan, yet I'm looking forward to going home. I'm taking the *Asama*

Maru, which leaves on July tenth. I want to stay with Emma in Honolulu awhile and wash diapers for her and feel very self-sacrificing and heroic while doing it. Then, guess I'll be home about August 20 or so.

I don't know what to do when I go home. Maybe I'll go to Cal and get a BA major in botany and take up Japanese to keep up on it. Really, my Japanese is very rough and I'm ashamed of going home because I can't speak decently. I might take private lessons before going home so that I'll at least know how to "*aisatsu*" [exchange greetings]. My Japanese is bookish—I can read pretty well—but cannot speak. Well—you'll find out soon how ignorant I still am. To know Japan I feel as though I'd have to stay five or ten years longer.

Right now I am in Osaka. We are leaving for Manchuria tomorrow. Mrs. Ito, my relative, went before me. There are two persons with me now—a Katsura *no obasan* ["auntie-of-the-wigs"] (sixty years old and looks seventy), and Takenosuke, who has charge of the make-up. The *obasan* is complaining this morning because we were left behind. I'm ignoring her and writing this. She has false teeth and washes them in her *ochawan* [ricebowl] after breakfast. I was surprised the first morning, because right after breakfast we have tea in our *ochawans*,[117] and here she was rattling something pink-and-white in her tea. I do hope she doesn't drink that tea up afterwards. She has charge of the wigs. Mrs. Ito said she doesn't like her. I tolerate her. The Takenosuke we call Take-chan. He is about forty-eight or fifty and has six kids in Tokyo. At first he reminded me of your Bill Something of MJC who looked like a skeleton, so I was rather attracted to him, but he's not at all romantic or mysterious or deep. But he is nice. Yesterday he took us sightseeing to Kyoto. Old people are all right to go around with when you are tired, but when you're rested and full of pep—they are so old and dead and boring.

It's fun to help Mrs. Ito with the kimonos. The kimonos are really beautiful. Works of art with gold thread and beautiful designs. They wear many layers of kimonos. I can't dress the dancers yet, but I kinda help around. Then I help them undress and fold up the costumes. Japanese dress is meant to be folded. They never hang up their clothing.

Mrs. Ito is rather modern. She smokes and uses rough language. She is sassy and lots of fun because she knows how to joke. Says just what she thinks, too, so that people either like her or don't like her—she is the type to be loved or hated, either one or the other and no in-between business. I surely like her. She has brains, too. George surely did like her. She liked him, too. But everyone in Japan seems to have liked George.

These old people in Japan are queer. For instance, there was a law that everyone had to be vaccinated for smallpox. The old people hate these queer

117. In those days, people customarily used the same bowl for their tea after finishing up their rice.

new-fangled ideas, but since they had to undergo the vaccination, they did. Then as soon as they came home they scrubbed off the vaccine as fast as they could. That's what this Katsura *no obasan* did. And so did Mrs. Ito.

My dream is to go on some plant-hunting expedition. I wonder if I could? But they usually take men—besides I'm Japanese.

I still can't get over the shock of how the men and women all sleep in the same room in the Japanese hotel. And think nothing of it. Take-chan is taking us to Kobe today.

April 29. Yesterday we went to Kobe. It was quite interesting. I never saw so many foreigners on the streets in a Japanese city as I saw there. Most of them spoke English but there were also Siamese, negroes, Italian soldiers, and Scandinavian-looking big men with sandy hair. The foreign women in Japan are usually homely. In comparison to them the Japanese women are beautiful and sweet.

Last night we went to Dotombori of Osaka. That corresponds to the Ginza in Tokyo. So many people—I was fascinated. In general, the people of Kansai (West) are tougher looking than the Tokyo mass. Here they seem more country-ish. And there is not that mass of weak, thin university-student class that there is in Tokyo. Here the students are in the minority. The men are mostly factory workers. So the black student uniform which is omnipresent in Tokyo is replaced by the factory suit and common suit in Osaka. There are fewer European-dressed girls here, too. Once in a while there is a smartly dressed beautiful painted girl in foreign dress who is escorted by a tall good-looking man—but that type is rare. Most girls go in bunches of threes or fours and wear kimonos and are not beautiful. I was really fascinated last night by the crowd. So many people—and of all types. But no foreigners.

I wanted to go to a movie but the old people didn't. This old lady gets on my nerves sometimes. She walks so slowly. And she has pockets under her eyes and she looks ugly and skinny. But when she laughs she is kinda cute.

We get on the boat today and sail for Dairen[118]—another land awaits our exploring—new sights—queer people—new food—climate. What will it be like? Anticipation is greater than realization, they say. But that was not the case with me and Japan. At first I was so disappointed in Japan, but now it is much better than I'd anticipated. After one gets accustomed to the squalor and dirt and learns to overlook it, then he can see the beauty of Japan.

Well—I'll see you soon. Remember—about June 10 is the last letter which you will be able to send me—so make it good. O—just think! I'll be seeing you soon!

118. Dairen (now called Dalian), on the tip of the Liaotung peninsula, the principal port city of Manchuria.

On the boat to Dairen, May 2, 1941

Dear Miye,

I am about two hours from Dairen now, on the boat. I have spent the last three days on this boat, having left Kobe on April 29. There is nothing to do—there aren't even any seats on deck. The women sleep and read all day. I hate to stay in the dark and unventilated room, so I'm usually walking around the deck.

So far I have fooled two men by saying I am from Tokyo. It is rather embarrassing and I have to think fast when they ask about my family. But I feel good that my Japanese is good enough so that people think I am a native Japanese.

For two days the sunsets have been just glorious. One evening you could see the golden sun gradually sink into the ocean. Another day the sun reflected onto the calm water so beautifully—the ocean looked like pure gold, which turned into bronze. Sometimes it looks like a huge, shimmering snake—you can imagine so many things while gazing at the ocean. It is fascinating—the water is such a dark lovely blue—it looks pure and yet mysterious. What wonders are hidden underneath its calm surface? And as the ship ploughs through, it leaves a path of luscious white bubbly waves—there is such a charm to it. The ocean beckons one and you can't help but feel like plunging into its purity.

Yesterday an enormous fish swam alongside the ship for quite a distance. It must have been six feet long. It was sleek and streamlined, black with white underneath. Every once in a while it would jump out onto the surface, then plunge in so happily. It looked like it was having so much fun. In my next incarnation I would like to be such a fish. And a big enough one so that I wouldn't have to be afraid that other fishes would swallow me.

In our room each person has a space of about two by six feet. In that cramped space we have to live, sleep and eat. Only Japanese could live in such a small space. But they say Chinese are even better at it. The cute little girl who slept next to me was from Shikoku, near the sea, and was sun-tanned. They say Manchurians have two or three wives. The richer a man is, the more wives he can afford.

You must be busy with strawberries now. How I'd love to have a sweet, juicy tomato now, or orange!

Mongolia, May 10, 1941

Dear Miye,

Greetings from Inner Mongolia! Wish you were here, too. I'm having a very interesting time. It is all so new and different.

Manchuria is big and spacious. And Manchurians are big and fat. They seem to be happy-go-lucky people. They talk with loud voices. Some middle-aged women still have tiny four-inch feet. It looks ugly and unnatural. They point their feet outwards and totter along. I can hardly look at them because it seems so inhumane. They don't seem to mind, though.

We stayed in Harbin about four days. I'm too lazy to find out for sure how many days we stayed. One day we visited a Manchurian temple. It was Buddhist. They had statues of the Buddha with peaceful, gold lustrous faces. I never saw any gold-faced Buddhas before. And these looked so serene—

We also went to a shrine of Confucius in Harbin. O—the gaudy coloring! It reminded me of Nikko.[119] However, my taste must be Japanese-y, because in Japanese temples, no matter how gaudy the colors, there is a sense of harmony. But here—no. Their bright red walls and dull orange roof combination is sickening. But I did like their jade green and royal blue designs on the ceiling. In the West no one would dream of using such bright colors for architecture.

The Russian graveyard was nearby, so we visited it also. Luckily for us, a funeral procession came along. It was Catholic, and the man in front carried a large cross. Behind him came two Manchurians bearing the lid of the coffin on their heads. Then came the priest in a long embroidered robe with three singers in back of him. They sang as they walked. It was beautiful sad music and the trio's voices harmonized well. Then came the coffin borne on a wagon all decorated with flowers. A horse pulled the wagon. Behind were the widow and other mourners.

May 31. Now I am on the *Nekka Maru* heading for Japan. We reach Moji tomorrow morning. From there I am going to go to Kumamoto [in Kyushu] where Emma's in-laws are. I am going to visit Emiko Fujita on the way. Am looking forward to seeing her.

One month's trip just flew! I learned and saw so many new things. But don't feel like writing. I am Tokyo-sick already. I hope some letters from you and my mom are waiting for me.

Only one more month in Japan! I'll be so sad when I leave.

Iza-chan sent me a card saying he entered the navy. He is learning to fly. Why does one feel so old and sad when coming back from a trip?

Excuse this short letter but I just don't feel like writing.

119. A small town north of Tokyo renowned for its picturesque scenery. Its beautiful, brightly colored temples are notably different from most shrines in Japan, which are typically unpainted.

Tokyo, June 17, 1941

Dear Miye,

Thanks a lot for your letters. Was starving to hear from you. Just returned to Tokyo on the fifteenth and went to Nagatas' yesterday and was so happy to hear from you. Before I forget—next time you write, please write here [Emma's Honolulu address]. Will be there from July 20 to about August 5, I think, so please write.

You know we students do not have to go back to America, and I was thinking of staying longer in Japan, but after I read your letter I couldn't even think of staying.

Two years! How it can fly! I'm so excited about going back now. I wrote to my mom and George and I don't know if any more stationery will go for 20 sen, so am economizing on space.

Gee—we'll have loads to talk about. I can't wait to meet you.

Stayed at Mr. and Mrs. Yanagihara's for two days. She is as merry and loud as ever and he is quiet as usual. Japan didn't change them. They treated me so well. I felt as though I were back in Modesto again.

I must make a round of my relatives before leaving. Am taking the *Asama Maru* on July twelfth. Am very busy now. Lily Matsushige is leaving tomorrow. I planned to go visit her today but wrote letters and the time flew. So I guess I don't meet her. It's funny how you can't meet someone who lives in the same city.

Ito-sensei is coming on the twenty-sixth, and I'll meet him there. His son invited me to Sapporo before returning home but I can't make it. I did so want to have another talk with him. Now that I can talk a little better and can get over ideas without too much fumbling for words.

Doubt if I'll meet Iza-chan again either. I do so want to go out with him just once more. You know he's in the navy reserve now—flying. He comes home on Sundays, but I'll have only two more Sundays in Tokyo.

Tonight Natsuko invited me over for dinner. She is leaving on the twenty-fourth and wants me to go with her, but I'm itching to go as early as I can. Tomorrow night I'm going book hunting with Shoji-san. Most of my luggage is composed of books.

Am staying at Ito-san's.[120] Want to meet Masako Yamada but she went to Osaka to attend Hiroko's wedding.

I am in a mess. My mom tells me to bring Masako back with me for George's wife. Darn it—I hate this business. Why do they have to get him tied down so early anyway. Masako is nice but not the type for George, I think. Besides, her family is coming to Japan.

120. Pending her departure, Mary went to stay with the Itos.

I want to go to Cal and continue my Japanese there. And maybe major in botany. They say there's more of a chance for Nisei in Honolulu. I'm tempted to stay there and go to college, but you pull me back. Also I want to go back East. I want to explore America now. If only I had the money. Sometimes I feel like staying home and helping on the farm and being *oya koko* [filial] and leading a quiet uneventful life. There would be peace there. But still there is a spark of ambition burning in me. They say that Nisei can't be anything, but I won't believe it until I've tried. And then I could always return to Japan. They need people who can speak English here. And I like Tokyo. Besides, from now on there will be many old maids in Japan. So I won't be the only one. All the eligible men get killed in China and they say the ratio is 27:1. Poor *ojo-sans*.

Please write to Hawaii. I'll be looking forward to it.

Tokyo, July 21, 1941

Dear Miye,

My dreams blasted! It was all so sudden. I was longing and dreaming of home—of meeting you after two long years. And then what—a cablegram. Just four days before sailing.

I wonder what is the matter? Are my family all coming to Japan? Why should they want me to stay? Must I remain forever in Japan? Never to breathe the free, clean and dry air of America again? Never to see you again? No! I don't believe it! I won't believe it.

No letter from home yet. No explanation. It's lucky that I am of *nonki* nature. Otherwise I'd be a nervous wreck from worry and anxiety.

I feel as though I'm living "on borrowed time." I really should be in Hawaii now. Wonder how Emma is. I should have cabled her but it cost six yen at the cheapest. I was too stingy.

It's been raining every day for over a month now. It is very cool. They say it is April weather. Last year at this time it was hot and dry. So dry that we didn't have water in Tokyo.

July 23. Still no letter! I wonder what happened?[121] A boat came in on the twentieth, too. I was so disappointed.

I'm inviting Youkiye and Masako Yamada and Kiyoko Shiojima to dinner tonight. This Kiyoko Shiojima is Shiojima-sensei's cousin. She attends Joshi Dai. I taught her some English. I get along quite well with her. We attended

121. Mary subsequently learned that her parents, feeling that the tension between the United States and Japan was somewhat lessened, had decided to let her stay in Tokyo a little longer to continue her studies.

lectures of Oriental Summer College together for a week. We eat out and go to shows together. She is cute.

I've just been playing and loafing around. I try to study but can't.

Last Sunday I met Iza-chan again. He looks handsome in his white navy outfit. I think he's a lieutenant or something. O—but he made me mad! I was planning to meet him Sunday before last but instead went to the country to [my] relative's. He was mad because I didn't meet him, so he gave some concert tickets to a school friend. Before he'd promised he'd give them to me. It's funny how I can dislike him so and then get over it.

There are no vegetables in Tokyo now. First it was the confectionery. Then the bakery and meat market. Now it is the *Yaoya*. My English is terrible—I know the Japanese but not the English equivalent [vegetable store]. We might be starving soon. They are building air raid shelters. I would hate to be in Tokyo when bombs drop here.

Something's in the air. It's awfully fishy now. They are calling everybody [up]. My teacher had to go. And people are not allowed to see them off or talk about it. There are rumors that Japan is to go [in]to the Dutch East Indies.

I am staying at Ito-san's. Two soldiers are coming here soon. There are so many pouring into Tokyo that they have to distribute them among homes. Month by month and week by week, Japan is feeling the pinch of the war. But the hard times are to be from now on.

The other night, Mrs. Ito, her daughter and I went to the "*yomise*" [nighttime outdoor market]. It was like a carnival. The stands are brightly lit. In the streets they sell potted plants, goldfish, caged insects, chopsticks, toys, etc. We bought ten goldfish and some plants. It was like a festival.

I wonder if my family is coming to Japan? And what shall I do? I am too lazy to work. Chances for marriage are slim. They are hard even for Japan-born girls, and Nisei girls have no chance, in comparison.

Go to school? And then what?

Youkiye doesn't like Japan. I do. I am so free here. And happy, most of the time.

I'm reading a good book called *Botchan*, by Natsume Soseki.[122] I have the English translation, but the Japanese original is much better. Much of the wit and humor are lost in the translation. But it takes so much time to read Japanese.

And I would be in Hawaii now!

Ito-sensei was in Tokyo for about a week. He gave me a telegram, but I wasn't home. Running around, as usual. I was supposed to meet him on

122. A popular comical novel published in 1904 and translated into English as *The Young Master* in 1922 by Sasaki Umeji.

Sunday but was late for the appointment, and when I got there he was no longer there.

It is four-thirty now. Those kids will be here soon.

Please write.

Tokyo, August 24, 1941

Dear Miye,

How are you? I haven't heard from you for ages. By the last boat I received only one letter. That was from Miyoko Suzuki. I was so disappointed not to hear from you or Mother. And they say that no more boats are coming in. I really feel exiled. Perhaps I'll never be able to return home—but then conditions can't remain the same forever.

Gosh, Miye, what are you doing? And what are you going to do with your life? How I wish you were here with me to discuss life, love and philosophy and religion like we used to. I really have no one to really say what I think to. No one who would understand my ideas and sympathize or discuss. The other night I dreamt about the Wickings (people I used to work for). It's strange how the past always haunts one.

Last night I got up at three and read a little. But soon became sleepy. I just loaf around now since summer session has closed. I'm staying at Ito-san's. Mr. and Mrs. Ito have been away since the fifteenth. So I'm here with the daughter and maid. Clean house a little, then read or study or just loaf around all day. I can't go out because they asked me to watch the house for them. Of course, nothing happens, but I feel it my duty to stay.

I say nothing happens, but everyday things do happen which are quite exciting. Two soldiers were boarding here since the thirtieth of last month. The maid and I had a time trying to think of what to feed them. Thank goodness, they left on the eighteenth. What a relief it was.

I really wish that you were here to talk to me. I'm too lazy to write. I've learned a lot about this Ito family that I never suspected before I lived with them. After you live with a family you learn all the drama of it. Mr. Ito is quiet and nice. I used to think that he was an ideal husband, but I've surely found out differently. When he gets mad, he's just like somebody with a fit. He shouts and every nerve in him seems to be quivering. He strikes his wife and daughters. Really—it frightened me when I first saw him. And Mrs. Ito—she surely does scold! I feel sorry for her daughter. I'm thankful that I don't have a mother like that.

As a rule Japanese are stingy. I used to think that Mrs. Nagata was. So is Mrs. Ito. And in Ito-san's case it's not one of necessity, as with Mrs. Nagata.

The Itos are quite well-off. But still—she makes the maid furnish her [own] soap and dustrags and thread. That might sound trivial to you, but in present-day Japan it is far from being trivial. For there are no cotton goods. Therefore, no thread. And the dustrags soon go to pieces, so the maid has to tear up her own clothes to use for dustrags. Also, the maid never eats what the rest of the family does. She said that many times she had no *okazu*, so put salt on rice and ate only that. And here the Itos could afford to let them eat what they do. And they have many old cloths. It's just a case of parsimony. Since I was a maid, I surely sympathize with them. They are treated awful in Japan. They go to bed about eleven and must get up at four or five. They can have no will of their own.

I've been considering staying in Japan. Because if I do go back to America, then what? There's no place for me. I'd be better off in Tokyo. Now that I am quite accustomed to it, perhaps I could stand it here. If only you were here!

It's surprising how the American best-sellers are practically all translated into Japanese. They seem to be quite popular here, too.

Last American picture I saw was *Young Tom Edison*. I saw it with Masako and Youkiye Yamada. I was surprised at Masako, too. Will I ever be able to truly judge people? At first glance she seems to be so quiet and angelic, but after you know her, you find out that she has a will and ideas all her own. She said that she used to be a tomboy. Now I believe it. But I'll never forget the first impression I got of her when I met her in Japan. She seemed so old, dignified and pretty. A sweet old maid. Her clothes are long (she wears conservative, long skirts). She has a lovely complexion. She wears make-up quite skillfully. But now, since I know her better, she seems to be just like me. Really wild and rebellious deep down.

She is funny and I do enjoy her and her sister. They came over the other night for dinner. We went to a show afterwards. Recently I've been seeing so many movies that I'm sick of them. The news changes every week, but sometimes I'd see the same news over and over. One I saw four times!

But now I have to be stingy, too. Every penny counts for me now. I never know when I'll get more money. I'm going out to the country. No matter how much I try not to, I spend my money in Tokyo. Goodbye—Please write!!

Yonezawa, August 30, 1941

Dear Miye,

How I wish you were here! I am now relaxing at an *onsen* [hot spring] near Yonezawa. I came yesterday with my two *obaasans* and Yasu-chan, my 22-year-old cousin. It is a quiet retreat in the mountains. We brought rice, vegetables and canned goods. We have a room in a hotel and all day long we eat, sleep, read and go in the baths. Yesterday those *obaasans* went in the baths about five times.

It's surprising how these Yonezawa people can eat. They even beat me! They tell me that I don't eat much, so you can imagine how much they eat in comparison. They have tea before breakfast. Then they have breakfast. Then at ten o'clock they have tea and cakes. Lunch at twelve. Tea at three again. Dinner at six. In between, if guests come, they always offer them tea and sweets or cooked vegetables or even rice.

In Yonezawa they still have food. Rice is not rationed and it is delicious Japanese rice. They have lots of vegetables. In Tokyo, the only vegetables we have are potatoes and dried onions. But the Itos brought lots of food from the country, so we have variety.

Yet, I feel more at home at my grandfather's place than any other place in Japan. Maybe they are the only people who really care about me. They are so simple and slow—dear old country people up in the mountains. It's restful to be here, once in a while. My *obaasans*' life is a cycle of eating, sleeping, smoking and visiting. They seem so contented—these people.

My grandfather gets up at five and first of all, smokes his pipe leisurely. Then he cleans out the *hotoke sama* [ancestral shrine] and *tokonoma* [alcove], placing fresh flowers in both. Next he does the radio exercises. It seemed so incongruous when I first saw him—a white-haired, bent and wrinkled old man swinging his arms so vigorously. Then it is time for his hot tea and *umeboshi* [pickled plum]. Then he goes out for a walk. When he returns he has one bowl of rice for his breakfast. The rest of the day he lies on the tatami, with his head resting on a porcelain pillow, and listens to the radio. Such is the life of my grandfather. His only pleasure is listening to the radio. The *obaasans*' only pleasure seems to be in eating.

I've been trying to read *Takekurabe*, a novel by Higuchi Ichiyo, an outstanding writer of the Meiji period.[123] Our teacher praised her and said she died at age 25 of tuberculosis. She fell in love with her teacher, only to discover—too late—that he was already married. So she sacrificed herself and cut off all relations with this teacher whom she loved. She lived in dire poverty. I saw a movie of her life. It was sad and well done. My teacher said that her writing is very beautiful. Only wish that I could understand and appreciate it. It is written in an old style that is difficult to understand. But still—even such as I can see that there is such a delicate and refined feeling in her writing. Many old classical Japanese authors have that. And it makes you feel good—

123. Like the other novels of Higuchi (1872–96), *Takekurabe* is about the life of Tokyo women, in this case, a young girl growing up in the red-light district.

as though you've come in contact with splendid people who have beautiful and pure thoughts and ideals.

When I begin to read them, they make me want to study. I want to be able to read those old classics. Even the Meiji writers would be all right. The modern literature seems to be so trashy. Just like the best-sellers of America. When I finish a modern Japanese novel, it makes me feel rotten—just the opposite of some classical writing. Or is it because I do not understand the latter that there is such charm and beauty in it?

Iza-chan gave me two of his magazines which the literary society of his university publishes. He was the editor. He gave them to me long ago, but I could not read them for pleasure then. It was too much work and agony then. Now I find them quite interesting. The poems seemed to be egotistical and empty. I didn't know what they were about. But I liked the stories. Iza can write quite well. He told me that I was unable to understand them because the writers had to be careful to hide their implications or the censors would not approve them. Once in a while I'd catch a spark of revolt against the smugness of the Big Shots.

One poem by Iza goes something like this:

> We are young
> We are burning with an inner fire
> We need no geisha and *machiai*
> Such as seems to be necessary for our elders
> For we have youth
> In us is a fire which cannot be extinguished.

I asked him, "What is *machiai*?" Do you know? He said it is something which every country in the world has and for me to use my imagination.

We went to Asakusa one time, and he pointed out a *machiai* to me. After that, I noticed many of them. At Otsuka and Ueno there are many of them. They are the licensed quarters.

Iza said if I were only a boy he would take me all over. He said that only men can eat the best food in Japan. Girls can't go to those places.

There is much that I don't know about Japan, especially the darker side. Since I am a female, I cannot poke my nose into many places. Is it better to be innocent? Or is it better to know? I often wonder. "The truth will set you free." So should we seek to know the bad as well as the good? If we don't know the bad, we cannot know the good. For everything is a matter of relationship.

What is dirty and what is clean? One time Iza said that he went skiing and ate the snow frozen on the twig of a tree. I said, "How dirty!" and he replied, "It's not dirty at all. There were no people around. Only where there are people is it dirty." That is not saying much for us human beings. Is nature clean, then? Japanese seem to think so. They surely are close to nature. I think that is one of the most outstanding differences between the Japanese and the Occidental. Japanese do not worship nature—they live with it—and are part of her. Flower arrangement and tea ceremony are a manifestation of this spirit of striving to live in harmony with the laws of the universe and nature.

It seems rather useless to write when I don't know if this letter will ever reach you. I wonder if it is just wishful thinking that makes me think Japan and America will never go to war? For what are all these developments if not in preparation for war—evacuation of Americans from Japan, no more ships leaving or coming, prohibition of the use of English in telephones or telegrams, etc.

[On July 1, 1941, Izaya wrote Mary this farewell letter, which she translated and sent to Miye in her letter of September 23:]

To Mary who is spending her few remaining days in Japan:

Upon reading your letter I was very disappointed. Are you not a little hasty in leaving Japan? As yet, you have not seen the most beautiful places; you have not read and do not know about the finest literature of Japan. After returning to the USA you must not say,

"I have been to Japan. And I have returned after thoroughly understanding her."

Mary, I can imagine that by now your eyes are glaring and your mouth is puckered from anger. You are probably longing to answer back. I also would like to hear what you have to say in reply. But please do not become too angry to read further.

Why must I—who love above all things: to play, climb mountains, go skiing, compose bum music, make friends with poets, construct radios—just why is it that one who loves to do these things must get up every morning at five and become oil covered and grimy working on machines everyday? Why must I—who want to live in a world of peace and art—why must I spend thought and energy in constructing fearful armaments—aeroplanes—and improving them to be more dreadful monsters which will butcher people and destroy beautiful cities and ships which took years to build? Can you understand this, Mary?

Do you think, "Izaya is being fooled by a handful of stupid politicians?"

Do you recall that you went with me to the palace on the night of the celebration for the 2,600th anniversary of the founding of the Japanese empire? You probably will never forget the multitudes gathered there to honor their emperor. Those thousands of people were not all very intelligent, but don't ever think that they were duped into assemblying there. You said, when you saw the faithful horde, there was some intangible beauty to be found there. That is the truth. Without doubt that something is one of the outstanding components of that beauty which the Japanese race possesses.

I am one of that Japanese race. And I am proud of it. I believe that this is not a matter of *theory*, but one of *affection* [love].

Mary, can you understand all of what I have written thus far? If you can, you are quite great. And being great, you will praise me for not fearing death; for sacrificing all selfish desires and loves for the sake of fighting bravely.

Mary, you are perhaps not angry anymore. There are huge aeroplanes soaring noisily above this room in which I am writing this letter. These many aeroplanes are used to bomb and torpedo the enemy. We are always prepared to fight at a moment's notice. No one knows—besides Almighty God—if I shall survive the next war. And if there is no God, then nobody knows.

I love the mountains of Japan. In the book which I once promised to give to you, I wrote the following in one of my novels: "Beautiful mountains—Fleecy, white clouds—Blue, spreading sky." Any Japanese who has spent even one day amid such a lovely environment would never hesitate to sacrifice his life even for the sake of protecting only these picturesque mountains.

So I must say goodbye to you, Mary, who tormented me—who went to concerts with me—who ate twenty "sushi" all at once—who never paid me any tuition. I shall probably never see you again. Goodbye.

Izaya

Tokyo, September 23, 1941

Dear Miye,

How do you like the above letter? I got ambitious one night and translated it. Iza-chan wrote it to me while I was visiting my grandfather in the country, just a few days before I was to leave Japan. It is Izaya at his best—in one of his rare moods. It is quite a masterpiece, don't you think?

Why don't I hear from you? It is almost four months since I last heard from you. What has happened? I have been careless about writing because they said no boats were going or coming. But I received mail from home recently. So I'm hopeful again.

Today is a holiday. It is the autumnal equinox.

Yesterday we saw the partial eclipse of the sun. They call it *nisshoku* [sun-eaten]. I went to church yesterday (for a change). I'd written to Masako Yamada and planned to go together, but she didn't show up. When I came home,[124] a boy, who is the son of a friend of Mrs. Ito's, was over, so we hunted up a piece of glass, smoked it, then went to the roof and looked at the sun through it. It looked almost like a new moon [sketch].

School is quite interesting.[125] A girls' school is not boring, as I'd imagined. The kids in our class are loud and peppy. There are seven Manchurians and four Nisei. We have just the language classes by ourselves, and have physics, natural science, mathematics, ethics, gym, etc., with the university classes. So it is quite difficult. Anyway—I thought I [would] never use all that science again, but here it's coming in handy. Although I forgot most of it.

Last Saturday I had lunch with Fritz Langer. I used to write about him—the German student. He was rather disappointed because he was dismissed from his job of teaching at the government Naval College. Now he doesn't know what to do. They fired all foreigners from the military schools.

There was an article in the paper last night that they discovered where some ham and sausage company had been mixing dogs and cats in their meat. How awful! And their meat had been going to the first-class hotels (Imperial, Dai Ichi, etc.), and famous restaurants. So I probably have been eating cats and dogs. They'd been doing it for three years.

Gradually they are getting stricter and stricter. Now they are saying, "*Kokumin kairo*."[126] Even girls who are staying home after girls' school are taken to China or to armament factories. The only thing which can release them after they are taken is marriage. The happy-go-lucky days are gone. Even schools are shortening their terms. The four-year university is cut down to three. Those who were to graduate next April are graduating in December this year. In the lower school they are not encouraging the students to try to go to higher schools. Just imagine—this is happening to Japan. To Japan, the country which always respected learning. "There is a shortage of labor. Studying is a waste of time. Cut down the students," is the attitude now. Japan is in a state of change. For better or for worse? Who knows? In some respects—better—but in others worse. It is better to do away with outworn customs and superstitions. But in doing that, isn't Japan losing much of her charm? One striking example is the stores. There is no politeness here anymore. Even since I came I have noted a striking change. At first, when I went into a store, they bowed and asked if they could help me. When I bought something they bowed and politely thanked me and said to come again. Now it is different. When you enter, no one pays the least attention. They don't even thank you

124. Mary was still staying at the Itos.

125. Mary had enrolled at Joshi Dai earlier in the month.

126. Lit., "Citizens—all laborers," a wartime slogan meaning that everyone must work for the war effort.

if you buy something. It is now the customer who thanks the clerk for giving him the "honor" of buying his precious goods.

I must study. But here I'm just wasting time. Just think: I have to make up three months' work and keep up with the class besides. We have semester exams in two weeks. And I'm so sleepy. Always.

September 29. We had "*Kinro sagyo*" today. It means work. The idea is German, I heard. The kids of school clean their own campus. We get down on our knees and pull weeds. We had no classes in the afternoon. We pulled weeds instead. Then they don't have to hire anyone. All the schools do that. The students clean out their own classrooms, too.

Last night we had sukiyaki at Masako's place for Hiroko. She used to board with us until she got married. They are going to go to Siam (Bangkok) next month. It was lots of fun. Masa is so thoughtful and unselfish. Got home at eleven. Haven't come home this late for a long time. I'm saving money by staying home. And studying.

Wonder when you'll get this letter? If ever—

Wonder when I'll see you again? If ever—*No*—I will go back! Japan, after all, is not the place for me. Or is it?

Anyway—I do hope to hear from you.

The "Dear Kay" Letters

1941–1945

[In the original "Dear Kay" collection, written as a term paper in 1947, Mary covered the entire period of her stay in Japan to present a brief, unbroken narrative across the years 1939–46. In this section the prewar material has been dropped, asterisks have been added to datelines to identify "letters" written in 1947 that reconstruct Mary's impressions of the war years (see the Editor's Preface), and some of the postwar letters that provide a context for the series of authentic letters of 1945–46 have been assigned new (earlier) dates.]

*Aboard the SS *Tatsuta Maru*, December 2, 1941

Dear Kay,

Such hectic days I spent since an unexpected urgent cable from home telling me to take the next boat home! On top of that, they did not announce that a ship would be sailing until a week before it left. In that short time I had to go to the consulate and get my passport approved, which required papers from the Metropolitan police, the local police, and hundreds of other places. Besides that, I had to buy presents to take home, see people to tell them good-bye, and write innumerable letters. What a mess it was!

Now that I finally made the boat I can relax and get rested. There are over one hundred Nisei on board here. Most of them are Nisei girls like me who are returning. There are a few white American teachers and missionaries.

*Aboard the SS *Tatsuta Maru*, December 8, 1941

Dear Kay,

I am coming back to you. Our ship has turned back, and we are heading toward Japan. We have no idea why.

What could have happened? Our ship boy says that Japan has declared war on the United States, and he tells us fantastic tales of a victory at Pearl Harbor, Japan's advance into Southeast Asia, etc. They must be empty rumors!

We are taking a zigzag course to avoid submarines. We have drills, and we are prepared to use the dust-covered life preservers. We sleep with our shoes and clothes on, for we may be torpedoed any moment. It is unbelievable that any moment may be my last. When I lie down on my bunk I think I may never get up again, for a torpedo would sink us within a few minutes. I always imagined that I would be so afraid if I were ever in this plight, but so far, there is nothing frightful about it. If I die, I die, and that is all. I must have absorbed some of the Oriental fatalism.

But if I live I will have problems. What shall I do if I go back to Japan? I haven't a cent to my name now, having spent all I had to get on this boat. Maybe Yokohama will be all bombed when we return. I am worried.

*Tokyo, December 20, 1941

Dear Kay,

Now I am facing reality. Those fantastic tales that I refused to believe while on the ship have all turned out to be true. When we landed in Yokohama, the police questioned us. We had to give them the time we would leave Yokohama, our destination, and our future plans. They say that all the white Americans were interned. Since we look like Japanese, I guess they thought it would be safe to turn us loose.

Why are these Japanese so elated about this war? They think it is marvelous, and every time the radio announces the latest victory, they go wild. Maybe they will not be so happy after a few years! I am so frustrated because my plans have been upset, and now I don't know when I will be able to go home. And what will happen to all the Japanese in America? Will Iza's prediction come true?

I have decided to continue school. I didn't know what to do until I saw Mrs. Sakai,[1] where I had been staying before the war. She was very sympathetic and even shed tears of pity for me. She advised me to stay at her home and help with the housework. I could tutor English for spending money. I guess that is the best idea. I would like to finish college, now that I have started.

1. Mrs. Sakai was a doctor who ran a small clinic. She wanted Mary to serve as her housekeeper and tutor her young son in English. As Mary makes clear, she was also a fervent nationalist.

I sold everything I could—the kimonos, dried mushrooms, and tea that I had bought for presents to take home. So I am not absolutely penniless yet. But now there won't be any money coming from home as before.

*Tokyo, January 10, 1942

Dear Kay,

During the winter vacation I have been toiling for Mrs. Sakai day in and day out and am so weary of it all! I knew my position here would be different from when I was a paying boarder, but I never dreamed it would be this drastic a change. She used to leave me alone, but now she constantly picks on me. Not only is she exploiting my labor, but she is trying to make a Japanese woman out of me.

For example, last night I was washing my clothes when Mrs. Sakai raps on my window and scolds me for wasting electricity. But I have no time to do my own washing except at night. Then when I hung out my clothes on her new bamboo pole, she was enraged, saying that I should use her old bamboo (as befits my low status). She said that where she comes from they cannot hang women's clothes on the same bamboo that they use for men's clothing. So I inferred that I had contaminated her precious bamboo by daring to hang my clothes on it. God, she is so petty!

I have been thinking, Kay, that maybe the American way is better. It is great to have class distinctions as long as you are of the privileged class. However, if you had the bad luck to be born in the lower class, you would be stuck there forever. Moreover, you have to be humble and grateful for whatever the upper classes do for you.

*Tokyo, January 20, 1942

Dear Kay,

This past month has been the unhappiest in all my life. I hate Mrs. Sakai! She is the most cruel, stingy and mean woman I have ever had to live with. When I look back now, the golden carefree days before the war seem like a rosy dream. I cannot even organize my thoughts. All I know is that I must get out of her clutches. When you came here she wouldn't even let you talk to me. And you later told me that you didn't like her looks. What a slave I am! She rules me with an iron hand, and I have to bow meekly to her since I have no alternative. How can she be so malicious? She gloats to me over the success of the Japanese army and navy as though she won these victories herself. She despises me as an American who is her helpless victim. Is it my fault that I am stranded here?

What a predicament I am in! But I will get out of here. Just this morning

Mrs. Sakai bawled me out for walking on the ridge of a tatami. What difference does it make if I step on a narrow black strip? She scolds me, saying no decent Japanese woman would ever do that. Even if I step over a newspaper that is on the mats, she becomes as mad as a wet hen. So whenever I walk in her presence I must watch my every step so that I won't transgress. To hell with her!

I might be able to take her insults if it were not for the mental turmoil I am in. Iza-chan's prediction has come true, and my parents in Central California have been uprooted from the farm and the house where all of us were born and raised. We Japanese in the United States were so naive about the racism of Americans! I guess people in Japan were able to recognize this racism and predict what would happen to us in case of war.

Kay, I loved our old farm. I remember how when I irrigated the crops I used to let the clear water run over my toes. I knew every inch of it—the places where poppies bloomed every spring, where the first strawberries grew, and where the various crops and trees were planted. In summer we used to find the ripest watermelons and drop them right there to eat only the delicious seedless portions.

And if even I have an attachment to the place, how much more heartbreaking it must be for my parents. My father bought it over forty years ago, then gradually paid for it with back-breaking work. Now after many years of toil, my parents deserve some rest. They have saved enough so that their future is secure, and their children are all grown up. But all this has been confiscated, I will have no place to go back to. My trust in America, my country, has been shattered. Now I cannot believe in anything. Kay, you are so kind to offer to let me stay with you and your mother, but I cannot impose on you. I will find some way out, somehow.

*Tokyo, March 20, 1942

Dear Kay,

What a relief to get out of that horrid Mrs. Sakai's place! I have a room with three Nisei girls, and we are as happy as we can be, under these circumstances.[2] I tutor two students and I have found some steady translating work, so my financial problems are solved for the time being.

Since I am free again, I see Iza-chan sometimes on Sundays when he comes out to Tokyo. He is stationed at Yokohama and says he never knows when he will be called to the front.

2. Actually, after living with Dr. Sakai through the first winter of the war, Mary moved to the Joshi Dai dormitory. Except for a brief interlude when she roomed with some Nisei friends in Otsuka, she stayed there during most of the war years.

We saw a newsreel last night of the bombing of London. How can people live through such terrifying experiences? Do you think we might be raided too? According to the newspapers, we are sure to be bombed before the war is over. Our neighborhood group is practicing air raid drills. I had to go out for practice this morning. Everyone hates them. It seems so pointless. What could a couple of buckets of water do in the face of mass destruction that would fall from the sky?

Isn't it shortsighted of the government to ban American movies? German and French films tire me, since I can't understand what they are saying, and it is so hard to read the Japanese subtitles.

Why don't you come over this Sunday? We are planning to bake some cookies with our last sugar ration.

*Tokyo, April 19, 1942

Dear Kay,

Did you hear about Tokyo being raided yesterday?[3] I was at the Waseda International Institute doing some translating. Around noon, I heard shots outside and people shouting excitedly. When I rushed out, I saw several people pointing up to the sky. There were puffs of smoke from anti-aircraft guns following planes which were flying low. I thought it odd that the Japanese were firing on their own planes. Then the siren went off, and no one knew what to do, but a student shouted to get under some shelter. We soon detected smoke rising on both sides of us. Later, we learned that a hospital near Waseda University had been burned. We never found out what the fire on the opposite side was.

It was all over before we knew what was happening. The papers said the "cowardly enemy" had picked out schools and hospitals for bombing, even machine-gunning schoolchildren at play. Wonder where those planes came from? They have boosted the morale of the people, for now they are confident they can pull through any raids.

Iza-chan is now stationed in Taiwan. I hope and pray that nothing will happen to him. He says he does not want to die, but he will do his best for his country. The last time I met him, he seemed so grim and different. I wondered what had changed him so much.

3. Under U.S. Adm. William F. Halsey (1882–1959), the famous "Shangri-la" task force sailed to within 670 miles of Tokyo, from where 16 carrier-based bombers, led by Col. James H. Doolittle (1896–1993), raided Tokyo. Then, because the B-25's were too large to land on carrier decks, they flew on to China, although some crashed en route.

Nagata Shigeshi, principal of Rikko Kai, with his wife and five of their seven children, ca. 1941. Mary lived with the Nagatas for all but a brief period before the war. She was particularly close to Yoshiya, Izaya, and Miyoko (standing next to her from left to right).

Mary's maternal grandfather, Kanazawa Manjiro, ca. 1932. Standing behind him are his sister-in-law Yae and Yae's adopted daughter; his sister Ise is seated next to him. Mary was disturbed by the traditional funerary rites for her "cutie pie grandpappy," who died during the war.

Okada Tomi with her children and her Aunt Yae. "Tomi-san," a maternal cousin who lived in Toyama Prefecture, was one of the first relatives Mary looked up when she arrived in Japan.

Mary with her classmate Natsuko at Kokusai, 1940.

Izaya and Mary caught by a street photographer during a *Gin-bura* (stroll on the Ginza), 1940.

The first-year classroom at Waseda Kokusai Gakuin (Waseda International Institute), the school for foreign students Mary attended when she first came to Japan. Among the close friends she made there were Natsuko Kitagawa (seated next to Mary), from Hawaii, and Eugen Hanisch, a Czechoslovakian (left, second row).

Professor Shiojima Hifumi, 1940. Mary earned spending money by tutoring his relatives in English. One of them, Kiyoko (far right), became a particularly close friend.

Mary's paternal aunt Teramoto Kiwa with her grandson (far right) and Natsuko, 1940. Auntie Kiwa, despite her own impoverishment, took Mary into her home in Wakayama when the government advised women and children to evacuate Tokyo before the occupying troops arrived in 1945.

On their trip to Manchuria in 1941, Mary and Aunt Ito Yae stopped in Dalien to visit her aunt's sister and children. Aunt Yae is on the far right.

*Tokyo, June 6, 1943

Dear Kay,

I was so happy to hear from you! I cannot picture you being stranded way out in Wakayama.[4] I do hope your mother recovers quickly so you can return to school in Tokyo.

Did you hear about Toshi? The other day she was reading an English book on the way to school when an ultra-nationalist Japanese man slapped her face and berated her with "How dare you read an English book! Don't you know we are fighting a war and we are going to exterminate America and England?" She was stunned and didn't know what to do. The others in the car only stared at her blankly. These small-minded Japs! Reports are that in America they are studying Japanese as never before, and look at them here—taking English out of the schools and abusing those who read the "language of the enemy." Well, we are definitely in the minority now, and it is no use to resist. Now more than ever, to be different is the unforgivable sin in Japan.

At least you have enough to eat out in the provinces. Our rations are becoming pitifully meager and I am always hungry. All we think and dream about is food. Once in a while, a restaurant will be open, but only for *zosui*, a soup supposedly made of a rice base with everything from weeds to fish bones thrown in. When they have that, there are queues of people waiting for hours. Speaking of queues, Masa and I got up at three this morning to line up for some rare cakes. The bakery opened at eight, but just before our turn, it was our bad luck to have them run out. Never again!

*Sapporo, October 6, 1944

Dear Kay,

Here I am way up north in Hokkaido.

It was so kind of you to have come to see me so often while I was sick in the dormitory! You don't know how much I appreciated seeing you with the flowers that you brought—even if they were picked on the campus. And the food your mother used to spare for me was delicious.

Now that I am up here, I am not starving any more. These people are just wonderful to me. I still feel very tired and have no energy at all, but the peacefulness here is soothing. I didn't know that jaundice was such a depressing disease. I'm sure my resistance was depleted due to malnutrition.

I don't know what has happened to me. I have never been so weak and sickly in all my life as during the last few years. I guess I have lost any incentive

4. Kay had gone to visit her mother, who was with relatives in Wakayama. Later they both lived in Tokyo.

to live. The future looks so hopeless. War drags on interminably. Was there ever a world at peace? It seems that I have lived ages during the war, always the war. Food is scarce. My clothes are wearing out, and it is impossible to buy any. I have only one pair of shoes left. I am just sick and tired of everything. There is absolutely nothing to look forward to. I don't even care to write anymore.

I weigh only 115 pounds. I yearned to be slender for so many years—what irony that it took a war to accomplish my heart's desire! But if I should ever get back to America I will never complain about being fat again! It is much better to be fat and healthy than slender, starved and sickly.

It is such a relief to get away from Tokyo and preparations for raids! But they are digging air-raid shelters even here. And victory gardens are planted along the sidewalks and in vacant lots. But people here look more well-fed. They don't have that pinched, hungry, nervous look that they do in Tokyo.

*Sapporo, October 20, 1944

Dear Kay,

I shall never forget how kind this Ito family has been to me. They are the one family who has not changed their attitude towards me since the war.

Rev. Kaoru Ito was jailed soon after the war started, as were all ministers, mostly of the Holiness church, who refused to renounce their faith. Mrs. Ito has been telling me about it. The Kempei [military police] grilled her husband for hours. The crucial question was whether he believed the emperor is God. I certainly admire these Christian leaders for keeping their faith in the face of persecution. They also interrogated Mrs. Ito for hours, and so intensely that her health has deteriorated.

Ito-sensei is in a very cold prison here and has only one thin blanket. Of course he gets little food, too. I remember that when I heard that he was jailed, I was furious. Whenever he used to come to Tokyo he would look me up, invite me to church and often we had dinner together. I like his preaching because he is humorous and he has good common sense. He was not fanatical like most Holiness preachers.

Japan is making a grave mistake by jailing these people who dare to defy the government line. Mrs. Ito told me that many liberal professors and writers have been imprisoned too. Japan can never win the war by suppressing these independent thinkers.

I think I'll return to Tokyo in a few weeks. After all, I must get back to school and work.

*Tokyo, March 20, 1945

Dear Kay,

Did you have a nice New Year's out in Wakayama? I couldn't help but think of the happy New Year's celebrations I had spent in Japan before the war. It was so much fun to make the rounds of friends and relatives, bowing to them and saying the traditional New Year's greeting. My mouth waters when I remember all the delicious foods each family had prepared for guests. What a contrast to this year, when I had to spend it crouched in a dugout, with not a bite to eat.

It doesn't make any sense how we have to scurry to the cold, damp bomb shelters whenever there is a raid, which is almost every night.[5] I am so weary of it all! When I was visiting you, it was wonderful that we could blissfully sleep through all the raids. Only in the morning would we find out that B-29's had attacked as usual, and what part of Tokyo had been hit. I would rather get a good night's sleep and be bombed in bed than have to scamper around in the dark and wait in those cold, dank dugouts, hearing bombs exploding in the distance and dreading when they would come closer. Remember how we used to go out and watch the fireworks at first? The way the tiny Japanese planes tried to attack the huge B-29's was like a tiny dog fretting a bull—and they were about as successful. Nowadays we hardly ever see any Japanese planes, and the B-29's fly serenely on unmolested. The Japanese try to make the best of it by joking about their foreign "guests" who visit us every night.

Did you read in the paper of how American soldiers ran tanks over wounded Japanese soldiers in the Philippines? And that one GI had made a souvenir out of a Japanese soldier's bones and given it to Roosevelt? But they never mention the atrocities that Japanese soldiers commit on the people of conquered countries.

[Tokyo, March 25, 1945]

Dearest Kay,

O, Kay, my world is toppling over again! What I had refused to believe has actually happened. All my wishful thinking has come to nothing. Where to go—where to turn now? I am lost—bewildered.

My mother-in-law told me that he does not want me anymore.[6] That he

5. U.S. bombers made almost 4,000 flights over Tokyo between November 1944 and the end of May 1945. The most devastating raid came on the night of March 9–10, when incendiary bombs destroyed two-fifths of the city and killed between 70,000 and 80,000 people.

6. With no prospects of employment and not knowing how long the war would last, after her graduation from Joshi Dai in 1944, Mary had made an arranged marriage to the brother of a classmate. This brief interlude was not covered in her term paper; the late 1944–early 1945 letters imply that she was living with various families and at the dormitory when she was in fact

said that before he left. Yes, it's true, and I had been unwilling to look facts in the face. Blind faith helps not at all now.

Why did I marry in haste? Yet everyone advised it except one friend. If only I had listened to him! It's come out just as he prophesied.

Kay—can they do this to me? Is a woman's love to be trifled with like this? I have really received a deep and lasting shock.

I must write, and yet I can't. Until now I was running away from facing the hurtful truth. But it is so—and now, maybe I have it off my mind!

I love you, Kay, and know you'll never leave me. Thank you for being such a true and faithful friend.

Let this teach me a lesson. I am too naive and trusting.

Good-night, Kay. I hope to be seeing you very soon. If only I could weep and weep! But such girlhood luxuries are now no more my refuge.

*Tokyo, May 26, 1945

Dear Kay,

I was so happy to get your letter because I was worried about you. Thank God you are still alive and in one piece!

Isn't it uncanny that when you are actually in a raid it is not as bad as you imagined it would be? I guess the same raid that burnt down our dorm hit your section. We knew that we would be attacked soon, for the bombs had been coming closer every night. As usual, the siren screeched just before midnight. Three of us Nisei, with the dorm matron, scampered to the same dugout. We could hear the men running, shouting that the fire was two blocks away. In a few moments the flames enveloped us too. Our dorm was ablaze and trees around us were crackling. It reminded me of movies of fires. We were uncertain what to do, but we realized that if we remained in the dugout we would be roasted alive. So we ran out to save our lives.

It was light and warm from the fires. Lots of people were running and screaming. I soaked my bonnet in water and ran to the side of a building for shelter. Then that building caught on fire, and we fled to another. Finally, we found refuge along the side of a building under a temporary roof made of sheets of corrugated tin. We huddled together and looked at the fire while munching on the hard biscuits we had saved for this emergency. How ridiculous and inadequate were the bucket brigades in the face of such wide-scale destruction!

---

staying with her in-laws—without her husband, who had returned to his job in Shanghai in January 1945. The date of this letter (which is not from "Dear Kay") has been changed. It was actually written from Wakayama on Aug. 25, 1945.

It was around four in the morning when the fires finally subsided. We found refuge in the chapel. Some women passed around rice balls for breakfast. For once, I was not hungry, but I ate mechanically.

I will never forget the desolate scene when it became light. Our lovely campus and splendid buildings were now in ruins. The dorm was a pile of smoldering ashes. I guessed where my room must have been and absurdly thought I might be able to recover my iron, but there were only ashes and sheets of corrugated tin. Trees were jagged black stumps. A hand pump was working, so I washed my hands and face. I saw a feeble old woman being helped out of a dugout. We were lucky that we were on such a spacious campus. In the adjacent sections with small wooden houses, many must have perished.

For miles around, there were only ruins and smoke and stench, the characteristic sickening stench that always follows a raid. The sun rose an angry, bloody red. I felt that nature must be horror-struck with the madness of man destroying his fellow man. No streetcars or buses were running, so I walked to the Nagatas'. Blackened corpses were among the ruins. The bigger buildings were still smoldering.

As I neared the Nagata home, it was a relief to find the homes still standing, the trees and hedges alive and green. I was so exhausted by the time I reached the Nagatas' that I could hardly move. I have been in bed for over a week now. I can still smell smoke in my breath and in my dreams I relive the terror of that raid.

I feel now that I don't care whether I live or die. At times I think death would be a welcome rest. It is only if we live that we must continue to struggle in this insane world.

*Yonezawa, June 6, 1945

Dear Kay,

I should have come north to my mother's hometown long ago to escape the nightmare of the constant bombings. How can you stand it in Tokyo?

However, they say that no city is safe in all of Japan. The smaller cities are now being bombed, and even a remote town like Yonezawa is digging air-raid shelters. The people are feverishly sending out their belongings to the country. Fools, I think, if Japan is so lost that even this remote village will be bombed, what difference would a few possessions make? But I guess people must have something close at hand to occupy their minds. If I have to die, I would prefer to die in Tokyo, where I am not attacked by fleas day and night. . . .

Even though Tokyo is half devastated, I still yearn to go back. I cannot be content to live out in the sticks with these ignorant people. At least Tokyo is a little closer to civilization—besides, you are there.

*Wakayama, August 16, 1945

Dear Kay,

Can you believe it is all over? Where were you when the emperor announced the end of the war? So we have managed to survive the bombs, the hunger, and all the other deprivations, but now what?

I heard the emperor's announcement at Rikko Kai, along with all the students assembled to hear it on the radio. People were stunned and didn't know how to respond. Later, Mr. Nagata said he knew that Japan could never win against the United States.

Yo-chan (Iza-chan's younger brother) died as a *kamikaze* pilot. He used to be so happy and carefree! I will never forget how he helped me in math all summer in preparation for the Joshi Dai entrance exams. I also recalled how one day he was very depressed because two of his friends had died during their training to become pilots. He said 20% of those who trained died during that time. And now it was his turn—but how sad, and just before the surrender.

They advised all women to leave Tokyo before the occupation troops landed. Mrs. Nagata is the only person I have talked to who seems unafraid of the occupation. She said that American men are gentlemen, and they will not loot and rape. Iza-chan had miraculously lived through the war. He showed me the small packet of poison that the navy had distributed to the officers. In case he should have been captured and tortured, the poison would have finished him off in two seconds.

What do you think of the bombing of Hiroshima? Rumors are that it was an atom bomb. Remember that our teacher said a professor at Tokyo Imperial University was doing atomic research until he was blown up by his own experiment? They said that one bomb could annihilate a whole island the size of Hawaii. I wonder if that really was an atom bomb? The papers say the destruction of Hiroshima was no worse than that suffered by other cities. I wish we knew what really happened.

*Wakayama, September 25, 1945

Dear Kay,

The letters from you that your mother brought this morning were like tidings from another world. Even your mother was surprised at the "pig sty" (as she called it) that I am living in, out here with my father's poor relatives. And I am sure getting tired of existing on watery *okayu* [rice broth] every day.

I wonder if my family is still living. Now that the war has finally ended, I feel sort of let down. It was rather romantic and exciting thinking that a bomb might put an end to all our troubles. And think of all the excitement of an actual invasion! Mrs. Nagata showed me her butcher knife and said she would use it on any invader. Japan was supposed to die *en masse* with the emperor, defending the sacred land with bamboo spears. But now we face the task of living.

You used to say that defeat would be good for Japan, that it would teach her a much-needed lesson. Now we'll see if Japan can rise from the ashes.

When did I see you last? I guess it was when I saw you off for Wakayama.[7] I took a train the next night. I found a little nook in between the cars and had to stand all the way, crowded in by people on all sides. It was a horrible eight-hour ride. People were afraid of what would happen when the United States occupation forces landed.

There must have been a million soldiers at the stations, so many little brown men with packs as big as themselves. They looked like khaki bugs crawling all over. There were several open freight cars set aside for them. As I saw the thousands of people running here and there, they reminded me of ants scurrying about in disorder after their nest had been invaded.

Did you know that the occupation troops will be coming to Wakayama soon? I haven't seen a white American for so long! I cannot believe what Toshi said, that the Americans will sterilize all the Japanese men, just as they did the Nisei men in the relocation camps. We are warned to keep out of sight or we will be raped. So many rumors are flying that I can't discriminate between the truth and propaganda anymore.

Kay, I'm really looking forward to seeing you in front of the Wakayama castle ground this Saturday, around 10. We have so much to talk about!

*Osaka, October 15, 1945[8]

Dear Kay,

[I was remembering] how we met Gene in Wakayama. It was a rainy day and we had gone for a walk. An army truck stopped and a freckle-faced boy asked with a Southern drawl, "You're a-gonna get wet out there. Wanna ride?"

7. Kay's parents were from Wakayama. She joined her mother there soon after the surrender.

8. When the I Corps of the U.S. Eighth Army moved its headquarters from Tokyo to Osaka, Mary and Kay went there to find work and took jobs with the American Red Cross (ARC). They roomed together in a Japanese house near the museum that had been taken over by the I Corps until Kay returned to Tokyo to resume her studies at Joshi Dai.

When we answered, "Sure, thank you," his blue eyes popped open wide and he whistled, "How did you learn that American? I ain't heard no gal talk like that since I left the States."

Then followed such carefree days in which we recaptured the joy of living. Remember the long ride he gave us in his "buggy," as he called his weapons carrier? He yodeled and sang and chanted his lines as barker in his carnival, "Only ten cents! A dime, this way to see the fat lady! Come one, come all—only two nickels, ten cents!" We laughed until tears rolled down our cheeks. He took us to your home and "carried" us all over the countryside. Remember how he would go to the gas station and ask, "How about some gas, buddy?" and if the GI was chicken and asked him for his trip ticket, he would shrug and say he couldn't find it. "I asked him first, so it's fair and square. I give him warning. Now if he don't give me no gas, I'll git it my way." Then in the evening, he would go out to the tanks and fill his truck with gas.

I see Gene [here in Osaka] off and on but he is not the same. He is sad and his eyes have lost their sparkle. He never sings or yodels while he is driving. I wonder why. Maybe the army is getting him down with their rules and regulations. Maybe it is the misery of life in this devastated city. Whatever the cause, the carefree and happy Gene, the GI from North Carolina, must be sick and tired of the army.

*Osaka, October 28, 1945

Dear Kay,

I have been thinking how different the occupation has turned out from what the Japanese had been dreading. Remember when we first went to Wakayama Bay to see the American sailors that everyone was talking about? There were the black ships—just as years ago when Perry opened Japan's doors from feudalism. The big, healthy and well-fed American sailors were all over the place. And the Japanese were mingling among them, bowing obsequiously and trying to speak English. Middle school students were hesitatingly experimenting with the English they had learned at school. People brought their fans, dolls and souvenirs to trade for candy bars. We started talking to some sailors who were the center of attraction of a small group of Japanese. One was a Southerner with lazy, easy ways. His buddy kept telling him to sing and he drawled, "Ah cain't sing no song."

And then you discovered Dr. Simms, the army dentist who was so eager to learn about Japan. I will never forget how delicious those first C rations[9]

9. Standard canned meals issued by the U.S. Army during the war. K rations, which Mary refers to in a later letter, were boxed emergency rations.

were that he brought to a picnic on the Wakayama castle grounds. He told us so many things and we were amazed at what had been going on in the outside world while we had been isolated in Japan. When we told him of our bitter experiences and how we hated the Japs, he told us that people are the same the world over.

Now I see so many GIs every day at this Red Cross canteen that I am rather tired of them. Most of those who come to the canteen are ignorant and shallow.

When I go home at night I often see cold and hungry Japanese looking wistfully into the brightly lit canteens, and in the shadows are painted girls waiting to lure the GIs.[10]

10. Beginning in late October, Mary was able to write her family again. In January 1946, she was thrilled to receive Miye's address from Blanche, and their correspondence promptly resumed, as presented in the next section. She also kept up a lively correspondence with Kay. Those letters and others are included as well.

The Postwar Letters
1945–1946

Osaka, December 24, 1945

Dearest Kay,

I miss you an awful lot, Kay. I have been very unhappy and lonely. I've missed you much more than I'd imagined. A part of me—and a very vital part—has been torn away from me. Perhaps the wound can heal, but it is very raw now.

Been phoning up Smitty[1] every day to get sympathy. When I told him that I felt lonely and blue, he retorted, "How do you think I feel?" He's always managed to cheer me up, bless his heart! Said he went to a sukiyaki party the night before last.

I haven't stayed at the dormitory yet.[2] Yesterday I went up there, only to find that they had stripped my cot of all its blankets. So I bustled around and found some, cleaned up part of the dirty mess around there, and got into bed. How I hated the yap, yap, yapping of those cats around me! They finally all left about noon. I took a nap. Then I got up and left and haven't been back yet.

Did you reach Tokyo in one piece? I heard from Ray that you got on the train all right. Please forgive me for not seeing you off. I felt awful that day. And the next day I felt like dying with a headache and stomach ache and cold. So I didn't go to work until Saturday.

I hear the I Corps is moving to Kyoto 15 January. (How do you like my

1. A GI friend of Kay's.

2. Mary's new employer, the I Corps, ran a dormitory for foreign nationals on its staff. She was housed there because, until such time as she could establish her citizenship, she remained a foreign national in the authorities' eyes.

army way of dating?) It's going to be a lot of bother moving, but Kyoto is much better for us, I know.

O, Kay, it made me so mad, or peeved, or something! You know what—that old *obaasan* of the Suemasas'[3] said for me to tell you that you could not return there anymore! Just when I'd been looking forward to having you visit me! She didn't like it because you took your *seki*[4] out of there. How narrow-minded she is! Well, anyway, I probably will be gone to Kyoto, so perhaps it doesn't make such an awful lot of difference.

Your mother hasn't come yet that I know of. . . .

So far my job has been very easy—too easy to be true. Best of all, the sergeant in charge said that I could use the office here at night or anytime to be warm and comfortable. Now I have a retreat. It is a quarter to two p.m., and he has not returned from chow yet.

I wrote to my brother-in-law[5] about you. I would appreciate it if you would look him up. He is in the Yusen building, the translation section. Name: Lt. Fred Suzukawa. I told him that you are my best friend and confidant in Japan.

It was certainly funny, Kay! Old Mancil Gray[6]—I found another letter of his to his dear wife. He gave her a snow job about GIs not going around with Jap[7] girls. That only about one or two out of a thousand went out with a Jap girl. The reason he gave was that if the Japs see a girl out with a GI they would mob her and beat her to death! I want to go up and pick on him and snow him under,[8] but never have the time since he is only up there when I am supposed to be working.

Kay, I am beginning to think that Gene gave me a snow job too. Fool that I was to believe him so simply and trustingly! I wonder if I will ever find out the pure and unadulterated truth about him and what he feels and felt towards me?

Merry Christmas, Kay! I do want to go to church but haven't anyone to go with. Smitty said that he wrote two letters to you but tore them up. I told him that you said you belonged to Smitty.

It is very cold and dark and dreary today. Thank goodness, I am in a heated office. The sergeant has not returned yet. At least, I'll get some typing practice.

3. The grandmother and head of the Suemasa family from whom Mary and Kay rented a room when they worked for the Red Cross.

4. Short for *koseki*, household registration. Rice rations were based on these registrations.

5. Actually, George's brother-in-law, the brother of his wife, Betty (née Suzukawa). He was a lieutenant in the U.S. Army and then stationed in Tokyo.

6. One of the two GIs Mary and Kay had met in Wakayama.

7. Mary and Kay used this pejorative in their exchanges as a way to communicate their animosity toward the native Japanese, and to distinguish themselves as Japanese Americans.

8. Army slang for giving someone a rough time (in this context).

Give my regards to Massy.[9] How is everyone up in Tokyo? I hope that you are getting enough to eat. Strange as it may seem, my appetite is not normal now. It's a relief, too, because I hate to be a glutton all the time.

Now that I have a warm place to go tonight (this office), I don't feel so forlorn and lost anymore. I must have some kind of anti-dorm-phobia. Just the thought of going there makes me cold all over.

The two captains[10] have just left. I wonder if my job is going to be this easy always? I'm going to get some reading and studying done from now on.

Goodbye, Kay, and be good. Don't worry about me. I've learned my lesson.

Osaka, December 27, 1945

Dear Emma,

I am enclosing a letter from your mother-in-law.[11] Hilo will probably be glad to see it. If he wants to write to her, I will gladly send it to her if he sends the letter to me. As soon as I heard from you, I wrote and told her the good news about you being well.

You may have noticed that I am using a different return address.[12] I lost my job at the ARC canteen. The ARC girl in charge did not like me. I was quite at a loss when I became suddenly jobless. But, thank goodness, I soon found another one as clerk in the signal office of the I Corps. The chief clerk will be here in Japan for some time yet and he kindly consented to let me use his return address. The I Corps is moving to Kyoto in the middle of January, while the Red Cross will stay in Osaka. Otherwise, you could use my Red Cross address. I like this job all right. I don't enjoy it as much as my other one since I don't contact people, but it is easy work, the hours are not long, and I think I'll get more salary than my other job. I got $80 at the ARC, and I'll get about $125 here, I think.[13]

9. Kay's Nisei girlfriend and roommate in Tokyo. Also called Mass, Marie.

10. In the Signal Corps office where Mary worked as a typist.

11. Hilo's mother was a Japanese national living in Kumamoto city in Kyushu. He was the only member of his family who had emigrated to the United States.

12. A word about the mail situation during Mary's last year in Japan. Overseas delivery, iffy at best, was complicated by the army's on-and-off policy on APO mail (the only available service before the international system was resumed in September 1946). Until late June or early July, Mary was able to send and receive letters fairly regularly, even when she began writing under her own name rather than using an official return address. Then orders came down banning foreign nationals from using the APO. Both Mary and Miye continued to write to each other even so, and at least some of Miye's letters apparently did get through. But Mary had to hold onto her own almost daily letters to Miye until the policy was relaxed in late August. Mary and Kay faced a different problem: their letters, like all domestic mail during the occupation, had to go through the military censors and were often considerably delayed.

13. Mary is translating her monthly salaries into dollars here. She was paid in yen.

My friend, Kay Oka, left for Tokyo about a week ago and I miss her very much. She is continuing her school there. That leaves me without any real girlfriends here, but I am quite happy. Living in Japan has taught me to adjust myself to almost any conditions.

At present, I am in the office during noon hour. It is raining, so I did not want to walk to the dormitory for lunch. We have an ARC canteen upstairs where we can get donuts and coffee. Besides, the dormitory is not heated, so I'd rather stay here. I haven't stayed there for a long time. It is so noisy there that I cannot stand it. About twenty Nisei girls stay in one big room. They are rather a wild group, and Kay and I did not get along with them. I'd much rather stay with the family I'd been staying with before the dorm opened.

Do you know anything about me being able to go back to the U.S.? I've asked around here, but there doesn't seem to be anything definite about it as yet, since they don't have [a] consulate here. I wrote to the Stanislaus County Courthouse and had them send my birth certificate. The recorder, Mr. Waring, was very kind because he enclosed a letter that George had written him from camp in Amache and also his answer to it. From George's letter I gathered that Japanese in America had a "rough time" of it.

I do so want to get back! That is my only ambition and hope now. Perhaps I can get back in a year or so, but then, I've been told that there is a chance we might not get there for the next ten years! That sounds like a death sentence.

The Japanese are surprised that the GIs are so courteous, kind, and gentlemanly. There is very little antagonism between the GIs and the common people. Japan has much to learn from the Americans. I still can't get accustomed to being treated like a human being after being knocked around by the Japanese. And I think it is admirable how Americans keep their promises. You know that the Japanese cannot be trusted to keep their word. However, I feel sorry for the Japanese now. They have never been taught to think for themselves. In school, it is all memorizing. We copied down notes and memorized them, then gave the same thing back to the professors in tests. Everything is so deeply rooted in tradition and custom here that one is afraid to be independent or original. I was getting that way, too. I was afraid to do anything because of what people would say. Can you imagine me being like that?

It is so pitiful to see the cold and hungry Japanese looking into the brightly lit and warm canteens! I wish I could do something for them, and yet, on the other hand, I just [think] they are getting what they brought upon themselves. And as I said before, there are only very few really sincere Japanese. Perhaps I am prejudiced, yet nothing can ever erase the bitterness I feel towards them for all I had to suffer here when I was down and out.

Why am I pouring out my woes to you? I should just forget it. Besides, I should not write all this because it will make you and Mother and Father feel bad. I am just writing the truth—perhaps if I get it off my chest I can forget it quicker.

Does Hilo have any chance of coming over here? His mother would be so happy to see him! She is a wonderful woman. Did I tell you that I spent about a week at her home? She certainly treated me royally, and I enjoyed myself thoroughly.

It always surprises the GIs when they discover that I can speak English. Sometimes I have fun pretending that I can only speak a little. [The] poor GI has the hardest [time] with gestures and the little Japanese that he knows! Words like *wakarimasen* or *anatawa kirei desu* or *arigato*.[14] It is funny how they have the idea that adding an "o" to the end of an English word makes it into Japanese. That comes from the Japanese saying, "cigarett*o*" and "chocolat*o*," "present*o*," etc. It goes to extremes when the GIs say it, for they say "why-o," "me-o," "name-o."

It really embarrasses them when they swear or make derogatory remarks about me and then find out that I can understand every word they are saying. Since no one can understand them, anyway, they become careless and say anything they think. On the subways there surely is a lot of awful swearing and "GI language" being spoken.

I am looking forward to going to Kyoto because that city was not bombed at all. Here, in Osaka, there is no place to go, since everything has been burned. Kyoto is beautiful with all its shrines, temples, and historical spots.

The pictures I had taken are going to be done this afternoon. I'll send them as soon as possible. The dress I'm wearing is the one Blanche sent to me. I'm certainly thankful for it. We civilian employees are going to get uniforms soon; then our clothing problems will be solved.

There are so many things I want, but when it comes down to writing to you, I forget. I'll just list the things I remember:

elastic
snaps
curlers (for my hair)
nail file

I really hate to bother you so much. At present, it is impossible to get the little necessities of life. We cannot be sure of sending inter-island now, or I would send your mother-in-law some things. They are usually stolen if we use the Japanese system. Kumamoto is an agricultural district, so I don't think she is suffering from lack of food. We get all three meals at the dormitory.

It is past one now. Guess I'd better do my work, for a change. Please write. I should write to Mother—next time I will.

14. "I don't understand," "you are pretty," "thank you."

Osaka, January 7, 1946

Dearest Miye,

It seems like a dream that I can correspond with you again! Blanche wrote to me and gave me your address. How happy I am that you are well! It's a wonder that I survived it all—at times I thought that I had seen my last. Please write to me quickly and voluminously.

It seems that I have so much to tell you that I don't know where to start. First of all—let me tell you that I love you with all my heart. No one has ever been able to take your place. During the darkest hours I used to take out your old precious letters that I treasured more than gold and read them and be comforted. "Dear old Miye—I wonder if I will ever see her again!" I would sigh. Now it looks like my dreams will come true. At least, I can write to you.

What are you doing way over in Washington, D.C.? Blanche told me that she went to see you and that you took her all over Wash and almost walked her legs off. It's just like you! O, Miye, I do so want to see you! Next to my family, I was most concerned about you.

Do you know what happened to the Modesto friends? I especially want to know where Thelma Christiansen is. She was one good, sincere friend. What happened to Alice Kerr, Jessie Moore, John Knorr—I can't remember any other names. And the Wickings. I loved Mrs. Wicking.

But I know where you and the rest of my family are, so all my worries are over. It's the awfullest to have that anxiety hanging over you always.

Before I forget—please send me a picture of you. I want to see how you look now. I'll send you one of mine as soon as I get around to it. I am fat again, thanks to the Occupational [*sic*] troops. You ought to have seen me during the war—believe it or not, I was actually skinny. You wouldn't have known me during the war. I was skinny, nervous, and a worry-wart. Imagine—a "nonki" person like me! Now, the people who knew me during the war years can't believe that I am the same person. I laugh now. I am getting to consider reducing again, too.

Right now I am working as typist at the Signal Office at the I Corps, Osaka. You know that I can't type, and I flunked the typing test that they gave me at the Military Government Labor Board, but it just goes to show how hard up they are for typists. I don't do much work at all. I am in the office with two Captains, three Sergeants (two clerks and one draftman) and a Pfc. It is working hours now, but since I have nothing to do, I'm making use of my time.

I often stay after working hours because it is heated in here. The only places that are heated now are the American Government buildings. And if I go back to my room, it is so cold. Kay Oka, my girlfriend, used to stay with me, but she is in Tokyo now, so there is no inducement for me to go home. I am rooming upstairs with a Japanese family.

Before this job, I was working in the ARC canteen as interpreter and information girl. It was fun. However, the ARC woman in charge did not like me and she fired me. It certainly hurt me—Kay was sore about it, too. She's no good, that ARC woman, and I'll get my revenge on her yet.

Now I like this job better, though. I am in a better atmosphere. You probably know how GIs are—fresh, happy-go-lucky. They used to act awfully fresh to me at times. I'm glad that I worked there at first, because I got acquainted with the GIs who work there. Now I can get food from them and I can bum rides from the drivers. Transportation is a major problem here. Commuters stand for hours waiting for the streetcar. And army vehicles won't give civilians rides unless they are authorized to do it. The ARC vehicles are. So I get around.

Perhaps you might be interested in what I was doing during the war. I was attending school—Tokyo Joshi Dai (Tokyo Women's College). I was majoring in English literature. However, I had to work my way through school, so I did not get much studying done. And the last year, we had to work in munitions factories.

That's all I did. If you want to know anything, just ask. I won't bother to tell you anything.

Did Blanche tell you—I got married as soon as I graduated. I don't know whether I ought to tell people. But you know that I never keep anything from you. It was hell. Living with the in-laws made a physical and nervous wreck out of me. I think that I was married in October. It was the Japanese way—had a *miai* [arranged introduction], then only saw him once again before I married him. It was fun on the honeymoon. I really had a wonderful time. But as soon as I got back to the family, all the love was gone. He wouldn't even speak to me after that. I was like a maid to the family. There were four girls and two boys in the family. The youngest was 18 years old. My husband went to Shanghai in January—alone, leaving me to suffer with the in-laws.

Well, it's all over with, thank goodness! I haven't heard from him since he left. I never was married to him legally. Kay insists that I was never married. She hates my in-laws thoroughly—especially that mother-in-law.

Everyone has left the office now. It feels good to be alone with my thoughts of you.

I thought that you or Elma might be married by now. Miye, I wonder if I will be able to get back to the States? It's like living hell to have to stay here. My one hope is to go back.

Since the I Corps is moving to Kyoto this month, I will be out of a job. I could go with them. I am thinking of going to Tokyo since my brother-in-law [*sic*], Fred Suzukawa, is there. He will take care of me. I hear that he is a pretty good interpreter. He is a second lieutenant.

I kind of hate to leave Osaka since I have a room to myself, I know the canteen fellows, and I have the right Japanese bribed. They don't do things for money—but for food or cigarettes, I can get my hair set, my clothes cleaned and pressed, and can even get sewing done—only I don't have any goods to be sewed.

I was working in the ARC commissary at first making donuts (supervising and interpreting) for Pamela Moore, an ARC woman. She liked me and we got along fine. Pamela kindly gave me some white material and I hand-sewed two slips and had two blouses made. Those were the first new clothes I'd had for a long time. Hannah Downs is the female who fired me. When I told Pamela, she said that she calls it "Chemical Affinity"—you just don't mix some people together, just [like] you don't mix some liquids together.

It seems so funny to go out with Americans.[15] Now I'm just getting the nice boys separated from the wolves. The latter are in the majority. Some of the boys remind me of the JC kids—they are most of them young, much younger than I.

Sometimes I think, when I get desperate, I'll marry a GI and go back. If that's the only way, I'll do it. We have a chance here since they are all so lonesome, and English-speaking girls are scarce. But God grant that I don't have to go to that extreme!

Well, Miye, I guess I'll sign off for the present. Please write! Give my love to Ada.[16] I still think of her as a little "squirt."

Osaka, January 7, 1946

Dear Blanche,

It certainly was good to hear from you! I can't imagine you as other than a little "shrimp." If Mother and Father couldn't even recognize you, how could I?

The same day I received your letter, I received one from Mother. Dear old Mother! Her letter brought tears to my eyes. What touched me most was her asking to be forgiven for letting me stay in Japan! I never even thought of it being her fault. It was just fate. And if I ever get back to the States, I'll be able to appreciate all its blessings.

Don't you have a picture that you can send me? I'll send you mine as soon as I can. Now that I have your address, I feel much better. Now I have everyone's address.

I just found out today that I won't have this job after this month. The

15. As Mary notes in the Author's Preface, at this stage of her life, she was so confused about her identity that "I even called only white Americans 'Americans,' as if we people of color born in the United States were not Americans as well."

16. Miye's younger sister, who lived with her in Washington, D.C.

I Corps is moving to Kyoto and when we get there, there will be four men coming into this office. I could get a job in some other office there if I wanted. But I want to go to Tokyo [near] Fred. My friends are all in Tokyo, anyway. Have you ever met Fred? My friend, Kay Oka, met him when she went to Tokyo and she liked him. She said that he looked like a grown-up baby. But that she felt very uneasy with him because of his air of indifference. He gave her lots of food—fruit cakes, chocolate, candies, and other things—to bring to me. We surely had a feast with these things.

The Japanese are having a hard time with the food situation, but since I work for the army, I get along fine. We civilian employees stay at a dormitory, where we get all three meals. It's all canned goods, but much better than we could get anywhere else. All the girls—about 20 of them—stay in one great big room. We each have cots. I don't like it because there isn't any privacy, so [I] stay with a family that Kay and I stayed with before. I hardly go to the dorm even for food—just live on what I can beg, borrow, or steal. The GIs are very nice to us, especially when they find out that we can speak English. And I used to work at the ARC canteen and commissary, so know the GIs there. We have a canteen in the I Corps Hq where we can get donuts and coffee anytime. As before, I still love to eat. And I'm getting fat again, too. During the war with the starvation diet, I was skinnier than even you were. But I'd much rather be fat, happy, and healthy.

Please tell me all about your school and your future plans. I'm proud of you that you won a scholarship. Keep up the good work. Are you staying in a dormitory?

Did George sell our old place? I used to dream of that old house and farm. I'd go over every foot of the place in [my] imagination. And as you said—the sunsets were really wonderful there.

I wanted to write to you yesterday. I've reread your letter so many times that I practically have it memorized now. Since yesterday was Sunday, I did not have to work. I slept until after 10, got up and was surprised to find the sunlight flooding into the other room. I am staying upstairs all by myself now. So I got up, cleaned my rooms, got some charcoal and boiled a little water [to do] a little washing. I had got up so late that the people downstairs had thrown away the bathwater. I always do the washing with that. The water is freezing cold now. And charcoal is so scarce that I dare not use any more than absolutely necessary.

The Japanese are surprised that the Americans are as nice as they are. I guess that they expected them to treat the people like the Japanese mistreated the people they conquered. When I was up in Tokyo, they told all the girls to get away from there to escape the clutches of the American soldiers. So I went to Wakayama. It's a good thing that their prophesies were far from true!

What I hated the most about those air raids of Tokyo was getting up out of a warm bed in the middle of the night. You know how hard it is to get me up when I don't want to. When I stayed with Kay for a month, neither of us would get up. Sometimes we would not know a thing about any raid. It's a lucky thing that we weren't burned in our beds. It must be true that Mother's prayers were following me.

Did I tell you about the raid that I was in? I was staying at the Aoyama dormitory at the time. The bombs had been coming closer and closer, so we figured that the next raid we would be doomed. The sirens screeched about 11 at night—after I'd got good and warm in bed. I had to rush about and carry the knapsack which I had ready by my bed every night. I wrapped up my quilts and threw them in the dugout, along with my umbrella and galoshes. With 3 other girls and the old dorm matron, we took shelter in a dugout. The fire bombs got closer and closer. First thing we knew, they were falling fast and thick on the campus. The men were shouting and trying to put out the fires. The fires spread. The entrance to our dugout was brightly lit with the surrounding fires. The dorm caught on fire. Then the trees began crackling. We were surrounded. But if we stayed in the dugout, the wood would soon catch on fire. Better to die running than be burned sitting still, we decided. After that, it was a series of flying from building to building. We would find refuge, only to have that building catch on fire. Finally, we found a comparatively safe spot on the side of a building. A shelter of pieces of tin was made for us quickly.

Luckily, they did not use any demolition bombs that night. The fire gradually subsided about 3 in the morning. We went into the chapel and slept on benches. The next morning they brought us *nigiri*—2 apiece. They said many died that night. We were lucky to be on the campus, for if we had been in the congested areas, we never would have come out alive.

As soon as it was light, I went to the dugout to find my quilts—they had all been stolen!

I was sick for about a week after that. All the smoke I had inhaled had upset my stomach. Believe it or not, I was the weakest nervous thing during the war. Malnutrition and worry had taken their toll. Now I am healthy and happy again, though.

The other night when I saw Kay off for Tokyo, I came back home at 11 o'clock. I was surprised to find all the poor homeless children and people sleeping in the subway. It really is a pitiful sight. Most of the homes of Osaka had been burned, so that many are homeless. I feel sorry for them, and yet, I'm so bitter towards the Japanese people that I don't care. Perhaps I should not feel that way about it. But Japanese are petty, small, and mean. It is only when they can get something out of you that they are kind to you. Many GIs think that Japanese are polite and kind. I thought so too—at first. What a bitter disappointment it was when I found out that their politeness is only on the surface.

Well, maybe I'd better quit griping. That's one habit we picked up from the GIs—besides much slang. Take care of yourself.

Osaka, January 14, 1946

Dearest Kay,

Why don't I hear from you? I hope that you haven't caught a cold again.

Do you know that I haven't received one letter from you since you left—not even the letters that you said you sent? I wonder what happened. If it's that you are busy with your work and play, it's all right, but I can't help but wonder if something else is keeping you. Did you make the trip up to Tokyo, anyway? I should have stayed with you until you got on the train, then it would have [saved] me the anxiety.

Kay, I still don't know what to do. Maybe it would be better for me to go to Kyoto. The place hasn't been burned down, so there would be places to go. My life here is rather going into a rut. I want something new again.

Yesterday I had quite a pleasant day. I went to church, for a change, and enjoyed it. I went to the I Corps chapel near the museum. The chapel was cozy. It felt good to hear church music again. I went with a Warren Ling, the fellow I met when I went to the show with Clark and his girlfriend. He is really a nice boy. His father is a minister and he has been brought up well. Though his name sounds like Chinese, he is a Swede from Wisconsin.

After church, we walked to the big canteen at Matsuzakaya.[17] Hannah [first] had Scotty, then Johnny try to kick me out. I showed my pass to them. I hope I get in Hannah's hair! They have fruits out on the tables, so I had oranges and a delicious apple. Warren is a lot of fun. Then we went to Donna's canteen, but she succeeded in kicking me out.[18] I'm through with those canteens. That is one reason why I want to go to Kyoto. Then we went to Warren's company. He got me a coke and sandwich and we went home. It certainly surprised me when he ate the *mochi*[19] that your mother had given me. And he actually liked it!

If all GIs were like him, they would leave a good impression on Japan. He said he hated to go in front of the line in the streetcar because the people had been waiting so long. And he has a very [good] attitude. People certainly stare at me when I walk around with him. He said that it is not strange for

17. A large department store that had been taken over for use as a PX.

18. The ARC canteen was off limits to Japanese nationals. From Mary's looks, the administration (and most U.S. personnel, for that matter) simply assumed she was a citizen of Japan.

19. A rice cake made of pounded glutinous rice.

them to do that because if an American girl went with a Jap soldier, everyone would think she was crazy. I hadn't realized before how people stare. Of course, I hadn't walked around with any GI much before, anyway, especially in daytime.

I didn't think I'd write over a page, but here I am.

Kay, I do miss you a lot. I have no girlfriends at all. And no satisfactory boyfriend. Sometimes I feel like packing up and leaving for Tokyo.

And yet, in a way, I do enjoy it here. I am free from obligations. I have lots of time. It is really luxurious, all the time I have. I can read to my heart's content. And I can keep up on my correspondence. (That reminds me—I think I'll write to Kimi-chan.)[20] It is wonderful not to have to do anything I don't want to. Here I don't have to go visit anyone I don't feel like.

I'm not going back to Tennoji[21] tonight. I do not have anything to give them. I think I'll read an Ellery Queen mystery tonight.[22]

Today I was reading poetry, and I came across the following, which reminded me of Ed:

"ON HIS SEVENTY-FIFTH BIRTHDAY"

I strove with none; for none was worth my strife.
Nature I loved, and next to Nature, Art;
I warmed both hands before the fire of life;
It sinks, and I am ready to depart.

Walter Savage Landor

I read poetry nearly all morning. Remember in Wakayama when we used to read poetry to each other? We were so innocent about GIs then, weren't we?

The colonel advised me to go to Kyoto. The captain told me that if I wanted a job with the 25th Division Signal Office, he would recommend me to the officer. The twenty-fifth is going to move in here.

Yesterday when I was leaving, Scotty called "Hello, Mary" from his truck. I looked in, and there he was with a Jap girl who was crying. Scotty looked solemn and sad, and said that she had troubles. But then it struck me that I didn't have to worry about "Shanghai,"[23] entangling her man. I'd hate to see Scotty caught by her!

20. A Nisei classmate at Joshi Dai. Her parents and brother had come to Japan from the States before the war. Their home in Tokyo was a refuge for Kimi's Nisei girlfriends.

21. The district of Osaka where Mary and Kay had rented a room. On her occasional visits there, Mary took gifts to her former landlords, the Suemasas.

22. A special edition of the popular *Ellery Queen Mystery Magazine* was distributed to U.S. armed forces in 1945 and 1946.

23. Mary and Kay enjoyed giving nicknames to co-workers who lived in the quarters provided by the army.

When I was outside Warren's company, a little boy, only about four years old, with a baby strapped on his back came to the gate. He was shabbily dressed and had a pail made out of a tin can thrown away by GIs. Warren said, "There's the man who begs scraps from the plates." He stands by the gate, and the GIs give him what is left over. It was so pitiful. And yet, scraps are much better food than he could ever get otherwise. Warren said he never writes back home about such things.

I wonder if time will heal the bitterness I feel towards the Japanese? I know that I shouldn't feel as I do towards them. Or was it their fault that they are now in this mess? They have never learned to think for themselves. But should we blame the people? I don't know. The chaplain said in his sermon that we should work for peace, or we would have another war in the next 30 years or so. The only thing the GIs think about is going home as soon as possible—they don't stop to think of their mission here. Warren said that in Germany, they called those GIs the "I-want-to-go-home" boys.[24] He said that they were leaving a bad impression on the people. There is [a] growing resentment against them, too. Although the GI is supposed to [be] an ambassador of good will, it [is] the GI who is drunk, loud, or flirtatious (is there such a word?) who draws attention. And someone like Warren goes by unnoticed. Since he cannot speak Japanese, the people cannot see how he feels about things. For example, he hates to go in front of all the people lined up for streetcars. Yet, who knows that he feels that way? They only see that he gets on before them, and they resent it—at heart.

Take care of yourself, Kay. I'm always thinking of you and missing you. I am quite a good girl now, so you don't have to worry. Warren is a good influence on me. I'm going to go to church with him as long as I am in Osaka. He said that if his father had heard the chaplain pray, he would have said that he was praying to the congregation. He lacked sincerity. In his sermon, he would pause and fumble for the right, impressive big word. His father must have been a wonderful man.

Osaka, January 19, 1946

Dearest Kay,

How happy I was yesterday to receive two letters from you! It was worrying me something awful because I had not heard from you at all.

24. Within months of the cessation of hostilities, thousands of American soldiers began demanding immediate demobilization and return to the United States. But the manpower needs created by the surrender of large enemy forces in both Europe and Asia and the occupation of Germany and Japan, as well as the transportation logjams arising in the attempt to repatriate the millions of displaced persons in the two theaters of war, caused long delays in discharges.

Kay, I should have realized that you would be so absorbed in Dal. Why is it that you do not hear from him? And then, I could kick myself for not phoning him. About two days ago I finally phoned him, only to be told that he has been transferred to Nagoya. His phone is Alice 158. They told me to call Warfare[25] first, then ask for Alice 158. I got as far as Warfare, but it took so long that I quit. It would be probably as easy for you to get him as for me. And the letters would get there just as fast if you sent them from Tokyo. I sent them from Osaka, without going to the RTO.[26]

It's funny how fickle and forgetful I can be. Now, Love seems so foreign to me that it is an effort to sympathize with you. When I think back, it seems so long ago that one man was all my life and meaning. Now I can't even imagine that someone could mean that much to one person. Yet, that must be the way with you and Dal. Only I'm afraid that it is one-sided. He is so brainy and silent that I can't figure him out. What should I advise you? I don't know. Anyway, I'll try to get him on the phone, and you do the same. After all, if he thinks more of Lee than of you, it might be best to drop the matter altogether. I think if I can't be first in a man's life, he is not worth fretting your love over.

Think I'm going to Kyoto soon. This office is moving on the twenty-seventh. The colonel and major, as well as the other people in my office, are very nice to me. It is satisfying to talk to the colonel and major because they are intelligent and respectable and they seem interested in me as a person—not as only a female.

I hope that your mother comes over soon. She will be disappointed that I am going to Kyoto. However, I don't think that I would [be] of much help even if I stayed here. Now, I don't get hardly anything. I don't know why, but something in me just rebels against begging for things anymore. Perhaps it is because I am not pressed by dire need. And I hate to collect more junk. I'm quite through with the ARC bunch. Gene is the only one who really lasts. Al is still nice to me, but I cannot get things from him when I don't go with him.

I am getting some reading done. I don't see Shanghai at all. Her brother went home already. He sent my letters, which was kind of him and very unlike a brother of Shanghai. The letter from my mother made me cry. Kay, I am blessed with a wonderful mother! She advised me not to tell anyone that I had been married. And she told me not to be bitter against those who wronged me. Isn't that just too wonderful? There must be a God—the God of mothers. He must have watched over all of us and protected us. And I received a letter from Miye—Imagine! She is married! Was married only a week before her husband went overseas, to Japan. His name is [Nick] Nishita. Wish

25. The office charged with overseeing the demobilization of Japanese military forces.

26. The Rail Transport Office, activated by the U.S. Eighth Army to run the Japanese railway system.

I knew where he is. Miye said that since she could not write to me, she wrote in her diary.

Homer had to use the typewriter, so I'll write the rest. Kay, I have a feeling that I'll end up in Tokyo. Who knows, perhaps I'll have to stay here the rest of my life. I might as well start planning my life with that consideration. Both the colonel and major asked me my plans for the future. I wish that there was something worthwhile for me to do!

Osaka, January 19, 1946

Dearest Miye,

It was wonderful to hear from you! I just received your letter which you sent through Fred Kobayashi yesterday.

I can't imagine you married, yet—I'm so glad for you. Will you please give me your husband's address?

I still go by my name Kimoto. My mother advised me not to tell anyone I was married. I want to forget it, too.

Blanche said you were a constant companion to her in camp, and you had a lot of fun. Miye, I know you're your old, true self. Please give me a lot of gossip of who married who, etc.

The same time I received your letter, I also got some from Blanche, George, and Mother. They really touched my heart. Especially my mother's. She told me I should not feel bitter towards those who had mistreated me. What a magnanimous attitude! Now I know that I should not be bitter against the Japanese, but I just cannot help it. I hope that time will cure it.

But I do hope they keep the emperor. He is an ideal and something for the people to look up to. I've had arguments with the boys in this office over it. Yet, he stands for the tradition, history, and all that is good in Japan.

Did you get my picture? Please send me yours. O—Miye—I'm so glad you love your husband! My husband was no good. And I had to live with the in-laws. If I had lived with him, it would have been much different. Imagine—Miye—he never even spoke to me! I was worse off than a maid to the family.

The diaries I'd treasured and poured out my heart to for five to six years were all burned in the Tokyo raids. That's the only thing I really regret.

Dear Miye—I'm so happy that we can correspond again! I've asked Emma and George for clothes. All I'd really like to have is some good, entertaining reading material. I have loads of time, now. And I don't go out, hardly, anymore.

Tell me where the rest of your family is. George told me that Masako had three children. Miye—all I want is to find a man to love and have a family for. But, again, ambition is beginning to pop out. In our family, I am the failure.

I wish there were something I could do—something worthwhile. The Japanese need someone now who understands both countries and languages. And there are many hungry and homeless. It is really pitiful. Every time I come home on the subway late at night and see the poor homeless crouching in rags there in the subway, I feel like crying. But I deliberately try not to think of those things.

The Japanese have never learned to think for themselves. At school, it was all memory work—no thinking at all required. The Japanese do not respect the individual. In fact it's better not to be individualistic. It will take the Japanese a long time to learn Democracy. Sometimes I get urges to help them. I wish I knew how.

Miye, I have not changed fundamentally. No—I tried to become Japanese and almost made a physical and nervous wreck of myself in the attempt. After 20, it is too late to change a person. I am still as honest, frank, unsocial, loud, moody as ever.

You know, if I wanted to, I could make a fortune doing black-market things here. But I'm just too dumb and honest to do it. Many GIs do it, too. The Japanese want the food, soap, clothing. And the GIs want money. I have everything that I really need now. And then, I can always ask my family to send things. Why should I wring their money from these people?

Write, please, Miye—a lot.

Kyoto, January 30, 1946

Dearest Kay,

I dreamt about you last night. I hope that nothing is wrong. I can't remember what it was all about, except that I was concerned about you.

How are you, dearest? My first enthusiasm over Kyoto has rubbed away, and I am beginning to be restless again. Wish I had some nice guy to go with. Right now, I am not going out at all. And I am getting tired of staying home. No one seems interested in me except the wolves—and I know better than to play with them.

I enjoy the walk to work. They have trucks for us, but I walked today. Every time I walk I take a different route. It is a leisurely 20-minute walk. I love to see all the different foods and gadgets they have out now. But I don't see how the people are living when goods are so expensive.

Gene got some battery acid in his eyes, and they had been bothering him. I went with him to try to get some colored glasses, but could not find any in Osaka. Day before yesterday, after work, I hunted for some and luckily found some, so took them to Osaka. At the Coffee Shoppe there was some antagonistic-looking Nisei girl working in the kitchen, and some GI from the

33rd Division. Just my luck that Chuck wasn't working that night! Gene wasn't there. So I went to the Transient Center searching [for] him. I asked where Al was, and he frankly answered, "shacking up." Roy and another GI were there with Carl. I thought that Al didn't care about women. No wonder he'd been so cool to me recently. If I don't give him what he wants, he gets it from some prostitute. It was rather disillusioning about Al, because he seemed like a good guy. Then Scotty came in. He wanted to know why he didn't hear from you. Will you please write to him? It would mean a lot to him, I'm sure. I asked him where Gene was, and he said that he was where he goes every night until 11 o'clock, and I know where that is. And I thought he hadn't been going to see Mickey! After I came all the way from Kyoto to give him his glasses, I was disappointed. Yet, I can't blame him. It made me very blue, nevertheless.

It's good that I have Dr. Simms' letters to boost my morale.[27] No, we don't sell out so easily! And if that is the only reason GIs want our company, we won't go! I often think of what Father Wilbur said, too. I wish I could find someone to go [to] church with.

Barney does not have a room in Daiken (our I Corps building) as he did in Sumitomo. I miss it, too. I don't feel at home in this building yet. Our office is on the eighth floor. It is nice and light. I miss the canteen. However, our meals at the hotel are sufficient.[28] We get about as good food as the time Charlie was mess sergeant. All canned food. However, we don't get cold corned beef anymore. Besides, we get table service. And laundry service, and ironing, too. The only thing we lack is a bath. We have showers, but I haven't tried them yet.

Homer suggested that they censor our mail because of the ARC envelopes we use. That is not the answer, though, because your letter in a plain envelope was censored. It is probably because we are civilian employees.

I must write to Kimi-chan. And Marie. If I feel like it, I'll enclose a letter to her.

Kyoto, February 5, 1946

Dearest Kay,

Just got through re-reading your letters. How wasteful it is for you not to send me your other letters! If you know how much I look forward to your letters—they are my one consolation and joy now that I am not in love or likely to be. You are so absorbed in Dal up to now that that is all you wrote about, but the last letters were just wonderful, and sounded just like you. I've been a

27. An army dentist Mary and Kay met in Wakayama. He kept up a correspondence with them after he returned to New York in January 1946.

28. Mary is referring to the army-run hotel where she was living.

heel about phoning up Dal, and you're probably sore about it. I don't think that he is here anymore, as you said. It is so hard for me to phone, too. I don't want to when someone else is in.

I took down a lot of notes while reading your letter, so that I would not forget to tell you. I always forget, then I think of them in bed or something. Your news about buying our ways home by July was startling and brought much hope in my forlorn breast. (How's that for some fancy words?) Yesterday I found out about going home from MG [Military Government]. The captain advised me to write to: The Honorable George Atcheson Jr., Political Advisor to the Allied Supreme Commander, GHQ, AFPAC, APO 500. (There's some outside captain who came in and took my typewriter, so I'll have to write.) Anyway, I wrote and told him about myself: name, date, and place of birth. When and why I came to Japan, what boat, where my parents were born and their present address. And I asked him how I should proceed to repatriate. I hear that we have to appear in person in Yokohama and they will decide each individual case after a hearing. I want to see Fred before that and get pointers on it. There isn't much hope of me accumulating a fortune to buy my way back: I have no Russell who brings me candy.[29] Really, I can't get anything anymore. I don't particularly care because I don't have to bribe anyone. The only thing is, I can't give your mother anything. Say—can't you use Russell's or someone's return address and send your things to Homer Clark? After you send it, let me know so that I can warn him. I feel sorry for your mother, too. And I know your mother would like to get the things.

When my mother wrote to me and told me to continue studying Japanese, I did so want to go to school. And I'm glad you are going. It is hard to study by myself. Your mother wrote to mine and I sent it.

They're taking orders again for uniforms. When I asked before, they said they'd run out of material. I feel just like you about disliking them [uniforms]. However, they can come in handy—especially when you want to impress the Japs. You have clothes to wear, but I haven't. I'm getting awfully impatient for my shoes. It's trying to have to wear these clattery "*geta*."[30] And I hope some clothes hurry and come from the States.

Today I sneaked out at 10:30 and cooked dinner for Pat and Paul—the two wolves down in the basement. They don't do any wolfing on me, so don't worry. We had: fried ham, toast, and butter, coffee. I surely ate a lot. They're quite nice. Pat is 31, I found out today. Paul looks older. They're always kidding each other. I prefer eating with them to going back to the hotel.

29. Russell was Kay's boyfriend at the time.

30. In wartime Japan, wooden clogs were the only alternative once a person's regular street shoes wore out.

I've got an awful cold. Wish I could go home. I hope the electricity is on. It went off this morning and was it cold! No electricity means no heat for us.

I'm enclosing some stamps. If I remember, I'll send you more when I get it.

Homer says let's go skiing this weekend. Don't feel so much like it. It might be fun, though.

When I went to Osaka, Sawa-san came over on Sunday.[31] He hates his job as interpreter for the police. He said his mother is sick. Wish he had a better job. And he said they have a hard time getting food. I felt sorry for him. I took him to that place where I used to work—you know, the Japs. Mr. Hasegawa was not in. I guess Innocent Little Boy Blue would not fit in with all those suffering in that "East End" district, as Sawa-san called it. Poor boy—when we passed all those little stands where they sold food, he said it was tempting, and I never even wanted to touch the dirty things! He let me read yours and Marie's letters, said he wanted to study more. Is escape what he is seeking too? If I were in Osaka with my present set-up I would gladly study with him since I have lots of time now.

Good-bye, darling, and please put the stamps on the letters and send them and cheer up a lonely heart.

Kyoto, February 20, 1946

Dearest Miye, my light and love,

How thrilled I was to receive your letters posted 24, 25, and 27 January. They sounded so much like the Miye that I knew and loved that I felt good all over. I can't get over it—how the years have flown and how different our positions are now, and yet we still can commune with each other.

I don't know where to start, so I'll just ramble on—

Thank you so much for the pictures. You are a beautiful pair. You looked different, but I can see the old Miye I used to talk, laugh, and get into mischief with is still there. Your husband is handsome. I hope that he is worthy of you. I am so glad that you are in love with him. It is good that he is coming back to you.

I can't imagine Ada being grown-up with lots of boyfriends. Sometime, will you send me pictures of the rest of your family? They must have grown up terribly.

I was transferred from the Signal section of I Corps to the Inspector General section, same building last Saturday. I am a typist here. At first, it looked like I would have to work here, but things are easing up now. Remember how

31. Mary and Kay nicknamed him Little Boy Blue because he seemed so innocent and trusting.

I never did like work? When you were out on the farm at Empire, I used to say, "I hate to pick beans," or "I don't like to hoe weeds," and I think it was Mako, remarked, "You don't like to do anything." Those old days—how I love to reminisce on them. Time has not improved my dislike for work. They kicked me out of Signal because I didn't have anything to do. I used to write letters, sew patches on uniforms for the men, get the mail, and run around the whole building. This morning all the clerks have had to go out on inspection, leaving me to my own sweet time. How sweet it is, too, when I can write to YOU.

There is another Nisei girl working here. She is from Canada, and her parents are here. They call her Suzie. She is quiet, rather cute, but she hasn't the wild streak in her like I have. So she is conventional and a good girl. You know me better than to suspect that I am that—although I do try to be, at times.

You asked about Iza-chan. He did survive the war. Too bad that I am not in Tokyo to see him and see how he is taking it all. His younger brother was killed in action at Iwo Jima, I think it was. Iza-chan was lucky, because he was always transferred just before things got hot. He married a country girl. He told me once that he had wanted to marry me. After the war ended, I did wish that I had waited for him. It's lucky that I did not marry him, though, because we are fundamentally very different. I find much more in common with GIs. Thanks for the low-down about Nisei marrying Nisei. In Japan, it does not seem so radical if we should marry an American. And the Nisei soldiers over here do not interest me at all. Of course, I never get a chance to meet any, either. I didn't think that there would be such a prejudice against intermarriage, yet.

I'm just starved for reading material. We do get *Life*, *The Saturday Evening Post* and funnies, and the *Reader's Digest*. At first, when I moved to Kyoto, I didn't have any friends, so I used to stay home and write letters and read. I had about a week of that. It was delicious—that privacy and all the free time all to myself. I wonder if I told you about our set-up in Kyoto? We Foreign Nationals (that's what they call us) live in a hotel, and we get our meals there too. We have furniture, army cots, ELECTRIC HEATERS (that's the height of luxury in Japan), wash basins, and so far, I have a room to myself. Some of the girls have had to double up. I told the manager that if I have to live with someone else, I'll move up to Tokyo. Our meals are much better than what we could get from the Japanese, yet it is all dried, dehydrated, or canned, and does not begin to compare with army chow. We get along, and I am quite happy here.

I have written to Tokyo about my citizenship. We have to appear in person before the consulate in Yokohama, and they are going to decide each case individually. I'm beginning to wonder if I can go back. It would be like being buried alive staying here. It is not bad now because I have the hope of going back, but if that is gone, I have nothing to live for. This life is so transient. I make a friend and he is gone tomorrow. I have never lived in Kyoto before, so do not have any Japanese friends here. I don't care for the Nisei or foreign nationals who are at the hotel. That leaves the occupation troops, and they are lonely and eager to be friendly to you. So I just live in the present and enjoy it as much as possible. You have your high-brow friends who talk philosophy—I envy you. It's so hard to find the people who are really congenial. Kay and I did discover one in a Capt. Simms in Wakayama. He has been a faithful correspondent to us. He is a Jewish dentist, and has returned to his home in New York. One of these days I'll send you his letters and you will be able to see why we are crazy about him.

Last night a Korean boy, Kay's friend, came to see me. It was the first Japanese conversation I have had in a long time. I think I'll see more of him because my world is too small now—bounded on all sides by Americans. It is so much more fun to be with Americans! This Korean boy's name is Kaneda-san. Kay and I had gone to his place before the troops came in. He had a small place in Kyoto, and we stayed for about three days and had lots of fun. At that time, we were both staying with relatives in Wakayama, and all we got to eat was rice—*okayu* [gruel] at that—and *tsukemono* [pickled vegetables] when it could be had. We made gluttons of ourselves, and I thought it was heavenly at Kaneda-san's place when we had white, polished rice, sukiyaki, pancakes with JAM (an unknown luxury to us for years), and I have forgotten what else, except that it was all like another world. He took us to a Chinese dinner, too. The Koreans had things, all the time. They do all the dirty work, and during the war when labor was scarce they were in demand.

Kaneda-san had just returned from Tokyo. He said it was sickening to see all the filthy-dressed beggars in the subways there. It must have been like in Osaka. When one went into a subway there, an awful stench would meet him. The homeless war-victims would seek shelter in the subways. They looked as though they had never seen water. That's one thing we do not have to see in Kyoto, since it was not raided. Here I can forget for a little about the rest of the suffering people.

Everyone is all excited about this new change of currency, and the limit to the money a person can withdraw from the bank.[32] It will hit the black market dealers hard. The GIs are worried because they will have to have their yen changed into the new, and if they turn in too much, they might investigate. Most GIs have thousands. I hope that the measure will stop inflation. I was talking to one of the Foreign Nationals at supper time; he's a German, and he said that nothing would stop inflation except getting enough goods out to

32. An initial occupation effort to check accelerating inflation came in February in the form of an abortive "new yen" currency reform. All existing currency was invalidated, and new notes were issued yen for yen, but with sharp limitations on the amounts that could be converted.

meet the demand. And they say that so many thousand must starve to death in Japan soon. The average Jap home now is eating *okayu* three times a day. I really feel sorry for them. It is amazing how the Japanese can change. I was talking to the plumber of the building here, a Jap, and he said that he has no use for the emperor, and that he was the foremost war criminal. The people go from one extreme to the other. Miye, I love the emperor and what he stands for, and I hate to hear people talk like that. I've probably said this before—the Japanese do not know how to think. They swallow whatever is handed out to them. During the war, they erased all the signs written in English because they said that Japanese is going to be the international language, and Japan is to rule the Orient. Now they are putting the signs back up again. It is all so silly and childish.

I don't know how I am going to return-address this letter. I can't use Homer Clark's [address] anymore since I am not working for him. Wish I could use my own name. I'll see if I can.

Had to do some work just now. It is afternoon now, and I am in the office with the colonel, who is typing a letter. It's amazing how your letters influence my thoughts now and help me to understand the talk around me. Please keep on writing. Letters are my greatest source of consolation and pleasure. I love to think of you, and the more you write the better filled-in will be the background of you. Such writing—my English has really degraded! Is there something I can send to you from here? If so, please do not hesitate to ask for it. I'd be more than glad to do anything for you. Dear Miye, I love you as much if not more than ever. My mother, too. I do not blame her at all for my predicament now. This has been a great experience for me. I have learned the ways of an altogether different people. And now I can appreciate the American way of life. As you pointed out, their ways are not perfect—yet, how much better they are than the Japanese!

Miye, I envy you your five friends. I'm not kicking, though. I am enjoying myself here. Does Ada remember me? I feel far removed from that younger set. Thanks for all the news about everyone, too. I wonder if you know what happened to any of the Ceres bunch? I suppose they are still there yet. Goodbye, and WRITE.

Kyoto, February 21, 1946

Dearest Kay,

How are you and Tiny getting along? You asked my opinion of him. Really, my dear, I have nothing to go on to form an opinion. However, it rather frightens me when he says that he is going to stay [on in Japan] for you. I told Chappy[33] that, and he said that if he ever stayed for a girl, and she changed her mind about him, he would kill her. I really think that he would, too. They are sacrificing a lot when they stay. And he could blame you for getting stuck over here. I can't understand him. You seem to be awfully fond of him, and he of you. He knows how to handle words. Yet, I don't know how much he has in him. Is he sincere? I can't find any sincerity in that poem, yet I can't condemn him for it since it is not that kind of poem. He must be an impractical poet. He must be a lot of fun, and very interesting.

I'm sorry. Kay, I just can't pass any opinion of him. What is his rank? Where is he from? What school did he go to?

Chappy said that he had to pull all kinds of strings to prevent another girl from coming into my room. Good old Chappy! Now, there are only one other girl and myself who have private rooms. I can just feel my privacy about to be snatched away. How come Flo has a hotel room? She must get around. Don't worry, dearest, there will be plenty you can do when you graduate.

Tell me, how has Mrs. Iwamoto[34] changed? I haven't done a lick of work this morning. It's really not bad here at all.

Kyoto, February 25, 1946

Dearest Kay,

My heart bled for you when I received your letters on Saturday. I never realized that Dal had broken your heart so. What did he do? Haven't you heard from him? Just what happened? I thought, smugly, that you had gotten over him. The dirty bum! How dare he be so mean to you? And that about Tiny surely burned me up, too! I thought that he was ideal.

Remember how we were so thrilled over Dal at first? I guess he must have grown on you much more after that. I never imagined that he would let you down like that, though. Kay, I wish that I could do something for you. I always thought that it was your affair, and that you could handle it. Please, please, Kay, don't take it so hard. Massy was mad about it, too.

Our hotel had a party at "Grand Kyoto" last night. I did not go. Just before he went, Chappy came to see me, and he said that he didn't want to go because there would be too many of the hotel gang there. It is wonderful how he dislikes them, at heart, just like I do. But outwardly, he gets along with them. I don't even do that. It is not worth the effort.

Kaneda-san came yesterday afternoon and brought over some translat-

33. The GI manager of the hotel for foreign nationals.

34. Mary and Kay's American literature teacher at Joshi Dai. Mrs. Marguerite Iwamoto was a Caucasian who had married a Japanese man.

ing he wanted done. It was easy, and I have finished it already. He was going to take me out to supper, but it was raining, so he went home instead. He saw your picture on my desk, and said, "*Natsukashii naa!*"[35] When I said that I hear from you often, he said that he wished that he would hear from you, too. Since he stayed around supper time, I ate later with Chappy and his GI friends. They surely piled up our plates! I could eat only half of it. I love fruit, and the others didn't care for it, so I ate three persons' worth of canned peaches. I was offered more, but felt like I would split.

Read the Bible last night. All of the Song of Solomons, and some of Isaiah. Feel like reading it now. Wish Kaneda weren't coming tonight, because I want to stay home and read and go to bed early. Chappy gave me a big tablecloth which I use for a bedspread. It is apricot-colored and I like it, only it doesn't cover my pillow. My heater broke, half of it, last night. Hope that it's fixed by now. And washed my hair last night. Surely feels good.

One of the Japanese men working in the building said that the Imperial University at Kyoto is going to open in April and will admit women. Such a temptation! If only I could stay in the hotel, or had some place to room and board, I'd like to go to school. It was gratifying to see his admiration and surprise when I said, as a matter-of-fact, that I was a graduate of Joshi Dai. Kay, I'm glad that you are in school.

Kyoto, February 26, 1946

Dearest Miye,

It was fun walking to work this morning. I looked at things, and thought, "I must tell Miye about this!" Do you know that you have made life much more worthwhile because I think of you, and that I must write to you all about it? They have trucks to haul us from the hotel to our office. I usually get up just barely in time to make it. This morning I got up before breakfast, and even went down for breakfast. We had three great big slices of French toast, and were they filling! Was so full that I just had to walk to work some of it off. As I was leaving our hotel, a GI who works in our IG office saw me, and asked me if I was crazy to be walking—I said it was for the exercise, and he said there was better exercise than that.

Did I thank you for the stamps? If not, thank you very sweetly. It was very kind of you, and just like you. I'll make good use of them. To get back to my walk—the stores were just opening up for the day. Some men, and women, too were sorting out their wares on the sidewalks. Went down one narrow street lined with little shops, selling tangerines, fish, pickles (*takuwan* [pickled

35. "Oh, how nostalgic!" or "I think of her."

radishes]—and how they smell). I just nosed around and felt so good to see life beginning in the morning. There were long queues for cigarettes. During the war, that's all we did—stand in line for this or that. I remember one morning, Masa Yamada and her sister and I got up about three in the morning to stand in line for some cakes—that was in the beginning of the war, when we could get such luxuries. Many times, we would line up and have them run out just before us. Would that get us sore!

In your last letter you said that you were a vacant soul now. Miye, how about me? I am much more a vacuum than you. I'm so glad that Nick is coming back. By the time this reaches you, you will probably be together.

Pardon my ignorance, but what is an MS?[36] I'm proud of you, Miye, to be having such a fancy degree on the back of your name.

Read some of "Isaiah" last night. Hadn't read the Bible for a long time, but your letters have inspired me to. Can't make much out of that prophet except that he loved righteousness and hated hypocrites. One of the few books which I have read recently is *The Robe* by Douglas.[37] Have you ever read it? It is about Christ. Think you'll enjoy it. It gives you food for thought, anyway.

My beautiful Bible was burned up in the raids. I was feeling so lost without a Bible—even if I don't read it, I feel safer if it is around—that Kay got one for me. Did I tell you that I went to Army chapel twice? Went to Catholic Mass with Kay and her boyfriend once. Don't know anyone to go with here. They had quite a nice I Corps chapel in Osaka, but the one here is just an ordinary room. Kay and I were taking lessons in Catholic-ism, or whatever you call it, from a Catholic chaplain. He surely was nice. He had the kindest, deep blue eyes that I have ever seen. I am prejudiced against Catholic religion because Emma used to be against it. I don't like it, anyway, because they say that we have to commune with God through an intercessor. I want to read the Bible and interpret it just as I want, and I don't want to have to see God through the eyes of any chaplain or pope.

I always thought that in critical moments, I would call upon God. However, during the air raid when we were in that fire, I didn't even think of God—I was too busy running from building to building, trying to keep from being roasted to death. It must have been God who kept us all safely through it all—I feel that whenever I read my mother's letters.

Do you ever get the *Stars and Stripes*? I just wondered, because they have some very fitting cartoons and articles in there, illustrative of how our "liberators" (as you called them) are acting and thinking. Next letter, I'll send

36. Miye was working toward an M.S. in agricultural sciences at the University of Maryland.

37. Lloyd C. Douglas (1877–1951), a best-selling author of the time. Another of his popular novels was *The Magnificent Obsession*.

you some of them. I'm enclosing an article about the want ads which is very close-to-life here in these islands.

It is 12:10 now. Have had my dinner. There are only two clerks up in the office now. Did I ever tell you about where I have dinner? It's a lot of fun. I go down to the basement of the building, where Paul and Pat cook for themselves (for dinner). They are in the Utilities department. I discovered them when I was working for the Signal Office and had to go down for some signs and some hasps (had to look that up in the dictionary). One time I went down about 11:30, and the very fragrant odor of hamburgers met my nose. I very eagerly followed the delicious smell, and it led me into the room where Paul and Pat were having dinner. Paul invited me to pull up a chair, and of course, me who loves food, didn't have to be coaxed very hard. That started it off. I said that I love to cook, so they gave me a steady job as cook and dishwasher. Now I get fresh meat at least once a day. They have things all fixed up around there, with electric stove, sink with running hot water, and even a shower. The soldier knows how to get around. If he is let alone, he fixes himself pretty comfortable. They weren't feeling so good today because they had taken shots yesterday for typhus and typhoid and I don't know what else. I much prefer to eat with [them] to going back to the hotel and sitting down to a tablecloth, and facing all those hypocritical people.

I just don't care for the people in our hotel. I only like our manager, a GI named Chappy. All the others are superficial and insincere. I know that I should try to be friendly to them, but it is too much bother. And if I can get along with a few sincere friends, that is all I want. Chappy is doing all he can to have me keep a room to myself. There are only about three of us now, girls who have rooms by ourselves.

Started reading *My Name Is Aram* by Saroyan[38] yesterday. It is cute, and rather light, entertaining reading. I feel a reading spell coming on. Think I'll stay in and read for about a week now.

Haven't heard from Dr. Simms since he returned. Some of the boys here haven't heard from home for four or even six weeks. I feel guilty to be so overjoyed when I get a letter from you—the others are so glum and envious. I get the mail, and when I come up every day without anything, I am threatened [with] all kinds of tortures. It is really too bad that they can't get mail to the men over here.

What do they say back in the States about Americans going with Jap girls? Since you are a married woman, I should not say such things, but it's surprising how few there are who remain true to their wives. I used to think that Jap

38. William Saroyan (1908–81), notable for his books on the life of Armenian Americans.

men were fickle and animalistic, but it seems that Americans are just as bad. I often wonder how much the women suspect. It is hard on the men when they find out that their wives are unfaithful to them. Should there be a double standard? I don't know—I only know that if my husband should be going around with other women, I wouldn't feel happy about it. And if I were married, I would be faithful. It is easy to make statements like that—but quite a different matter to keep, I suppose. Your Nick looks like he would never look at another skirt. And if I were lucky enough to be your husband, I wouldn't even dream of anyone else. That's true.

Here I am going on the fourth page already with my trivialities.

Feel quite dry now. I know something I was going to tell you—the soldiers over here say, "Don't touch my moustache" for "*doitashimashite*." They nearly all can say, "*ikura desuka*" [and] "*takai*."[39] It's funny seeing a GI trying to talk to a Jap. It is mostly motions and gestures and finger pointing, interspersed with "you," "me," and other simple words.

The tailor was at the hotel with some uniforms. Mine wasn't done yet. They are grey wool. The girls wear slacks. I don't want to wear a uniform, but since my clothes are all pre-war, it will be better for me. I hate to make myself conspicuous.

Did my picture ever reach you? How long does it take for you to get my letters? Yours only take about two weeks.

Enough of such trivialities. Keep happy, Miye.

Kyoto, February 27, 1946

Dearest Kay,

How is my sweetpea getting along in this wide, cruel world? Thanks for the pictures. I can't help but admit that I was disappointed not to find a letter for me. Do you know that you had Scotty's letter in an envelope addressed to me? I thought it was for me, and didn't discover my mistake until I'd read half the page. Then I couldn't resist the temptation to keep on reading to the end. I sent it to Scotty through Japan mail, to the Matsuzakaya ARC. Hope it reaches him.

They certainly are feeding us a lot now. Last night we actually had steak—the first time that we had fresh meat there [at the hotel]. I had breakfast there yesterday morning and felt overstuffed and uncomfortable all day. We had pudding for dessert last night, and I barely got it down, I was so stuffed. The mess sergeant is going to stay at the hotel for good. I didn't have breakfast this morning, but still full. Kay, I hope that you are getting enough to eat.

39. "Don't mention it," "How much is it?," "Expensive."

Kaneda-san came over last night. He didn't come night before last when I had expected him. Why is it that I get so bored and sleepy when he comes? And I have the hardest time trying not to show that I wish he would go home. It's good for me to see him because it broadens my horizon. He is an enterprising young man, and I expect him to go far. He said that if he went to Korea now and started some factories, he could make a fortune. Perhaps that is what your father is doing.[40] There must be some reason for his silence.

Is Matsubara-sensei[41] teaching? His classes were ones that I truly enjoyed. He loved literature and you could feel the atmosphere change when he started to read or lecture about it. Last night I was reading *Hamlet* when Kaneda came. I enjoyed it, too. Shakespeare surely has a wonderful vocabulary. As I read it, I thought of you and the passages that you must find entertaining. Homer Clark gave me a handsome volume of Shakespeare's tragedies. Someone said that Shakespeare grows old with you. That is very true. I like him much better now that I am old and experienced, you know.

How do you like Miye's letters? Please return them. I am enclosing another. Thought I had sent this one, and was surprised to find it the other day. Can't wait for her magazines and reading material to get to me. Have your packages come from your sister? Wish mine would come. I bought some shoes in Kyoto for $750—no, I mean yen. Feels wonderful to wear shoes for a change.

Kyoto, February 28, 1946

Dearest Miye,

O, I am so darned tired! It must be nearly five now, and I've been typing all day. Now I am so tired that I can't even think. Hate to go home yet because my Korean friend might come over, and he does bore me so—keep wishing that he would hurry and go home. The best way to avoid him is not to be there. He gave me an idea, though, for which I am thankful. He suggested publishing a book on English Conversation. He is at the head of some Korean youth movement, and he said that he would publish it for me and see that it sold. Such books are in demand now. It is such an effort to think, though. Haven't had to for so long that I don't know how. One is not required to use her head when she is a typist.

Walked to work again this morning. Saw some beautiful fresh fish out in the markets, and suggested to Paul and Pat that we have a fish dinner sometime. They were not very enthusiastic. They said that prices were so high that

40. Kay's father had come to Japan with her mother, but he didn't live with her.
41. Professor of English literature at Joshi Dai.

they couldn't afford it (that's a lie!) and besides they didn't know how fresh the fish was. We had fried chicken today, and it certainly was good. I don't mind not having fish, because it is so messy to prepare and smelly too. I wrote down the sign on the barber shop; it is: "Barber shop, most clean and sonorous store."

As I look out of the window, the city is grey and a faint mist hangs over the rooftops. Kyoto is nestled among hills. When I look out from my eighth-floor window, I want to go sightseeing, but when I see the crowded streetcars, all desires vanish. I had a lot of fun before the war when I came to Kyoto to go sightseeing. Somehow, I can't get into the mood anymore. Everything is no longer quaint and different and attractive.

Do they have any books around there about learning Japanese? It might be a good idea to make a book on beginner's Japanese for the soldiers. They certainly want something like that. Do you require written requests to send books? And Miye, my love, would you do me a favor? Could you send me some brown shoe polish? I hear that if you send something airmail, it is not necessary to show a request for it. If it is too much bother, never mind. Shoe polish is hard to get here—even the soldiers have a hard time getting it. Thanks a lot, Miye.

Kyoto, March 1, 1946

Dearest Kay,

Did you see that article in *Stars and Stripes* about Nisei not being able to go back? In case you never, I am enclosing it. What a blow to my hopes and dreams! Now, I guess that the only way to get back is to marry someone. O, well—I rather expected it to come out this way. Life isn't so bad here. Where there's a will there's a way, and you know darn well that I have a will to go back home!

I've been staying in this week. Kaneda-san came over last night. I enjoyed his company, too. Do you know that he gets the privileges of a foreigner here? I told him that we who had been abused and kicked around before were on the upper hand now. He said that that woman, you know, the one who cooked for us when we visited him—the young one, was a fallen woman now. He got her a job in a factory where she made 400 [yen] a month. But she fell into bad company and took up woman's oldest profession. Now she makes over 100 a night. Over 3,000 a month. Kaneda was sore about it and said that he didn't want to have anything to do with her. Still she keeps it up. Many soldiers patronize her, too. What price honesty and chastity now? It is the dishonest and unchaste who are making the money now.

Talked to a soldier today who said that he liked Osaka better. I teased him that it's because of the girl he left behind him, and he said that there are more girls here—just go to the Shijo station around six or seven and there [are] hordes of them. That gave me an idea—wouldn't it be fun to pick up someone like that, pretend that I didn't understand English, and see what the average Jap girl there goes through? I've often wanted to do that, just for the experience. I've been afraid to, because I know what the soldier is after—and I'd hate to risk it.

Kyoto, March 2, 1946

Dearest Kay,

What joy when I found your two fat, fat letters waiting for me! I just lay down on my bed and laughed and wept with you. And just yesterday I complained to you that I hadn't heard from you. Thanks for sending back Miye's letters and pictures.

One of our clerks is going home tomorrow. I have a funny premonition that Pat is going soon, too. And it makes me sick in the stomach. I'll be lost if he goes. He's the most ideal yet. The best thing is that I'm not in love with him, or he with [me]. We just like each other.

We are getting our new money today. Yesterday we had to turn it in. I only get to change 1,400 [yen]. I'm glad that I'm not rich—otherwise, I'd be worried now. There's one boy at our hotel who has 12,000 and doesn't know what to do with it. I wonder if your mother will be inconvenienced? The Suemasas probably had to do a lot of thinking and scheming and seeing the right people to get connections. [Mrs. Suemasa] wrote to me and asked why I didn't come to Osaka. They must be running short of chocolates.

It was certainly interesting about the well-bred Joshi Dai student falling for the soldiers. My, my, so the Occupationists have won the women of Japan from the very high-toned educated females to the loose women of the street. Sometimes I wonder if the occupation is doing any good, after all. Personally, I am glad that our "liberators" (don't you love Miye's irony?) are here. But for the good of the country—I wonder. Perhaps it would have been better for the Japs to have worked out their own salvation. Now they rely too much on outside help.

My neck muscles ache this morning. I told that to Serge at breakfast, and he says, "maybe it's from necking." He gives me a pain in the neck—that's more like it.

I'm so glad that you can go to Brownie's place and cook and eat like that. It must be a lot of fun. I love the way you described evenings with him. I see that you have changed, too, in your attitude towards married men. After all, they will all leave us behind, so what difference does it make if they are married or not? It's dirty to try to hide it like Tiny, too. Besides, men our age are mostly married, anyway. That's one thing I like about Paul and Pat—they are my age. I can talk to them and understand them better than these very young men who haven't seen life yet. Chappy is 26—which is enough to make him good company.

I just delight in your handwritten letters, as Dr. Simms often commented. You have such expressive and neat handwriting that it is a pleasure to read it. What a relief it is not to have those sticky—what is the English equivalent of *shitsukoi* [persistent]?—Jap girls near me anymore. O, they used to make me boil with rage—inside, of course—when they would come to me to get their compositions and translations corrected. And it is a disappointment about Kazue. Kay, I'm proud of you for seeing it through. At least, you are not being swayed by immediate returns. I love Mrs. Iwamoto for saying that you will be "better equipped." I want to write to her. Did you know that two letters I wrote to her long ago came back to me? Guess I'll address it to the school next time. It is such a pity about her shabby clothes. Shakespeare advised, "Costly thy raiment as money can buy" (I got some words wrong there). It is true—clothes are a very important morale booster, just as a good dinner is. I can't wait until the clothes come in and I'll be able to strut around in "stateside stuff." The vanity in me.

I really enjoy Shakespeare now. I like *Hamlet*. It was so funny, the passage I read last night. Some fool was trying to find out what caused Hamlet's supposed madness, and Hamlet surely told him off! He asked the guy can he play a flute—the dope says no, and Hamlet says, well no more can you sound me off. I know that I don't explain it very well, but it was really clever and funny. There are passages that I want to quote to you. There is one about men being matched with beauty and yet going to bed with garbage. So many of the Americans are doing that. Like Brownie. And lots of these brass hats and others who have lovely wives at home go out with Jap garbage. I guess before when I read Shakespeare, I couldn't grasp the significance of some of his pointed sayings.

I told Chappy that I was upset yesterday because I was convinced that I'd never get home, and he said that he wished he were not married, because then he'd marry me—even if it was only to get me home, and if I didn't love him after I got there, he'd let me go. I echoed his, "You're snowing me, honey," as he always says to me, but he looked sincere and I think that he really meant it. It is wonderful to have someone tell you things like that you love to hear.

It made me so very, very angry (do you know how the Jap girls say that?) when I heard that someone had told Col. Duncan of our IG office on Chappy—said that the hotel was going to the dogs, that the food was lousy, etc. It was like sticking a knife in his back. It is not true, either. That place is heaven compared to Osaka. You remember how I raved about it. If they have any complaints, why don't they tell him straight to his face? So the Headquarters Commandant came to the hotel to look up Chappy. Was he sore! (I mean Chappy.) He said that he's going to find out who it was who talked, and he said that he hoped it was a man—and a big man, because it would be a pleasure to knock him flat. Chappy is short—maybe no taller than I. He likes boxing and goes to the company to practice. And he always has sores on his knuckles from fighting someone. Just as it heals, he socks someone else. They're yellow through and through whoever did that squealing—and they have nothing to complain about. Chappy goes out of his way to do us favors, and look how they repay him.

Kyoto, March 4, 1946

Dear, dear Kay,

My heart goes out to you when you write like you do—Kay—what is it we are yearning for and searching for and longing for? For a while we might think we've found it, yet, how disillusioning when we find the gold to be dross. Ah—a cigarette hits the spot now. "To see the world through smoke," as you so aptly put it. Life is so realistic and ugly and sharp—one needs smoke and haze to soften it.

Tonight I would like to get away from it all and go commune with Nature. It was on a night like this—years and years ago—that I would wander out in our field with my little understanding dog—and go lie down on the sand and gaze at the wonderful heavens. The velvet black dome of heaven studded with diamonds. How I love the stars! The same stars are over you and I and our loved ones. On a night like this, not so long ago, Teruko Kawai[42] and I would wander out on the slope—away from the imprisoning, stifling, worldly dormitory and our match boxes of rooms—and we'd talk and talk and look at the wondrous stars. But now I am imprisoned. I have no one to commune with. You are far away. Teruko is far away, probably nursing her "Moses."[43] Miye is so far away—and I am here alone, cramped in by four walls.

I want to soar and fly, as Milton did in spirit. Get away from the petty earth—from dirt and squalor. I long to fly among the universes and—what do you call it—darn it! I can't think of the right word, just when I wanted to be grandiose. Back to earth again with a thud. I left my glove on the top of my lampshade and got a nice burn on the thumb. It's the glove you gave me, so it hurts!

Just came back from seeing a Western at the Kyoto Theater with Pat. Why

42. A friend and classmate from Akita Prefecture. She married Odashima Sueyoshi.

43. Teruko's first child. She had named him Moses because she hoped he would lead the Japanese people after the war.

is it that I always feel restless and dissatisfied after I leave Pat? I hate to hear him talk and gloat over what he's going to do after he gets home. Can't help but contrast his bright and happy future to my bleak and unpromising one. The years stretch out without a glimmer of hope.

Yesterday Kaneda came about 3:30 and we went to his place on the car that his Korean Youth Party uses. We had chicken sukiyaki and boiled chicken, which was quite good. If I weren't spoiled by the delicious steaks, chops, etc., that I get from Paul and Pat, it would have been delicious. Two of his friends came and I enjoyed it. I didn't appreciate the place like I did when we went—we had such a perfect stolen holiday then! I thought of the time we were there. Kaneda said, too, that he wished you were there.

That visit opened my eyes to all the blessings I have now. I was cold there, even if he had an electric plate and *shichirin* [charcoal stove] going. And the sink was dirty, and he didn't have the conveniences we have. Thank God for a heated warm place to work and stay. No—I guess I should thank our "liberators" (I love that!).

Do they have any heat at Joshi Dai?[44] I didn't think so from your description of all that you were wearing. Kay—I admire you for sticking it out. It takes guts and of the right kind. Remember that I'm always thinking of you and loving you and being proud of you! I try so hard to try to control my pride when I nonchalantly say "my friend is going to Joshi Dai." You are going to stick it through, Kay. It's wonderful to think of you studying when the rest of the Nips and Nisei are chasing worldly pleasures.

Kaneda had two lovely pictures of you—one by yourself, sitting and looking down with a background of country, some hills or something; the other with a group of people I didn't know, probably Koreans? Anyway, [the shots] looked just like you and I felt awfully lonely all of a sudden.

Isn't it consoling to know that among the transient and fleeting friends that we come in contact with, you and I will stay forever? Like Tennyson's poem about the brook—"For men may come and men may go, but I go on forever." Let GIs and brass come and let them go, but we will remain true forever.

Finished *Hamlet* this morning. I like him. He was always in doubt and wondering what to do. I think that you'd find many points that coincide with yours and mine in him. Now that I'm home, I'll quote the passages I was talking about before:

> "So lust, tho' to a radiant angel link'd,
> Will sate itself in a celestial bed,
> And prey on garbage."

44. All the radiators had been removed for metal scrap during the war.

"Frailty, thy name is woman!"
"O God! O God!
How weary, stale, flat and unprofitable
Seems to me all the uses of this world."

Changing the subject, here's a passage from Isaiah I have in my notebook that I just love: ". . . and they shall beat their swords into plowshares, and their spears into pruning hooks: nation shall not lift up sword against nation, neither shall they learn war any more."—Isa. 2.4.

My darling, I've written myself out of my very temporary depression. I love to write like this—just rambling on, in the privacy of my room with no one to bother me. It is ten now and I feel like reading. Chappy let me pick out some books from a box they got—I found *The Years* by Virginia Woolf. I can't recall where I heard of that—but I do know that I've been wanting to read it for a hell of a long time! O—that makes me feel wicked and free to say that. I like the way Miye writes "damn," too, don't you? Tho' it did give me a slight shock at first.

There are hordes of brass that flock here for the gals. Tonight I saw one of them with a col. Brass have a lot of privileges, but I bet the EM [enlisted men] have a lot more fun—the ones that want to. The other day I was drinking with Chappy and his friend Jimmy (he's a clerk in IG) and Bud (one of the stuck-up [staff] of our hotel) and their respective girls, and Jimmy told me something very true. I said the EM do more for their girls than brass, and Jimmy says, most officers are not in a position to do anything. It's all right if they have the right connection—how few of them do. Jimmy's former girl, when she was going with him, used to get cans of food and fresh meat, bread, etc. She left him for some brass. All she gets now is a nice soft bed at the Station Hotel. Now she wants to go back to Jimmy. Says Jimmy "What the people want here now is food—you can't live on love." That is frankly put. I guess it inflates their female egos to go with brass—that's all it inflates, though. Not their stomachs. I rather like Jimmy. He's the only wild man in our section. Our chief clerk, Henry, is a good boy. "So are they all, all honorable men" said Shakespeare. To listen to GIs you could retort, "So are they all, all good boys." To get back to Jimmy, he said it's too bad I met Chappy first. He said when we were in Osaka, he asked Clark about me and wanted to go with me, but was afraid to ask because I might turn him down. How women love flattery! And I am not exempt.

So Kay is a sophisticated woman of the world, now? Act your part—life is a stage. Do as you want, Kay. I've had a lovely time ranting on to you. Wish I'd write like this more often—I love to put my soul into it. Good night, my love.

Kyoto, March 5, 1946

Dearest Miye,

They say that the mail going out is just as delayed as the mail coming in. Wonder when you'll get my letters? I've been busy ever since all the brass have come back from their inspection trip of Okayama. Haven't had time to write at all. Now I am stealing time. No one is in the office—it is noon hour. I get off early for chow and come back just when everyone else takes off.

Felt like writing to you last night. Now I am no longer in the nice, gloomy mood when the writing spell comes on me. Am quite content with the world again. Last night went to the movies with Pat—some western picture with lots of shooting and riding and excitement. Didn't care much for it. We went late—that didn't make much difference because I didn't want to follow the story anyway. The Kyoto Theater is just a block from our hotel, which makes it very convenient. This morning I had to type up a bitch about the Civilian Employees (foreign nationals) being able to sit in the officers' section. They say that if enlisted men are not allowed there, neither should CEs. Red Cross gals and nurses get to sit in the officers' section, naturally. And any girls who go with officers. Do you hear much back in the States about the army caste system? It is really undemocratic and unfair—the officers get all the privileges and the EM only the dirty work and indignities. I haven't met an officer I like yet. They all are so self-contained and superior in their own sight. O, I take it back—I do remember one lieutenant that Kay and I liked. He told me that he is a wild man—and I found it to be true. He was a West Pointer. You ought to see how the brass flock to our hotel for the girls. Just last night I was surprised to see one of the mediocre girls—Nisei—with a colonel. And me with Pat—a lowly T/5 [technician fifth grade]. We have a lot of fun, though. I am too boisterous and unrestrained and natural to go around with any sophisticated brass.

There was an article in *Stars and Stripes* about Nisei repatriating which I am enclosing. Miye—do I have to stay in this hole forever? God forbid. However, it looks like the only way I'll ever get back to you is by marrying some GI when and if they allow it. Woe is me! I was very upset and moody when I read that—and I am not among the 100 they talk about. My gleam of hope receded farther and farther away until I could barely see it.

Also, I am enclosing a translation of a letter from Iza-chan. He thrilled me when I received his letter! It was just before supper; I took it to the supper table, and it moved me so much that the food just would not go down—and I left with the supper half untouched. Poor Iza-chan! "The country I love" he said. Yes, he does love Japan. And when I was staying at his place, he taught me to love Japan, too. Its history and emperor and literature and arts. Japan did not have for me only sadness—no, I did learn a lot here and enjoyed myself here. Now that it is all over, I remember how I used to go out with Iza to the Ginza and walk and talk and eat. I loved it. You probably remember my letters at that time. I'm glad that he survived it all, too. One of these days I'm going to translate letters from Teruko Odashima, a Joshi Dai friend of mine. She is my only true Japanese friend that I've made in my stay here. When I read her letters, tears come to my eyes. Japan is not a dying country as long as young people such as Iza and Teruko are left. I haven't written to Teruko for a long time, since it is so hard to write in Japanese. Some day I'll tell you all about her. She reminded me of you. We used to sneak out of the stifling Joshi Dai dormitory and look at the stars and talk and philosophize.

Went to my Korean friend's place Sunday afternoon and we had chicken sukiyaki. He has a Japanese home. I was cold, even though he had an electric plate and charcoal burner going. Thank God, I don't have to freeze in Japanese homes anymore! You get only your hands warm—the rest of you is as cold as if you were outside. And courtesy dictates that you take off your coat inside the house. How I hated wearing layer upon layer of clothes in winter to attempt to keep out the cold! Sometimes I actually had ten layers of underwear, sweaters, jackets on. All my wardrobe was on my back.

It is 12:30 now. I must get back to work. Anyway, I feel like working now after writing to you. Wish the mail situation would clear up.

Good-by, now. Hope you're happy with Nick now.

[This is Mary's translation of Nagata Izaya's letter of February 16, 1946. She sent copies to both Kay and Miye.]

Dear Mary,

How are you?

I have finally found a solution to the mental turmoil and anguish I was in after our nation's defeat. Now I have planned a course for my life which I shall follow. At present I am working at the Tokyo Shibaura Electrical Co. where I was working until I was drafted. I am trying to make up for the time lost during the war. It is a fact that one of the greatest shortcomings of the Japanese was our scientific backwardness. What I want to do now is to help rebuild our country by some scientific contribution.

Our country is faced with the problem of providing a livelihood for millions of people on small territory. In order to meet the need, I suggest the following:

1. Encourage emigration
2. Manufacture goods in large quantities for export and import food in exchange
3. Diminish the population

4. Invent means of making food by a simple process

This is the only way out. Other proposed methods of salvation, such as: changing the form of government, abolishing the emperor system, introducing Communism or Democracy—these would have nothing to do with solving our problems.

Of the above, number three can be accomplished either by birth control or mass killing. Birth control will not show any appreciable effect for five or ten years; besides, it is opposed by Christians. Mass killing is the better way out; yet, it is completely out of the question. Number four is something we should strive for, but there are many difficulties to be overcome. This leaves only numbers one and two, which must be left up to MacArthur.

Japan is treading the road to destruction.

Mary—do you realize this truth? Japan, your father and mother's country which had in store for you only misery and sadness. On the one hand is America—a bountiful land of plenty; on the other is a land congested with the fatherless, the homeless, and the starving. A country which has lost its last means of survival, a country hated and attacked by all the world. This is Japan. This is Japan, the country I love. "It is Japan's fault that she has been reduced to this," the victors tell us by newspaper, radio, and by starvation. Yes, it is true.

Mary, I am quite well.

I thank God that my life has been spared to witness these troublesome times. You probably remember that I continually complained of boredom before; well, I am no longer bored. Formerly, I was always doubting; now I no longer doubt.

I have written just as my pen flowed. Be well and happy, Mary. I pray that your parents, brother and sisters are all healthy. And just as you were independent and thought for yourself previously, I hope that you will continue to do so.

Good-bye. I look forward to seeing you soon.

Sincerely,
Izaya

Kyoto, March 9, 1946

Dearest Miye,

Tonight I am in a low mood and long for communion with some loved one. It's Saturday night and nearly all the hotel has gone out—to drink, dance, or to the movies, or to make "love." And left the hotel to darkness and to me.

It was so disgusting, and pitiful too, Miye, the way the GIs were drunk tonight, cursing, yelling, and raising hell. Are they "ambassadors of good will"? Not when they carouse like this! I wonder again if this occupation is doing any good at all. Why force an unwilling soldier to stay here wasting his life? He does no good at all. He sells on the black market, seduces the women with chocolate or gum, bitches about the rules, or the delay of mail or not being able to go home, gets drunk and acts in a disgusting way. Is this what the occupation was meant for? If so, better leave Japan to work out her own salvation. Such representatives of Democracy only confuse and antagonize the people.

On the other hand, I see the average soldier's point of view, too. He is forced over here through no fault of his own—away from loved ones, among strange people with queer customs and with a language he cannot understand. He is lonely and restless. There isn't much work to do to occupy his hands or his mind. Why not make money and have a good time if he can? The girls here throng to tag after a soldier. If they want some fun, why not give it to them? No one will know.

O, why is the world like this? At first, I believed the American soldier was so happy-go-lucky, generous and kind. He does feed hungry women—but for a price. The average soldier must be bored stiff—so he seeks stimulation and diversion from wine and women. And the officers are no better. The officers can black market in a big way. And they can send their money home.

Thank God that I like to read. I enjoy myself more staying home and reading than seeing some third-rate picture or gadding about. They don't give the army any good movies. The war is over, you know.

Anyway, I do feel better that I have unburdened myself to you. I can't wait for your reading matters to come.

Good-night.

Sunday morning. Just came back from a heavenly little walk to a snowy Paradise. It's been snowing all morning and staying in was getting on my nerves, so I put on my *geta* and got all bundled up and took off. The Imperial Palace is only two or three blocks up the street. How glad I am that I discovered the place! It is like a park. And today, the snow was on the lawn and trees, making it look like a pure, white garden of Eden. The first steps inside the gate left me breathless. Naked black trees crusted with pure white. The virgin whiteness of the snow contrasts with the sinewy blackness of the trees. And the pines were lovely with their faint, rust-colored trunks, dark green leaves overlaid with frostings of snow. I walked and walked and was so happy! Thank God for beauty! What a feast for the eyes that was! Now I have a refuge to go to see Nature. Until now, it was all streets lined with tiny, crowded shops and houses. How I longed for a place where I could breathe and see the open sky, and commune with God! That Palace is the answer to my longings. When I feel that "the world is too much with us," I'll fly there to my refuge.

And how pleasant it is to come back to a warm, private room! Coming back I went down a narrow street and the awful years came back—when I had to shiver with the cold and live in dirty, small hovels like the ones lining the street. Why don't the Japanese make themselves more comfortable? Their houses are like ice-boxes. The cold just eats into you and numbs you so you can't do a thing. And I am thankful that I no longer have to bear the cold, the inconveniences, and the smells of the Japanese house.

I love today—a quiet day at home. I am becoming a hermitess again. O—I wish I had the ambition and energy to write! Once in a great while I want to, but it passes before I get to work. Good-bye, Miye, and please keep writing.

Kyoto, March 14, 1946

Dearest Miye,

Walked home from work this afternoon. When I was crossing the street, the Jap cop strode over to some poor man and was bawling him out. The guy was wearing glasses, and he looked scared. I don't think the Japanese will ever change until a new generation is educated properly. The police have always been arrogant bullies. And the people have always accepted it, apologizing when scolded, yelled at, and beaten up. If I had seen even a little spark of rebellion in that be-speckled man, it would not have [seemed] so pitiful. I hate the cops of Japan.

I was thinking, as I slowly trod my way homeward, I am a failure and I will never get anywhere. I want to write—yet, I hate to take the effort. It is so much easier to take life easy, and to float lazily down the stream of life.

I do wish that I would hear from you. I don't even get letters from Kay very often. And I write to her every day or every other day. 'Tain't fair! I did receive a letter from her yesterday which she mailed on the second. The censors had been keeping it. Wonder why they are censoring our mail, anyway? Weren't our liberators supposed to come to give us free speech?

Today I was just simply thrilled when I bumped into Chaplain Hyams—Dr. Simms' friend whom we had met in Wakayama. He is the Jewish chaplain. I met him when I was going on the elevator at our Daiken building. But for the life of me I could NOT remember where I had seen him before. All I could remember was that he was a chaplain, and I wanted to talk to him. Finally, the light dawned. Kay and I had met him while we were working for the Jap MPs in Wakayama. Dr. Simms had come with him. He is very interested in music. While in Wakayama, we played some Jap records for him, and he kept asking so many questions about the music and what it meant that he nearly drove both of us to distraction. Are all Jews that way? He wastes not a second, shooting question after question at us, and we are hemmed in between him and the Japs and nearly tearing our hair. It's awfully nerve-wracking to interpret. Thank God, I am no interpreter. You have to always be all attention, and the right word doesn't come to you at the right time, and it is torture. It seems unfair that interpreters get paid the same amount as a clerk and even less than a typist. And the Japanese have such roundabout ways of saying things. The Japanese usually spiels off a long-winded speech if someone asks him a question. Why don't they get to the point at once? After I listen to all the why's and wherefore's for tedious long minutes, I sum it up in short sentences in English.

Chappy told me this morning that after every date night at the Kyoto Theater they have to DDT the place because there are so many lice crawling around. Otherwise, they would have let the GIs bring in girls every night. Now I hate to go on date nights. How I hate lice! I had them during the war, and what misery I was in! They were breeding in my clothes, but I was in the country at the time, and had to wear all that I had, making it impossible to get rid of the dirty vermin. And they got in my hair! No matter how often I washed my hair, they would hatch out the next day. I thought I'd go crazy! Someone wrote a poem, "To a Louse."[45] When I read it, it made shivers go up my spine.

Kay is going to visit me during spring vacation, and my heart is singing with anticipation. I want to talk and talk and talk some more with her. How I wish that I could do that with you! We'd have volumes to tell each other. Miye—will that blissful day ever come? I dare not even think of it because it makes me feel so dissatisfied and restless. I MUST get back there! And I will, too—Just see if I don't!

Took a recess right now to wash my undies. It is such a comfort to have a room all to myself, to have furniture and running water all for my private use! In a Jap home, all this would be impossible. One always has to "*enryo*" [act modestly, be self-effacing] with the Japanese. And how I hate it! I was getting pretty good at [it] towards the end. I could take the smallest piece, do the dirty work that no one else wanted to, sit on my feet, and bow SO humbly. It reminds me of the story of the man who almost got his horse trained to eat nothing—only when he had nearly succeeded, the horse died. Yes, my dear Miye, the in-laws had me almost Japanified—but my life was almost wrecked in the process. Kay is so mad at them that she says that if she ever sees that sister-in-law of mine, she is going to punch her nose in. And I believe she would do it, too.

In the family that Kay and I roomed with in Osaka, there was an old

45. Robert Burns (1759–96), "To a Louse (On Seeing One on a Lady's Bonnet at Church)."

grandma who ruled the family with an iron hand. She was the mother of the man of the house. She didn't get her way with him, but his poor wife had to obey her and serve her hand and foot. Poor persecuted bride! And she must have been over 35 years old. I bet she wished in her heart that her aged mother-in-law would kick the bucket. But she dare not say it or show it! Upstairs, we'd often hear the old grandma calling her daughter and bossing her around, as if she were a child. Then, when the bride becomes a mother-in-law herself, she takes it all out on HER helpless bride. A vicious circle. No, it's not a circle—it keeps going down from generation to generation.

Damn it all, anyway! The sooner such harmful customs are done away with, the better. What Japan needs is an Emancipation Proclamation for the slaves of mothers-in-law. Japan cannot progress as long as her women are repressed and inhibited as they now are.

They are going to open up the Souvenir PX at the I Corps Headquarters tomorrow. Pat was saying, watch how the officers and Red Cross women take the pick of the goods there. And when the EM get around to the counter, there'll be maybe some plastic ashtrays left. (They are going to sell silk.) He says that's what happened in Tokyo, and officers are no different here. I'd like to get some of that silk, but know I will not. We cannot buy anything there. And they do not sell it in civilian stores, or what they do sell is sky-high. There is no democracy in the army. An officer is a privileged character. Did I ever tell you what some GI once told me about the army—"It's not WHAT you know it's WHO you know." Someone with friends in strategic positions—like the kitchen, QM [quartermaster corps], PX, etc. can get practically anything he wants.

I bet I bore you with such stuff. Well, one advantage of letters is that if you don't want to, you don't have to read it. Which is more than you can do to people who bore you with long-winded stories.

Speaking of bores, my Korean friend has not been around. They had a meeting yesterday—I hope he survived it. His party is for Democracy, so the Reds are after them. He said that he expects Russia and America to fight soon over the Korean problem. I rather miss him when he doesn't come, because I used to keep in contact with what was happening to the world around me through him—and from a different viewpoint. He said that lots of Jap veterans were holding up people with guns which they haven't turned in yet. They are unemployed, defeated, and have taken the easiest way of solving their problems. How glad I am now that I am not a native here!

Isn't Isaiah written beautifully? One advantage to getting old is that you can enjoy and appreciate many books that you couldn't when young. Reading the Bible used to be an odious duty, but now I find pleasure in it. Although I still don't understand much of it.

We were very busy up in our office today. I hardly have time to write during working hours anymore. End of the page. So I'll call it an evening. I've enjoyed it.

Kyoto, March 22, 1946

Dear Kay,

Today from the window of the 8th floor I watched the jeeps and army trucks go by in front of the Daiken. How come the Americans are here? Is it a dream? But this is Japan—*Kami-no-kuni*, the land of the Gods. Why should foreigners be here? One year ago such a thing was undreamed of, fantastic, impossible! Why, Japan, in her 2,600 years of history has never been defeated! Before surrender, the men, women and children of Japan will commit suicide. Ignominious defeat? No! Death—honorable death is the only way out. Remember, Kay, when they gave us all this propaganda? Proud Japan has been humbled. The vain Japanese have tasted defeat. How much do the people remember? If they fall for one set of lies, what will prevent them from falling for another? Gullible people! The people are so easily swayed. That makes me wonder if democracy is right. Is the majority always right? Not necessarily.

When I was looking down on all the U.S. army vehicles and the soldiers and officers of a foreign land, the incongruity of it all came upon me. What are they doing here, anyway? What would Kusunoki Masashige say? And Michizane, and Emperor Meiji?[46] And now the people are clamoring to string along with the occupation. Well, one has to get along. What if your principles and ideals fall? Remember, Kay, all that we once believed in—where are they now? Where is the ideal of Japan—the land of beauty and cherry blossoms and picturesque mountains. The land of one family with the Imperial Family as its head? Now they are trying to "humanize" the emperor. These grown people act worse than children at times.

O my God, my God, why hast thou forsaken me?[47] I wonder if there is a God? There is a law in the universe, but is there any one personally concerned about each individual? If so, why does he allow so much inequality, meanness, and hate to exist?

Here I am in Kyoto, where Murasaki Shikibu[48] wrote *Genji*, where the

46. Kusunoki Masashige (1294–1336) was one of the greatest military strategists in Japanese history. He is revered as a model of loyalty to the emperor. Sugawara no Michizane (845–903) was a leading court scholar, poet, and political figure of the Heian period who challenged the Fujiwara family and died as an exile in Kyushu. The Meiji Emperor (1852–1912) held the throne during Japan's transition from feudalism to modern statehood.

47. Mark 15:34.

48. The court lady Murasaki Shikibu (978–1014), whose masterpiece *Genji Monogatari* (The Tale of Genji) is generally considered the greatest work of Japanese literature and thought to be the world's oldest full novel.

emperors lived with their concubines, where the gay court was in flower during the Heian Period. And I am a descendant of the Chosen People? What is it all about? Will I ever find an answer to my groping and seeking? "Seek and ye shall find,"[49] said the Master. And He had compassion on the multitude. Why? Because He came unto His own, and they knew Him not.[50] God—I want to feel your presence again. I get so tired of this sordid existence, this ever-earthly life, tied to the flesh.

Dear Kay, I want to go home SO MUCH! Why should I stay here and vegetate in the land with so many bitter memories? Yet, my bitterness towards the Japanese has worn down. They can't help being so little, stingy, and cruel. They know no other way of life. But I cannot have compassion on them. They are too self-satisfied and smug. I want to have nothing to do with them. I want to fly back to a refuge and home. Kay, are we fated to forever wander and roam with no place to really call our own? With no one to really love? God, you know that I am tired of this transient life. How many soldiers really care for us? Very few. And why should they be sincere with us?

All I care about now is going back. And yet, it's myself I have to live with. Fundamentally, it will be the same wherever I go. Or will it? Yes, environment has a lot to do with what you are. But I do not belong in Japan. Neither do you. If we go back East in the U.S., there will probably not be so much racial prejudice.

Last night I read your old letter you sent with your mother when she came to Sakada to my aunt's to see me. And I wept. Dear, dear Kay. Why should there be so much meanness in this world? Your poor mother, having to care for the child who was the offspring of your father and his mistress. When I get old, I hope that I will never have to suffer like that. I guess she made a mistake in staying over here. Just as we all did. However, we are young yet. Must we pay for it the rest of our lives? God forbid!

Later. O, happy day! I received two letters from my mother and two from Miye. My mother's made me weep. How lucky I am to have such a dear mother! She said that she cried when she saw my picture, that I looked the same as when I left San Francisco, so many years ago. And she warned me that father is 67 and she is 63, and that it is our responsibility to care for them. She has such complete trust in God! She says she believes that God will return me to her. What a comfort to see her simple faith!

49. Matt. 7: 7.
50. John 1: 11.

The Amache Relocation Camp in southeastern Colorado, 1944. Only after the war did Mary learn that her family and Miye, along with all other people of Japanese extraction in the Modesto area, had been sent to this detention camp in August 1942.

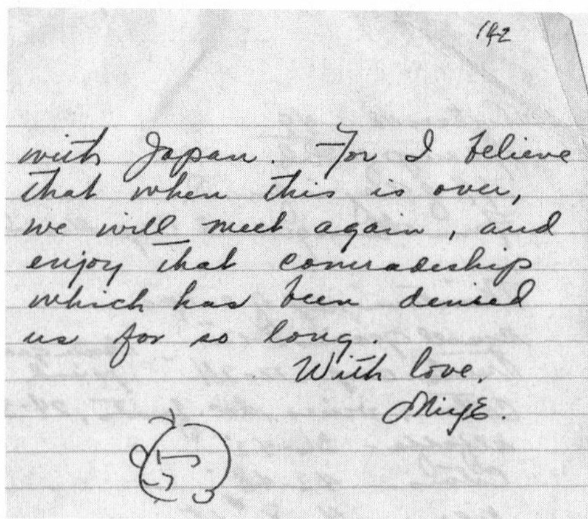

142

with Japan. For I believe that when this is over, we will meet again, and enjoy that comradeship which has been denied us for so long.

With love,
Miye.

The closing paragraph of the journal Miye kept for Mary during the period when they could not correspond, from December 1941 to February 27, 1942, a few months before all Japanese in the Modesto area were sent to the Merced Assembly Center en route to Amache. The drawing was Miye's favorite caricature of Mary.

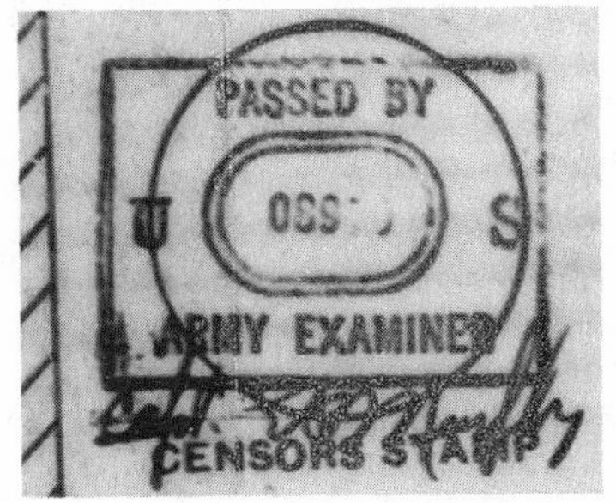

A U.S. censor's stamp, Second World War. The occupation authorities randomly censored domestic mail in Japan, often causing long delays in delivery. Mary and Kay, who railed constantly at the nosy "buttinskys" who held up their letters, eventually hit on the idea of reusing envelopes with a censor's stamp of approval to circumvent the system.

Osaka, late 1940's. Like Japan's other large cities, Osaka—where Mary worked for a time during the occupation—was heavily bombed in the closing months of the war.

The Reverend Ito Kaoru of the Holiness church, who with many other ministers was jailed early in the war for refusing to acknowledge the divinity of the Japanese emperor. His was one of the few families, Mary wrote, that did not change their attitude toward her after Pearl Harbor.

Miye as a graduate student, 1944. Released from the Amache camp under the relocation program of late 1943, Miye moved east to study for a master's degree in agricultural sciences at the University of Maryland. She was completing work on her thesis when Mary was finally able to get in touch with her again, in early 1946.

Mary and Kay Oka in Kyoto, ca. 1945. Mary and Kay, another American citizen stranded in Japan by the war, became close friends at Joshi Dai, where Mary reenrolled and lived through most of the war years. Common witness to the arrival of the first U.S. occupation troops in Wakayama, they kept up a lively correspondence after they went their separate ways in 1946.

Odashima Teruko and baby Moses, 1946. Mary was enchanted to learn from her "only real true Japanese friend" during the war years that she had named her son Moses because she hoped he would lead the Japanese people when peace came.

Newlyweds Miye and Nick Nishita, 1945. Unlike Mary's family, which did not return home after the war, the Nishitas went back to California soon after Nick got his discharge from the army and Miye completed her graduate work.

José Luis Alvarez ("Sr."), 1946. Mary counted among her good friends in Kyoto this former diplomatic representative of the Spanish Republican government who had been left to fend for himself in Japan when Francisco Franco came to power.

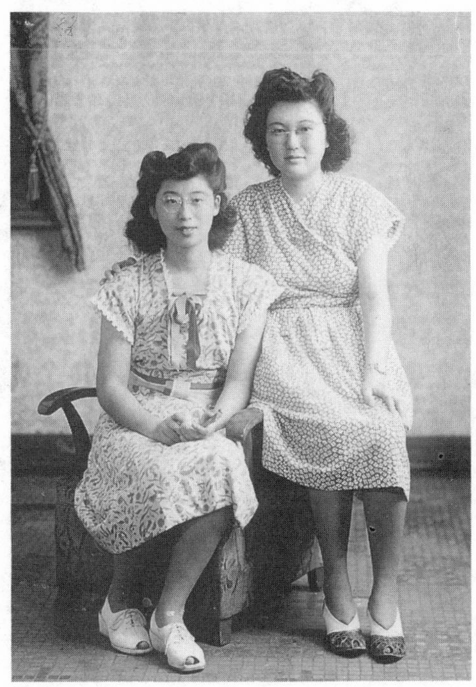

"Dear Kay" and her friend Marie ("Massy") in Tokyo, ca. 1946. Kay was much slower to get her citizenship reinstated than Mary; she was not able to return to the States until late 1947.

Mary sporting new "iron shoes" in Kyoto, 1946. Forced to use *geta,* the traditional Japanese wooden clogs, for lack of anything else in the war years, Mary was happy to return to Western wear as soon as she could. Shoe polish was one of the first and most prized items she received from home.

Mary and some of her U.S. chaplain-employers at a Buddhist temple ceremony, May 1946. The officer flanked by the two Japanese priests is Father Gefell, for whom she later wrote an account of the visit. Note Mary's Army-issue uniform, a welcome addition to a much-depleted wardrobe after the war.

Mary posing for a photograph before her proud achievement, the public library she helped organize in Kyoto in the last months before she returned home. Officially opened on October 3, 1946, it was jointly sponsored and run by the U.S. Army's Civil Information and Education Section and the Krueger Foundation.

Kyoto, March 27, 1946

Dearest Miye,

Darling, I love you and your very frequent letters. Thank you, thank you, ever so much. You don't [know] how you boost my morale. And I need it. At the same time I received the first letter since the war from my father, and such a feeling of homesickness came over me, and the tears flooded my eyes, and my throat felt like it would just choke. God, help me back to the good old USA!

Kaneda-san, my Korean friend, came over the other night. I was wondering what happened to him because he hadn't shown up for quite a while. He was interesting and had something to say. He'd been busy interviewing the Provost Marshal in order to get a Korean friend out of jail. I flared up in righteous indignation when I heard about it. It happened like this: Many GIs were in a house of prostitution (which is off limits), and so were some Koreans and Japanese. A Sergeant was flirting with a Korean's girl, so the Korean got sore about it, especially when GIs are not supposed to be in there, anyway. So he slapped the Sgt.'s face. The Sgt. called a Jap police, and had the Korean and four Jap men taken to jail. There they have been for 20 days. The brother of the Korean came to Kaneda and told him the circumstances, begging him to do something about it. So Kaneda got all riled up about [it] and sent a man to see Captain somebody about it. The Captain absolutely refused to see him. So Kaneda came to Daiken to the Provost Marshal. They were going to have the hearing yesterday morning. I wonder how it turned out.

Kaneda was provoked about it because of two things: 1. That any American, of a highly civilized nation, could do such a mean trick; and 2. That the Japanese can be so mean and petty and a "Brown-noser" enough to turn in an innocent man, just because a GI asked him to. No Jap policeman has to take orders from a soldier. I don't think they do; I'll have to find out about that. But to think that the Japanese do anything, regardless of whether it is right or wrong, only to please the Americans, since they are in power now. Don't they have any sense of decency or right?

Another thing he talked about which I thought was of interest is that a Jap man who is in charge of keeping a secret store of gasoline and silver in the mountains came to him, asking him what he should do with it. The owner wants to make a fortune from it, I suppose. Since Koreans are foreigners now, and Kaneda is in charge of liaison, he could procure it at the low standard price. I think Kaneda was kind of drunk, that's what loosened his tongue so. He said there are hundreds dying of hunger now—at the stations, and all over the country. Why should a man who has such riches bury them for his own selfish ends? If he would divide his wealth, how many could be saved from starvation and want and misery.

I never realized that there was so much hidden wealth. I bet there is a lot of it. And these rich are keeping it and hoarding it for their own good. "The poor ye shall have always with you."[51] You could rationalize that way. It is not right, though.

There are many brightly colored posters for the candidates running for Parliament pasted on the telephone posts, buildings, and signboards now. I'd like to listen to one of their speeches to see what they have to say. One of the posters had, for the battle-cry, "Where is the 100 billion yen of income tax going? Do capitalists and *narikin* [the nouveaux riches] live on two *go* one *seki* of rice per day?" Everyone knows that the rich do not live on the meager rations. Neither does anyone else who can beg, borrow, or steal something else. One *go* is less than one cup. About two-thirds of a cup. Imagine living on less than two cups of rice per day. Besides, there is very little other food. Everything is so expensive that it is prohibitive. One egg costs five or six yen. I wonder what the people are doing. Kyoto is rather well off. Yet, you often see people hunting around in the garbage. However, you don't see people dying in the streets of hunger, as they say it is in China. In Osaka, they pick up many dead every day. Perhaps they do here, too, except I don't see it.

Think I'll beat it. Must write a short note to Kay, too. Write and keep on writing, Miye. If you want to make me happy. Kay calls me "Butterball" now because I am so roly-poly. I don't care. In fact, I rather like it. At least, I am full of energy now. During the war, I hated to do anything because it would take effort and energy, and that would consume the few calories we got. I'd think, if I do that, I'll get hungry. And the cupboard is bare. No more.

Kyoto, March 29, 1946

Dearest Miye,

I can't believe that it is nearly April already. Time just flies, doesn't it? Soon you will be back in Sunny California with your Nick. I feel all content and satisfied in every cell of me when I think of you being in love and happy with Nick. You deserve someone like that, and he is lucky to have you. And I'm not "snowing" you, either.

Last night, Pat took me to the show *God Is My Co-Pilot*.[52] Have you seen it? That is one of the few pictures that gave me food for thought. It was about an army pilot who joined the Chinese army and fought against the Japs. It was interesting to see because I have seen war pictures—and air-fight pictures—put out by Japan. It was interesting to compare and contrast the two. In one the villain is the Jap, and in the Japanese picture, it is the American who is

51. "Ye have the poor with you always." Mark 14: 7.
52. A 1945 movie starring Dennis Morgan.

cruel and the person to hate and destroy. I didn't like how they used a Nisei pilot, "Tokyo Joe," to fight for the Japanese side. He talked to the American pilots and insulted them in their own slang. I wonder if there really were any "Tokyo Joes"? I told Pat, in case there were any Nisei like that, it would have been better for them to have died in action rather than to see humiliating defeat and occupation, after all they lived and fought for had been annihilated. While I was watching the picture and saw how they made fun of the Japs, it made my blood boil. Yes, we have too much racial pride. But they did not treat us right in California, and you can't blame some of the Nisei for turning against the US. The Nisei in America who were loyal to her must have hated to see how their brothers who had come to Japan had turned against her. Yet, towards the end of the war, they drafted foreign Nisei to fight. They took them regardless of whether they were American citizens of Japanese ancestry.

In the Japanese pictures, the highest good is loyalty to the emperor—to die for the nation and the emperor. That is their religion, whereas in the American picture they showed an Irish missionary, and faith and belief in God. Another difference was how the Americans showed scenes of the soldier's wife tearfully parting with her man, and her grief when she thought that he had died. A Jap picture would never show that. A woman is never supposed to show sadness that her husband has died gloriously for the emperor. Of course, human nature is the same everywhere, and the wife or mother is just as grief-stricken here as anywhere else. In public, the woman has to hide her emotion and tears.

Being in Japan so long, I was almost catching on to that hypocritical hiding of my emotions: to smile when your heart is breaking, to show a wooden face when you want to jump and shout for joy. It's no good, though. Happiness is stifled when it is not shown. Love cannot grow when there is no outer tenderness shown. Yet, I must be conservative and Japanese-y because it is distasteful to me to see these soldiers with their arms around the Jap girls. And I can't stand for any GI to do that to me. It seems so cheap.

Do you know, Miye, being in Japan has taught me to appreciate the LITTLE things in life. And it is surprising how much one can do without, if necessary. Somehow, you continue to live. Or is Exist the better word? It's not jewelry, silks, and luxuries that really count. Necessities, such as pencils, paper, good washable cotton material, sturdy socks, and shoes, needles, pins—these little notions and things that one could find in Woolworth's are more important to daily life than any finery. At times, I would have exchanged any precious jewel (if I had any) for a good, sturdy safety pin. And so, what are riches? I want to have just enough money so that I don't have to worry where my next meal or clothing is coming from. Right now, I feel so rich [compared] to before the troops came. You don't know how wonderful it is to not have to worry about what to eat or what to wear. Men's life shouldn't be burdened with such trivialities. No wonder Acheson[53] said that democracy would not work in Japan until the food problem was solved. Even to get envelopes and stamps with glue on them is a luxury to us. Jap stamps have no glue on them now, and they are not even perforated.

I cannot for the life of me picture the kids we used to know all grown up. As Peeno and Henry, and Ada. If I ever get back, I'll be "old Aunt Mary." You can talk about having children. To me, it is fantastic and nearly impossible. There was a time when I wanted to have kids—lots of them. Now I never think of it. What's the use? I hope that you have lots of them—lucky kids. Japan is no place to rear children. At least, Miye, we have a happy childhood and adolescence to look back to, no?

My dear, I am so gratified that you cannot dance, either.[54] I had an inferiority complex because I couldn't. Now I don't feel so bad. I have tried to learn, but I am afraid that I was not made to keep time to music. One time I got a spurt of ambition, when I was getting afraid of getting too fat, to learn how to dance, then I might be able to reduce. However, Pat is my best friend now, and he doesn't care to dance. We go to shows or shop around and walk and walk. Consequently, I have never learned to dance.

My Korean gives me rice once in a while. Anyway, living on a rice diet for so long has made me dislike the stuff. I prefer American food to any kind of Jap food now. They don't have the right ingredients and seasonings now to make any tasty Jap food. Our mess sergeant at the hotel said that soon we would have fresh meat. Hope so.

Today Paul and Pat had an argument about the women of Japan. Paul said that some Jap lecturer had told them that the women should not be allowed to vote until they got equal rights as men. Pat says, Voting is one of the rights. If they get that, other things will change. Paul said that women should be taught politics and how to vote. Pat: They are educated enough here. They are not as backward as some people make them out to be. I think the women of Japan will wake up soon, and voting is one big step towards their liberation. Yes, the Japanese are educated, but the education is of the wrong kind. It is all rote and memorization. Why, in girls' high school, they take at least 14 subjects a week. They get such a scattered smattering of knowledge that it does them no good. And they take the greatest pains to make their notes look neat and

53. Dean Acheson (1893–1971), then Assistant Secretary of State, later (1949–53) Secretary. His remarks in September 1945, on the eve of his confirmation as Under Secretary, to the effect that the occupation forces were the instrument and not the determinants of U.S. policy were taken by some as attacks on MacArthur and set off a debate within Congress on the general's authority. The affair presaged the policy conflict between Truman and MacArthur during the Korean War, which ended in the general's dismissal as supreme commander of the UN forces.

54. Dancing was forbidden by the Holiness church.

immaculate. In Joshi Dai, they spent all their time in recopying their notes. They don't know how to study. And they surely cram before tests, and how they cheat! Some girls in our class got caught in the act. The prof gave us the test questions beforehand, so three or four of the girls divided up the questions among them, each looking up a few. Then they pooled them together and copied off each other. That is a common occurrence. During the test, they took all the answers to the questions, laid them under their test sheets, and started copying. Another prof happened to take charge of the class, and he went around and caught them. There was talk that they were going to flunk the whole class and not let us graduate. So we all got together and held a general confession, and some representatives told our advisor that it would never happen again. It raised quite a scandal in the school. Now, isn't that a fine way for the women of the highest institute of learning in Japan to act?

All the Nisei girls used to get so sore at the Jap girls. They would come to us to copy our English notes, and to have me correct their English compositions. But would they help us in the Japanese classes? Not if they could help it! We really got disgusted with them. For composition classes, they would hunt up something in a book and copy it verbatim.

Enough yapping for one day. Keep writing, dear.

Kyoto, April 1, 1946

Dearest Miye,

I love you back in the good old California setting.[55] I hope that you and Nick are happy there. Just received your letter of 19 March today, and was all a-tremble with excitement and love for you. I wanted to write right back, but, like a good girl that I am not, I did all my work first. I was all done when I read your letter, and I was so happy that I burst out in one of my loud laughs.

Miye, whom my soul loveth (or do I have the words from *Song of Solomon* right?),[56] your Mary has her Kay with her now, and the world is ALL RIGHT. She burst in on me yesterday afternoon, just as I was dozing in my siesta. Was I ever surprised and happy! Boy, were we happy to see each other! Marie, the friend with whom Kay is staying, came here with her. We surely made a lot of noise and racket with our shouts and gossip. Everyone of us love to yap, yap in loud voices, and how we went to it to our heart's content!

Tell me—O, dear—I forgot what I was going to say because I was so ab-

55. On Nick's discharge from the army, he enrolled in graduate school at the University of California. Mary assumed here that Miye, having completed her thesis, had moved back west to join him. Slow communications prevented her from knowing that Miye was having trouble with her thesis adviser that delayed her degree.

56. "Tell me, O thou whom my soul loveth." Song of Solomon 1: 7.

sorbed in the chief clerk giving vent to his wrath on poor Amy. She says she is unhappy here at the office. I don't blame her. I have developed a nice crust to my delicate feelings, so that whatever the darned clerk says does not penetrate, and I can smile so naively and do just as he desires. Pat says, "Chief clerks are all that way—so important in their own eyes. When they get out of the army, they'll probably end up as pencil pushers in some obscure bank or so." My signal clerk used to be self-important, too, but he was an easy-going Southerner.

The clerk just pounced on me because I didn't put my initials on one copy which was going to AG [the Adjutant General's office]. My Japanese humility was forgotten, and I barked back, "How should I know? I've never learned anything like this!" So he gave a TM [technical manual] to me and told me to read it. Wish I'd seen it before. Then I wouldn't have to ask Suzie all the dumb questions, or got chewed up by the dear clerk. He says it, then it goes away, just like a quick storm, so it could be worse. Now it seems that the sun is shining again. Also, he said that I should not do anything else during this "period." I always knew his mind belonged back in high school, and that subconscious remark proved it. What the heck—if I have no other work, should I waste my time? No, if he is going to prohibit me writing letters when I have the spare time, I shall find another job. And that's that.

Kay and Marie were saying that they have Anti-GI Complexes now, and I don't want to ask for favors from any of them.

It suddenly struck me, what I've been itching to tell you. It looks like we can go back! I heard of a girlfriend in Tokyo who reinstated her citizenship, and she will probably be able to go back this fall. And I hear that if someone is in the States who will pay for our passage, we can go much more easily. Now that Kay is here, I think I'll take a day off to go to Wakayama to get some of my necessary papers. It seems too good to be true. Don't know what I'll do after I get there, but I want to go anyhow.

Thanks a lot for the shoe polish. It hasn't got here yet, but I am hoping. It's wonderful to be able to ask without entailing a big obligation on oneself.

One of these fine days I'll get my picture taken uniformed and send it to the people I love. Until then, let it be known that the uniform is grey wool and patterned after the GI ODs.[57] Except our slacks, of course. Eisenhower jackets.

Do you know the Jap expression, "*Shinzo-ga-tsuyoi*"?[58] Ask your Nick about it if you don't. Don't have time to explain. Anyway, that is me all over. But Kay surprises even me with the *tsuyoi*-ness of her *shinzo* [her strength of heart]. She is going to work for the I Corps for a month so that we can be together. And it is heavenly.

57. Olive drabs, the GIs' green woolen winter uniforms.
58. Lit., "The heart is strong"; connotes courage and audacity.

Some people are getting ready to go. I pop out of here on the minute. The other girls faithfully stay and finish up. Not me. My *shinzo* is *tsuyoi.*

Good-by, my darlink. Sorry I didn't have time to write more. More yapping next time.

Kyoto, April 2, 1946

Dear Miye,

Kay and Marie like Chappy (our hotel manager) a lot. Last night he came up to our room and stayed until 11:30. Chappy is really good-hearted. He is short and cute, and is SO lovable! Kay aptly said that Chappy is like a little dog who puts his paws to you and begs you to love him. I am glad that he likes my girlfriends and takes care of them. Yesterday they took him sightseeing. They went to the zoo and a great big monkey got mad at Chappy and threw water on him, so Chappy, not to be beaten, took a brick and threatened. That made the other monkey on the other side of the bars madder than hell, and he splashed water over all of them. It was so funny the way they came home and told me about it. Marie wouldn't let him kiss her good-night, shouting, "Two girls is enough for you!" Good old Marie! She is going steady with a T5 in Tokyo. She is so straightforward and good-hearted and loud. She is good through and through. Big and fat—even more than me. And it makes her madder than fury to see any wrong done. We all talk loud and laugh and yell our heads off, and how I love it.

Here's another comment from my Kay: "Well, I still wish some boys would fall so much in love with these yellow-skinned, black-haired, slant-eyed damsels that they would divorce their American wives because I am getting plenty sick and tired of always being on the receiving end when I'd like to be on the giving end too. I don't care—I just don't care."

How's that? That's an awfully far-fetched wish. You know something that you and I and Marie and Kay have very much in common is our sense of right, and hatred for anyone who dares violate it. After all, it isn't right that we Jap gals are always "on the receiving end." What do the American womanhood suffer? And believe me, the GIs are going to leave plenty of broken hearts behind. I heard of a Jap girl who grieved so much that she came around to the barracks and stayed in one spot for THREE DAYS straight because she was so grief-stricken. Now if that isn't infatuation, I don't know what is. And the merry, carefree soldier was overjoyed to go home—so much so that he didn't even tell her good-by. She had to find out from someone else that he had left her flat. And the cruel tall tales they tell them! That they will come back after them to take them to bountiful America, as their lawful wives! Snowjobs, snowjobs!

It suddenly dawned on me that education is not so much, after all, in a way. The boy—Gene—who discovered us in Wakayama and brought us up to Osaka had very little education. So has Chappy, for he said that he'd been working since he was twelve years old. Yet, there is a fine, rare sincerity in those two boys that I have not found in any other GIs. And of course, not officers. Does education take away the naive gold of sincerity that we brought from heaven? Somehow, with those two, you could believe that there is something GOOD and fine and worthwhile in man. And Gene had the most expressive eyes that I have ever seen. He really did a lot for Kay and me. He used to run a carnival back in the States. He said that he wants to see people happy, and wishes that he could help them to become so. He really loves to help people. I'll never forget how tenderly he used to care for that little orphaned boy who came to his truck to sleep at night. He was homeless. Gene would open cans of C-rations for him, and the little boy would gratefully say, "*okini*" (the Osaka dialect for "thank you"). It was a moving sight, because you could just feel how Gene loved the child and pitied him. One morning they found him all stiff and cold in the truck. They took him inside and warmed him and then took him to the police, where they could take care of him. Another GI took him because Gene was busy, so that GI got all the thanks and credit. Kay and I were mad when we heard about it, because it was Gene who had taken care of the homeless orphan, but when we let out some of our steam on Gene, he only looked sad, and said, "It doesn't matter who gets the credit. I was only too glad to help a child in trouble. It was getting colder, and I knew that I couldn't take care of him, so it's better for him to be turned in where they can take proper care of him." Wonderful Gene! Later, we found out that he goes to church, and he used to teach Sunday school. When we were in Wakayama, how happy we used to be! Gene would take us out for rides, and he would sing and yell and bark like the carnival barkers do, and we would laugh until the tears rolled down our cheeks. What fun we had! Just riding in the open country roads, with Gene at the wheel shouting, yodelling, and singing "The Salted Dog." After he got back to Osaka, he never sang like that. He was one wonderful person, and it makes me regain belief in mankind when I recall that there was one person like that among all these wolves.

Inspiration from Kay: "Mary, my darling, do you happen to remember that first sailor we talked to? I just happened to think that he was utterly charming in his slow-going way. I think that he will forever leave an impression on my mind. I don't know what made me think of him, but occupation—Allied forces—what the white men are doing brought me suddenly back to that day when I first saw a white man after five long years and made me contrast my emotions when I was so surprised that when I landed in Yokohama, all I saw was Japanese and I couldn't figure out that one country could have so many people of the same race. Ah, nuts, I guess I am getting funny in the head again."

Yes, dear Kay, I do remember. With the very same feelings as you, I think. We were working for the Jap MPs as interpreters at the time. They said that the beach was thronged with American sailors. It sounded so exciting! Kay brought up the fantastic idea of going for a walk to see what we could see. I conservatively warned, You know how they cautioned us to be careful of the Occupation Troops! But Kay is the Bronco that will not be Broken, and she pulled me there. First, we asked the men in our office if they thought it was safe for females, like us, to go, and they said, "Be careful of your step!" We got on a streetcar, all set for adventure. There, in Wakayama Bay were the Black ships—just as at the time Perry first opened Japan's door from feudalism. And along the beach and road were groups crowded around sailors. One or two sailors would be in the center, trying to talk to the interested people who flocked around. There were a few Nisei who picked up conversations with them. We walked up the street to where there was bargaining going on. The people brought their pictures, dolls, and fans to trade for candy bars. We got into the midst of one such group, and when they discovered we could speak both languages, we were the go-betweens, nearly being crushed in the crowd. But we got wonderful delicacies—chocolate bars—for our trouble. How we marvelled at them! Then, we extricated ourselves from the bargaining when a Jap cop came along to break it up. And we talked to the memorable first sailor. He was so thoroughly American—and Southern with his easy, lazy ways. His buddy was with him, and kept picking on him to sing for the audience gathered around, and he would drawl, "Ah cain't sing no song!" O wonderful days—soooo long ago when we first came in contact with the Occupation Troops. Now, it seems like we have always been with them. A GI here, a GI there, here a GI, there a GI, GI, GI GGGGGIIIIIs everywhere. Our life is made up of GIs forever.

You sort of expect an officer to be above the EM, and it is a let-down when they are not. Yes, they have more education. Yet, some of them are quite dumb. Why, even in our office, there are officers who make the most obvious spelling mistakes. I could write up those inspections just as good if not better than they. And I could take the dictation that Amy and Suzie do, because they go so slow. We used to have to take notes in class faster than the way the officers give the dictation. Shhhh—don't let them know, because I do not know shorthand, therefore, I cannot take dictation, therefore I cannot work on Sundays. See my reasoning? Just like Pat. He says he knows only plumbing (he's the building plumber) and only a little of that. In reality, he knows everything about plumbing, and a lot of carpentering, and other things, too. But if they ever find out, they love to make others—EM—work, you know.

Pat was planning to be a lawyer and went three years in Chicago, but financial troubles prevented him from finishing.

[Kay said,] "When you write to Miye, give my love to her, too. Don't you want a Nick? I do. Something made me think that as superior as these Nisei seem, no one has written a book that has been published yet. Which also makes me think that in the world of Art, the Japanese have done wonders in the French school, and I remember that in the seven great artists in Seattle, at least two of them were Nips. But why have we no writers? I am sure that a lot of us are more sensitive and more nervous and more liable to conditions and situations than a lot of these *donkan* [dull-witted] Americans are and yet no one has ever started to write anything of any value. And who is this Richard Wright, a Negro who wrote *Black Boy*, and a lot of Negroes have succeeded in their respective fields, even though we do speak of the Jigs and the Coons, but no Nisei.[59] All right, Mary, this is where we put in our bid and I'll be damned if I don't get something published in even a third-rate love story mag. Ambition—no, necessity. [It's] been done before, and we are two out of thousands that have been chosen for this work. My that sounds like hot inflation, doesn't it?" Now, isn't that inspirational? Only, what could the matter be, I just can't buckle down and write. The short story I started (damn my ribbon) for you is collecting dust in the closet. If anyone can write about Nisei, it surely is us. And look at all the unique experiences we have been through. We must do something about it.

[Last night] I was reading Isaiah 9 (yes, I'm STILL on it) and there was something to the effect that He had not created the world in vain. I wonder if that applies to us? I love the economic use of words in the Bible—but O, how descriptive and fitting! In the February *Reader's Digest*, it said in one article that we should read only the best books, and the ones that give us the most pleasure. Miye, I am so glad and proud of myself that at long last the Bible is actually giving me pleasure, and I can begin to appreciate its truth and beauty. It is really written beautifully. That is about the only reading I do now, and I read only a few chapters per night. Remember back in Modesto, how you used to pick out the darndest passages and show me, and we would giggle in church during the boring sermon (if I weren't sleeping)? Like where a man fell from the window because he fell asleep during Paul's sermon? Miye—don't you love to reminisce on our youth together? I love it. Now, as I look back, like Wordsworth, it all seems

> Apparelled in celestial light,
> The glory and the freshness of a dream.
> It is not now as it hath been of yore;—

59. At the time this was written, few Nisei writers had developed much of an audience outside the Nisei community. See the Introduction.

Turn wheresoe'er I may,
By night or day.
The things which I have seen I now can see no more.[60]

And when you wrote of how you used to come to my place and get a slice of cake with lemon filling, and we were only 18 then, how my mind's eye went back to those happy, heavenly days. But, "Where is it now, the glory and the dream?" How we used to philosophize and argue and laugh. Yes, "Heaven lies about us in our infancy!" Do you know that even Orion does not give me the supreme thrill he did before when I was an adolescent? Sad but true. O, lovely days, and lovely dreams of long ago. And yet, not so long ago. No, at times it seems like yesterday. It came to me as a jolt, your "We were 18 then." Why, that is nearly ten years ago! How Mrs. Wicking loved those cakes. Bless her heart! I love her. Sweet old American women are God's gift.

Kay says that she wants to have lots and lots of kids. Just oodles of them—all over the house. Wonder if her dream will ever come true. She told that to Chappy (he has only two) and he says, It takes money to raise kids. Impractical, dear Kay! As for me, such a wish seems awfully far off and impossible. Yet, I love kids. Maybe I can play with all my little nieces and nephews, while Ma and Pa sit nearby. I remember your rollicking, boisterous family, led by you. What a family it was! You certainly revolutionized the quiet, staid families who came in contact with you. And it's due to you, for you led and ruled that family.

Damn it all, anyway, Suzie and Amy came nosing around wanting to know what I was doing, and I said, nonchalantly and shrugging my shoulders, "Writing letters." They said, "How can you write so much?" I said, "If it's to an intimate friend, I can just ramble on and it's like thinking out loud." Amy: "Let me see a page, as an example." So I tried to pick out the most harmless page, and showed it to her. Amy: "You must be educated!" Me: "No, I only like to write." Suzie: "You could write books." Me: "No, if it's only rambling on like this, I could do it forever, but books are different."

Kyoto, April 3, 1946

Dearest Kay,

This morning I feel so good and overflowing with energy that if I were a rolly fat rat, I would chew any pencil that you thrust into my cage. Pat was telling me last night about the rats he used to take care [of] for some doctor who used them for experimental purposes. He said that a protein diet makes

60. William Wordsworth (1770–1850), "Ode: Intimations of Immortality." The following quotations are from the same poem.

them too, too energetic, and if he poked any pencils into their cages, they chewed them up ferociously.

And NO WORK!! It is just simply marvelous and I bask in the sunshine of timelessness, as you say. This morning I went to the Chaplains' office and obtained a BIBLE. Sally gave it to me. The other clerk there said that they gave Bibles away—they are the Gideon Society and that is a giddy office. I said, "And Giddy people there." I feel right sassy this mohnin'. And best of all, it is exactly like mine. Darling, now will you get one for me, so that I can have one at the office? I'd like to know who is giving them out, because I want to thank them. A Bible is one of the greatest inspirations and comforts to me. When I get to be a rich old Aunt Mary, I'm going to join whatever society they have for giving out Bibles to the Heathens. Ambition Number Five. Now let me read my Bible.

You know, I'd like to have known Isaiah. I bet he was giddy and a dreamer. And the injustice going around him must have made him boil. I bet he had a lot of fun raining curses on the people warning them and trying to scare them about the Might of God. Look at this:

> None calleth for justice, not any pleadeth for truth: they trust in vanity, and speak lies; they conceive mischief, and bring forth iniquity.
> They hatch cockatrice's eggs, and weave the spider's web: he that eateth of their eggs dieth, and that which is crushed breaketh out into viper.[61]

Wonder what he was referring to when he said eggs, and spider's web. What is a cockatrice?

[Later,] Damn it, Damn it, and DAMN IT! Why are women just a bundle of emotions so unstable, fluctuating from the height of happiness to the depth of misery in such short time? Just went down to get the cracklings and sandwich for Marie, and Paul says, "How many sandwiches do you have in there?" I said, airily, "One." The Fuehrer: "That will never happen again!" What the hell difference does it make? And then he insulted me about my size, and it made me so mad that I just ran out of there and slammed the door.

Darling, it is so wonderful to have you only two stories below me here. No, it is three. But it is so close, so close, and I think of you so near and I am comforted. The afternoon was started off wrong because I started to ask Sgt. Henry if I could get the afternoon off, and he anticipated my question before I even popped it, and complains, "No, I've let one person off, and that is all." What difference does it make? He does not rule me. Maybe eight hours while I am here, but he does not own my world. And if I have not a lick of work to do, does it make any difference if I warm this seat until four o'clock?

61. Isa. 59: 4, 5.

On the dot of four, I am amscray-ing, too. No one is doing anything, and it is so stupid to sit here when I want to get a perm. Promised Chappy that I would get one.

I can understand that Marie gets lonesome. In her letters she has confessed that she is not happy. She is so good. She deserves a cozy home with [a] loving husband and kids that she can fuss over and scold and spank and be jolly with. With the weather, my spirits have drooped. And only this morning, I was so up in the clouds. Down to the dirty earth with a dump.

I loved your "Your country is desolate, your cities are burned." Isn't that Japan today? Strangers are devouring her and her women.

Think I'll write to Miye and pour my woes on her. Sgt. Henry was singing "The White Cliffs of Dover" today, and it brought back so many nostalgic (is that the right word?) memories. "Tomorrow when the world is free." Remember the house? How we wouldn't get into the shelter, but excitedly watched the anti-aircraft, and the bombs coming down? And the nights. Was it worth it? Only time can tell. It certainly was an unforgettable experience.

How happy I am that we will be together tonight. Chappy is certainly taking care of you and I have nothing at all to worry about. The mountains surrounding are hazy and dull greyish blue. And my soul is blue. And grey.—

Kyoto, April 5, 1946

Dear sister Blanche,

Thank you ever so much for your letter of 22 March.

Blanche, my dear little sister, you do not know what you are saying when you write: "If it should turn out that you had to stay on that side of the ocean, I think it would be a great privilege and a challenge for you." They say travel broadens the mind. Yes, if you have never been outside of America, you cannot imagine the squalor—the mental depression—the pettiness of Japan. Who cares for privileges and challenges at the price of one's own soul?

I am no martyr. Or even a missionary. Once upon a time, I could have dreamed of facing challenges—those sweet, impractical dreams are gone forever. I'm sorry, Blanche, I shouldn't destroy your gossamer illusions. I have had them in my younger days. Now, Japan has hardened and calloused me. I have no love for the Japanese. I do not want to help them. I know that is pretty harsh to condemn all of them. Dr. Simms told us that all people are the same all over the world. But these people are not my people. They would accept a foreigner much more readily than a Nisei. We do not belong here. We are square pegs in a round hole, and every time we twist or turn, we hurt ourselves and the Japs around us.

Wow! I shouldn't have ranted on like that. Perhaps time can heal some of the grudge I feel towards Japanese. Right now, I have an anti-Jap complex, and let me glory in it. Emma knows how it is here, and she knows how awful the condemnation—the sentence—would be to have me stay here all the days of my life.

Perhaps I could forget the sufferings and wrongs I have suffered. I hope so. After all, I wasn't the only one. But I don't see how my distaste for these people could ever metamorphize into philanthropy. I tell you that I am quite happy and content here. That is because it is such a contrast to what I had to go through—living in dirty Japanese homes, the continuous inhibition, the everlasting *enryo*, the arrogance of the men, the inconvenience of not being able to get the little comforts of life, and the agony of pinching on the very necessities of life.

I love the way you said that you were stirred up with conditions in America. That's what is good about America. You can get stirred up—and you find people who agree with you and admire your guts. And I can see why the GIs are dissatisfied too. They have had education in the school of war. And they are not afraid to fight. I'm glad to hear that they are cooperating with the pacifists.

However, my dear sister, I don't think such generalities mean anything to you. Yes, I know, all is not rosy and easy in the "land of freedom" where you are now. But there is such a difference—such a contrast. There, you don't have to worry about the real necessities of life. Now it is such a comfort to me to be able to ask you or Emma or Miye to send me something. Life is too precious and short to be fretted away over the trivialities which are so much missed when not present, or unable to be obtained. "Man shall not live by bread alone"—true, however, without food, life can be desperately miserable. Honestly, when you are hungry, you can't study or concentrate on anything.

I shall never forget how that woman doctor I worked for used to starve me. And Japan is full of such people. Even during peace when food was plentiful, these parsimonious housewives limited the food given to their maids. And the maids had to be content with a few bowls of rice. She was lucky if she got a piece of pickle to go with it. While the family she served was eating meat, and delicious foods. There is so much injustice going on around you that it makes you boil. But you dare not say anything, and gradually, you harden yourself to accept it as inevitable.

I told Rev. Ito that your group had offered to send some families food, and that I had sent you his name. He was so happy about it. He said they are looking forward to it already. I really feel sorry for him. The cruel imprisonment took its toll on his health. He says that he can hardly travel now, and he used to love to travel so much. I went all over Hokkaido and even up to Karafuto with him. He cared for me like a father. That's what made me so mad at

Japan—the injustice of locking up such an uprighteous man just because he was brave enough to stick up for his belief.

You know, I was talking to Marie, my girlfriend who came down with Kay to Kyoto, about the GIs. She says, I bet we know the GIs better than the people back in the States. I think so. We see so much of them. And I think we see them for what they really are—without their reserves up. You don't see any of the racial prejudice among them that we had in California. Except for their prejudice against the Negroes. It's sad how narrow-minded they are towards the Negroes. Somehow, I feel as though we and the Negroes have a vital cause in common. I have heard soldiers say: "We'll have to fight another war—one against the Niggers, when we get back." And other such inhuman statements.

I'm glad that you are studying and making good. I guess all of us girls got the love for studying from Mother. How are you and the cat coming along? And the less said about my husband, the better. For me, he does not exist. Now I am tempted to elaborate. Well, he was tall (nearly 6 feet), dark, and handsome, and aged 30 when we got married, I think. He liked sports, loved to talk and read. Everything seemed ideal—he had diversified interests, loved his family, was healthy and intelligent. He was working for a Jap Shipping Company branch office in Shanghai. His parents thought that it was time he settled down, and he said that anyone whom his mother chose was all right with him. The name of the family is Kinoshita. I had met his sister through a Nisei friend. Two of his sisters were Joshi Dai graduates; his mother had graduated Doshisha Girls School in Kyoto, and his father had spent many years in America. I liked his sister a lot, and the family too.

Everything seemed too good to be true. So, like a fool, I was rushed into marrying him after only talking to him once and seeing him twice. We had a wonderful honeymoon up in the mountains—it was lovely mellow fall. But as soon as we got back to the family, I came down to earth with a bang. We lived with his four sisters and his parents. And, can you believe it—he NEVER spoke to me! It was torture.

And as the days went on, the sisters began to talk about me behind my back, and it was continual *enryo* always. I had an inferiority complex because I do not know all the rules, the "p's and q's" of Jap etiquette. I could have stood the mental torture, the hunger, the injustice—if only he had loved me. But he definitely did not. And I tried to live up to his ideal of a shrinking Jap bride. And how I worked my head off like a fool. I was their maid, and did all the dirty work. If I wanted to go any place, I was so afraid to ask my mother-in-law for permission. He only took me out once. And that once he walked with such long strides, and kept ahead of me. Doggone it, I was going to stand so much but no more.

Now I don't see why I stood all that humiliation, that uncertainty, that cruelty. For cruelty does not consist only of beating or slapping a person. No, it is more lasting, effective, and unobvious when it is slowly applied to the mind and heart. The Jap bride is supposed to: take the smallest piece (if she is honored by having anything offered to her), get up the earliest, go to bed the latest, never express her own opinions, especially if they contradict the opinions of her superiors (everyone is superior to the bride), always smile—never show anger (she should never be angry, in the first place), bow humbly, lick the dirt—O, it's awful. And my DEAR husband never so much as looked at me, let alone talk to me. He completely ignored me. Being a maid to the family would have been much better.

I married him with the understanding that he was to take me back to Shanghai with him. Even that could not be. He left in January, I think. We were married in October. After that, it got worse and worse, living with the in-laws. You wouldn't believe that I was a skinny, nervous wreck. If I heard a pin drop, I would jump for fear. Before he left, he gave me 100 yen and did not say a thing. He never wrote to me. After the war ended, my mother-in-law told me to go some place else. We had never been legally married. In Japan, they do things like that. It is not necessary to get a license to get married. We had a ceremony in a shrine. And it seems like I was divorced just as easily. So now, do you see why I said "the less said about my husband the better"?

I've poured out my sad story to you. Thank God, it is over. And a new, brighter life is beckoning me on and on. Time is a great healer. Now, I want to forget the last five years. Yes, maybe remember it only for the sake of writing about it—but not remembering it so that it will embitter me.

Keep on writing. You don't know how much joy I get from your letters.

Kyoto, April 5, 1946

Dearest Kay,

I was going to write you a long, long letter when I got started writing to little sister Blanche, and got inspired to write four pages. It must be nearly ten now.

Poor child—wonder if I destroyed her sweet pink candy illusions? I poured out my wrath about Japan. And I told her about my dear husband, the Kinoshit.[62] It was kind of fun, going over the stupidity of me to have stood all that humiliation, mental torture, and starvation. What was wrong with me, anyhow? I must not have been myself. And remember how, even long afterwards, I used to jump at everything, out of nervousness and how you used to get madder than hellfire about it?

62. Kay habitually used the derogatory name Kino*shit* because she was incensed at the Kinoshitas' treatment of Mary.

No work to do today. It is nine. No, it is ten. Doggone it—Kay, I wished that you could eat with me. It makes me mad, yet, if I look at it impartially (like our wonderful Massy), perhaps they have their side to it too. And I know you—you are too proud to stoop to such people. At least, Chappy has a heart of gold. I am so glad that you like each other. Kay, have you ever thought: it's like meeting people you've read a novel about, to be seeing the people I've raved to you about.

Well, I must go. Don't let him work you too hard. xxxxxxxxxxx

Kyoto, April 5, 1946

Dearest Miye,

"As cold waters to a thirsty soul, so is good news from a far country." Proverbs 25.25. There, isn't that a fitting quotation to begin with? Now, following is my testimony:[63]

I was lonely, sad, and forlorn. Every day brought me no news. No letters from the people I love. Then the mails got through. I heard from Miye. Furthermore, I kept on hearing from her—sometimes short, sometimes long, sometimes magazines and books, and TODAY, Shoe Polish! I shall now have my shoes shining like a real soldier. Thanks be to Miye. God be praised. Amen.

Remember, Miye, how our church people used to give testimonies? And when the fire would smolder out, how hard a time Yahiro-sensei used to have to get anyone to testify? If it's not spontaneous and voluntary, there's no sense to have testimonies, do you think?

But really, I was overjoyed to get your shoe polish this morning. And doubly glad because Kay is here, and we can share the treasure. She says her B.F. [boyfriend] (a colonel) emphasizes that shoes should always be shined. And just this morning, I confidently told her, "When Miye sends me my shoe polish, we can have dazzling shining shoes." It came so soon. I was surprised. And this afternoon, a letter came from you too. At first when I read about you coming to Japan, I uttered an exclamation of "God forbid." Not that I wouldn't love to see you. But what would poor Nick do? And I don't want you in Japan. You'd be so disillusioned. Although it would be educational.

I'm the only one in the office who gets so much mail, and do I gloat over it! I whoop and yell when I see a letter on my desk, then I tear the envelopes open with the broadest superior grin on my face. Then I cram them into my drawer, and later, like a miser counting his gold coin, I sort them out and gloat and gloat. Now I definitely do not feel like an orphan that nobody loves.

63. Holiness church members were expected to give testimonies at meetings, usually based on passages from the Bible.

Today when I came back from chow, Kay was up at my typewriter banging away. She wrote me a letter, saying that these two females in the office were whispering to each other as though they had a secret about me that everyone knew. And just this morning a CE asked me who Mary Kimoto was, because he had heard about me. When I asked him what, he sniggered and wouldn't tell. Then just now, when I went down to see Kay, her clerk says, "I'm jealous of you," and gave such a meaning sly look. What's it all about? Kay comforted me with "If people talk about you, it means they are thinking about you. And that is better than being a nonentity." That made me feel a little better, that salve on my wounds. Why should I exist in such a way that people would not even talk about me? I want to live fully, and to taste life to its fullest heights and depths. Why should I be afraid of a few waggling tongues?

Kyoto, April 6, 1946

Dearest Miye,

Your shoe polish is just wonderful! Now I feel so well-groomed, to the tips of my toes. I kept raving about it, then when Kay used it this morning, she said, "Why didn't you tell me it was such good shoe polish. It's simply marvelous." I retorted, "I was raving over it, and I only rave over good things." So today, two girls went forth to brave the world with shining shoes.

Today is Army Day. They had a parade which marched in front of I Corps. Of course, we all stuck our heads out of the windows and gaped. There was a certain mighty beauty in seeing the armed soldiers march, all in unison like so many sticks making up a big machine. When they passed in front of our General Woodruff, they saluted. I thought, "A leftover from the Prussians." And I recalled reading how the Germans are impressed by such shows of power. Wonder what the Japanese think about it.

Nothing to write today. It just feels good to write to you every day, even if I don't say anything. Last night I could not sleep, so I quit trying and got up around twelve and read Lord Byron's poetry until two, when I was able to heed the call of Morpheus. I love Lord Byron's poetry about Nature, and his message that we are strengthened by communication with her. Wish I could remember some of the beautiful lines I read. Like, "There is a pleasure in the pathless woods/ There is a rapture in the— " (I have forgotten).[64] All I remember is that I was enchanted by it. And I wondered how a playboy like him could appreciate Nature. I don't care much for Shelley, and Keats will do. Of the three, I like Lord Byron best. They are all together in our literature book *British Prose and Poetry*.

64. "There is a rapture on the lonely shore." *Childe Harold's Pilgrimage*, Ch. 4, st. 178. This is part of the passage with the famous line "I love not man the less but Nature more."

Yesterday, after work, Kay and I wandered around and had a lovely interesting time. We went window shopping. Saw, or rather smelled, some of the most exotic, oriental incense in a satchel. I said I loved it, but not ten yens' worth. Kay copied down an explanation about pearls. I can't figure out what [the writer] was trying to put over. It was a long-drawn-out story about salmon, and about putting shell in an oyster to make the pearls. We saw some Negro women with a man—probably they are in the "Harlem Varieties" USO show tonight. One girl was cute, with a different hair-do. Her hair was straight, and worn up. The other was fat. All the Japs stared at them and good-naturedly laughed. Then, we went into the Red Cross donut stand, and Kay saw an Italian GI whom she had met at the cabaret. He was feeling happy from some intoxicating drinks. He said he'd introduce Kay to his wife, at the counter. We oh-ed and ah-ed, "Is your wife here?" and he took [Kay] to show her [his wife's] picture at the counter. Joke was on us.

We walked and snooped around, seeing the city. Everyone would stare at us, going down the street loudly gabbing in English, but what did we care? They have some of the most [beautiful] lacquer ware and china out now. It's a pleasure to gaze at them. And most of the shops have ridiculous "English" signs out now.

Chappy had invited Kay to sukiyaki dinner, but we had got home so late that he went alone. Tonight he is going again. He said the place was beautiful—a rich home. Kay invited herself and me to go with him. Don't know if I will. I'd like to see a nice Jap home, and how they treat us. Chappy told Kay that he likes me a lot and that he is jealous of Pat, and doesn't see what I see in Pat. Chappy is so warm and soft-hearted. He has a heart of gold. In that way, he is better than Pat. He says, "If you go to Mass. I'm going to look you up." What a contrast that is to Pat. The latter doesn't even want Kay to have his home address. He said that when he gets out of the army, he wants to forget everything and everyone connected with it. Chappy is much better hearted. But then, Pat is better educated and better read. With Chappy, we have very little to talk about. Kay says, "Is it necessary to have the same things to talk about? If you fell in love, that is all that is important." Yes, to a certain extent. But you can't live on love. And the more things you have in common, the more your love can develop, I think.

The clerk just went down to see if there is any mail. He announced after he came back that the Post Office is closed. Heck.

Kyoto, April 10, 1946

Dearest Miye,

O, Miye, I am undergoing emotional turmoil. I feel like I am in the dark, black night. Shapeless dark and sinister arms are trying to pull me under. They are trying to make me forget the light, the heaven of my youth. My ideals, my longings, my dreams. O, God, help me and save me. My head aches. I long for home. O Miye, how I long to see the dear, dear people whom I love with all my heart. My mother who bore me. My father, brother, sisters, and YOU. Will that glad ecstatic day ever come? If there is a God in Heaven who has kept his children through the black, evil days that we had to go through, surely He will continue His blessed Guidance yet.

Tonight, I long for home and those whom my soul lovest. Why was I fated to be cast out here all alone and so far away? Is there any justice?

Miye, I try to be brave, to forget those things which are inevitable. Yet, at times, my thin resistance breaks down and goes to a million smithereens. "Put on the armor of Faith," didn't Paul say?[65] I need some armor stronger than the puny self-defense that I can erect. Every day finds me only older and sliding farther into perdition. The times when I see the Things That Are More Excellent are getting fewer and more far between.

My dear, I am so tired, so tired. Mentally, physically, emotionally. I want to become Nil. Just a nothingness, and float around doing and feeling nothing. I want to forget the ache in my heart. That awful gnawing in the pit of my stomach continually murmuring, I want to go home, I want to see my loved ones. I want to bathe in the bliss of forgetfulness. Forget that I even exist. Forget the wrongs around me. Forget. Forget all in a blessedness of peaceful nothingness.

Maybe I shouldn't even send this. Perhaps it might make you worry.

[Later.] Dear Miye, would you please send me a book of Greek mythology? I'd like to have something small and simple. Gee, Miye, I hate to bother you when you are busy. If it is too much bother, forget it. I want my *Walden* bad, but this Greek mythology is a passing fancy. Yesterday when we were out on Biwako [Biwa Lake] sailing, I didn't know the god of wind, and Pat said it was "Oleos."[66] Couldn't find it in the dictionary, and felt dumb and dissatisfied.

The cherry blossoms are out in all their glory now. They were simply lovely yesterday. I love the faint, delicate pink of the petals. I wonder if I ever wrote to you about the thrill they gave me one year—that was the time

65. "Let us put on the armor of light." Rom. 13: 12.

66. Actually a goddess, Athena.

I learned to love them. No, I guess I never [did], since it was after the war. How it all comes back to me now. That winter had been so hard—so hard. For war had started, I had been dumped back onto the land I had wanted to leave, and I had struggled and cried as I had never before in all my life. That winter was really hard. I worked at the woman doctor's home while going to school. Had to work like a maid, and take the indignities of a maid. That winter had been so cold—my hands had cracked from using that icy cold water to scrub floors on my hands and knees. But I had stood it and gone through with it. Life was beginning to start anew for me, for I had found some work as [a] tutor and translator; so I left that witch of a doctor. And I used to go to the Ueno Library to get material for translating. After I climbed the hill, lo and behold! A whole row of lovely cherry blossoms met my eyes. How beautiful they looked to me! It meant that the cold, cruel winter was gone. Hope lay ahead. Warm weather was coming, and less of a struggle against the elements. Honestly, Miye, tears just flooded my eyes when I beheld those harbingers of Spring and Hope and New Life. Delicate cherry blossoms, bringing me Beauty and Joy. They have survived the cruel winter too. Life goes on, and joyfully. The message and comfort and delight I was blessed with by those blossoms shall dwell with me all the days of my life.[67] I have never before or since received such a thrill from the cherry blossoms.

Kyoto, April 13, 1946

Dearest Miye,

Just in case your DT[68] got the better of you, I am sending a copy of this letter to Maryland. I was so disappointed when I received your letter of 3 April saying that you hadn't heard from me when I had been writing every single day. Then I figured that the letters had been going to Richmond. Well, when I write a letter, I feel so much better if I know that it is going to reach you soon, and maybe give you a little pleasure. I hate to think of the letters piling up at Richmond, and you going home to no letters from me. Because I feel so good when I hear from you, and perhaps you feel the same about me. The solution of the problem, think I, is for me to write to two addresses. If the letters go to Md. after you have left, let them burn them up, because I am making a carbon copy, sending one to Richmond. Isn't that bright?

Miye, my love, I liked your poem so much that I immediately made two copies of it, tacked one up on the stand near my desk, and gave one to Kay. Who wrote it? It sounds like Omar Khayyam. And the other quote you sent

67. An allusion to Psalms 23: 6: "Surely goodness and mercy shall follow me all the days of my life and I shall dwell in the house of the Lord forever."

68. Miye's thesis adviser, who was giving her a hard time.

me about the true lovers of God and the most ascetic are joyful. I love the things you send me. You don't know how they inspire me and thrill me. Coming from you gives it a special flavor.

After I typed the first page of this letter, I went with Kay to the third floor where they have opened up the ice-cream bar. We can get: ice cream, pie, coffee, donuts. Only they say that it is off limits to civilians. Or rather, to foreign nationals. We intend to go down until we get kicked out. But I really don't want any, since we get plenty of food now. And then, we snooped around the Special Service, and lo and behold, *Walden* was right out on the table. Well, I had a sweater on, and all of a sudden, it was bulging in the most unbecoming angles. Anyway, Miye, you won't have to send me the book, as I had requested. (Have some work now.)

That was done quickly. Helped Suzie correct some errors. The lieutenant was around asking for some help, and when he mentioned dictation, I popped up with, "I can't take shorthand." One of these days, I'll probably be sorry that I wasn't more willing to work my head off, but at the present I want to forget "past Regrets and future Fears."[69] I'd much rather rattle off to you than be doing some inane typing.

I have been wanting to write to you about the interesting incident Kay and I witnessed. We were strolling home from Daiken to the hotel, window-shopping and ambling along, airing our views, when we were attracted by a big mob of people all crowded around a man. We tried to find out what he had. Everyone was so intent upon listening to him that no one would inform us, so we strained our necks, and got on tiptoe, trying to look over the heads of those around him. It was out on a vacant lot, in a busy section of town. All he said that we could hear was, "For those who can't afford it, I will give these to you free. For others, they are two yen apiece." And he started to sell envelopes, brown and small. How they clamored to buy! Mostly men—there were young boys, too. They fought to give him the money. Kay asked several men what it was, but they only looked embarrassed and puzzled, and did not answer. That made us all the more curious. Finally, when Kay asked a woman, she received an answer. Each envelope contains about five pieces of onion-skin white paper, of size around two by four inches. Purpose: Write any question you want answered on the paper, heat the paper by holding it above some charcoal, and there will appear the answer [to] the question. We were dumbfounded when we heard that. If that isn't a fake, I don't know what is. And of all the stupid gullible people! That goes to show how willing the people are now to believe anything that comes along. Put some paper in an envelope, and sell it for two yen. And two yen must count, now that the amount a person can draw out of the bank is limited.

69. *The Rubáiyát of Omar Khayyám* (Fitzgerald trans., 1959), verse 16.

After we left that bunch, we snooped in at a little store where they make stripes, etc. for the GIs and officers. Kay tried to get an eagle for that colonel of hers, but they didn't have any. Then we got interested in [the man's] wares. He had a little tiny store on the corner of the block. I saw a coin I wanted, since I had lost one just like it that the major in our section had given to me to find out what it was. [The shopkeeper] gave it to me, making me very happy. Then he showed us some imitation (although I never knew it was imitation) coral, and gave Kay and me some pretty carved hair decorations. We were thrilled over them. So Kay gave him some chocolate candy that she had in her purse, and he was happy, making all three of us happy. We had an interesting visit with him. Kay later said that he must have been eccentric. We felt as though we had found a kindred soul. You should have seen his carefully kept trinkets on the wall. He had everything, from coins, charms, dolls down to samisen stands. No, take the plural off—he [had] only one of each.

One officer has gone home already, two are ready to go, and one more is leaving very soon. The one who is leaving soon is a warrant officer, and I liked him. He used to give me candy once in a while. And he was quiet, and worked hard and inconspicuously. I liked to do his typing because his writing was legible, and he used good English—in fact, he used some words that I was not familiar with, which immediately made me feel respect and awe for his superior vocabulary. He's wrapping up some boxes now, and I'd like to help him, only I'm afraid to because others will think that I am "brown-nosing."

Last night I read a good article about the enlisted men in the army, in *Life* mag. Said that the reason hardly any EM want to re-enlist is because of the caste system. That certainly is right. Why must they have it? It humiliates the EM something awful. Dr. Simms was very much against it. Pat is so bitter towards all officers. He says an EM is not allowed to have any self-respect at all. He didn't mind it so much during the war, but now it is all nonsense. You can feel that underlying bitterness and hatred in all thinking—or even unthinking—EMs.

By the way, I heard from Dr. Simms yesterday. He said for you to be sure to look him up. He even gave me his phone number to give to you, but I left it at home because I thought you would go to Calif anyway. He said he'd take you to some Japanese dinner. O, I do so wish that you would, could see him. My life has been so enriched by his friendship and his kind fatherly advice. I am glad that he is home.

We like to think that if we have found a friend, we can rely on him forever. No, the GIs are so transient. How they come and go. But some of them are so nice—they ask us to come and see them if we get back to the States. Our mess sergeant at Osaka even gave us directions how to get to his home in New York. What a contrast to some who refuse to let you have even their addresses!

Kyoto, April 16, 1946

Dearest Miye,

What a load off my mind! I just wrote to Alice Ushihara. I hope that I hear from her soon, and when I do, I'll let you know. And I was cleaning out my very messy drawer today when I found your relatives' address. What do you want me to do about it? I guess I should let them know that you-all are safe and sound, but remember—in physics we learned the law of—O, what was that—one of Newton's laws stating that a body at rest continues in that state until acted upon by force, and a body in motion continues in motion—Is it the law of momentum? Anyway, in obedience to this law, I do not exert myself until absolutely unavoidable. Your question as to whether I wrote Alice pricked my tiny, shriveled-up conscience into writing.

We certainly did have a good time Sunday evening when we went to the show. We went early—Kay and I. Since we could not lure any stupid GIs (or cared to), I took her, and she took me. We sat down, and aired our crazy views on life in loud voices. (We had gone early to get good seats). All GIs around us—no dates are allowed at USO shows, but we foreign nationals are allowed to go to any show. Soon the GI in front of us looked back and started talking to us. "Ah, there was our victim for the evening," thought we two dames. And did we give him the woiks. He asked us, in the course of our loud conversation, what we were. I informed him, innocently, that Kay was half Korean and half Chinee, while I was Gypsy. He wouldn't believe it—can you imagine, Miye, he dared to doubt our veracity. He said, "You told me you came from California. Go on!" (He was a Norwegian from South Dakota, and looked as though he had been scrubbed with soap, so clean and blond). Me: "Why, of course, there are gypsies in California. First I went up and down the state, then crossways, then diagonal." Such nonsense continued, and all the GIs around were astonished at our giggling, and loud chattiness. He said, "You're giving me a line," and Kay looked so prettily hurt, and pouted, "Why we have no lines, only curves." He said that we were making a fool out of him, but he always came back for more. Said he made no headway talking to us, because if he went one step forward, he slipped two back. It was a lot of fun, and both of us were in [a] merry mood for mischief. You know, it's so darn much fun being crazy. And to shout big words and astonish the soldiers with our huge vocabulary. Just between you and me, I believe that we can speak better English than most of them. Beat them at their own game.

Yesterday, I bought myself a new pair of shoes, and have I been gloating over them! No, they are second-hand, but they are toeless and cute. O, yes, my dearest, would you please send me some black shoe polish? These shoes are black, and I want to keep them nice and shining. They make my feet look small. Today, when I complained to Pat and Paul that my feet hurt, Paul says,

"Well, if you tried to get a quart in a pint bottle, what do you think would happen?" What price vanity.

Sunday night, after the show, Kay and I went on such a heavenly walk—it was really out of this world. I want to write to you about it, yet words fail me. It was a lovely quiet moonlight night. We walked to the Kamo river,[70] and the dark murky waters were touched with gold from the precious reflection of the moon. It was all so quiet, peaceful, and fantastic. It seemed as though we had lost our earthly ties, and had floated up to a new, and vague, dream Paradise. Then we saw a willow tree, lit by the streetlamp. It seemed as though it were made of frail glass, of creamy-pale-green hue. And as we gazed, it looked as though it had frozen, and we were enchanted with the wonder of it all. Then the breeze moved the faint-glistening glass leaves, and we were mystified with the wonder of life and motion. For all of a sudden the tree lost its glassiness and sterility, and it became alive, vital, and breathing. We saw in it a kindred soul, and the mystery of our lives was inherent in the form before us, communing to us in the language of the universe.

We continued our little stroll into fairyland, following the edge of the water. We had to cross a canal which plunged over a dam into mighty froth and pure white suds of joyful living. O, it was wonderful, and all that we could say was, "Isn't it beau-ti-ful!" We came upon a tiny, dainty Niagara—so frail, yet wide and sure of itself. And we followed up the river, flowing so silently on in black, cool comfort.

Our thoughts were suddenly brought back abruptly by coming up to the bridge, right ahead of us. How were we to get up? Kay blithely climbed up, and I followed, thanks to her pulling me. How she ever made it, I don't know. It was way above our heads, and there was no place to get a foothold. My hat's off to her.

So ended our little peek into enchantment. But as Wordsworth says, "They flash upon that inward eye, Which is the bliss of solitude."[71] The memory of that night will be with me forever, and I shall treasure it as one of the precious gems in [my] chest of memories.

Miye, it is so nice and quiet in the office this afternoon. It is ideal for writing. I am lucky that I get time to write like this. Some girls never get a free moment.

But I must go, and I shall write again. Kay received a heart-warming letter from Dr. Simms. I was going to copy it, and send you one copy, but I couldn't find it this morning.

Good-bye. I wonder where you are now.

70. The Kamogawa, the river running through the old Heian capital, often mentioned in Japanese literature.

71. From "I Wandered Lonely as a Cloud" (1807).

Kyoto, April 17, 1946

Dearest Miye,

Say, will you do me a favor? Bawl me out good and proper for mental and physical laziness. Otherwise, I will never write no story for nobody. Just can't buckle down to it. At times, I lecture myself, but to no avail. Mary will not listen. She snubs her better self, and forgets her in some worldly pursuit. Now, coming from you, it might be a little more effective.

Read parts of *Walden* last night and got consolation from it. Was in [a] pretty bad mood, way down in the dumps after leaving Pat because he doesn't care at all about me, and I do [care for him], and it isn't fair. And I'm so tired of being alone, of being left by GIs who don't care at all, of struggling for myself. I want to settle down, and never move again. I want a little cottage with blue ruffled curtains and potted geraniums at the window, with a husband to love and be loved by, with a little farm, with chickens, pig, cow, with a great big family—just oodles of kids. To heck with dreams and fighting and thinking and arguing and wanting to be something I am not. Gee, Miye, last night I wanted to go for another enchanted walk down the river. But I was afraid to go by myself very far, so I was looking down from the bridge, when some GIs came along and put their filthy arms around me. That broke all my poetic atmosphere, and it was displaced by distemper. That surely made me mad! But I can't blame them, because a woman out alone at that time of night is a suspicious character. One good thing about the GIs, they will leave you alone if you spit blood like a horned toad, or ruffle up your feathers like [a] hen with chicks, or throw out your needles like a porcupine. And that is why I am infinitely afraid of Jap men—they have no sense—they will chase and scare the living daylights out of you, and no spitting or ruffling or needling will discourage them.

Why, I've plumb forgot to tell you that I phoned up the Yokohama US Consulate today and got an appointment to register to repatriate. Guess what—it is set for August 27. They ask us questions, then they send it all back to Washington, where each case is decided. Maybe, maybe our dreams will come true. O, the very thought makes goose pimples come out all over me.

This is all that I am going to write today. *Owari* [The end]. That is what the Japs say when they finish their speeches, and it is so dumb. I suppose you know that thirty-eight women were elected to Parliament—or is it Diet? Among them Mrs. Ichikawa, the birth-control advocate.

Kyoto, April 17, 1946

Dearest Kay,

How goes it on Earth?[72] Have you met Satan? If not, why not, for "And the Lord said unto Satan, whence comest thou? Then Satan answered the Lord, and said, From going to and fro in the earth, and from walking up and down in it."[73] Now, surely Satan is going up and down and to and fro, and you must have met him. NO, I'm not referring to the devils—they keep their place in Hell.

Quote: Col. Duncan gets all excited. He doesn't know what he is doing. He gets all flabbergasted. Unquote. Guess where I got that? None other than Sgt. Heeennnrrrryyyyy.

O, Kay, I am so tired. But I did done and went accomplished a lot, a mountain of work, no a heap of pleasure, a book of letters, for I wrote: 1. Dr. Simms, 2. Kenneth John (formerly a clerk in Signal), 3. Elsa (a former girlfriend along with Miye), 4. Miye, 5. You. Now ain't that a lot for one day? All I want to do is write Kimi-chan but I am completely exhausted, worn-out, run-down. (Wait a minute, I'll get my big blue book and I will bowl you ovah). Now I'll give you the woiks: Kay, I am drained, empty, depleted, used up, consumed, spent, tired, fatigued, debilitated, enervated, prostrated. There, you never [thought] that one hooman beem could be all those things, did you? Well, here she be in person.

Twenty minutes more to go. And I am hungered. Wait a minute, I'll look up that passage in the Bible. Wonder if I can locate it. In my hunt, I came upon this gem:

> Behold, I send you forth as sheep in the midst of wolves:
> be ye therefore wise as serpents, and harmless as doves.[74]

Heed that, my love, and never wilt thou get your little heart broken.

Kyoto, April 19, 1946

Dearest Kay,

Gee, I love Thoreau. He gives me so much consolation, and strikes a resounding note. And his: "Do not seek so anxiously to be developed, to subject yourself to many influences to be played on; it is all dissipation," is what I had been thinking, yet was not able to formulate it into distinct words like he did. That's what I thought deep down that time when you said that we must get

72. A reference to Kay's place of work. Mary, whose office was a floor above, was in "heaven," and the basement was "hell."

73. Job 1:7.

74. Matt. 10:16.

experiences in order to write—like going out with GIs, picking them up at the station and pretending that we could not speak English, just for the sake of the experience. By some experiences we lose more than we gain.

When I read him, I resolve to live a higher and better life. To search after truth and good. I love his, "Do not trouble yourself much to get new things, whether clothes or friends," because it coincides with my laziness to develop myself socially. And God does see that I do not want society.

Thoreau was the advocate of the simple life. My mother was like that. I used to clutter up my room with junk and trinkets, and she wouldn't like it because she said that all it did was collect dust. And I like the Japanese idea of decoration—like the story of the man who had a scroll, a vase, and a—what was the other one? And he took them out one at a time. Yes, that is one thing good about Japan—their idea of beauty in simplicity.

Kyoto, April 20, 1946

Dearest Miye,

I wonder where you are now. Are you still in Maryland or have you moved to Richmond with your Nick? I can't fill in your background, and it is hard to think of you with undetermined surroundings.

Gee, Miye, please continue to write to me. I'll miss your letters so much, to heck with rules and regulations. I haven't heard of it officially[75]—only rumors, so that I am ignorant. And if I've gotten away with it so far, perhaps my good luck will continue. This time, please address me at Chaplains' Section instead of IG Section. But I am only getting mail from you and family now, because it's better not to spread my correspondence too far, and besides, it's only you that I really care to hear from.

Pat left yesterday. Somehow, the place seems so bare and missing without him. I try not to think of it. But I did get very attached to him, and now feel quite lost. My tranquility and peace of mind are gone. That dull ache inside me—the stricture in my throat—the restlessness and sadness gnawing in me—these must be due to missing him. God, if I could only have a good cry and get it over with! But no, it just keeps coming back in spurts. And whenever I have nothing to occupy my mind, I think of him, and it hurts.

Now that both of your shoulders are drenching, let me give you a little sunshine to dry them off.

Miye, I am so thankful for you and for my family. No matter what happens to me, I know that you will always be faithful unto death for me. It seems to me that childhood upbringing has an awful lot to do with one's character.

75. That is, of the ban on foreign nationals' using the APO.

And as I've told you before, our common childhood and adolescence surely did mould us into one form.

Yesterday, Kay and I rode with our truck driver all over Kyoto. It was a lot of fun. He took us to the hotel, then we asked him if he wouldn't take us for a ride. Said that he had to take some English sailors around, so we tagged along. There were four Aussies, and were they inebriated! We went way up the mountain to a cabaret, but it wasn't open yet, and by that time, Kay and I kept hollering, "I wunna go home," so the driver took them down to the station. It was funny, hearing their King's English, and we mimicked them. They asked us, "Are you from the Steyetes?" (to rhyme with "heights"). One of them we couldn't understand at all. They didn't like for us to talk their way, saying, "You distahb us." On the way, the driver hit an old woman, knocking her over. I felt sorry for her, but am sure that she was not hurt. She was more frightened than anything else. These people have no traffic-consciousness at all. She was jay-walking, or rather, hobbling. They put their heads down and take off. It's a wonder that more people are not hurt than they are. Guess that's why the speed limit is 20 miles per hour.

That MP just came up and told me that the MP at the gate would like to take me to the show tonight. Think I'll go because I hate to be by myself and moan and groan. If I go to a show, I can forget it for a little while.

Jimmy, the clerk in our office, let me read a letter from his aunt. It surely was a homey, nice letter. That's what the soldiers need to keep up their morale. Honestly, I think letters like that are the greatest contribution a woman can give towards making the occupation a success, for they keep the boys in touch with the best of America.

Kay just called up, saying that she didn't want to go. Had to hang up because the Col. is in now, and I'm not supposed to get phone calls.

Good-bye. Give Nick my regards for me.

Kyoto, April 23, 1946

Dearest Miye,

Two letters from you, and I am happy again. I love all the good, sound philosophy you put into them, too. Now you must be getting ready to go to Berkeley. Did you see Dr. Simms? I certainly hope that you did.

Sunday, I promised my mother I would go to church on Easter, so I was resolved to go, but I was feeling so dead that I did not force myself. But, as you said, my conscience does prick me at times, so Kay read about the resurrection in all four gospels. That eased my little, shriveled-up conscience a little. When we were in the midst of our private services, a Jap friend, Mr. Sawa whom we call "Little Boy Blue," came to see us, so we made him suffer through the reading. He was too polite to say anything. Let me find what Thoreau says about church. Aw, heck, I can't find it. I'll come upon it some day, and give it to you. It is about hypocritical people sitting in stuffy churches when it would be much better to worship God out-of-doors.

Kay and I hitched a jeep ride with a nice GI who took us riding way up a mountain. It was so beautiful to look down on the green, neat valley below. He was nice and we liked him, Kay especially. He was on restriction because he had a fight with a lieutenant. He said that if more of the GIs would stick up for their rights, things would not be so bad.

I'm not missing Pat as much as I thought I would. I did miss him a lot for three or four days, but by now, I have forgotten him somewhat. There are so many men here. Now I am going with an interesting GI named Scotty. He is from Kansas, is the son of a prof, took mechanical engineering at Kansas State, is five-foot-seven when he stands up straight, which is seldom, has a moustache, and in general, reminds me of Chiaki-san. He had a strict religious upbringing, had a nervous breakdown in college, is talkative and has a good vocabulary. He is in charge of Special Troops Supply in the Daiken Building. He wanted to go with me before I started to go with Pat, but I kind of gravitated to Pat. Now that he has gone, Scotty said that he would be his replacement. Tonight I think I'll go to the movies with him. We went once before. And then, on Sunday, we picked him up when we were riding. He does things on the spur of the moment, just like us. We brought him back to the hotel, then tried to psychoanalyze the poor victim, until he cried for mercy. But, anyway, I am so flattered when someone is interested in me that I do not put them off too much.

I'm so glad that I found out you are going to Berkeley at the end of the month. I hope a lot of my letters are there waiting for you. Now I can fill in a background for you. Nick needs you. He must be a brilliant boy. Well, he'd have to have brains to appreciate you.

This morning, in my gadding about, I went to see that Chinese soldier in the pharmacist section of the dispensary. He lent me some best-sellers a couple of years back. I'm interested in him. He said that he is a lieutenant in the Chinese army. He came from Shanghai. I want to talk to him. And then, we discovered some very interesting foreigners in our hotel the other evening. A Mr. Wilson is a Swede who has been in Japan for thirty-five years. He was Little Boy Blue's English teacher in college in Osaka. He was a true scholar, athlete, and all-around man. He was so very interesting. And his friend, a Spaniard, was interesting too.[76] They are individualists. I love people who are

76. José Luis Alvarez, who had come to Japan in 1935 as chargé d'affaires for the Republican government. Unable to return home when Franco seized power, he supported himself by teaching Spanish in a university in Osaka and at the Army School.

not afraid to be themselves. I asked the Spaniard for a history book of Japan, and he asked me if I would swear to God, Allah, and Buddha that I would return it. I said, "If I only had a Bible here, I'd swear on it." Then, there was a Shakespeare there, so I put my hand on it, and solemnly swore. He said, "That is like a Bible of Literature, so it will do."

Enough of such chat. I hope that you are well and happy. If you saw Dr. Simms, tell me all about him. And what you did. They haven't said anything to me about not getting mail, so please continue. I am hearing only from you and family. They can't do anything to me because I am a civilian, anyway.

Kyoto, April 24, 1946

Dearest Miye,

I have your letter open before me now, and my eyes lit on, "Hurry and get that best seller done." Miye, you have me feel like a really good-for-nothing. Why is it that I can't get it done? I can't even begin on it. What do I do with all my time, anyway? I go to shows altogether too much. I don't want to go, but Kay begs me so much, that I often give in. Wish she had someone to take her. Well, she has on Thurs. and Friday.

Last night I read a little more of *Bernadette*.[77] Somehow, I can't concentrate at all. Just today I was talking to Sally, the boy who works in the chaplains' section, and he said that he didn't know what was wrong with him—he couldn't remember anything, or get anything done. And Scotty says he feels that he is going to lose his mind. He told Kay that when he was in the Philippines, he had a nervous breakdown so that he wouldn't have to go to the front lines. And that he had it on purpose. You know, he has brains. He says, "I loathe physical exertion." He said to call him [a] *character*, and he surely is one, if there ever was one. Reminds me faintly of "Feebly-growing on his chin."[78] Remember?

Are you going to get your degree? I'm right proud of you, for I trust that you now have MA tacked on the back of your name. Ain't that wunnerful?

I really envy you for all the famous actresses you are seeing in the flesh and blood. How I wish that I could go with you to snoop around NY and New Orleans, etc. Be sure to tell me all about it. Your Nick must be a brainstorm. I like him so much, and know that you are happy together.

I don't remember Grace at all. Who is she? In fact, I remember very few people. Did you read that article in the *Reader's Digest* quite a while back, no it wasn't—it was in the March 1946 one—about how to enjoy a bad memory?

77. *The Song of Bernadette* (1942) by Franz Werfel (1890–1945).

78. Mary's debating partner at Ceres High. He was in the same graduating class as Miye and Mary at MJC. The name originated in their vast amusement over the two readings of "down" in a sentence he had used: "He had a feebly growing down on his chin."

Well, I sure enjoyed it. I have a bad memory, and have an inferiority complex about it until I read such uplifting articles.

Kay didn't come to work today. She was feeling sick. When she called me up at noon, she said that she was in bed sleeping all morning. She lives so intensely that she has to rest up once in a while. If I have learned anything through age, it is that my poor body can't take all the punishment it did when it was young and gay. So I take it easy. Health surely is important. I've found that out through sad experience.

The other day, the clerk comes around and says, "I don't see what you have to write about. Look, we do the same things every day, and it is all boring." Perhaps so, in his case, but for me life is new and different and interesting. And if it is to you, I could write and write and write. Just what I am thinking would fill pages. The girls here say, "What do you write about? Teach us how to write letters." Things like that can't be taught. Look at me with my Holier-than-Thou attitude again.

They say that we have fresh eggs, ice cream, and fresh meat and vegetables at our hotel now. I haven't eaten there for the last two or three days. For one thing, we haven't been paid for the last month, and I have exactly one yen left to my name now. It's fun to be so poor, when it doesn't hurt me. I eat with Paul in the basement here, and they eat on Tuesday nights here so that they won't have to go back to the company where they give lectures, and keep the GIs from leaving. Why do they do that on Tuesdays when it is date night at the theater? The stupid army, as usual. Well, I cook for Paul, and we are both satisfied.

We've had very little work to do recently, thank goodness. I've got it quite nice here. Am very free, and go gallivanting all over the building. Have discovered some rather kindred souls. I must have told you about that Chinese lieutenant in the dispensary. He gave me *Frenchman's Creek* and *The Chiffon Scarf* since I told him that I wouldn't have time to read *Gone with the Wind.*[79] Doubt if I'll read them, the covers are so cheap-looking. Some night, I'll curl up in my room and read. I guess after I get to the Chaplains', I will have more time to read.

Kyoto, April 25, 1946

Dearest Miye,

This morning I feel wonderful. And I'm in a writing mood. So I love nothing better than to write off to you, whatever comes into my mind. Just finished typing the letter from Mr. Sawa to Kay and me. Thought you might

79. All three were novels by women. Daphne du Maurier, who wrote *Frenchman's Creek*, is probably best known as the author of *Rebecca. The Chiffon Scarf* was a work of the popular mystery writer Mignon Eberhart.

like it, so made out a copy for you, too, which I am enclosing. We call him "Little Boy Blue." He is very cute. A Japanese boy of about twenty-two who is growing up. He has been protected and comes from quite a good family. He is what you call "*ojohin*," I guess. Refined, quiet, thoughtful. And best of all, he likes us. Of course, we like him a lot, too, though perhaps very maternally. His letter was nearly all in one paragraph, which I did not realize until I had typed over half of it. So when I thought of it, I made a new paragraph. He wrote it in English. It's very good for a native here.

Did I tell you about the time he came to see us? He came once on Sat. evening, and we talked with him and Mr. Wilson, who was his English teacher in college in Osaka. It's so funny the way Little Boy Blue speaks English—he uses words like they have in literature and the dictionary—not the everyday, trite expressions which we always use. For instance, he said, "I am oblivious." We looked at each other, and couldn't make out what he was trying to put across, and he, seeing our predicament, added, "Forgetful." I told Kay that I was going to have pad and pencil the next time we spoke in English to Little Boy Blue because he said the funniest things, and some of them apt. Once he told us not to be so ribald, and that sent us scurrying for our dictionaries. I know that you'd like him. He says that Nisei—especially girls—do not give the Japs a good impression. And I asked him to teach me Japanese. If only he didn't live so far away—in Osaka—we could see more of him. Poor boy, he looks so lost and like he is living in the clouds. But he has a sense of humor, and he tolerates us.

I like Japanese boys like him. Too bad there are not more of them. He took the entrance exam to the Imperial University in Kyoto, but does not know if he passed it yet. Hope that he did.

Last night we had such a good time. First of all, about six o'clock Mitchell, a GI who drives a jeep, came after us, and we went with him to a stationery shop that Kay had found, where they paint pictures on paper. It was raining cats and dogs, but we had a roaring good time. He's crazy, and in the right way. We went to the store, and in there were hanging lots of rag dolls. Well, what does Mitch do but buy whole bunches of them. Poor woman, he was almost depriving her of her decorations. Foreign nationals are not allowed to go to cabarets, but he offered to take Kay—me having a date with Scotty, he couldn't take me with his friend. Up to now, all GIs had refused to take us since they have the ruling, but Mitch says, "Those MOPushers (MPs) in front only need the right kind of handling." So he took her. We like people who are not afraid to defy rules and regulations.

Here it is afternoon, and my inspiration and vitality are at an ebb. You know, I could write a book on Scotty, but yet, on second thought, perhaps I couldn't. How he loves to talk. He was going to take me to the show last night. But it was raining cats and dogs. We started out bravely towards the theater, which is only two blocks away. We began to be soaking wet, so the first shelter we saw, we crept in. It was all so crazy. We stood out for quite a while, until he suggested that we go in the store, so we did. It was a camera shop, and they were very nice to us, letting us sit in their easy chairs, and bringing us hot tea. So we just sat and gabbed. Mostly gabbing on his side, and listening on mine. He doesn't like it because I stick up for Japan, and says, "What nationality are you, anyway?" I retort, "You say that you invariably stick up for the underdog, just for the sake of a good argument, and I can't resist doing the same." He is only twenty, but looks at least twenty-five. Wears his hair long, and has a mustache and glasses. Quite a queer.[80] He fascinates me. Too bad that he will be going home in a few weeks. He said that he used to read the Bible a lot before, and that he took a three-year course in it. I don't know how much to believe of what he spiels off. Anyway, he gives me mental stimuli, which I need very badly. And his interests correspond very much to mine.

Tonight Francis is taking Kay to the show. O, I never told you what else happened last night. Well, the people at the store seemed to be getting ready for bed, so we bid them *sayonara*, and ventured out in the rain again, back to the hotel. It was past 9:30. Bet the poor kid got soaking wet going back to the Daiken bldg. where he stays. I went up to my room, but Kay was not home yet. So I put my hair up in curlers when Francis came. He didn't recognize me until after I'd talked to him a while, then he burst out, "O, you're Mary!" I asked him to the parlor, but he says, "I'm wet all over, and if I should sit down, it would soak in." He's not afraid to be himself, and we like him for it. Yesterday was his last day of restriction for talking back to a lieutenant. Hope he doesn't get himself into any more trouble.

So you see, I just can't get down to writing or reading or studying. In a way, I'm glad that Pat went home, for otherwise I would be spending all my time with him and missing out on talking to Scotty and some other people.

Work keeps interfering when I want to write to you. So I think I'll quit for the day. My hair is a mess—just flying over all creation. It is three, and so only one more hour until freedom. Good-bye, and keep Nick happy.

Kyoto, April 26, 1946

Dearest Miye,

It's a beautiful morning, and if I were a bird now I would fly to the very top of some luscious blossoming tree and sing and chirp to my heart's con-

80. Mary meant "what a character." At that time she was ignorant of the sexual meaning attached to the word.

tent. If I were a rooster I would hop to the top of the fence and crow. If I were a peacock, I would expand my tail feathers and strut. But being only a homo sap, I climb only to the top of the Daiken and type out my heart to you.

The morning started out wonderfully. Took a shower, had a delicious breakfast, rode to work with Mitchell, and gabbed and laughed all the way. Then, after we got to Daiken, Francis was there driving the truck for the brass, and we chatted with him. Waiting for the elevator, we met Homer Clark, the Signal clerk, and yapped with him. I left Kay, and when I reached the office, Sgt. Henry tells me to go down and get Jacko, the Jap driver. So I went on down, and stopped in on Scotty and his replacement, yapped again, and then brought up Jacko. And here I am.

Last night, what a bore that blind date turned out to be! He was a country bumpkin from Oklahoma, quiet, and uneventful. Never, never again will I ever go with someone I don't know! But then, Francis was with Kay, so we had fun. They came around six. Having an hour and a half before the show, we went for a walk to the Kamo River. Our little blue, pure stream had changed overnight into a rushing, muddy torrent. It's because the rains came. Then we followed the other canal up to the lake-like place, and Francis's eyes alighted on a big canoe on the opposite side. Says he, "When I see a boat, I go crazy!" and he climbed over barbed wire fences to get to it. It was a huge thing, about thirty feet long, and rowed by a single oar in back—a Jap way. Poor Francis didn't know how to work that kind of an oar, and he was sweating away. Johnny was the other guy. He pulled us along the shore. Then, about that [time] Francis had found out how to work it. Now that really is a marvel, and very American. He tries everything. I heard that it is quite an art to work one of those things, too. A Jap, if he knows nothing about it, leaves it alone. He has very little initiative or curiosity. All the people living around the lake came out to see the soldiers rowing that boat. Thank God, it was getting dark. Francis said that he had never worked so hard since he joined the army.

You know what—this surely made us mad! Francis said that Father Gefell, the Catholic chaplain, had reported on him! Of all the mean tricks! You see, Francis took us to the Chaplains' because I had to go see about my job. While Kay and I were in the living room talking to the fathers, Father Gefell looked out of the window, frowned and said, "Why, that's the driver who didn't get the truck for us this morning." Later, Francis said that he had driven Father Gefell around, and that he was a good guy, and talked to him. Then that dirty Father Gefell reports to Francis's commanding officer that he had women in his jeep, which is not allowed. Now if that isn't dirty, I don't know what is! My estimation of the chaplains has taken a sudden and decisive drop. And just when Francis had done us a favor, too. It wouldn't be so bad if I hadn't got a ride from him in order to make it on time to the Chaplains'! But Francis takes it all so nonchalantly. He tosses it off with, "They've got the rank, why shouldn't they report me? When I first came into the army, I used to get mad at all the dirty deals they gave me, but now I am used to it, and I don't get mad. They want to get me mad, so I don't and fool them. They can't do anything to me—only a Pfc." You know, Francis is just wonderful. And he never mentioned it until last night. He's so natural and carefree and happy. How much better it is to be like that than a brown-noser with stripes or brass, always afraid that he will be busted.

Tonight I fully intend to stay home. I've been gadding about altogether too much for my own good. I like Scotty a lot, though. He certainly interests me. Such a queer. I bet he would be interesting to know in a couple or five or ten years—as yet, he is young and undeveloped.

Wish Kay weren't leaving so soon. I'll be alone again. No one to holler around with. Whenever we go to the dining room at the hotel, we are the only ones who make any noise. The others are eating so politely and smugly and wearisomely. Last night, we pounced upon Sensei, which being interpreted is Teacher. The Spaniard. He told us we made too much noise, and put his finger to his lips and looked sly and cute, with his round blue eyes sparkling. We spoke to him in Japanese. He says some of the most inspirational things. He said that we could go to the classes in Music Appreciation of the army, because he had asked if we could. Isn't that nice of him? He said that it would do us good, that it would aid us towards perfection. And when we informed him that Kay is going to go back to school in Tokyo, he says, "*Kokoro no chikashitsu kara*—Congratulations." "From the basement of my soul—Congratulations." Now, isn't that right clever? Further, he says, lots of people think only of the immediate future, of earning money, but that it is better to go to school, for someone who has had learning sees things through different eyes. For instance, like a piece of paper, one who is learned, sees it as it were, with X-ray eyes. We went away from him all inspired and feeling as though we had taken a breath of pure and heart-warming air.

It's time for me to go to chow. Good-by.

Kyoto, April 26, 1946

Dearest Miye,

I love you, Miye. You tell me that I am not fat. I love you to pieces. You are the only one who feeds my vanity. And I love it, but I love you more.

Received your wonderful letters of 16 and 17 April today, and was I happy! The more I get of your letters, the more I love them and you. It's just like Nick to send you my letters. Here I was worried that you might not be getting them. I should have trusted him more. O, I'm so glad that you have found a man worthy of you. Take care of him, and grow fruitful and multiply. Honestly, I think your kids are going to be blessed with a happy home life, understanding parents, and inspirational surroundings.

Wrote to you this morning, and here it is afternoon, but your letters made me so happy that I couldn't refrain from writing. At noon, Kay and I phoned up Chappy at the hotel, and chatted a lot. I asked him who they had in the Chuo Hotel, and he answers, "O, a lot of grouchy people with square faces that you have to see around the corners." Don't see how it all makes sense, but it sounded funny and apropos, so I laughed. Then Kay got involved talking to the operators, who stay in the switchboard in the basement of Daiken. It's fun just gabbing to people you can't see.

Mitch told Kay that if she found two GIs who had not fraternized with Jap women, he'd give her 100 dollars. One clerk in our section allegedly comes up to that standard. Perhaps he does—he's a very nice kid. Mitch said that he had, and he was ashamed of it. Pat said that the women are out, most of them, for the money. I wonder just how many hearts really are broken. Now if the soldiers get VD, they get three weeks restriction. And MPs pick up Jap women after eight o'clock if they are wandering on the streets. (I have a faint idea that I have written this to you before. Excuse, please. Vely soly.) And Paul was mad at the women because even if a soldier keeps her in a house, she goes out and shacks with others. O—the whole subject is very disgusting.

At noon, Kay surely got that major in here madder than all hellfire. He was so mad that he was all red in the face, and could hardly walk straight. Well, that serves him right. Did I tell you about it? He wanted Kay to get a Jap bath for him, and when she did, she has to pay for it. If that isn't just like cheap, stinking brass for you. They are so used to getting something for nothing that they try to get away with it always. Today he asked Kay when she was going to take him sightseeing, and she practically told him that she wouldn't. Then she says that she has had dates for the last three nights, and she adds, "You'll miss your chow, *Sir*." I couldn't resist adding, "O, yes, Sir."

Sorry that you are not going to see Dr. Simms. We feel so close to him. Somehow, I feel a tie between us and Jews and Negroes and all persecuted minorities.

To answer some of your questions: When the war ended and it was known that the American troops would occupy Japan, people warned all young women to flee from Tokyo, where they would come first. So I went out to Wakayama to the country under the wing of my relatives. It was awful there—the dirt and squalor and filth. But I did not care—life was not at all hopeful or interesting to me then. You would never believe me when I tell you that at the time, I was skinny, nervous, and undernourished. It all seems like a bad dream now. It sends cold shudders down my spine to even think of those days.

Only one aunt is living. My grandfather is dead. Poor old man—he died without even hearing from Mother. It was a little after his death that Red Cross letters from Mother came. My cousin telegraphed me that he was in serious condition so I got on the train to go to Yonezawa that very night. But when I reached the little hut, [he had already been] sent to the crematorium. I'll never forget that experience. My dear old grandfather. I believe that he was the only [one who] really loved me, from the "basement of his heart." He used to send me ten-yen checks while I was working my way through school, and how welcome they were! He'd enclose a short, short note, saying it was getting cold in Yonezawa, that he is enclosing ten yen, and for me to take care of myself. But I could read all his love between the lines.

After the funeral, I discovered some of the letters that Mother had sent to him. I couldn't help the tears flooding my eyes, and overflowing when I read them. Yes, that's an idea—I think I will translate them. My mother used to ask for forgiveness for not staying by him and taking care of him. Then she'd write about our old farm, what crops she had, about Emma, George, Blanche, or yours truly—it was really wonderfully simple and so true and loving. How I wish that he could have heard from Mother before he died! He was a gentle, quiet soul. At one time, I even thought of writing about him. He had a hard life.

I wish that I had the composition I wrote in Japanese class about him. His life was one long hardship. He married when he was only sixteen, and when he was only eighteen, his wife died, leaving my mother and her brother. So, he worked hard, trying to support them. He didn't remarry for a long time, for he knew that a stepmother could never love and care for his children properly. He had a fish market, but he loved to read books so much that he paid more attention to his books than to the change that he got from his customers. At that rate, he went bankrupt. He worked at the railroad. His son grew up, only to die, then mother announced that she was going to the faraway land called America. He was left alone. Before his son died, he had taken a wife and had two children. The grandson, whom he loved, left him to go to a better land. The granddaughter,[81] who should have taken on the family name, left the family to marry a student. Again, he was left alone.

Finally, after much work, he made enough to retire. Then it was that he succumbed to temptation. A woman snared him. For her he built a home, gave her the family treasures, lost his spotless reputation. But he had a hard life. One can't blame him. This was the only way he could have even a bit of pleasure [that had been] denied to him for so long. This woman left him, after she had squeezed all she could out of him, for another [man]. So, when

81. Tomi-san, Mary's cousin, who lived in Toyama.

I came to Japan, he poured his pent-up love and loneliness upon me. He was quiet, and did not ever express his emotions. But I could see it—*donkan* [insensitive] though I am. It was really a blow [to me] when he left this earth.

They had a Buddhist funeral. I hate that chanting and ranting—so gloomy and forlorn and hopeless. The next morning early, we went to pick up the bones. The teeth all went into a special little box which my cousin has enshrined in her family altar. The other bones all went into a wooden box. Imagine—Miye—they picked up the bones with chopsticks, and thought nothing of it. Japs surely are realistic. You could see it all out on that metal tray—all the flesh had been cremated, leaving nothing but his bones. It made me shudder. Something so barbaric about picking up the bones that had been Grandfather so few days ago. And the people talked and gossiped while they were doing it. I thought it was sacrilegious. At the graveyard, it was worse. My cousin's husband carried the box containing his bones—an unpainted, crude box—from the crematorium to the graveyard. There, a boy in ragged clothing dug up the tombstone of some ancient ancestor and put my grandfather's remains there. As simple as that. No music, no flowers, no sentimentalism.

A cold dreary autumn day it was that this handful of relatives buried Grandfather with such simplicity and coldness. It made me wonder—what is the worth of a man? Would anyone care that he had gone? Only very few—and they would forget soon. But after that, I felt alone—dreadfully alone. Even if I seldom saw Grandfather, I had him to rely upon and I had him to go to for refuge and love. Among all the hypocritical, scheming people I knew, he was the only one I could always be sure of. Dear, dear Grandfather. Yes, he is dead and gone, but his memory will be enshrined in my heart forever.

Maybe you have something there, when you say that maybe the reason the Nisei GIs are so aloof is because they don't want to hurt the girls. I don't know—I only know that they are aloof, and that I have no way of meeting any. When it's so easy to get acquainted with an American GI. They stick together, too. Well, I never did care much for Nisei boys, anyway. And I don't think that I could ever get acquainted enough with a man here to be really serious about it. So why not go with boys that I like and have fun with? Like Scotty, now—I really enjoy being with him. He says the most unexpected things. But he does think. In a way, I'm glad that Pat went home because I spent too much time with him, and I needed a change.

I had another picture taken, but at present am broke so that we cannot get them—Kay and I. You know, I repeat—we surely have it nice here now. We get our quarters free, our meals for twenty-five cents, and transportation free. Hereafter I am going to save all my salary for my old age.

The lieutenant was in to the Chaplains' to see whether and when I am going to be transferred so that he could make out the necessary papers for it. I told Tuttle (Pat's replacement) about the dirty deal the chaplain gave Francis, and he was very understanding and fatherly about it. He says, among chaplains, as among any other group of people, there are good and there are bad. However, among chaplains the majority are good. However, they are human, and it is wrong to expect them to be perfect. A man has to study at least twelve years to become a priest, so he has learning. Now, it was nice of Tuttle to tell me all that. He's a good guy. He comes from San Francisco, is twenty-nine and fat and a Catholic. He never spends his money on women, but is faithful to his wife. He surely is a good influence. Paul doesn't make all his nasty cracks like he used to. And he's so appreciative of my cooking, it makes me feel good.

Kyoto, April 27, 1946

Dearest Miye,

How are you? I am not fine. I felt lousy this morning. We did not see anyone we liked. We are spoiled. We only like to see whom we like to see, and to heck with all the others. Our Sensei told us not to be that way, for we would become Egoists. That was paternal of him to admonish us so.

Here's my morning report: Went out with Red last night. He's just a kid, but a redheaded, cute little boy. He said that his hair was white until he was fourteen, and it was just like a white dog—getting dirty right after it was washed. The show was *Along Came John*.[82] Then later, we went walking down the river with Kay and Francis. Sat near the rocks, and Red chatted away about his post office, and little incidents that happened around there. Felt like I was with a little cute five-year-old boy who wanted to tell his mommy everything that happened that day. Was rather pleasant, but don't care to go with him again. I want to see Scotty.

Kay and I went to see Scotty this morning, and he surely looked the picture of The Morning After. His shirt was all wrinkled, his hair was flying, and he wobbled all over, and his hands shook when he lit a cigarette. But he attracts me very much. And I'm too proud to ask him to take me out. So I wrote him a letter, and just gave it to him, telling him that I liked him. Then, I saw him later, and he winked at me, and I felt good.

Sometimes I wish that Pat were still here, because he was always there, and I never had to think, "Where shall I go? Who shall I go with?"

Well, from the beginning part of next week, I shall go to the Chaplains'. Wrote up a buck-slip this morning concerning my transfer. That's just right—I'll leave the hotel just when Kay does. And from then, I am going to buckle down and study. If the reserve and politeness of the Chaps does not stifle me.

82. Mary means the 1945 movie *Along Came Jones*, with Gary Cooper and Loretta Young.

Francis is an interesting kid. He told Kay all about himself—that he was a gangster before. Ain't that sompin? He can take care of himself, all right. As you said, there [are] all kinds in the civilian army.

Yesterday I went to the dentist in the dispensary because my gums bleed, and he said that I have gingivitis. Now, you call it hard names and I feel civilized. He cleaned out my teeth, and they feel so good now. It's marvelous how much difference a little something like that can do. I guess the natives in Africa felt this way when white men came to doctor to them. All for free, too.

We got some stationery, which I am sending. It's too puurrty to write on. Must quit or I can't send this for six cents. Goo-by.

Kyoto, May 1, 1946

Dearest Miye,

Your sweet letter of April 24 just reached me today. Just think, you're in Calif. by now. And by Nick. It's so wonderful to have you near him again; now I can think of you just like in that picture.

Doggone, that letter came back again today that I had addressed wrong. Was going to drop it in the post box again, only, my better judgment prevailed over my stubbornness, and so I am wasting an envelope to send it to you. And yet, I am not wasting it because I am writing to you anyway.

Yesterday I got paid, so right off, I went down and bought a whole stack of envelopes. Now I can write you a lot. Blanche wrote to me, too, telling me all about her cat that she is dissecting. It seems that I talked too soon in saying that I might be able to go back—I don't know at all. Only hoping.

Last night I went to the Army school and took Spanish, from our Sensei. We have classes three times a week. Hereafter I am going to study a lot, and be able to talk in Spanish. Yes, I agree with you that a liberal education is desirable. How I do wish that I could take all those courses with you! I'm going to take as many classes as possible, instead of wasting my time with GIs. No one is in my life anymore. Was interested in Scotty for a time, but he has a dancing girl who he goes to dance with, and so I don't want to bother with him anymore. He'll go home within a week, anyway.

Don't have time to type letters anymore. I do a lot of filing, and some typing. It is raining cats and dogs now.

Adios, my fine amigo, no, it is amiga. I want to take French, too. It's fun to study now. And there are lots of people around me that I can practice with.

Kyoto, May 2, 1946

Dear Kay,

Just did some interpreting for a Jap man whose store was to be used by the army for a pro station.[83] My heart went out to him, for he had quit his job in order to put up a novelty shop, and was just getting started when his store would be taken from him. Capt. Dale told him to go to the Liaison Office to protest. He has gone, but they tell him that whatever the army orders must go through, regardless. He said that the Liaison Office had never seen his place, or cared at all for him. Here is one of the tragedies of defeat. It surely struck home to him. He started to cry when we told him that there was nothing that could be done: the request had gone through the MG and Liaison Office, there had been no objections, so they were justified in demanding it.

Poor man. He has to get out by tomorrow. I told him, just think of those who lost all their possessions during the raids—think of those who were maimed, or whose beloved ones had died. And the army does not just take it outright—they go through the regular channels.

Yet, sometimes I wonder. What difference would it make in the long run, whether they took a place by brute force, or more subtly, by going through official channels and red tape. They get what they want in the long run. Perhaps the defeated nation could get over it more if they did take it by brute force. Then, they could at least hate their conquerors. And they would be awed into silence. This way is getting the same thing through more shrewd and civilized ways. So the wound is deeper. In this way, the man's hatred is turned towards the officials of his own yellow race who are so obsequious to the army, who never fight for him. But if he thinks further, he will know that officials could not protest—it would be senseless, and do more harm than good. And his hate would be turned in more fine and vital, hurting ways on his conquerors.

Kyoto, May 4, 1946

Dearest Kay,

Thank you so much for the letters. I loved that letter on the napkin—it was very effective with the Oriental background. I must write to my Blanche on napkins, to give her a bit of the Quaint Orient.

I can't believe that you have been here for a whole month already. Now that I am going to lose you, I'm sorry that I did not treat you better. It's too bad that you have to go back to Hell in Tokyo. I've been emancipated so long that I have forgotten what Slavery was like. Just like the children of Israel used

83. Prophylactic station, where the army distributed condoms to military personnel.

to complain to Moses that their lot was better in captivity in Egypt, so often I look at myself bitching and marvel at how short memory can be, and how much time can heal the wounds inflicted thruout the war years. But to think of you going back to it is very pitiful. But grit your teeth—it's only a little while.

I should not be writing. Up to now, my conscience has ruled, and I haven't stolen time as I've been wont to do. Say—Sally's going, and so am I!! No, it's only 11:30, so I'll have to sit here like a dummy. No, I'll sit here like a pert typist and bang away.

Wasn't it lovely to play on the piano? Really, your playing of "Minuet in G" was so beautiful, and you put so much feeling into it that I thought of long, long ago when I used to sit in class in high school—about my soph year—look, no gaze, out of the window, and hum that tune while watching the majestic, fluffy clouds sail along in the blue sky. I have loved that tune. And I love it yet. It made tears come into my eyes because it was so beautiful.

Now, Kay, you get some piano and you practice! See! That's orders. It's a crime to let all that go to waste. And we can write letters—our letters that we love—to each other. I'll be lonely and blue and melancholy when you have flown away. Which is a good mood for writing.

I wonder why I have no time to write letters anymore? I'll have to rediscover the knack of "goofing-off." Hope I've made a good enough impression by my diligence the first week to steal time off hereafter.

Kyoto, May 4, 1946

Dearest Miye,

It makes me just sick because I have no time to write to you, my beloved. During office hours, I am always working, or busy doing something. Then, I'm attending classes three times a week, so that I am plenty busy. I don't know where all my time flies to. Last night I went to a movie with Kay and her BF and a dumb kid that he brought along.

Here it is Sat already, making one week of work at the Chaplains' Office. Someday when I have time, I will write my impressions of them. At present, it is more favorable than I had dared to hope. The trouble is that people expect them to be super-humanly perfect, when they are only men like the rest of them.

Yesterday, I had an interesting time because I went with the chaplains to a Buddhist temple to witness some kind of dedication ceremony. It was a lot of fun, especially because I did not have to bow and act like a Jap, as I've had to for years. Now I could stick up my nose at them—but I didn't, I only acted natural. And they had to excuse me for being that way, since I had on my uniform complete with cap, and had four American officers with me. One chaplain kept making wise cracks about it. Then, the second part of the ceremony, they lit a bonfire, and chanted in unison. One of these days, I'm going to write up on it. Yesterday afternoon I was all set to write and was all brimming over with inspiration, when I had to do some typing which took all afternoon. It's a crime to stifle an ambitious thing like me with stupid typing, don't you think? Do I love myself! O, well, you're the only one I can talk like this to.

It was noon before we left the temple. So we got to all go to the Miyako Hotel for dinner, that is where the majors on up stay. It was a beautiful place. I was scared that I would have to sit with the chaplains and watch my p's and q's, but luckily, according to the caste system, I was relegated to eat with the driver—an EM. We sat in a hi-ceilinged great big dining room, and it felt so good. And outside, there was the garden, so verdant and fresh.

Seems like no one is going to bother me. Hope that I can continue writing. There's a lot of junk to file away. Let that wait. I'm doing something more [important].

Kyoto, May 6, 1946

Dearest Sweetpea [Kay],

You know, it seems so strange and unbelievable that you are not on your earth. And that you will not be home in our room. So much *our* room. So another chapter of our book has ended. And you are going back to your hell up there, while I crawl back into my shell here.

Received a letter from Miye today. Went around to tailor, a printer, and another shop with Chaplain Connelly this morning, so that I was late in cooking for the D[evil]. Tuttle (Pat's replacement) had gone to the CIC for work, so that Paul and I ate together. He was very nice. I never knew it was possible [for him] to act so much like a decent man. He said that he took night courses in electrical engineering at Penn State, so that raised my estimation of him. I'd much rather eat with him than go back to that snobby, smug place. I hate to go back for supper now.

I'm so happy—Father Connelly said that I could attend Spanish classes on Tuesday and Thursday from 3:30! Now, I'll have my evenings free. And the classes ought to be more interesting. I got a binder for Sensei, too, which made me happy. Wish I could get some ink for him. He's so wonderful!

Kyoto, May 6, 1946

Dearest Miye,

Kay left today for Wakayama to her mother's and so I am by my lonesome again. She is leaving for Tokyo on Wednesday. My world is falling down again.

Yesterday we had the most entertaining time with our Spanish teacher—Señor Alvarez. We lured him to our room and had such an interesting chat. He is so cute and original and funny that he has us roaring all the time. He flattered me by saying that I was too advanced for the beginners' class in Spanish that he has at night, and that I ought to go in the afternoon to the higher class. Which I am going to do. It is so much fun to talk to him in Spanish—even though I have to grope for words, and even then, I have to say the most simple things.

We are lucky to have discovered him. He is the only man in my life now, and I am glad that we have found someone so like ourselves. I'll write more about him when I get the inspiration.

Kyoto, May 6, 1946

Dearest Miye,

You know what? It's just plain getting me down the way I've been neglecting you, and here is where I balk. Now, Mary, you stay here until you write like YOU should write to your beloved Miye, and not a one-page letter like you have been sending as excuses for letters. So here goes. If not in quality, in quantity, I shall be the letter-writing Mary of yore.

I feel good because the people in the kitchen of the Ice Cream Bar on the third floor of the Daiken building just gave me some ice cream and coffee. The manager, a short, chubby Jap in white jacket and cook's cap, was up at the Chaplains' Office this morning, and I did some interpreting for him. When I found out that he belonged to the forbidden-to-foreign-nationals ice cream bar, I asked him if he would give me some if I went down at four. He smilingly said yes, so I went on down just now. He wasn't there, but the KPs willingly served me. And I even got seconds. So it made me feel good. And just this afternoon, Sgt. Henry of IG Section went down with Al (my clerk now) and asked me "Do you want to go?" I said, "Yes," and started to go when Cecilia, the typist who is a Portuguese, but cute and intelligent, said, "You can't go." I felt like retorting, "I can too, because the manager said so!" but I controlled myself like a Jap maid should, and quietly sat down. So I feel like I put something over [on] them. I took down a piece of candy that Mr. Lewis, our warrant officer, gave me, in order to bribe the manager. But sad to say, he was not there.

I heard something very typically Japanese about that manager. He seemed so chubby and jolly when he was speaking to the chaplains that I would never have thought that of him. Which follows. Well, Paul, the T/4 [corporal] electrician who was Pat's buddy, said that the first time the manager came into the building and started putting up his store, he had all the workers stand at attention when he spoke to them, and had all of them address him respectfully as "Manager." Now, Paul said that he couldn't stand to see that. Once when he was around, one of the workers failed to stand at attention, so the manager took a terrific swing at him. Luckily, the worker ducked, then he stood at attention, scared to pieces. Paul saw that, and was mad. Well, after the manager got through with him, he saw Paul, and started to holler at him. That really got Paul sore, so he took him down to the commandant's office and had the interpreter tell him that hereafter he was never to make the workers stand at attention and call him "Master." He surely put him in his place. You know, when I hear incidents like that, my heart warms up to GI Joe. Surely, they are showing what democracy and equality means by such ways. It used to make me so sore the way the workers always had to bow and humble themselves before their superiors. But then, when I stayed in Japan a long time, it just got to be the natural order of things, and I failed to think it was humiliating for the one who was being exploited.

Today, I had to go with Father Connelly and [did not get back till 11:30]. I didn't know what to say because Father Connelly insisted that he would take [me] back to my hotel. I guess I wasn't very tactful when I protested, "But I want to go back with my friends." When I told Paul, he said, "Why didn't you tell him that you eat at the Daiken?" Me: "O, I thought the fewer people knew about it, the better it was."

Well, Paul had the potatoes boiled and the coffee made, so that all I had to do was fry the pork chops and set the table. They surely have a good setup there with electric range, running hot water, and everything very nice and clean. It was fun eating with Paul. I never realized that he could be so nice. I'd much rather eat with him than go back to the hotel and eat with those smug, self-righteous, dull Nisei. You know, they try to be so ultra-fastidious, and it makes Kay and me sick. Just to be ornery, we holler and laugh and make a racket in there. And we are the only ones who make any noise at all. Now I won't have Kay. That is why I don't feel like going back tonight. That ice cream will hold me. And our mess sergeant—Sgt. Pool—bawled us out this morning, saying that if we didn't come down for breakfast, that meant that he could draw that much less rations. Well, I didn't get up in time for breakfast, and I never eat lunch there anyway. And today I won't eat supper there either.

After this, I am going to school and practice on the pianer. It is so comforting to play, even if I can't play. What the heck—I am playing for my own benefit, so who cares if I can't put in all the trills and chords. The melody is what is important. That's what I love about practicing the pianer. It just carves the melody into one's soul. And you live and breathe and suffer and rejoice along with the composer of long ago.

Yesterday, I surely enjoyed the Kreutzer piano concert. After it was finished, Sensei (Señor Alvarez) says, "*Kokoro no ofuro desu ne!*" ["It is a bath for the soul!"] to hear such wonderful music. He says if we do not hear something magnifico like that, we do not live. O, he is wonderful. And when we were going to the concert, we walked through the Imperial Palace grounds, which were perfect in their green freshness. O, it was like a verdant Paradise. He says, "I must come here and think on things eternal." We asked him, "Have you ever been in love?" He: "I don't know for sure. At times I have had a funny feeling." Kay: "Do you want to be near her at such times?" "No, not exactly. How do you explain it—perhaps it was love, and perhaps it was lack of vitamins." We roared at that! He was here through the war years, too, and starved with the rest of us. Miye, I know that you would enjoy him. He always says the most unexpected things. He said that his sister was so full of life that they called her "Miss Typhoon."

And he dresses in fatigues. Kay is always getting after him for it, and he is always laughing it away. He says that people see him around school with his fatigues, and tell him to move tables and things, and he obligingly does it. Can you imagine—a Doctor, a professor, a diplomat who represented his country to one of the then first-rate powers of the world—a learned man—willingly moving tables for some stripe-happy GI. He gets a big kick out of it. He told us that when the director first interviewed him, he wore his dirty old fatigues, and when he was introduced as "Dr. Alvarez," the director looked all over to find the doctor—he never supposed that the humble, dirtily-dressed man could be a famous, learned doctor. So the director put him on for ¥600 a month. He said nothing. (Even dumb typists get ¥1,200 a month.) Then, he had to fill out blanks for the CIC, stating his rank, schooling, etc., and so he put it all down truthfully. What do you know—all at once his salary skyrocketed to ¥2,800 a month!

I think it would be fun to be a great man like that and yet wear camouflage and fool everyone, and see their embarrassment when they found out. He was surely laughing away about it. His fatigues' pockets are bulging and they are dirty, it is true, but he always has a clean shirt on underneath, and he is immaculately clean otherwise. He is very fastidious about keeping himself clean. Yesterday, he had to go wash his face before he went to the concert, and he had to brush his teeth after supper. He is a character, and a respectable one. I mean that [as] "one who commands respect," and not in the other way.

While I am in the writing mood, I'll get something else off my mind that has been stewing for quite a while: namely, the temple we went to. It won't be polished, since I am writing as I think. Miye, I kept thinking, "This will be SOMETHING to write to you about." And to Blanche, for she is so awestruck by the world about her, and she is so thrilled with whatever I write her about the quaint and exotic orient.

Well, this was both quaint and exotic. A Buddhist priest led us there. We were led to the main ceremony room. The ceremony was already in progress, with all the monks (about forty) seated in the middle, in front of (facing) the altar, the officiating monk chanting his weird sing-songs in front of the altar, the candles burning, and the believers all seated around. You have heard that weird, other-worldly chanting of Buddhists. And every once in a while, a bell would ring, a drum would beat, adding to the clamor and chanting. We couldn't tell when one chant ended and when another began, although I did have a program in my hand. The costumes of the monks is what made it all look so colorful and fantastic. The monks who were squatting on the tatami had on yellow silk costumes, with fuzzy round balls strung down suspender-like, of purple, green, or red. Then, in back hung a piece of fur from their waist down to the hem. On their heads were black, round (about three-inch-diameter) caps, tied on with string around their chins. There was one monk with a beautiful green costume on—it was gorgeous, for it was stiff silk, of pea-green, and with the light, it would show up orange. On top, he had a kind of wide band of purple with white flower patterns. I wish I had a picture to show you—in color.

After the first part of the ceremony, the priest who took us there allowed us to go close to the altar. There were large tapestries hung on both sides, with Buddhas woven in.

On the low tables in front were piles of rice-cakes of white and pink, fruits, and other foods. The tablecloth was simply gorgeous. It must have been woven gold, in the most artistic and colorful gold-and-red designs. There was a candle burning on the middle table. The priest told me that that fire is the essence of the Buddha that they worshipped.

The second part of the ceremony was more varied and interesting. Everyone went out to the garden where a big pile of wood was in the middle. It was completely covered with pine (or some kind of evergreen) branches. There was a little square all set off, with the green pile in the center. At first, the yellow-costumed monks had to march around to the front, where one monk asked the first [yellow-costumed] monk all about himself. I wish that I could have understood all that he said. He explained all parts of his costume. O, I forgot—the procession was led by one of the monks blowing on a huge horn, made out of shell. It sounded other-worldly. After the monk had given an account of himself, in elaborate classical Japanese spoken slowly with much dignity, he was allowed to pass, and all his followers. They went around the square and sat themselves down in two rows of chairs in front of the pile.

Then, after much more chanting, two monks got big, about three-ft.-long bundles of dried bamboo and lit them with the candle from the sacred altar. They set fire to the pile. All the time, the monks kept on chanting rhythmically. As the fire gained in intensity, the chanting seemed to quicken its pace and ardor. Then, one monk took out a sword, brandished it in front of a long oblong box, and threw it into the fire. That was supposed to symbolize the destruction of all evils.

It was lunch time, so we had to leave before the ceremony was all finished. I wish that I knew what it was all about. I bet they don't know themselves. As much as I could draw out of them was this: The ceremony was to celebrate the independence of that sect from another. They believed that they should train themselves in the mountains. There have been believers of this sect from 1,300 years ago, but this sect had to unite with another during the Meiji Era, when Western civilization came in. And just last month, they declared their independence, so that in this ceremony they announced their independence to their Buddha. So all the monks had come down from their mountain to this most holy of holies to partake in this unique ceremony.

Well, one of these days, I might try to find out what Buddhism is all about. I tried one time, when we had to take it in school. There have been profound books written in English about it. But it all gets me mixed up. I did write up about Nichiren Shonin[84] in our religion class, and it was fun. The legend is that when he was to be beheaded, a stroke of lightning smote the sword of the executioner from his hand. He was a noisy radical, and the rulers did not like him.

The chaplains wanted me to write up about it [the ceremony], but after I came back, I had to do something stupid—I think it was typing out a stencil. And they muffled all my inspiration. But it takes more than that to kill my ambition![85] And Miye—listen to this. Hereafter, I am going to gather material and write. Now that Kay will be gone, and I do not have any girlfriends, and Pat is gone, and I do not go with any GIs, I'll be able to snoop around the second-hand bookstores, and I'll stay up in my office, so quiet and light, and I'll type and type and type. And I'll get something out! Just see if I don't! And Sensei inspires, and you from across the sea, with your letters, keep my fire burning, and by heck—I will write something!

Wow! What a sudden and rare burst of ambition. I like this office better than any I've been in yet. Going around interpreting gives me lots of interesting experiences, and gives me contacts. The people in the office are congenial. The brass are all in another room, and they do not harass us too much. I work from 8:15 to four, and I can go to Spanish lessons on Tuesdays and Thursdays, and I can practice on the piano after work to my heart's content, I eat with Paul and Tuttle downstairs, so what more do I want?

84. The holy man (1222–82) who founded the Nichiren sect of Buddhism.

85. Mary wrote "Visit to a Ceremony at the Shogo-in Buddhist Temple" for Father Gefell a few days later.

Kyoto, May 8, 1946

Dearest Miye,

It seemed so wonderful to hear from you in romantic New Orleans![86] Just got your letter last night, and was thrilled to get it. Just think—you are back in Calif. now. How happy Nick must be! O, Miye, I am so happy for you. May you be fruitful and prosper.

Here I am stealing time during the noon hour. It feels good to be all alone in the office. You know, Miye, I must be a hermit in disguise—I love to be alone. That's why I am dreading it so much when I have to share a room with three other girls. I think I'll go crazy. I can't figure any way out at present. I'll stay at the office after hours, I'll go to school, I'll practice the piano—then I won't have to be home so much. It's awful when you hate to go home, and when you can't call a place your own.

You know, Miye, this week has been heavenly. I've discovered the Army School, and how I love it. And I like my Chaplains' Office much better than any other. I am hardly at the hotel at all. I used to go to meals there because Kay was there, but with her gone to Wakayama, there is no attraction there at all. So I stay at the office, or I go to school and practice the piano. The day before yesterday, when I was practicing, an Italian boy, Johnny, came in and played some opera pieces for me. Then we walked home together. At the hotel he played the few classical records we had there, and we stood up by the phonograph and were entranced. It is so wonderful to have found someone who likes the same kind of music that I do! While the record was on, I asked him a question, but he was so absorbed in the music that he didn't hear me. Now, isn't that perfect? He is very young, and doesn't talk much, but still I rather like him. Anyway, he's a good boy who goes to bed early and doesn't drink.

The boys in our chaplains' section are good boys too. It's a relief to be with such. They go to church, and have ideals. You don't hear much about such soldiers—it's those who seduce Jap women and get drunk and make a bad name for themselves that get the publicity.

Guess I'd better get back to work. Before anyone comes. I'm enclosing some things. The article about the temple—it took all afternoon and this morning to write. I haven't thought for so long that it is surely a hard thing for me.

I'm looking forward to seeing *Bells of St. Mary's* this Friday. I've heard so much about Ingrid Bergman that I am dying to see her.

Tell me all about Calif. Miye, when will the day come when I can set foot on that blessed land again?

86. That is, en route back to California.

Right after I got through with the last page, I received a phone call from a Lt. Warwin of Tokyo, saying that he had a job for me as a translator in Tokyo; that I would get my meals and uniform, and would get around ¥1,700 a month. And if I get my citizenship papers cleared up, I would get much more. O, the sun is beginning to shine again. If only I had seen about my citizenship before! I am going to Tokyo—probably in about a month, I think. I never stay put. And it will get me out of having to share rooms with others. Or maybe I should stay put. But it is so stupid to stay here as a file clerk and typist. I wrote up to Tokyo saying that, and my qualifications, and that I wanted to do something more interesting. Well, I hope this will be an advancement. My schooling here was so much fun. I wonder if I will have it so good up there? Anyway, it will be a change of scenery to move again. Too long in one place makes me stale.

Now I'm all excited about it. I do want to do something worthwhile. There are some girls in our hotel who are going to work in civil service. I do envy them.

Kyoto, May 9, 1946

Dearest Miye,

Today I received a letter from Emma, and she wrote it on the second of May! It's unbelievably fast. She is having troubles, and I felt so sorry for her. She lost her job; Hilo couldn't get in the army because he was overaged; they might have to go back to Hawaii. I do pray and hope that he will not have to come back to Japan. God forbid!

Kay left this morning,[87] and I am all alone again. I shall go quietly back in my shell. Chappy said to me, "You never acted crazy like that before Kay came." Yes, I know, I was nice and quiet in my little shell.

But I'm going up to Tokyo in about a month. I think that will be better for me. And I'll get a civil service job as soon as I get my citizenship cleared. Keep your fingers crossed! Today I wrote to Fred and Mrs. Nagata, asking them to find a place for me to stay. It shouldn't be so hard for me to find a place since I would never eat at home, and that is the biggest problem confronting the people now.

Today, the general was expected to inspect the basement, so I didn't cook for Paul and Tuttle. Had a few sandwiches and fruit. So I had a lot of time, and I went to the I&E[88] reading room, where I found a *Harper's*. There was

87. Kay had gone to Wakayama to see her mother, then stopped back in Kyoto before leaving for Tokyo.

88. Short for CI&E, Civil Information and Education, one of nine special administrative sections established by the occupation authorities. Its mission was to "effectuate control over Japan's education, religion and media of expression."

an interesting article about MacArthur's First Year or something like that. He knew what he was talking about. Why can't I write an article like that?

I packed up your *zori* last night, and will send it off tomorrow, if I remember. I'll have to remember to get some wrapping paper and twine from AG for it. It's wonderful to be working for the army—you can get so many necessities like that.

Today, I am definitely not in the writing mood. The day is dreary and cloudy, my head aches a little, and Kay went home. All summing up to leave me way down low.

I'm all excited about going to Tokyo. I'll feel more at home there. I hope the job will be interesting, and not too hard. Perhaps they will be disappointed in me, because I had to give myself a big build-up.

Spanish lesson day today. Last night Kay went dancing with Scotty. He couldn't get over it—me asking him to take Kay out. Well, I'm not going to ask him to take me out—I'm too proud, and it ain't worth it. So I stayed home, took a shower, washed my hair, packed up some junk to send to Tokyo. It felt good to have a hammer in hand and do a lot of pounding on the box. I must have looked a sight with my hair all frizzy.

Well, I must close since I am not the least bit inspired.

Kyoto, May 11, 1946

Dearest Miye,

Everything is happening and I feel so rushed and popular. And after I told Kay that I would stay home all the time after she went! It started off when Rev. Ito came to Kyoto yesterday, and was I surprised to see him at our office! He waited around for me, then after work, we went down and had supper with Paul. Atsushi, his son, came later, and we had a merry feast. I was so happy that Paul let them eat there. He's got a kind heart, after all. He said that he sees through people and treats them [accordingly]. Well, his judgment was correct with these people. If anyone was a true and loyal friend, it was the Ito family. When things were the worst, they gave me a warm, helping hand, and I shall never forget it. Rev. Ito was looking as spry and merry as usual—he was imprisoned for three years in a dirty, cold prison, and he said that he had not yet regained his health.

Rev. Ito had to go to Otsu for a service, so he left early, and Atsushi and I walked home together. He wouldn't come into our hotel, saying that the Nisei there were snobby. I don't blame him. It was surely good to see him again. I've had a lot of fun with him. He looked small, thin, and very fuzzy-haired, but as I talked with him, I found his old charm returning. Did I tell you that he was the only one who opposed my marriage? And it turned out just as he had warned. Fool that I was. When we talked about it yesterday, he said, "O, well, it was all right for the experience." I don't know if you'd like him. He's definitely a sissy. And he loves to talk.

Excitement No. 2 was this morning, when Freddie Suzukawa popped in. He is the cutest, curly-headed, smiling little boy! He doesn't seem like a lieutenant at all to me. We have a date tonight. Gee, but he's cute. He had breakfast at our place. It was so funny, after he'd had his cereal, he was looking around, and in the meantime, the waitress had brought him his eggs. All of a sudden, he looked down, and said, "When did she bring this?" I laughed, and told him that it was a long time ago. He said naively, "And I was going to complain about the bad service." He's going to be in Kyoto for four days. Wish that Atsushi and he had come at different times, though.

And then, last night I went to the show, *The Bells of St. Mary's*, starring Ingrid Bergman. I loved it. Went with Señor Alvarez. He said that it was the first show he'd seen in eleven years! Imagine! And he only went because Kay told him to go to the movies, because they make him younger. After we got out, he said, "They showed one face too long—no good." I noticed that during the show he kept looking around and changing his position, so I thought that he was bored. And I thought it was wonderful! He said that he has no sentimental side at all: that is the reason that he has stayed single so long. I can't figure him out. We went for a lovely moonlight walk near the river. It was really beautiful, with the hazy half-moon, the reflection in the dark water, and everything so quiet. As we walked down the street, he paused near the tree, and put his hand to his heart, and exclaims, "Ah, Luna! Luna Hermosa!" And then he says, "Now is the time for romance." And he laughs, as though it is a big joke. He said that he is going to look it up in a book, and find out how it is done. Afterwards, when he was serious, he said that he has read so much that he has no sentimental side left to him. I tried to get his story by asking him if someone had stolen his heart, but he got off on something silly. It's funny—he doesn't like to discuss serious things, like how it is in Spain, the politics, etc. He wants to always joke and laugh. But maybe I am giving you a wrong impression. I'm glad that we have discovered him, because he is very congenial.

It's time to go. So good-bye.

Kyoto, May 12, 1946

Dearest Kay,

Last night went with Freddie to the Grand Kyoto [Hotel], and that chicken MP at the door wouldn't let me in. So we snooped around that district—all *machiai* and tea houses. On the corner, we snooped into the Ichiriki[89] and caught a glimpse of a beautiful, painted and graceful geisha. Fred says, "At least I can say that I poked my nose into Ichiriki." He's a lot of fun to go with and I like him a lot. He stops and talks to everyone—chauffeurs, mama-sans, girls, and anyone. He tried to get them to bring out a geisha, because he wanted to talk to one; but they refused. Then we went to Gion and the cabaret there. Couldn't get in there either. Came back about ten and sat around till 10:30, when he left. He is staying at the Station Hotel. Have a date to go to a dance at the Burako Hotel this afternoon if it doesn't rain. And I'm taking off this Monday to take him sightseeing. Hope it's good weather.

I'm going to church with Atsushi Ito this morning. As a girl working in the chaplains' section should. Last night, poor Sensei [Alvarez] looked so sad and alone—I felt sorry for him.

And was I happy! My sister's package finally came yesterday—the one she sent to the ARC! It contained: a rose, bright sweater, a blouse, a fingernail file, a fountain pen. Gee, it surely is a relief. And I love the new clothes!

Guess I'll go down to breakfast. I still have my room to myself yet. Wonderful privacy. Poor Sensei—he hates to live with all those mundane people. He says, "One must live with a person who has had the same education as yourself." There's something to that.

I surely like Fred. He has a superb vocabulary. When we were going through the off-limits areas, he says, "This is a bachelor's paradise and the bane of the old maid." I made a mental note to look up "bane." He doesn't look twenty-six, either. Said his sister Betty is a wonderful cook and he'd like to "sink his teeth" into something delicious she made. Said she's a perfect housewife. George is lucky to have her.

I thought I had so much to tell you, and here I'm running out already. Mitch is driving a staff car. I miss him. Haven't seen Francis since you left, either. Paul tried to make love to me, and I just teased him to be ornery. I rather like him, though. I keep telling him to go home to Fusae.[90] He said Pat's wife used to write him only once a month at the most and that he's the henpecked type. Fred said the Nisei girls here look sad. You can't imagine how I rejoiced and gloated over that! It's the cat in me. Sensei misses you, I know. I don't make a fuss over him. I can't get over Miye telling me to "go steady" with him. You don't "go" with a teacher like that. I think he tolerates and likes us like he does children—not as an intellectual equal, and never as a lover. He comes from an old-fashioned country. He says the Gomis family is rich and that he [Gomis] would never marry Babs—but they are good friends.[91]

89. A famous Kyoto nightclub.

90. The Japanese woman he lived with.

91. Gomis was another Spaniard who lived in the hotel and a friend of Alvarez's. His girlfriend Babs, a Nisei, roomed with Mary for a few days.

Somebody says this, someone says that—enough of such. I'd better go down for chow.

"Say—tell Kay that Allied nationals get to buy PX supplies and they get the use of the commissary (clothes). Find out about it." Unquote Fred.

Kyoto, July 17, 1946

Dearest Kay,

I am in [a] writing mood. How I wish I had the typewriter! Fool that I am—when will I learn that if I play with fire I'll get burned. This time, I think I got off with being singed a little. I'm not going to allow any GI to break my heart!

Russ. I was beginning to be fond of him. Tonight I walked up to the Red Cross to catch him. What do I see, Russ and [a] girl, girl and another boy, all four packed in the front seat. It didn't dawn on me at first—I went up and then saw that he had acquired a new gal-friend. With hurt pride I crawled into the back, and bitchily thought, "The joke's on you, my dear. You thought Russ would beg for you, forever. Stop aching, heart—it's only your false pride that's hurt. You didn't *really* care for him—you and he are so different. It's better for him to go with a girl who has no scruples—better for him to go with someone he can get something out of—better for him to go with a girl who has girlfriends that can go with his buddies."

I'm glad it happened. But, O, Kay—it makes me sore! What is it that makes me sore? It's the idea that we can be just mere playthings—to be picked up at will and thrown away when unwanted. And I thought of you and Brownie. What will happen when his wife comes? You know as well as I—he'd never give up his wife and family for you. And you will suffer. Damn it! We're always on the suffering [end].

Here I am with a typewriter. But then, I'm down in the hotel office with a lot of distracting people around. Dear Doll, I felt so blue today. I went and walked along the dark streets, then onto the Sanjo Ohashi. There, the bridge was broken just right for me to sit down, so I leaned against the pillar and dreamed and observed the people parading by. How I wish that I could describe the various emotions flitting in my soul. Then, if I were a poet, something would have been created. I loved the murky darkness of the Kamogawa way down below, and yet, how gently the waters flowed. How peacefully and utterly regardless of the stupid people walking above. Entirely unaware of the penguin-like pregnant women trundling along by their skinny spouses, of the little children toddling along blissfully in their little clattery *geta* with hands grasped by their elders, of the painted prostitutes, searching for lustful victims, of the drunken men shouting and laughing, barely able to stumble along, of the average girls and men, of the Kyoto middle-aged women, so correct in their expensive kimonos, daintily picking their way. No, the waters below are entirely separate from these fickle humans. God—what did you create man for? What is the purpose in all these people? Japs everywhere. What are they talking about? Most of them aimlessly wander along, saying nothing. But always can be heard bits of conversation: "the occupation," "speaking English," "Nothing to eat," "Nisei." What do these people think about? What are their lives worth? Thus I wondered as I blankly gazed at the passing parade, there in the dim light on the ancient bridge. Then, fast-striding soldiers would break my train of thoughts. Back to reality. Soldiers. Everywhere are soldiers. They have become an integral part of the average Jap's life.

Then I thought of Massy. Poor girl! She gave her heart to a man who only wanted to take her for a ride! And me, still smarting from the lashes to my delicate pride when I saw that I had lost my man. But who cares? Better to give him up now while I am not much involved. And it is only fair. But it is always a shock when a man goes with someone else. Although I think it only natural if I go with another man. Let's look at Russ's point of view: I get mad at him for something entirely beyond his control. Besides, I soon go [out] with "Pedro,"[92] and I am seen going with other GIs. Why should he only go with me? He's only out for a good time, so why not take any girl who wants to go with him? Mary thinks she is too smart. She's always giving him a hard time. So I don't blame Russ at all.

But then I realized the truth of what you had prophesied: Sr. will be a friend forever. He will not pick us up and then throw us away. Isn't he perfectly wonderful? O, I've been mean to him! Just as I was mean to you. But that's why I want to be alone now. He called up tonight, and wanted to know what I was doing. I said I was staying home; then he asked whether he should come over. I hesitated, then cruelly and point-blank said, "No." My conscience hurt me after that, for he immediately slammed the receiver down. Last night, I was feeling blue, and poor Sr. was so worried about me and wanted to know what was the matter. I wouldn't tell him, but just maintained a stubborn silence. I want to be alone. At that time I was still wondering between Sr. and Russ. But tonight has settled it. No more Russ for me.

Swee'pea, what is to become of us? Even if I go back to the States, I don't know what to do. Seven years wasted over here. Just think, if we had gone to school that long back in the States, we could have at least a couple of degrees after our names. But then, what are those letters in back of one's name. No, Kay, we must not let these years be wasted. We have experienced a lot here and

92. Russ's derogatory name for Alvarez. In this letter Mary begins routinely calling Alvarez "Sr." (for Señor).

we must not [let] it be in vain. When I got the lovely things from my brother, I thought, "I am the failure of our family." My brother is making money and is raising a family. Emma has her family. Blanche is studying to become a doctor. Only me, O—I am good for nothing! But I won't mooch on the rest of them! Just see if I don't do something! Today, during noon period—no, it was yesterday—I looked over the vocational guidance books in the I&E reading room. And I thought, it is about time that I decided on a vocation. As far back as I can remember, I've wondered what I could be. And I still haven't hit my work. Will I ever?

Sent you *Masefield*[93] today. Hope you get it safely. If it doesn't reach you, I'll give you mine when you come this way. It is blissfully quiet now. Would that it were this way always!

I have fallen in love with the Kamogawa. I long to go to it now, and be consoled by its gurgling, its blackness, its frothy white. But I am afraid to venture out at eleven in the night. No, it is 11:30 and all is quiet. Now is the time for witches to venture out on their broomsticks, for rats to dance, for fairies to dance in the moonlight, for imps to work their mischief. Lovely river, how I love you! Now, if I knew enough about it, I would compose an ode to it. Maybe I shall if I get up enough ambition. Let's see—Joyful river, happy river, serene river. No, they do not express anything. Today, when I was gazing at the water, I thought of Tennyson's "Song of the Stream," about how "men may come and men may go but I go along forever." I have a rendezvous with my lover, the river. No, I am the lover, and the river is the loved. She is apathetic. She does not pay the slightest attention to my adoration. But last night, I became one with her. I jumped into her refreshing waters, and played to my heart's delight. O, it was really innocent joy to feel the clean waters in every pore of my body! She was too inviting, and I could not resist her call. And she left me clean and cool. Before I was restless and sad and alone, but she comforted me. I went with Sr. to the river, but my mind was turbulent, dark, melancholy, and I was deaf to Sr.'s entreaties to let him in on my sorrows. Then, some man jumped into the river and swam. It looked so tempting. I sat and envied him until I tore asunder my bonds, and in I splashed—with my slip on. O, it was pure joy to feel the cool waters about me. I splashed and laughed and sang for joy. In childish enjoyment of the water, I lost my troubled state of mind. Good old nature! How I love you, dear, dear river.

It is going on to twelve. But I'd still like to write pages and pages forever. You know, Kay, it doesn't look like the people are starving. Those on the streets look well-fed and content. Or is it only a mask? I guess those unfortunates who are starving haven't enough energy to walk the streets. The girls fascinate me. Tonight I saw a beautiful creature accompanying a GI going

93. A collection of the works of Britain's poet laureate John Masefield (1878–1967).

towards the cabaret. She is a success. Hair set just so, fine-featured face, the best in clothes that Jap dressmakers have to offer. She walked with confident stride, and Japs paused to look after her as she passed. But yesterday I saw two bawdy prostitutes—dirty and cheap. With worn-down shoes, unkept hair, thin, uncared-for dresses. And there are a surprising number of cripples on the streets now. Hunchbacks, cripples. Tonight I saw a Jap veteran in white kimono with the Red Cross band on the sleeve. What does he think?

Dearest, I have such a yearning to write. Yet, I can't. What is the matter with me? It seems like there is a message I must have out of my system. I want to tell everyone something, and in an effective way. Yet, what is it? All these people. Tonight, you should have seen the crowds on the streets. The sidewalks were packed, and I was fascinated with them, going against the stream of faces. What are they out for? They are so restless that they cannot sit still at home. How pitiful it is. People without purpose—people without an anchor. They are wandering, searching, grasping.

Babs. She surely is a good sport. Her heart must be bleeding. Her Gomis is leaving for Venezuela by the end of this month. Yet, she laughs it off. Sr. said that she is *erai* [strong]. Yes, I think so too. No moping around for her. She must be well in her thirties, said Sr. Also, Sr. said that the natural path of a woman is to become married. In their thirties, women feel their utter loneliness. But what are we to do? There are no eligible men floating around. And we don't want to marry just anybody.

I have almost forgotten my sad mood. Think I am pulling out of it. My back aches now, so I guess I'll go to bed. Washed my hair, and it feels so nice and clean. Larry just came in and said I could take this typewriter up to my room. He's right nice to me. And today I got on the bus with one of the Chinese boys, and he asked me how do you say "*saboru*" in English. I told him the slang expressions, "cut" and "ditch." He said that he wanted to learn slang. You know, if we ever get that book out, it will be very helpful to lots of people. He said that he was going to buy a dictionary of slang, but it didn't have GI slang in it. So mentally I patted you on the back.

I really feel like a "*monomochi*"[94] now. Tomorrow night I want to wear my new dress and wow them when I go to the show. Vanity. Might as well show off my new clothes now, while they are rare things among the females here. And I'll put on your lipstick thick as the time you bowled Kaneda over. He was so awe-struck that he couldn't find his tongue. Waren't that fun? Gee, Kay, we've had a lot of fun doing a lot of crazy things together. I wouldn't have missed it for the world.

The pageant of Japan. Going on under our very noses, Kay. If we don't write, who will? Let's write anything and everything, and save it, and use it.

94. Lit., a person with a lot of possessions; more generally, a rich person.

I'll be darned if I am going to waste my precious time on foolish GIs! What will that get me? Better to sit with typewriter in front. And to look, and observe, and write. Tonight I regretted that I had no pad and pencil with me. Hereafter, I am going to carry one with me. Writing is work, and I am going to sweat over it. Sr. told me off, and said that I do not exert myself to the extent of my abilities. True. I know it is. I am too lazy.

It is twelve and they are locking the door. You know, while I was typing here, some gals ran across the office, hid their faces, and ran upstairs. That's guilt if there ever was. They were in nightdress. Probably Paul and Chappy are satisfied now. Although I am not accusing anyone. And Russ told me that a certain gal and another stayed overnight with soldiers. I didn't know who it was until the other morning I sat across from [her]. And it suddenly came to me that that was her name. She looks like she would do something like that. She is sour and does not have any friends that I know of. And she doesn't look like she has any uplifting interests either. She is a type, I guess, but not an interesting one. Those GIs must have all these girls here classified. It was kind of fun getting some of the gossip from Russ.

We didn't have any dessert tonight, and Chappy says, "I guess Pool blackmarketed the dessert again." He said it so matter-of-fact that it was funny—Now it is twelve. I would love to have a rendezvous with Kamogawa. She must be beautiful now, under the light of the moon. I have really fallen in love with her. I'm going to get my descriptive powers going on her. It is so nice and cool here. I know that up in my room it is stifling hot. Gee, I wish I had a cigarette. Think the office boy is waiting up for me. Sr. doesn't like for me to smoke. He said it is impossible for him to leave Japan. It's a pity, really. Gomis is going to Venezuela. By way of the U.S. Gosh, Kay, I wish I could type on more and more and more. But I'll have to think of the little office boy. You know what, Kay, I bet in order to get any literary work you have to be in love with something—a man, beauty, nature, truth, or something. If you love something or someone, the work cannot be held back. Look at the Bible—I bet those men were in love with God. Therefore, the inspired work. I've got to take myself by the nape of the neck and reform. I saw a very good book yesterday, *The Secretary's Guide*, or something. It gave many good points in English. I bet that man is waiting for me. So I will stop, even if I hate to.

Kyoto, July 18, 1946

Dear Kay,

I haven't lost Russ after all. He just happened to have those girls up in front with him. And I think he still likes me. So here I am with my problem yet. I know that Sr. is more faithful and sincere, yet I gravitate towards Russ.

Why is it? Sr. has the brains. I admire him. It must be only the devil in me, pulling me towards the easy path. Because with Russ I am so light-hearted and content. While, if I am with Sr., I mope and think about Russ. What a fickle heart hath a woman!

It is seven at night, and here I am up in the office. I was going to write, but I rode up here with Russ, and now I have lost all inspiration and the sad mood. Sr. is coming tonight, too. I must get home before he does. It's awful—I can't concentrate at all. So guess I'll stop with this. I tried anyway.

19 July. Why, O why, don't I hear from you? And now that I can't write to my family or Miye, you'll be the ONE and only to correspond with. But as Miye did during the war, I think I'll write to her and keep it until the happy day that we can meet.[95] That's a very good idea. It will be sort of a diary for me, too. I'll fool them wise guys that wants to prohibit us foreign [nationals; *sic*] from doing anything.

I've been carrying around Rupert Brooke and reading it while waiting and [during] odd moments. I don't know about him. I like some of his verses, but some of them I don't care at all for. And there doesn't seem to be anything very lasting about them. I mean, they don't deeply move me or leave a deep impression. I could read them and forget them easily. But then, he has beautiful ideas, and lovely ways of expressing them. Maybe he has to sort of grow on you. I like John Masefield more for his variety and his story-telling style.

I've been wanting to read Walt Whitman, but it seems that something always interferes. I wonder why Sr. likes him. Last [night] I defended myself with him. We surely had a fight. I really don't blame Sr. for getting angry and disgusted with me. I know that I am a fool. I knew that Sr. was coming, so I should have come home early. Instead, I was gallivanting around with Russ. I made a date with Russ to go to the movies tonight, and Sr. wanted me to break it. I wouldn't do it. It's very true what Sr. says—Russ will go home very soon, he only wants to have a good time, he will forget all about me. But I let out all of my pent-up bitterness on him, especially when he said, "What is your responsibility to God?" I muttered, "What's the use of being good, of being conventional, of trying to improve oneself? What has it got me so far? And what will it ever get me? I'm sick of it all." Look at us, Kay, stranded over here for seven of the most precious years of our lives. Is there any justice? How can we talk about our responsibility to God when there is so much ugly injustice going on about us? O, I'm sick and tired of it all. And I only want to forget everything. Sr. looked sad, and said that he felt sorry for me.

Walt Whitman said,

95. Miye kept a journal of "letters" to Mary all during the war, which she presented to her after she returned to the United States.

> I think I could turn and live with animals, they are so
> placid and self-contained,
> I stand and look at them long and long.
>
> . . .
>
> They do not make me sick discussing their duty to God,
> Not one is dissatisfied, not one is demented with the mania
> of owning things.[96]

I don't see why Sr. likes Whitman. When he told me, "Where is your dignity, where is your responsibility?" I tried to tell him what Whitman said about animals not caring about their duty to God.

But just think—what has the struggle been worth, anyway? Why did I work my way through school? Only to become a typist for the army? Merely a substitute for a machine. We've been cheated out of seven years of our lives, and what is the world to judge us? I told Sr. I believe in myself, and what do I care what others think. It's not my fault that I am stuck over here.

Poor Sr.! He was so disappointed in me! He's really wonderful, and I ought to be shot for hurting him as I do. Why do I do it? It would be much better for me to go steady with him, for he respects me and I know that he likes me now. But I think he let me know too late that he likes me. He took me for granted too long. Now, I am not content with him. Aw, I'm tired of analyzing all this. I do know that my head tells me to stick to Alvarez, but my heart says no. After all, emotion does rule. When I saw him in class yesterday, I was struck with distaste for his fatness, for his sloping shoulders, his femininity. But what should that matter? It's his brains, his kindness that should count. What are physical characteristics anyway? But he thrills me no more.

And Russ. I am not satisfied with him either. He is cute, and yet, we really don't have anything in common to talk about. But he is all attention again. I told Sr. that he doesn't take care of me like a girl likes to be taken care of, and he says that he's never been with women, so [he] doesn't know the first thing about it. If I was going to marry Sr., it might be different, but that can never be. Perhaps my friendship with Russ is temporary, but with Sr. it will be also. One thing I have found out through experience: I can only go with ONE person. And Sr. and Russ surely hate each other. I must make a decision, yet, I can't for the life of me. If I knew that Russ is going with someone else, I guess I could give him up. But as it is, I keep thinking of him.

So here's your Mary going around in circles in her merry way.

Here are some quotes I liked, which were in some English book: "To make your meaning clear—that is the secret of good punctuation, good usage, good speech, and good writing!" "My point of view is that, in everyday life,

96. "Song of Myself" (1855), verse 32.

good English follows clear thinking rather than that system of rules called Grammar which youth loathes and maturity forgets." They are by some unknown [i.e., not famous] persons, so I didn't bother to take down the authors. I like them, for they are very sensible.

I've got on the cutest dress today. This morning my morale had hit a new low, so I tried to boost it up by wearing a new dress. It surely did get boosted, too. The cat in me was purring away in content when the gals like Flo and Ray gave me envious dirty looks while I ignored them completely in my purty new dress. And it is flattering to see that men look at you twice. Clothes surely make a difference. As Babs kept repeating, my sisters surely made wonderful choices of clothes for me, for everything goes together. And they are all so simple and smart. I love them all. Another good thing is that they button up in front, making it easy to iron them, for I can unbutton them and get them out flat. It certainly is wonderful to have a family now.

1:30. Got a letter from NYK today saying that they had no records of the passengers on the *Tatsuta Maru*.[97] They took long enough to answer it.

So good-by. Why don't I hear from you? Hope my letters are reaching you, at least.

Kyoto, July 19, 1946

Dear Miye,

I found my little pad, and I am going to carry that around with me hereafter and jot down whatever strikes me. I used to do that. Now my ambition is gradually ebbing back.

Like I've wanted to write about the two little bedraggled orphans who are always out in the street, sitting along the sidewalk, begging. They have a sign which explains that they are victims of an air raid, their belongings were burned up and their parents are dead. Now, two of the little tots sit in the dirt, with filthy dresses on, sucking their fingers. They have a little pot in front of them in which people who are so moved contribute towards their upkeep. Poor little things! And yet, I don't know why, but they arouse no compassion in me. Maybe it's because I suspect that their parents wrote the sign and come around to collect their "earnings." I only gaze on them in wonder at how dirty human beings can become, and still exist. They are such a dirty brown, their hair is dust saturated, there are cakes of dried mud on their feet. And they have been out in the street corner for it must be nearly a month now. Isn't there somewhere they could go? Once I read an article about how

97. As part of her effort to document her citizenship, Mary wrote to the line on June 24, 1946, inquiring whether it had a passenger manifest for the ship's December 1941 voyage.

it is doing harm to charitable organizations to give to beggars, and ever since, I have never felt pity for them. But that was in America.

It's 4:25, so I think I'll go, and then I might be able to catch the bus. Good-bye.

Kyoto, July 20, 1946

Dearest Miye,

Heard the best news last night. We might be able to get back by next January. They are going to send us Jap-Americans back from January! Just think—only half a year! Boy, did my heart skip a beat, and frolicked just like a lamb. Just think! I'll be back to good old California, and I'll be able to see your little baby,[98] and your Nick, and of course, YOU!!! Gee, it won't be long now. I have now fresh impetus and stimulus to stick to it until that happy day.

It is probably only a rumor, but it is surprising how some rumors come true. That's the way everything used to start and spread over here. The government must have started things only as rumors, and when people had gotten used to the idea, they would announce it.

This morning I was reading John Masefield. I like him much better than Rupert Brooke, both of whom I have in the small editions, and carry around with me. I find in Masefield a depth which is lacking in Brooke. And his style is so narrative, and so easy to read, that it is like following a stream from its very source as a pleasant spring onto its various curvings, rapids, serenity, in and out, until it reaches its destination in the vast ocean.

Father Dunn is still away. I do miss him. He has character, that man. Guess I'd better not discuss the people around here because I am leaving these things in the office. Wish I had a box that locked.

Think I'll quit and write the letter for Al. Gee, I do wish that I could send this out right away. It is Saturday, already.

Kyoto, July 20, 1946

Dearest Miye,

Just received your 20 July letter,[99] and now feel like I'm on top of the world. At least, Miye, you believe in me. You like my writing. That is what counts. I can't remember, for the life of me, what I wrote on the Fourth of July. Your Nick surely did flatter me, though. I'm so glad that you found each other. He must be wonderful.

98. Miye, then expecting, had promised if she had a girl to call her Mary.

99. A mistake. Mary was supposedly responding on the 20th. The date was perhaps unimportant to her at a stage when she could only accumulate her letters to Miye.

Also heard from Blanche and mother today. Emma is to leave on the fifteenth, they said, so they must be in Monterey by this time. Emma is so darned sensible, that it surprises even me at times. Like, I wanted to have Emma send me an affidavit saying that she was my sister, that I came to Japan to study, that I got on the last boat to the US but was unable to make it on account of the war, that she would take responsibility that I would never become a public charge. That's what Kay had her sister send her. But what does Emma do but have the affidavit say that I can take care of myself. And in the letter accompanying, she states bluntly that she doesn't expect to support me, and knows that I can support myself. I thought that was just like her. She is so straight! If you don't understand her, I guess you could be hurt. Like, when I sent her a brooch, and she bawled me out because things are so expensive over here. That made me rather sore, but then, when I thought it over, I know that she had my good at heart, and never meant any harm.

Now I am beginning to climb out of my slough of despair. Maybe I am not a failure. Even if I am only a typist now, I have a lot of time that I can call my own in which I can write and read to my heart's content. Which is more than I could do if I had a better paid job. Money isn't everything. I know that; yet, it is helpful to have some. And I'm surprised that cotton is so hard to get. I'm glad you told me how things are. When I used to be in the States, cotton was so plentiful and cheap that it is hard to picture the situation now. I bet you'll have to hunt a lot now. And you, in your condition, and working so hard too. I ought to be ashamed of myself by being so brazen as to ask you for so much!

Miye, you have surely put me into a writing mood. And I am almost so disappointed in not being able to write to you that I could write the War Department. Why can't we use the APO, anyway? Foreigners can, and so can Nisei who have their papers. It takes so long for us to get our papers. Why cause unnecessary suffering? Especially when it won't hurt anyone? I enjoy writing to you, for you are so appreciative, and I can write along, just as I think.

We don't have to work forty hours a week yet. I treasure your letters all the more when I know that you are writing it out of rare and precious time. I wish that I could give you some of the time I have so much of!

Another delicious weekend ahead of me. This is the leisure I have always craved, for time I can call my own. And not have to spend on things or people I don't care [for].

I do hope that the doctor confirmed your suspicions. Little Mary. I love to think of her. What are you going to name it if it is a boy?

Kyoto, July 20, 1946

Dearest Kay,

Chappy said last night that the only thing wrong with Sr. was that someone should make him jealous, then he'd be all right. Well, I guess he's getting what's good for him. He took me too much for granted.

Jimmy's here!! Aren't you glad? He's in MG now, was transferred. He was as full of life as ever. Last night after supper, I saw Jimmy, and exclaimed over him, and went to Chappy's room with him. There we had cokes and whiskey. It was too strong for me, and I didn't care for it. Jimmy says, "Tell Kay I got several letters from her, and I'm sorry I didn't answer. But I got a letter from mother bawling me out for not writing. I haven't written anyone for five months." He was looking so suntanned, I said, "Where did you get your suntan?" He answers, "That's no suntan, that's my natural color. I'm black!" He and Chappy went out together last night.

Went to the show *Mr. Smith Goes to Washington* last night, but walked out because it didn't interest me, and Russ had seen it before. I wonder why—movies bore me now. I can't sit quietly through them, I get so tired of sitting. I'd rather be practicing or washing or taking a shower or walking or gazing at Kamogawa. Met a girl last night in the shower who came from Kainan,[100] and she's from Washington, or Oregon, or someplace like that. She is taking piano lessons and can play quite well. She said that the pianos are all full in the evenings. I guess it's the best time for me to practice when I go—after work until 5:30. Mrs. Hoshina[101] was telling me of two GIs who began piano only a couple of months ago, and now they can play quite well. They practice about three hours a day. I like to hear about GIs spending their time profitably like that. It's encouraging.

Here's some gossip. You know Mary, of RTO [the Railway Transport Office]? That sweet young thing. Well, she had been living with a GI in a hotel and night before last, he was picked up by an MP for being out at 11:30. They discovered that he has been AWOL for two months, or something like that. He's been in the army 38 months, and his record is bad. He is supposed to be married to Mary. I think she made a poor pick, though. He's in the stockade now. Russ said that she looked like she had been crying yesterday. I said, "They have to get married by the consul now." And Russ said that it was a Japanese wedding. O, well, who cares? It's their affair.

Hurray! I just got a letter from Miye, Blanche, and mother. What a morale booster letters can be! And amidst all my self-blame and disgust, Miye's praise of me comes like a balm. Listen to it:

100. A city in northwest Wakayama Prefecture.
101. The Japanese piano teacher at the Army School.

"Your Fourth of July letter came today and I let Nick read it because it was so beautifully written, sounding just like you at your best and no mention of Sr. Nick was amazed at your intelligence and said you're no ordinary woman but a very brilliant one. Aren't you flattered? You're no failure. You're the most interesting Kimoto and that's better than making a lot of money. You've certainly experienced a lot and my ma says you're the most lovable. And my child would be honored to bear your name.

"I admire your getting up early to practice the piano. You really are extraordinary. If I got up early I'd do some Martha-ish thing like the washing.[102]

"Your observations on the girls at the hotel were too keen and biting. I had to laugh because I could picture each type. They seemed to parade across my mind as you described them."

(Isn't Miye wonderful? At another part she says, "Nick said, 'You sure fixed things up good for me,' when I told him about the baby and then [he] laughed and laughed. I told him he could pick out a Japanese name for her. Now he's always talking about 'our kid' this and 'our kid' that.") Isn't it just too perfect about them having a happy event in the near future? I feel good all over when I think of them in their cozy little home.

What would I do without you and Miye? I've been feeling so rotten lately, feeling like a complete failure. But now I think I am slowly but surely climbing out. That surely was flattery, coming from Nick. I don't remember what I wrote to her on [the] Fourth of July. And I thought my description of the girls was flat. Well, if she liked it, my poor efforts are not all in vain. I hate to think I am the failure of the family. And I won't be, if stubbornness has anything to do with it!!!

Aren't you ever coming to Kyoto? Even for a few days? Now that Jimmy is here, won't you come? I want to see you so much! "Absence makes the heart grow fonder" is true where deep friendship or love is concerned. It is only with passing acquaintances that it does not hold true.

Another weekend ahead of me. It is so wonderful to be able to call your time your own!

Kyoto, July 20, 1946[103]

Dearest Kay,

Both Peggy and Amy have their citizenship papers now! I'm happy for them, but very envious too. Amy got hers a month ago, and she didn't say a

102. An allusion to Luke 10: 40, a passage in which Martha complains to Jesus that she has to do the serving while all her sister Mary does is listen to him.

103. Mary was clearly in a writing mood, with two letters to Miye and now a second to Kay. By her own date line, she started this letter at 4:30 P.M.

word to me about it! I asked them why didn't they get civil service jobs, and Amy says, "Things don't come as quickly as that!" So they are no better off than we are. Except that they can write to the States. Just think, Kay, by the time we get our papers, there will be so many applicants for civil service jobs that we won't get any. Listen, if you see any opportunities to put in an application or get any pull, please let's get in on it. I'll be darned if I'll continue to work as a foreign national after I get my papers! Just think of all the privileges we are missing out on—pay in dollars, PX supplies, commissary, mail, and the rights of an American citizen. But by the time we get our papers, if I can go back, I'll take the first boat home. I'm sick and tired of this place.

I got lots of gossip today. Had such an interesting talk with Mrs. Hashimoto, the art teacher, and Mrs. Hoshina, the music teacher. Mrs. H.[104] said all her family is crazy. They used to live in Chicago. All her family is back there yet. Her brother married a Russian-German girl, her sister married a German boy. She said that her sister loves cats and dogs, and has no children, and that her husband is a psychologist who gives lectures, and that their home is always wide open and noisy all night long. And when Mrs. H. comes to their place, they say, "Here's the little Jap." Mrs. H. is fifty years old, but very interesting, and she can talk just like an American, and is witty and intelligent. She told my fortune from my hands. Said that I had an offer of marriage last year (I let her think that was true), and that I would be married in the near future, that I would live long, have lots of property but not money, that I have moods of sadness, though I cover it up. She loves to talk, and did just that for nearly an hour, before my music lesson.

After the lesson Mrs. Hoshina (O, I never noticed, both of them are Mrs. H.'s. Well the above refers to Mrs. Hashimoto) told me about the officers, saying that most of them have private homes with temporary wives. Girls from good Jap families, for they are afraid of picking up VD. And that officers want women who can't speak English, for then they can keep their tracks covered more. You know, I think that is one reason why they don't go with girls at our hotel. For we can speak English, and everything we do (as well as do NOT do) is noised all over the town. Besides, we might go back to the States and make things embarrassing for them. Mrs. Hoshina said that some families charge 1,000 yen for their daughters FOR ONE TIME! Can you imagine! Why, that's more than I make in two months! And that a friend of hers is a doctor, and that he is having a lot of women and girls come to him in distress. You can guess what for. And lots of them are high school girls (*jogaku-sei*) who WANT to have American babies. Mrs. Hoshina thought

104. Mary catches herself in the next paragraph, realizing that she's named two women whose names started with "H."

it was terrible. I conventionally agreed. Yet, I wonder. Will the standards of morals change with this huge impact? I wonder how those officers get their girls, and why these good families allow such things. Is it that the Japs admire officers and are willing to offer their daughters as presents? I never knew that it was so widespread. The officers keep it secret, too. That's why Mrs. Hoshina said that she prefers to teach young GIs, for they are cute little boys who have other things besides sex on their minds.

Today I saw an officer with his wife walking in front of the Red Cross. She had red hair and was—gee, I can't find the word—anyway, she didn't look pretty, for her skin was too tanned, her dress was too loud, she had an unsatisfied look on her face, which was smeared with too bright lipstick. I've heard that men who have been in Japan for a long time go home to find that American women lack the delicate beauty of Japanese women. I think I know what they mean. Jap women are so fine-complexioned, so dainty and neat. That is, the well-to-do ones. They don't have that aggressive, mean look that American women have.

I rode on the bus from Red Cross to Daiken with a load of drunk Australian sailors, and the profanity embarrassed me. I feel so self-conscious when I am with a bunch of GIs, among whom are those few who are drunk and swearing. I know the sober GIs are embarrassed. And that makes me so too. Russ told me last night that he heard that you cussed a lot. I suppose he heard that from Francis. The latter had a gal riding around with him the other evening. Now, Francis, Johnny, and Russ drive at the same time.

Saw Mrs. Rubini this morning, and she told me to come to her room tonight and she'd show me pictures of herself at her prime, and newspaper clippings. She must live in the glorious past. O, yes, another thing Mrs. Hashimoto told me was that I would not spend a lonely old age, although I wouldn't have many children. I feel so sorry for lonely old people, and hope I am never like that.

Look at all I write you, and I don't hear a thing from you! I'm beginning to rebel!!!

Again, I say I will close. Tell me about Steve[105] when you write.

105. Steve Brody, a civilian employee of the ARC. Kay worked for him in both Osaka and Tokyo.

[Chafing at the prohibition that kept her from writing overseas, Mary sent this letter of protest to the U.S. authorities on July 22, 1946. A follow-up, sent nine days later, is not included here.]

Theater Postal Officer
GHQ, AFPAC
Tokyo, Japan

Dear Sir:

I have been told that we Japanese-Americans who have been stranded in Japan from before the war, and who are working for the Occupation Army cannot use the APO. Could you please give me the facts on the matter? Are we forbidden to use the APO? If so, I wonder if the matter could not be reconsidered.

Only a short time ago, I heard that a foreigner who lives in Kobe, Japan, wrote to the War Department asking if foreigners could use the APO, and he was given permission to [do so]. If foreigners can, why cannot we who are American citizens use the American channels of mail—the only way we can get in touch with our loved ones? There are not too many of us here, and the volume of mail would be negligible.

I shall present my case, since I know of it better than any other. I came to Japan to study the land of my ancestors and to study the language. I had not the slightest intentions of giving up my American citizenship. The war broke out as a surprise, catching me over here alone. For dreary long years, I was cast out here with no word from my parents, brother, sisters, and friends. It was a happy day indeed when peace finally came. From my brother-in-law, who is a member of the Occupation Troops stationed in Tokyo, I received word that my family were all well. I was so relieved and happy that tears flooded my eyes. If only I were allowed to write to them, how much happiness would be mine! At present I am working as a typist for the Chaplains' Office of I Corps in Kyoto.

"As cold waters to a thirsty soul, so is good news from a far country" (Prov. 25:25), states one of the wisest men who ever lived. It is a well-known fact that letters are one of the most effective morale boosters for members of the Occupation Troops. Should it be of any less importance to us who are stranded over here? No, to us, who have never even met our loved ones for six or seven years, they would take on a proportionately bigger importance! And also, is not correspondence a means towards the making of "one world"? We who have suffered here the war years know and understand the Japanese people. With this experience added to our background of American upbringing and schooling, surely we can contribute towards mutual understanding, and thus, the shortening of the occupation and the prevention of future wars.

History shows that it is the minority that has always suffered. We Japanese-Americans who are over here are no less loyal to the land of our birth than the famed 442nd Infantry Combat Team, composed largely of Nisei. Rather, having witnessed the disastrous effects of militarism and a life inhibited by old customs and traditions, we realize the advantages and freedom of the American way of life. And what is to be gained by prohibiting us to use the mail? Perhaps the mail will be a few pounds lighter, but what difference would that make in the tons of mail that are handled? It is like a drop in a bucket. And if we are working for the Army, I should think that we could be granted this privilege. Even if we haven't got our citizenship cleared, why not give us a little bit of innocent and constructive happiness? It takes so long to get our papers cleared. Should we pay the unjust penalty of being victims of events over which we had no control?

I appeal to your sense of humanity and justice in asking that we Japanese-Americans who work for the Army be granted the privilege of using the APO, even if we do not have our papers cleared as yet. Such permission will mean the greatest happiness to us who are separated from our loved ones.

Very truly yours,
(Miss) Mary Kimoto

July 23, 1946

Dearest Sweetie-pie [Kay],

How perfectly wonderful to hear from my long lost gardener! I was nearly dead from the drought, but thanks be to Allah, you have refreshed my soul! I have taken life, my leaves are resurrected from their wilted laxity, my flowers have bloomed, and here I am so green and fresh! I knew that you were writing! Three big letters from you today, and I thought I'd die of the pleasure. "O ye of little faith," didn't Christ say?[106] I thought God must be faithful, just like you, always writing and caring for us, but here we fret and complain and distrust Him. Now, if I were a chaplain, I would make that the theme of next Sunday's sermon. But thank God, I am not, and I do not have to elaborate and put over the moral.

Dearest, I am so sorry, so sorry that you have no time to call your own. I wish that I could divide some of my wonderful leisure time with you. It is so lovely and quiet and peaceful here in my little green pond and I can really call my soul my own. I hate to think of you way up there in a dirty, dusty, hot place so busy and so unsatisfied. But I do admire you for sticking it out. Really I do.

What is the idea of calling yourself a skinny frog (you had me worried, for

106. Matt. 16: 8.

I took it literally), then a couple of letters [later] telling me that you want to wear one of those hideous girdles? I hate those things, and for the life of me, I shall not confine my natural curves in such restraining tortuous garments. I hate restraint, be it mental, spiritual, or physical. And let's not hear any more of that. Even if you are fat, I know of a few people (half of our hotel) who are twice the circumference as you in vital spots, so that's that.

Good ole Steve is one wonderful person whom I shall never forget. Somehow, he is so tied up with Gene and the better things—I don't know how to express it—you know, those olden days when we were so impressed with the handsome, valiant, generous Americans. Days gone forever. But Steve was really so sincere, and he never would take credit for worrying about us. I loved the way he used to kid around with us, then all of a sudden get serious and come to the point. Yes, always with a phone in his hand. I loved the way you described him hanging up when they started mushy-mushying[107] him. I don't want him to leave Japan! No more than I wanted Dr. Simms to. Where is he going next? Be sure to tell him every time I write that I said hello to him.

I like your Lt. King, too. He must be a lot of fun. And it was so nice of Brownie to want you to be his wife's companion. I hope she is a sweet little wife and mother, and you will be able to go to their home as a refuge. That would be ideal. But what I've seen of dependents over here leaves a bad taste in my mouth.

You know, Kay, this seems too good to be true. Namely, starting tomorrow, all military personnel work from 7:45 to one in the afternoon. Babs said that her major said it included foreign nationals. Won't that be just too wonderful? Think of all the time we'll have. Babs and some girls were talking about it, and saying, what will they do with all their time? That is the least of my worries. I could never have too much time. Last night, when I told Johnny about it, he pops up, "That's a lot more time for me to practice." And that's just what I thought. I went to practice last night, and all four pianos were occupied. One girl from our hotel on one, a Jap on another, and Johnny on another. Forgot who was on the other one—O, I remember, it was Ishida, the foreign national who is a graduate of Ueno.[108] So I sat and listened to Johnny play until one of the others left. He can play a beautiful piece by Chopin, and I love it. It's one he has been working on ever since I first met him. I love to hear him play, for he puts everything he has into it. He stopped for a while, and said, "Listen to that Nisei (Ishida) play. He really can play." I told him, "I'd rather hear you because you bang away so hard and put everything you've got into it." While Ishida can play more complicated pieces, I wonder

107. A play on the Japanese telephone greeting "*moshi-moshi.*"
108. Ueno Music Academy in Tokyo.

if he has the passion and love for the music that Johnny has. Maybe he has in a quiet way. But why have that in a quiet way?

I'm reverting back to type, the heathen Japanee. You ought to see me running around with only my birthday suit on. But it feels so free, cool, and unhampered. The nudists have something, after all.

You see Negroes around Kyoto every once in a while now. Yesterday, when I was coming up the side elevator, the door wouldn't open, and a Negro GI who was waiting on the same floor, told me, after we got on, "Tell the boy to bring the elevator on the same level as the floor. I used to be an elevator boy myself once." I liked that. Somehow, it touched me. He was so democratic about it. And he was not ashamed of the fact that he used to be an elevator boy. But he smelled so nice, like a beauty parlor, that I carried the aura with me back to my room even after I left him on the elevator. The trouble with people is that they generalize, saying that Negroes are no better than animals. There are a lot of whites you can say that about. There are educated Negroes, and there are illiterate ones. Why should they be classed according to color when there [are] many more important characteristics by which men should be classed, if they are to be classed at all?

Sr. certainly is patient with me, and keeps coming back. Yesterday he came up to the office and he showed me the pamphlet that the I&E section had mimeographed for the school. It spoke of Spain as taking all the gold and precious materials from her colonies, and a lot of junk like that, but didn't have a word about how the US took half of Mexico away from her. Sr. was all excited about it and said, "*Kenka shimasu*" ["I'm going to fight"], but he went to see Chaplain McCandless about it first, then Chaplain McCandless calmed him down, so that he didn't feel like going to I&E to fight. Sr. said that Chaplain McCandless is a wonderful person. I am beginning to admire him more and more.

It is just like your mother to keep a record of accounts. No wonder you like to see a job well done, and do your work well. Childhood training. But I liked your quote from *RD* [*Reader's Digest*]. I saw the cover, but that was all. Yes, too many mothers are too careful about keeping collars white and tidy, and don't give a hang about keeping their children happy. Just this morning, I was reading Masefield about that. See if I can find it. There, I've found it. Wonder if you have got the Masefield I sent you yet? It's in "The Everlasting Mercy," page 48. You see, this drunkard found a little boy who had lost his mother and was crying. So he told him stories,

> Of where the tom-cats go by night,
> And how when moonlight came they went
> Among the chimneys black and bent,

From roof to roof, from house to house,
With little baskets full of mouse.
All red and white, both joint and chop
Like meat out of a butcher's shop.[109]

The little boy was delighted with his tales, and forgot about his sadness in losing his mother. Just then, his mother came in sight and slapped him for listening to a drunkard, saying,

Some day you'll break your mother's heart,
After God knows she's done her part,
Working her arms off day and night
Trying to keep your collars white.

Then she gets after the drunkard for associating with her little boy. And all the time, the boy had been in wonderland, listening to the wonderful tales.

While I was in the middle of the above paragraph, Al started talking, and said that he heard that I knew all the truck drivers. That's not true. He said that he defended me. Good for him. But then, he gave me advice that truck drivers as a rule do not have good reputations as far as girls are concerned. Yes, I guess that is true. I think I'll break up with Russ. I don't care for him especially, and he's getting too insistent.

Kyoto, July 24, 1946

Dearest Miye,

I feel wonderfully alive this morning. It started off well because I saw Watanabe, the Nisei boy who comes to Spanish class, on the elevator. He is a character, and Sr. thinks a lot of him. Said that one night he saw the kid Watanabe bicycling down the street with a big cross at his neck. He asked him if he were Catholic, and Watanabe answered, "No, Christian." He comes and goes to class whenever the notion strikes him. And has the cutest, open grin on his face. Very young—he must be around eighteen at the most. Last time he came to class, he walked up behind the teacher and put away his dictionary, then he talked to Sr., right in the middle of the class, and told him that he had graduated, and was to be stationed at Osaka or Nagasaki. So I was thinking, I'll never see that character anymore; then I ran into him this morning, and was so happy over it. I like little kids like that that I can tease.

Nearly all the office force is here now, so I think I'll do a little work.

Here it is 11:30 already. Cut two stencils and had them run off, then folded the leaflets. That bunch down in AG Publications surely is funny. There's a

109. From "The Everlasting Mercy" (1911), verse 61. The following quote is from verse 65.

GI named Miller who is the highest in rank there, and he's the only one who is serious or does any work. The others always have an I-don't-care attitude. There's Poncho, as they call him, who is a Spaniard with typical round face, black hair, fair skin, dark eyes. He's always trying to talk to me in Spanish, but I can't understand half what he says. So easygoing he is, and it's a wonder when he is there, for he is always fooling around somewhere else. And then there's Tarnish, a blond from Kansas, or someplace where they have cornfields, and he looks it. Rather small, but quite a good worker, and good-natured too. He gives the impression of having slant, cat-eyes, and altogether, reminds one of a light brown cat, a tom-cat that minds his own business. Russell is the third of those who are the staff of Miller's. He's blond, heavy-set, older than the others, and slow in his ways. He always tells me when my dresses are too long, or when my slip is showing. Looks like a well-settled storekeeper, and would look at home in a storekeeper's apron, with hands on hips and viewing the world go by in a small town. He would give little kids candy and gum in his matter-of-fact, slow way. Set in his ways and his petty prejudices.

That's enough. I'm tired of thinking. There's still half an hour to go. It seems like Saturday today. I'll close for now.

Kyoto, July 25, 1946

Dearest Kay,

Wonderful letters from you—gifts from heaven were in my cubbyhole. I grabbed them, and regardless of the fool Pool's instructions, I read them greedily thruout my dinner. Getting both mental and physical food at the same time.

My gosh, is his real name Samson? I thought you were just kidding at first. And I'm so glad and at ease now that you gave me such sensible advice about Russ. What you say is very true, and you have me see it all objectively. And dear Mr. Brody. I could just hug him for taking you to the concert and for getting indignant when they asked you for your pass.

Just went down to the Language section to return the book. Everyone looked at me, and the lieutenant who told me how to procure a dictionary said "Hello" to me. I felt so important to draw all their eyes. Yeah, me too, I wish I could find a nice Nisei boy to go with. But they are all so darned young, I feel like a grandmother beside them. That Watanabe I borrowed the dictionary from said that it would cost me five yen for borrowing it. I said, "After my ship comes in I'll pay you." Don't you believe it, Kay, for when my ship comes in, I'm going to board her and sail me home!!!

Last night I went to Spanish class and Sr. came home with me. We had quite a lot of fun. For I missed my supper, and I was ravishing hungry; then I thought of the lone K ration I had. Out it came, and down it went in a moment's time. It tasted good, too—especially the ham and eggs, the can of it. I bet the damned censors will prick up their donkey ears when they read "K ration." Haw, haw, I guess I only had one, and that is gone now. So there.

One thing of interest I learned in Spanish class was that their expression for "giveaway" (I forgot what the dictionary termed it) was "describe donkey's ears," which comes from the Aesop fable about the donkey who tried to fool the animals by putting on a lion's skin—but his ears sticking up gave him away.

I don't see why you raved about my letter so much. It was done in the mood, though, and I guess that is what counts. Someone like me ought to have lots of loves and get her heart broken innumerable times, then I would write and write. But as it is, I am happy, fat, and the mood to write does not visit me often.

That Watanabe is really cute. You know, there's something to what you say about picking out the people you want to go [with] and asking them. I was doing that after a fashion. But it didn't occur to me that that is a good rule to follow. I have asked D'Aconda to take me, but he said he is always busy, although he did say he would take me sometime. Sr. predicts a brilliant future for him. But it's hard to draw him out—the Yale graduate with the perpetual smile.

And Johnny, the Dago. I must write up a description of him. He has charm in his dreamy eyes, so luxuriously set by curly thick eyelashes. Just think—he was practicing the piano from two yesterday afternoon until six when I saw him. And last night, while we were having our Spanish lesson, I could hear him. He really loves music with all his passionate Italian heart. People like that grow on you.

Larry is going to begin taking piano lessons from Mrs. Hoshina from tomorrow. Do you know that no dates are allowed—Jap dates—from next week at the Kyoto Theater? I feel like going to see some brass about that. Why not?—O, but it's too much bother. And I really don't care so much—it's just that I feel sorry for people like Mrs. Hoshina and Etsuko. The other Japs can go hang.

On second thought, I think I'll just let this letter go with this. Or shall I? Got into an argument with Al about letting Jap dates into the theater. He says that GIs are out with Japanese girls for only one thing, and it is disgusting. Now he is going on about how much he thinks of Cecilia. Al the dreamer. Wonder if he'll ever wake up? In a way, I hope not!

So my dear, I'll be leaving you. How could I be of such little faith that I doubted for an instant that you'd not write to me? Good old Steve, I'd like to write to him. Think I shall, and would you please give it to him?

Kyoto, July 26, 1946

Dearest Kay,

Ha, ha—the men have to move out of our hotel! So ole Pool and Chappy look like they've lost their last friend. Well, I think there shouldn't be any men staying in a hotel full of women anyway! They've had it too good up to now. It was going a little bit too far.

The Chief of Staff inspected our hotel today, and that's why the men have to go. I went to get my pay today and the bank clerk said you hadn't got your money yet. Why don't you go get it if you're hard up? But then, I guess you wouldn't get much after they deducted your meals and uniform. But still you'd get at least ¥500. And they hadn't given me a raise, either! I must go see that stinker-butt Gorrez about it!

There, I feel much better with the typewriter than with a pen. So I'll get started on what I wanted to comment about that dancer. Well, good for her, I guess she got what she wanted. But I wonder if she is happy. I very much doubt it, especially when you say that she does not love him and that they have fights. What do all those clothes and jewels mean, really? They only add fuel to the fire of greed and vanity which are hers. Do they essentially change herself—her fundamentally prostituted body and soul? Of others I do not know, so I try to judge from what I have observed in myself. Yes, when I have a new dress the novelty and self-assurance are wonderful. But soon, you and those around you become used to your new dress—it is not new anymore and does not attract attention. After all, it is yourself that really counts. Fine feathers do not make a fine bird. That dancer might be able to lure rich men, yet is money everything? Give me a poor man, wise and content, any day to a rich man who is greedy and self-seeking. Didn't the Great Teacher Himself say that it is as hard for a rich man to enter the kingdom of heaven as a camel to go through a needle's eye? There are exceptions, I'll admit, but the majority of the rich are without character and without real happiness. And isn't a woman most happy when she loves and is loved? Look at the dancer—perhaps she is loved, but how disgusting it must be to live with a man you do not love. All the clothes and jewelry in the world cannot make up for the craving and loneliness in her heart. Yes, Kay, it does seem unfair to see a woman without scruples making a success—worldly success—when so many more deserving and honest women suffer. I guess that is one of the strong points in the argument for a future life, for the life here is unquestionably unfair. There ain't no justice. But then, deep down, I like to dream that there is justice. Look at her case. I do not believe that she is happy. And what are the joys she knows? Merely the vanity of dressing well, of gloating over her jewels, the physical pleasure from sexual contact, the animal pleasure of eating and drinking. But are those pleasures not soon numbed? Don't we grow immune to them? If we continually eat only the best food, one can easily become tired of it. What does she know of the inspiration received from reading poetry, the delight of true friends, the heavenly joys of motherhood, the satisfaction of knowing that she is doing what is true and right? No, I would rather live my life in my way than exchange it for any rich Spaniard, jewels, or clothing. What profiteth it a man if he gain the whole world but lose his soul?[110] Just think, Kay, would she enjoy that concert with Mr. Brody like you did? Could she appreciate Rupert Brooke? Personally, I think her life must be barren, and I rather pity her.

Well, I have said my say about the matter. It was rather interesting I must admit to find out what had happened to her. What is it that women like her have that attracts men? She must have what Helen of Troy, Cleopatra and others have. As for me, I am quite resigned to my lack of that essential sex appeal. If I haven't got it, that's that, and I do not mope about it. Life is too short for that. I can enjoy myself in my own way, with my chosen circle.

I think Cecilia is wonderful and, as Al said, she grows on one. She doesn't like all the gossip that most of these girls seem to thrive on, either. But she says that her roommate is always so full of it. You know, Cecilia has ideals, and I think she lives up to them too. She said she doesn't mingle with the others much either. And Al was saying that she told him of all they had to go through. I guess it wasn't easy for her widowed mother to raise up two daughters. There must be something in religion, for those who do go to church are different. And those church-goers who are bad are the exceptions.

You know, Kay, I was thinking that here I am getting all excited about racial prejudice and any kind of discrimination, but I am just as bad. For look at me among all these girls. I don't really know anything against them, yet I look down on them. I got to thinking that after Cecilia and Al were saying how nice Florence Nitta is. And she really is sweet. I don't know anything against her. And Terry, the other night when Sr. was getting some ice water down in the lobby, she was so nice and ladylike towards him. Maybe she is nice after all. Who am I to judge? Even mentally, I have no right to look down on them. Their superficial, ultra-politeness at the table gets me down, too, and if I see someone with even a little glimpse of congeniality in him, I talk

110. Matt. 16: 26.

loudly and laugh with him. Like this morning I was talking to a little boy who works in G-2 [military intelligence]. I thought he was kind of different, then I found out that he is Chinese. He wants to take piano lessons, too. He said that he had been taking economics in Teidai of Kyoto.

Well, I guess I ought to go and eat too. Babs just went now. But then, I can't let all this paper go to waste. How I wish I had a portable I could call my own! I know, I'll get Larry[111] a ribbon. I think that's what's wrong with this typewriter.

Chaplain McCandless is leaving tonight. I did like him and admired him. There was nothing petty about him. I liked the straight, unflinching wide-open look he used to give me when I talked with him. Last night, I met another GI who stays at the school. He seemed to be a little above the mediocre class. Said he teaches electricity, and also a group of college girls the American way of life. One incident he mentioned I'd like to pass on to you. One time a young boy of eighteen or so pushed a feeble old lady off an over-crowded streetcar, and got on himself. Eddie (that's his name) saw that and definitely did NOT like it. So he drove his jeep out in front of the streetcar and made the boy get off and let the woman on. He said that old woman was so thankful that she had tears in her eyes. The reason he told me the incident was because we got to talking about Japs and how they don't show their emotions. He said that old woman surely did. Eddie used to be a salesman back in civilian life. He said that you could look an American in the eye and tell just about what he was thinking, but not a Jap.

Well, I guess I've got my two cents' worth. Now I'll go down and eat, then off to school for Spanish and piano.

Kyoto, July 27, 1946

Dearest Kay,

Gee, I'm so excited! Listen, honey bun, I might be up to see you again! Really! Ain't it wonderful? Now, please tell me what times you work at the [Quartermasters'] club, and your doings as much as you can predict. Let's see—I'd better begin at the beginning. You see, I can get a two-week vacation, only don't tell anyone. Say that I have an ailing grandmother, and I have to go and be by her dying bedside. Anything, just so it won't get around that I am getting a vacation. So I am planning to go next Saturday, August 3, up to Akita to Teruko's place, if I hear from her, and also to Yonezawa to my country cousin's, and then, on the way back (or up) I'll stop in at Tokyo. That will be

111. A Chinese civilian who worked in the office at the hotel. Mary was grateful to him for allowing her to use his typewriter and a spare room.

so much fun! And I'll get a lot of new impressions. Yes, my little pond is quiet and nice, but I like to get out and see the wicked, wide world too. Now you be sure not to go gallivanting down anyplace when I drop in. Say, can't you come back to Kyoto with me when I come back? That will be around 17, 18 of August when I come back down here. Which would be perfect, except that I couldn't take off after that, for Cec will have her vacation from then, I suppose.

Ha, ha, the men have to move out of our hotel! O, I forgot, I have already told you. Well, that Chappy—I wonder if he was always like that? I definitely do NOT like him anymore. He was like a king there. Growing so fat and sensual. Now he has been dethroned. They have to sleep in the same room as six other GIs. Until now he had a palatial room to himself, with rich curtains, feathery bed, electric fan, icebox always stuffed with drinks and food, women. What more would a man want? It was really quite disgusting. All he lived for was his senses, I'm afraid. He was the law at our hotel. Well, it might be catty of me, but I am rather glad that they kicked the men out. It's not good to have a few men among all these women, anyway. Even the married couples had to go to the Station Hotel, along with the men foreign nationals.

Kyoto, July 28, 1946

Dearest Kay,

Gene is just simply wonderful! Good old Gene, he came up to see me today. Kay, I was a fool for not going with him steady. Compared with all the mediocre and low GIs I have come in contact with, Gene stands out like a pure jewel amidst all the imitations and glass. I hadn't realized fully how wonderful he really is. And he asked me if I had forgotten him! How can I? As long as I live, the memory of dear Gene, faithful, sincere, happy—will ever hold a cherished niche in my heart. For Gene represents some of the happiest days which we have spent in Japan, this God-forsaken land in which we had suffered for so long. And he is leaving in two weeks. O, I will really and truly miss him.

Kay, I hate to believe that Scotty is a stinker. But then, it was Scotty who led us to suspect Gene with his hints and open statements about Gene going with Mickey. I want to believe Gene. He said that there was nothing between them. He took her home four or five times, and went to see her when she was sick. And Gene wanted me to know before he went back that there had been nothing between him and Mickey. Gene—did we wrong you? I don't know. At that time I thought it would be better if I didn't go steady with him anymore. But look how faithful he is. He will be our friend forever. And always the same old Gene.

Doggone it, here's the fool Pool and I'm afraid he is butting in my business, so up I'll go. Kay, my dear, church this morning was really inspirational.

I like Chaplain Newby a lot. He isn't afraid to say what he really believes. He has fire and convictions. He pleaded for tolerance and faith, and his words were so apt. No more other churches for me. I have found a preacher whom I admire. No platitudes and dry theology for me. His words live. Well, here I go. My back aches. It must be old age.

Larry was saying that he wants a job in Daiken, and for me to find one for him. I don't know how to go about it. He likes to practice piano. I'm glad that I have someone to go with now. Also, Larry said that Chappy is mad now and wants to go home. He told Larry and Henry (the other office boy) to transfer to the Daiken bldg. I hate to see Larry working as only a typist, though. He ought to be able to do something better than that. Also, something else Larry told me: Pool never stays at the hotel—he has a house of his own where he goes to sleep. I never knew that. Chappy looks rather lost now that he has been dethroned.—It has been so nice and cool recently. Today I wore my white skirt that I had the Japs make for me, and my white blouse, and Al said that I look like a nurse. I don't like the skirt because it is too full. And makes me look very hippy. Maybe I'll take it up to my cousin's and fix it on her sewing machine. I'm so glad that now I have lots of blouses to wear, especially when I travel it will come in handy.

Now what was it that I wanted to tell you? I don't know, a hundred things come popping in on my mind, so I'll jerkily tell you whatever comes in mind. Went to the RTO the other night and asked the Lt. there about the military cars running up north from Tokyo, and he said that he didn't know—the best thing was to go to Tokyo to find out. I want to make plans, and on my vacation every day counts. Well, this morning I asked the Jap side, and they dully muttered that they didn't know. Undaunted, I went to the RTO again, and the boy told me to ask the Jap man they had in the office. Of course, he didn't know, but I looked around in the office, and there, right by where that lieutenant had stood to tell me, I found a schedule of the GI trains. Well, of all the nerve! What is the matter with that Lt. anyhow? Saying he couldn't tell me, when it was right before his very nose. Some people don't know the slightest thing about their jobs. It is disappointing to find how lax some people are about helping someone in distress. That's one thing, among other traits, that I so admire in you. If someone comes to you in distress, you do everything possible to help him. And Mr. Brody is that way too. I can't understand why some people can be so calloused to the troubles of others.

I found out that there is a train that goes up from Tokyo to Fukushima, then on up to Sendai, Aomori, Sapporo. And the GI there said that there were no others, except the one going to Nagano. So I don't know what to do. Wonder if it would be easy for me to get a ticket on the Jap train from Fukushima to Akita? If I have my travel orders, that ought to make them snap. Well, I haven't given up yet. I'll get there some way. But it is so complicated, and I hate to think of the heavy luggage I'll have to tote around. And of having to give presents to my relatives in Yonezawa.

I was so glad that Gene came yesterday and took me to my relatives'.[112] I was all worried about it, for I didn't know where it was, and so I bought a map of Kyoto and tried to locate the place. I hate to ride the streetcars because there is so much tedious waiting, and besides, they are always so very crowded. Then, Gene came to the rescue. It's wonderful, too, how he never is afraid of rules and regulations like so many of these chicken GIs are. He says he gets away with almost everything. By the way, Scotty was in the stockade for a day (until Pat got him out—good old Pat) for speeding. Gene was driving in front of him, but they didn't catch him. He said they have to catch you before they can arrest you. I told Gene that he had done so much for us, and he says, "I didn't do anything for you. I could have done much more. If I had gone through brass tacks." Now, isn't that just like him? How such a modest statement contrasts with what the stinker Mancil Grey has to say! He told me once that he really did a lot for you, then he went on to say everything—how we had a whole truck full of stuff that they had given us. What exaggeration! On the other hand, Gene said, "Tell me one thing that I have ever done for you." See, he didn't think he had done anything out of the way for us, when he really had. No, Gene, I'll never forget you and your giving, kind heart. He was saying, "People have more fun than anybody (like he used to say in Wakayama), it's no good if you have fun by yourself—it's giving others fun that's really worthwhile." I guess that is why he loves his carnival so. It's giving so much fun to people! He said that he is out of practice now. We drove way up the mountain, up by a little stream, so clear and beautiful and green and quiet. He says quietly that he likes places like that. And there are many times when he has drunk water from streams, kneeling on the rocks and drinking like a dog. How I wish that you had been with us!

As I was starting to say, we went to find my relatives' place. We did finally locate it, after asking lots of people and going back and forth and around in circles. They lived in the company compound, where they have lots of houses alike under one roof. All the kids of the neighborhood must have flocked around us. There were as many kids surrounding the jeep and jabbering their hellos and "goodu-byes" than the time we went to Kanedas'. My relatives are a sweet young couple from Yonezawa. They used to live in Tokyo, and I have gone to their place during the war. She is really a sweet country Japanese bride, having the best of the qualities of a Japanese woman. So modest, quiet, sweet, thoughtful. It does my heart good to see her. But they insisted on giving me

112. Tomi-san's half-brother and his family.

some cans of food, and I really didn't want to take it because I have plenty to eat, while they must be barely making it. However, during the war years when I was half-way starving, I used to go there and eat, and how good it was! You see, they could get things from the country, so they were relatively well off. But then, I thought, it's just like the Bible says, to those who have, more will be added, while to those who haven't, it will be taken away, what little they have.[113] It's not right. I don't want anything from them, yet they insist on giving it to me. If it were the ordinary Jap, I'd know that they were giving it to me in order to get something back in return. But during the war, when they knew that I could never give them anything, they used to be so generous to me! I hope that I can help them out now.

Kyoto, July 29, 1946

Dearest ~~Kay~~ Miye,

Here, I got you mixed up with Kay when I have just written to her. I was just discussing with Al my age. He didn't know that I was so old, and I told him how old Kay was and he says, "Gosh, you're old fogies!" Of all the nerve! But I don't care. I'm glad that I'm not one of these silly young things that flutter around here. I really feel sorry for some of the young girls in our hotel, being left to the dissipating influence of unscrupulous GIs. It is bad enough when you are old enough to take care of yourself. How unbalancing it must be to these impressionable young things. Like Cecilia talks about her roommate, Mickey, who is only seventeen years old. This Mickey gets all kinds of gossip from the others, and tells it all to Cecilia. Now Cecilia comes from a very devout Catholic family, and has strict upbringing, I am sure. She has character, and yet, she is sweet too. But she said that she used to be pretty much to herself, and didn't indulge in the gossip that most of the girls at the hotel seem to thrive on. Now she is hearing from Mickey the doings of everyone. It's rather pitiful that Mickey should be the receptacle of all the slander and gossip. I am afraid that it will not do her any good. Anyway, this is no life for a young girl to live—so superfluous, so unstable, so unnatural. I would hate to have had to live in such [an] environment during my impressionable years. Now I am calloused and stubborn, so can shut out the world and live as I want.

Just received [your] July 21 letter. O, I'm so glad to hear from you, even if I can't write regularly. Last night I went to the movies and USO show with Russ. He was feeling rather sick, so he was quiet. I felt sorry for him, for he kept yawning away during the picture, so we left before the movie ended. It

113. "For he that hath, to him shall be given; and he that hath not, from him shall be taken even that which he hath." Mark 4: 25.

was *Kitty*.[114] Rather interesting because the scenes were in England in the eighteenth century, and the language was different. Otherwise, it wasn't much. Wish I could have seen *Kitty Foyle*.[115] And will I ever see *Gone with the Wind*?

Kyoto, July 29, 1946

Dearest Kay,

Heck, I wasn't supposed to work here after all! Chaplain Newby is staying this afternoon. Now all my enthusiasm about writing you a book is gone. But I must tell you that I really enjoyed your wonderful letters.

Let me see now—what were some of the things I jotted down in my mind to tell you? O, I really feel sorry for the poor fish that Hannah Downs landed. She actually got married. But, then, I don't feel sorry for him, for if he's a fool enough to marry her, he deserves the misery he'll have to go through. I suppose you know that Pam Moore went back. And Mancil Grey has gone somewhere else. Al re-enlisted, and should be back soon. Scotty will be going back with Gene and Regan. Lily the loud-mouth, as Regan called her, is still there.

Kay, you were right in not liking Pat. In retrospect, I can see that he was no good, and I was a fool for going with him. At the time, though, that was the path of least resistance. I cooked for them, and it seemed so natural to go with him. So maybe I should take your advice about Russ. I don't spend too much time with him, though. At present I don't feel like going with anyone. I don't even care to see Sr., either. He does not attract me at all. That fire surely was quenched quickly. And as only a friend, I don't know, he doesn't interest me. Perhaps I am too sure of him, and I feel that he will be here forever, and that makes me indifferent to him. But you know how I am—I love to be alone.

Was talking to Chaplain Newby. He said that he doesn't like the way some of these Protestant churches compromised their beliefs during the war. And that Major Moore is up in Tokyo. Say, why don't you look him up? I don't know where he is, though. Say, did you meet him, or didn't you? I can't remember. I liked him, but I couldn't think of anything to say when I saw him.

Chaplain Newby said that every family of Japs he has met so far had wanted to get something out of him. I am rather in awe of Chaplain Newby, for he is the God-fearing, strong type who will not stand for nonsense. You know, Kay, when you quote me, I am so surprised that I ever wrote anything like that! It's strange what I do write when I feel like it. I loved your description of the people in the Ginza, too. And I like Samson, Jr. What a fitting name for your strong man! I surely laughed over his saying that he

114. A period piece on a Pygmalion theme, starring Paulette Goddard and Ray Milland.

115. Ginger Rogers won an Academy Award as Best Actress in this 1940 film about a young white-collar worker and her troubled love life.

would pick up two Nips and bash their heads together. I liked your conversation, too. Do more of it. You know, Kay, we ought to be more versatile—do everything from conversation, description, to just personal observations and whims. That's a wonderful idea of coming down after our appointment.[116] Then I could loaf off with you, for I expect to come down to Kyoto before my two weeks are up. Maybe we could even drop in on your mother.

I think I see why Samson said that you are more Jappish than Massy. It's merely that you have more depth. You are many-sided, and some people see the side of you that seems oriental, and they say, without thinking, you are like a Jap. Now, I think that is a compliment.

July 30. Cecilia is going to take next week off. Said her mother advised [her] to take only one week because they need the money. But you know me, I don't give a hang. So I think I'll take off on the seventeenth and come back to work on September 2. I'll go up to Yonezawa, then be back in Tokyo by the twenty-seventh, maybe stay one day or so, then come on down to Kyoto. Then we could go to Wakayama for the weekend or something. I'd like to go to Odawara and see Harley Yamada's sister who came back from China.

Now I have your letters in front of me, and I am re-digesting them. But for heavens' sake, I don't see why in the world you read my letters over so many times! But I can count on you to do the unexpected.—It's been rainy the last couple of days now. The tail of the typhoon. Hope the typhoon didn't work havoc with the precious rice crops. If Japan is God's country, why doesn't God see to it that it doesn't suffer so many disasters? If it's not an earthquake, it's a typhoon, or drought, or war or something or other. God-forsaken country is more like it. *Kami no kuni* [Land of the Gods, i.e., Japan]. Remember how we learned about it in Jap lit? Wonder what Nishio-sensei thinks now? Did you ever have lectures from him? I loved his lectures on Jap lit, and I'll never forget how enthralled I used to be with his words. But I can't remember a thing he has told us. However, I do remember the divine feeling I used to get, the inspiration, the patriotism he would indoctrinate us with. I wonder if he's a-hurting now? If he really believed all that he used to teach us, and *Kami no kuni* and stuff, he must be suffering. Or has he changed face like the rest of them?

I can imagine you riding all over on a motorcycle. That's even worse than me on the front of the bus. Except that you are in a big city and everyone can't recognize you and talk about you. It must be fun. Why do you pick on Samson for going with a Jap before you? He is only frail flesh after all. No, I guess he isn't, on second thought, he is the Strong man who carried away the Gates of Gaza, or is that what it was? Even his namesake had his Delilah.

116. At the U.S. consulate at Yokohama, where they hoped to clear up their citizenship status.

It's a coincidence, but I know a French Indo-Chinese too. I was wondering what he was. Perhaps I have told you about him. His name is Pham, and I took him last Saturday to have music lessons from Mrs. Hoshina. He likes it very much. Said he used to play the violin. And the two Mrs. H's laughed when I said that I brought a student for Mrs. H., but didn't even know his name. He's very little, not even five feet, and he looks like a Jap. I used to think he was a Nisei, but wondered because he seems to have individuality, and he can't speak English too well. He has a good sense of humor, and I like to talk to him, although I have never carried on a long conversation with him. I think you'd like him too.

Am I rattling off to you this morning! Just like an old Model T. Do you know what—I'd better leave this country before I get bald. My hair is getting thin on top. And my grandpa's sister was real bald-headed, and my mom said I was like her. Heaven help me! Wouldn't that be a calamity? You with your deafness, and me with my bald head, what a couple of rags we will be! But don't worry about deafness, Kay. I don't think you are deaf. I can't hear lots of things either, but just nod and let it pass.

Ha, ha, I betcha you put the carbon in the wrong side to the paper you were writing on one of the letters! Many's the time I have done that, and cursed myself for my stupidity. I loved your "Heart-wring sight" (Oops, I spelled that wrong) about the little family, motherless and burnt out. Things like that really touch one's heart. And you wrote it up well, too. Keep it up. Let's have more things like that. Only, how about putting in more descriptive detail? I have seen such shacks, so I can picture it very easily. But there are some people who are not so fortunate (?) as to have seen those pitiful, brave little tin shacks that sprang up after air raids. How about a description and filling it all in? I'd like to have a word picture of that. Next time I travel I want to write loads. I don't know why, but when I went to Tokyo last, I didn't feel like writing at all. The dirt, the clamor, the prejudices of it all stifled any writing instincts. Next time, I hope to override such outside influence.

Thanks to your advice, though, I have decided not to go steady with Russ. I have been thinking it is silly to go steady. Why bind yourself? I thought I told you what he looked like. Guess he's around five-foot-ten or so, and must weigh at least 165 if Al does, for he's better built than Al. Here, I'll copy for you what I wrote up about him, then that will save me thinking it up again. Tall, well-built, athletic-looking, with dark brown wavy hair always well-greased, brown eyes, straight nose, and pimples on his face. He is a good-natured, carefree GI who likes to kid people and have a good time. Everyone likes him, and his buddies swarm to him like bees to a flower. Only, he is far from being a flower. There is nothing flowery about him—his actions, talk or looks.

Russ looks healthy, and like he belongs in wide open places. He is quite good-looking, and girls like him. Always his mouth is busy, either in chewing gum, or talking or laughing, or all of them at once. He starts sentences, then looks at something else, his attention is arrested by that thing, and he forgets what he was going to say. He is like a little boy in that respect. He is very attentive and generous to the people he wants to be that way to.

Our little boy likes to have things all planned. He has a simple, one-track mind, and when he sets his mind on something, he keeps at it until he gets it. But he is so easy-going that sometimes he falls asleep and misses bed-check. Someone ought to invent an alarm wristwatch for sleepyheads like him.

There, do you have a better picture of him now? I think you would like him. Well, I've written enough for my thirty sen.

Kyoto, July 30, 1946

Dear Miye,

I don't know when Sgt. Henry will pop in, so I'll write on until he comes. Yesterday I went to practice, then it started to rain. Didn't have an umbrella, and it was pretty far to the bus stop, so stayed at school. Then, around six, the GI who stays at the hotel and has a girlfriend at the hotel said he'd take me home at seven on the car. Well, when seven came around, he hollered to me that the car had a flat. Johnny was there practicing from one in the afternoon. He hadn't had breakfast, lunch, or dinner. Had come to practice right after work. I kept telling him that I wanted to go home, and he kept persuading me to stay and listen to him play, for he liked to play when I was around. [That] flattered my vanity, so feeling like I was one of those women in books who inspire musicians, I stayed until nearly eight. Then the rain let up a little, so I didn't get too wet.

I was feeling real blue last night, though. Probably due to the dreary weather. And also, something Johnny told me. He said that someone had said awful things about me. Now, why is it that people must forever be talking? When will we be freed from petty gossip and buttinskys? As Cecilia said, no one in our hotel can lead a private life—your whole life is public. And it made me so mad because I was so wrought up over something so trivial. I know that people gossip, and I should overlook it. Yet, I can't. When someone tells me that people are talking about me, it upsets me so. I sat and watched the grey low-hanging clouds sail by while Johnny's piano playing just touched my heart. There was a Nisei boy next door who was playing away, and Johnny would stop playing and listen to him. I told Johnny that I would rather hear him play than the Nisei because, even though the Nisei could play better, he only played the notes while Johnny put everything he had into the music. A passionate Italian music lover is Johnny. He's a good boy, too. Said his father was strict with him, and he always had to hand over every cent of his pay to him. I bet his father is a character. It's so funny when Johnny imitates him, that Italian accent. And Johnny is so Italian looking, with his big nose, his curly eyelashes, his curved eyebrows, his so-expressive brown eyes. I like Johnny. He's so young, and he loves music so much. To look at him you wouldn't think he is a pianist, for he is far from thin and pale.

I'll never forget those moments in watching the lovely grey and white clouds. At times I felt like I could fly up and play among the clouds—getting away from this convention-bound world, this petty world with its ugliness, hate, and troubles. Up into the grey beautiful world of nothingness. I want to take wings and fly up, up, right on until I reach the very realm of the angels. What is man that thou mindest him? And created him a little lower than the angels.[117] A LITTLE lower? The prophet must have been an optimist. No, we are much lower. However, the angel in us does come out at times; we look upward and long to be freed of our binding fetters, to rise up and be in a holy kingdom. The kingdom of God. Will it ever come? Is there one? I don't know. But I find myself being drawn towards religion again. This time, if I search, I feel that I will find the REAL thing. Not the emotional, evanescent feeling for God that we had in our adolescence. More the real belief that was mine in childhood when I would gaze at the heavens and know that there was a God in Heaven who cared for me.

I was thinking, Miye, what is very much needed in Japan now is an orphanage for all the innocent victims of the air raids. Some soldiers have written to the *Stars and Stripes* about it. Why isn't something done? The Catholics have an orphanage, but it is small. The other night Colton, the CID man who comes to Spanish class, was saying that they picked up a little boy on the streets and took him to the hospital. They found that he was starving. He said he doesn't see why more attention isn't paid to the starving children around here. Doesn't anyone have the initiative to start something like that? I guess most of the people are too busy taking care of themselves. I wonder how you'd start anything like that? It is work really worth doing. Maybe I ought to find something like that to do over here, where my services are needed, instead of going back to the States where I would be unneeded. Work like that is always plentiful here. What is it about the harvest is ripe but the reapers are few?[118] You know, it would be fun, and worthwhile, to found an orphan asylum and to mold the younger generation of Japan. But it is such a huge task. Wonder if some social-minded persons are considering something like that? And instead of military personnel wasting their money over here on worth-

117. "What is man, that thou art mindful of him? For thou has made him a little lower than angels." Psalms 8: 5.

118. "The harvest truly is plenteous, but the laborers are few." Matt. 9: 37.

less women and beer and hi-priced souvenirs, wouldn't it be wonderful if they could contribute towards the upkeep of an orphanage? I'm sure that many organizations back in the States would be willing to help such an institution, too. If I knew of some such place here, I would willingly give them my extra clothes and material. I don't know about now, but when I was in the States, we used to have so many old clothes and stuff around that we didn't know what to do with them. How helpful they would be to the people here now!

Kyoto, July 31, 1946

Dearest Miye,

Just got through writing another letter to the Army Postal Office, GHQ AFPAC in Tokyo. I just betcha the dirty censors are holding up my last letter. Yesterday I received my certificate from Commander Hetfield in Tokyo, a student of Emma's, and he thought it was so queer that my letter had taken so long to reach him. The censors had got his letter back to me, too. Damned buttinskys!

You know, it's fun to write to people like the Army Postal Officer and tell him what you think. So I guess that is good reason for the existence of the gripes column in *Stars and Stripes*, for after once you write in and tell someone your troubles, it just folds up like the Arabs and as quietly steals away. Only that isn't really true. I still have my trouble in not being able to write to you! Hereafter, I'm going to make a pest out of myself and write lots of people, whenever I get mad enough about anything. And it pays to go see about some things, too. One of the foreign nationals made a big uproar because we were forbidden to go to the USO shows, and he got results—we can still go. And one time they said that we couldn't ride elevators. Now, we work on the eighth floor, and before I walk up those many stairs, I'd rather stay away from work. At my age, too! So I got all excited about it and went down and saw the colonel, the Headquarters Commandant. He said we could use the elevators, and even had one of his men escort me to the elevator and put me on! He had a smile on the corner of his mouth. I bet it's not often that girls come in to him so brazenly and demand that they be allowed to use the elevator! Well, I grant that that's one thing good about Americans. They think a person has a right to say his say. And they don't shoot you down in cold blood for saying something either.

Last night I had a lovely time at home all by myself. I took two showers, ironed a skirt (have to do something else at the same time, for the iron is so small it gets all cooled off before I half finish ironing), sorted out my various junk, started to pack, read from *Modern British and American Poetry*. I like Robert Frost and Conrad Aiken. Read some women poets, and they have delicate, finished ways of saying things, but they have no depth. For the first time I see what Frost is trying to say in "Mending Wall." I had that in my *101 Poems* from a long time ago, and liked it though I couldn't understand what he was trying to say. Frost is fighting against barriers, bonds to freedom, walls—international walls. But I like the way he writes so conversationally, and so naturally. Yet, there is depth to what he says, although it takes time to sound its depth. I like his "Tree by my window, window tree." He loved nature. When I read his poetry I can get the delicious feeling that I get from direct contact with nature.

This morning just flew! Here it is twenty after twelve already. Sr. was in this morning, and I gave him the stencils I had run off for him. He wants me to meet him at four at school to translate some songs that Homer Clark gave me to do. Said Chaplain McCandless offered to get him any position in the US teaching Spanish, but he refused. Why? There's no future in Japan! Why doesn't he get out of here? Eleven years here, and he dislikes most of the Japanese, too, yet, why is it that he stays? He is wasting his talent here! Why doesn't someone wake him up?

I feel like studying poetry now. Think I'll read all of that book. That is much better than going to shows or just shooting the breeze with anyone. And it is nice and quiet at the hotel from around 7:30 since nearly everyone goes out.

Kyoto, July 31, 1946

Dear Kay,

This morning when I was waiting for the bus in front of the Kyoto Hotel, there was Lt. Reilly, of I&E, talking to a little dirty waif. The boy said that he hadn't eaten since yesterday noon and that he was hungry. I told [the] lieutenant, and he said, "I wonder if he would go to a restaurant and buy something to eat if I gave him the money?" So I asked the boy, and he nodded. The Lt. gave him ten yen saying that he felt sorry for him. O, before that the kid said that he would hang around the place but no one would give him anything. Said he had no home, his father was a soldier who had not returned from the war, his mother was dead. I wonder just how much of that is true. There was a man, a Jap, sweeping outside the stairs, and he told the kid not to tell so many lies. Lieutenant wanted to know if the Kyoto municipality didn't have a home for these orphans. I asked the boy, and he said they half starve you there and make you work. There's something definitely wrong with this picture someplace. If it is so easy for him to bum off ten yen from someone, why should he go to an orphanage? Even if the orphanage would be better for him. I wonder just what that orphanage looks like. If only it could come to the attention of those interested, there would be many improvements, I am sure.

Gosh, I feel dead this morning. I didn't even hear the breakfast bell go off this morning, and when I did wake up, it was twenty-five to seven already. So I hurriedly washed, ate, then dashed off to catch Russ on his round. On the way, we picked up three soldiers who had Jap girls clinging to them. Cheap prostitutes, probably, and I tried to get my eyes full.

Father Gefell brought me a letter from one of the girls studying to become a nun. She wants to learn English conversation. I hate to teach. I hated to teach during the war when I had to for a living. But there is a satisfaction in it. And I can't turn her down! So I guess I am stuck. It will do me good to associate with a sweet little thing like her. It's a lot of bother, though, and I hate to begin, for it is so hot, and I hate to be tied down to anything. I want to be as free as the air. With no responsibilities. Guess that isn't the right attitude.

> Man acts more like a poor bear in a cage
> That all day fights a nervous inward rage,
> His mood rejecting all his mind suggests.
> He paces back and forth and never rests.

That's by Robert Frost, taken from "The Bear." There's something about a big black bear that is very fascinating, isn't there? It reminds me of the article in *Life* quite a while back, about the bear in a cartoon. He is dragged out of hibernation and made to work in a factory. It was so funny!

Today I will do the filing! I've got enough to keep me occupied the rest of the day. After I once get started, I like it, but O, it is hard to get started! I'd much rather write letters. Father Dunn just called me and asked me if I saw that article in the paper about "Relocated Nisei May Be Reimbursed." So I read it. Say, that is justice in action if that goes through. Good for our side! I'm so glad that the Nisei proved their loyalty, too. They must have made quite a name for themselves.

There was another article about missionaries returning to the East. But not to Japan. Guess they will be coming to Japan soon. The field here is ready for missionaries. The Americans now have a prestige as they never had before. Just [because] you're American, they will look up to you.

Father Dunn offered to take me to Osaka, so I'm off.

Kyoto, July 31, 1946

Dearest Kay,

Why is it that I hear gobs from you all at once, then I have to suffer a drought again? I was thinking of a way to overcome that—the next time that I get five or six little brown envelopes all at once, I'll save them and open them one at a time, every day. But I know I won't have enough self-control to do that. Just like, you know, during the war when we were always in a state of half-starvation, when we'd get some food, we'd eat it all at once instead of saving it and having a little at a time. Honestly, I used to get so disgusted with myself, for if I had something to eat, I'd gobble it down all at once instead of prolonging the pleasure. Now, if I have some candy or something to eat, I let it pile up and forget all about it. Like I have a little box of candy in my drawer now, and when I offered Cecilia some the other day, she was surprised and exclaimed, "Do you STILL have that?" I could never do that if I were hungry. Do you see the moral? I am so hungry for you that I am continually yearning for you, and when little bits of you come wrapped up in brown envelopes, I devour you all at once. I know I'm always complaining, but I do wish that I'd hear from you daily, or at least once in two days. For I know that you write every day to me.

Yesterday I got my feathers all ruffled up. Here's how it happened. You see, I went to practice, then along come two more foreign nationals. That Pham, the little Indo-Chinese, was one of them, so I talked to him and told him to call me in time so that we could get back to the hotel by chow. Well, we did get back, and barely in time. They have a rule that if we don't get in before six, we can't eat. I ran straight into the dining room and barely made it, but the others dilly-dallied around so that it was a few minutes after six when they came in. There were two Nisei boys at the table already, and also Hauchcorne was there. Well, old Pool was in the kitchen and saw what time it was when we came in. There was only one piece of cake left, so he told them to give it to me. Then, when they saw the other girl come in, he had them cut it into two for us both. The Nisei boys had been there before six, so had Hauchcorne and I, and so we were entitled to dessert, along with the rest of our meal. But the Nisei didn't say a word, only quietly slipped out as soon as their main course was finished. But not Pham. He said that he should have dessert. I didn't think of it until then. But the injustice of the case stared me in the face. Why shouldn't they get dessert? They ought to open a can of fruit for them, at least. Pham went up to the kitchen and demanded that he have some dessert. I took up his cause for him. Old fool Pool was there, and I argued with him. He knows how many will be there for supper, for those who don't eat tell him at least one meal beforehand. And something like cake, which comes in sheets and is cut up into pieces, should be cut into enough pieces to go around. I know that we were in the right. Then Pool says that Pham came late, so that he didn't have to feed him at all. And that the next time he comes late, he's not going to let him eat. Now, if you ask for justice that's what you get. On the other hand, if you quietly back out like the Nisei did, you are still in favor with the king of the kitchen, Fool Pool. It's not that they were so hungry, or that they wanted dessert so bad—no, it's the principle of the thing. I offered the men part of my cake but they wouldn't take it. Something about the whole thing makes me mad. I know that if Gomis had been treated like that, he would have raised the roof. And the weakness of the Nisei who didn't say a word nauseated me! Is it better to take injustices without a murmur? Perhaps you don't make enemies, but I do not admire such jellyfishes.

It rather surprises me that you got all the parcels. Now there's only your slacks to get to you. Guess you can trust Jap mail now. Only it's a mystery what ever came of my *ido shinkoku-sho* [change-of-address form]. Told [the] Suemasas about it and asked them to have it traced. I don't care particularly, but at times I think of all that is going to waste. But not really to waste, so it doesn't matter.

Listen, Kay, when did we move from Wakayama to Osaka? O, I know—I looked it up in my diary, and discovered it was 28 October 1945. Have you filled out all those blanks?[119] I don't know who to put for the persons in the US who could vouch that I was born and where. So I put down Miye and another person. And I haven't any idea when my pop went to America—I'll have to go to Wakayama this weekend and find out. Or maybe I'd better write. That might be better.

[Later] There, I did write. Also, I got an inspiration and wrote to your mother on a card from Boston. Thought she might like it. And I told her that we might drop in on her the latter part of next month. Your mother has done a lot for me, and I like to see her once in a while. I feel sorry for her out there with all the country people.

Saw Russ this morning, and he was feeling as devilish as usual. I like to see him that way, more than quiet and sick and unnatural. Last night I stayed home and had a lovely time all by myself. I sorted out some of my junk. And started packing—ALREADY. Got some old junk I'd like to unload on your long-suffering mother. My mom told me not to bring anything back to the States. So I want to gradually get rid of my unneeded junk. Also, I read some poetry, and surely enjoyed it. From *Modern British and American Poetry*. I liked Robert Frost and Conrad Aiken. If I had my book here, I'd quote some for you. In fact, I had it all red-pencilled what I wanted to pass on to you. I love some of that poetry. At last, maybe, I am beginning to enjoy poetry.

Here 'tis, the bottom of the page. I'm going straight home this noon.

119. Mary and Kay had obtained citizenship forms to fill in, preparatory to an appointment with the Office of the U.S. Political Adviser on August 27.

Kyoto, August 1, 1946

Dearest Kay,

It takes the longest time for Father Dunn to get away! Here, around nine he asked me if I would like to go to Osaka, and I said of course, so he said he'd go in a few minutes. Here it is 10:30, and he is still not ready to go. O, well, that gave me impetus to get some of that filing done that I'd had on my mind all this time.

It will be fun to go to Osaka again. Wish it were Saturday, for I must go then to see Gene. Just think, that might be the very last time I might see him. It will be the very last time I'll see him in Japan.

I have that poetry book with me now, so I'll quote to you:

> Ah, when to the heart of man
> Was it ever less than a treason
> To go with the drift of things
> To yield with a grace to reason,
> And bow and accept the end
> Of a love or a season?
>
> —Robert Frost,
> from "Reluctance"

That surely is the opposite of the Oriental passivity and willingness to bow to fate, no? But don't you feel that way about it too at times? The stubbornness to take fate, to bow to the hand of time?

While I was typing, I thought of Mrs. Hoshina. She was so downcast yesterday because she said that she would have to start teaching at nine in the morning and wouldn't get through until nine in the evening. And that she couldn't bring rice for two meals, and that the last time she went to the Red Cross they kicked her out. Isn't that mean? The ARC woman who used to be in charge let her go there, but the one now in charge will not allow her. What difference does it make if one lone woman goes, especially when she is in such distress? She wondered if there weren't anything that could be done about it, and I told her that I was afraid not, for what those ARC bitches say goes around here. They've got the officers around their little finger. No one will stick up for her. They will all side with the ARC woman, right or wrong. My woman, right or wrong. There ain't no justice.

I saw Sr. at school yesterday and he waited for the bus with me for the longest time when I was going home. He said that he was very jealous, and that if he didn't go home and get in a tub of cold water he would be all in smoke before tomorrow night. Isn't that cute? He says, why don't I go steady with him. He really does have the cutest sparkle in his eyes. Well, I knew I'd gravitate back to him.

Kyoto, August 2, 1946

Dearest Miye,

Your purse came just in time for me to travel. It's just what I wanted. Miye, it must have cost you an awful lot to get all those things! I wish that I could repay you in some way for it all.

Yesterday, I had such a perfectly wonderful time! Went with Father Dunn and two Sgts. who came down from Tokyo, to Osaka and to Kobe. We went in his staff car. It is about an hour's ride to Osaka. We went to the chapel, where Father Dunn let me off and Cecilia's mother took me over. She took me to the foreign nationals' dorm for lunch. Their food is not nearly as good as ours. I like our cozy little place better, for there it is so spacious, and there seems to be such an impersonal air about the place. The service is very bad, too. Then from there, we drove on to Kobe. The chaplain there is so big and fat and jolly, and so generous!

This morning I put all your letters back in my folder, but I guess I'll have to get them out again. I'm staying this afternoon, so I think I'll write again. Father Gefell just gave me a lot of typing to do. That will keep me busy. Sr. comes over once in a while, whenever I let him. He came last night. We went to the band concert together. It was wonderful. But we didn't stay for the movies. He has the weekend off, and was wanting me to go someplace with him. Too bad I promised Gene I'd be in Osaka! But then, I guess I am still too convention-bound to go with a man anywhere over the weekend, although I know Sr. can be trusted. He outlined the most interesting plan for us, too. Beautiful scenic spots around here. O, well, another chance will come if it is meant for us. I knew that I'd gravitate back to him.

Kyoto, August 3, 1946

Dearest Miye,

I feel so dead this morning. That ride to Kobe surely tired me out. I've been tired for the last two days from it, but it was worth it. Yesterday I had to type out a lot of things for Father Gefell, so I didn't even feel like writing to you. Then the phone rang, and of all people—it was Homer Clark, of Signal office. He wanted me to go to his office, just on the other side of the building, only two doors away. When there, he told me that he was trying to get Kokura in Kyushu, and he wanted me to "Moshi Moshi" to the operator. I did just that. Then, after I hung up, I started talking to Homer. He really is a character. He has his own set [of] opinions, and woe be to whoever has different ideas! Looks older than his twenty years. I jabbered with him for a while, until quitting time, then came back to the office, and started putting ink into a small bottle. Just then Homer came, I looked up fascinated, and the ink spilled all over my dress. He let out an "O!," I looked down, and there was my pretty new dress all splattered with ink. He said to go wash it out quick, then brought me some soap and hydrogen peroxide (is that HO?). It was marvelous how the latter took it out. But I felt so silly going home with the front of the dress all wet ("at your age, too," said Homer). Babs said it was a good thing it wasn't the back.

Homer had an iron, and I begged it off him. Now he wants me to do part of his laundry for him.

Took the books to Sr., but he wasn't in. When Gomis came to take Babs to the show, he told her how excited Sr. was over getting his books and pen. Haven't seen him since. Wish he'd come to the office. He'd better write to you, too. I know he's just bursting with happiness over getting his beloved books.

Dear me! It must be near the bottom of the page. Gosh, Miye, I know that you spent so much to get my things, and I feel guilty for not being able to pay you. Especially when Little Mary is coming, and inflation is on in the States. Hope you feel better by the time this reaches you.

Kyoto, August 4, 1946

Dearest Kay,

I don't know what, but I feel like something so vital is going away with Gene. Something warm and good is leaving and only the hard shell is remaining. Remember the happy carefree days in Wakayama? How Gene used to whoop and holler and how we'd laugh and laugh! I told Gene and he said he never acts like that anymore. I think that is Gene at his best. Weren't we innocent then, Kay? Good old days gone forever! Now I am left flat, and I can't even write. Gene, Regan and Scotty were supposed to leave this Tuesday, but they are taking the [GIs who are] fathers instead. But it won't be long now. I feel so tired, so infinitely tired. I want rest and peace and quiet. Not as young as I used to be.

Heck, I don't even feel like writing. So I've neglected you the last three days. Not that I don't think of you—you are ever in my thoughts. Kay, will we never find a home? Are we destined to be wanderers forever? Heaven forbid!

5 August. Dearest Kay, I do not feel like writing. But I am going to send this off only to ease my conscience. I had a lot of work to do this morning. Checking up on the registration of graves in Guam, Leyte, [and] Okinawa which Father Dunn had. That's going to take me a month.

Kyoto, August 6, 1946

Dearest Miye,

I feel like a *narikin* [nouveau riche] walking back and forth from work with your super purse of many compartments. I love especially the handy compartment in back where I can insert my letters to mail, so that I won't forget them, or my little New Testament, which I read while waiting for the bus. And I like it because it is so generously made, and because it is rectangular. Now I've got a part of you to be with me perpetually.

How's Little Mary getting along?[120] I hope she won't be a problem child like I was. I'd love to be your kids!

Here I am so early this morning that the elevator wasn't even running! However, just after I walked into Daiken, the elevator boy came and he gave me the first trip up of the day. You know, Miye, I'm swamped with work now. Father Dunn gave me hundreds of thousands of names—the registration of graves—to check over and type out. They include Guam, Leyte, [and] Okinawa. I don't know—I get such a queer feeling when I check any names—to think that that person gave his life, for what? To think that loved ones back home are without hope of ever seeing him again. Why is it that some were taken and some were not? I told Al, "I'm glad that you didn't become one of these cards." What are touching are these "Unidentified No. blank" cards. It would be of some consolation to know where your son, husband, or father was buried. But if you didn't even know that, how awful it must be! To get back to the point—I am so busy with those cards that I don't have time to write. And if I write personal letters during working hours, my conscience objects. Especially since Father Dunn has been so nice to me. So I got ambitious this morning and came just to talk to you.

Practiced quite a bit yesterday. Went around four, and stayed until quarter to six, then I practiced after Spanish class last night. I'm mean. I wanted to avoid Sr. coming over, so I gave the excuse that I wanted to practice. When he comes over, he stays until 11:30 or so, and I get so sleepy! I was thinking that I'll never find a man I will be able to live with. At first I might be all enthused over him, but it wears off so quickly, and I get bored with them. Capricious old maid am I.

Only one more week and I'll be on my journey! And Teruko is waiting for me! This time I don't think I'll even stay in Tokyo. That big metropolis frightens me with its dirt, noise, and foreigners. You know, even Osaka frightens this little country mouse. As soon as I leave my quiet little Kyoto, I feel lost. I don't like big devastated places. But Osaka is bravely building up. Shacks are springing up all over. And in the empty lots, ruined territory, the weeds are

120. This is simply an inquiry after Miye's health. Her baby was not due for several months.

sometimes nearly shoulder high. Thus nature tries to make up for the sins of man, hiding man's cruelty upon himself. I guess that is what those poets meant when they talked about grass covering the graveyards and battlefields —that grass is gentle and kind, covering up the horrors and stupidity of war.

All fathers are going before anyone else. Soon there will be no more combat men left in Japan. The fool Pool, our mess sergeant, left last night. And the hotel manager, Chappy, will leave in a week or so. He's been quiet since he has been dethroned from his former tyrannical state. He has to stay around the office now that he hasn't got his luxurious room any more. Bill, the clerk in our office, is going soon, perhaps next week. I like Bill. He's quiet, but humorous and *majime* [earnest, serious]. A churchgoer. There was an article in the *Stars and Stripes* about Bible-packing GIs who go around and give English lessons and conduct Sunday School. That certainly is encouraging. Some of them are coming back here to become missionaries. That's just what Japan needs now. GIs who go to church are most of them better than those who don't. I'm discovering that fact.

Kay said that there were only seventeen who went to Hongwanji[121] in Tokyo for some festival or other. And before they used to flock there by the thousands. She deplored the sudden change of faith of the Japanese. From one extreme to the other go the Japanese. Now if they only had enough white missionaries, they could convert the country to Christianity. It might be a good thing, for even if the majority would only be surface Christians, there might be some who would really become good Christians. I might be prejudiced, but I do believe that Christianity is much better for a people than Buddhism, or Shintoism. At least, it gives a person ideals and a moral code, which is more than oriental religions do. Well, it looks like I have reached the bottom of the page already. Think I'll get ambitious and cut a stencil for Sr.'s lessons. It's nearly time for everyone to come traipsing in anyhow. So goodbye for now.

Kyoto, August 6, 1946

Dearest Kay,

On second thought, I think I'll write to you, you poor neglected angel. But I'm glad that you have found a refuge in the office, and are happy there. Your letter was censored, so that I got it later than the one you wrote after that one. I don't know how you and Samson are getting along now. How come he can take you around on a motorcycle? Russ said that no one is allowed to ride motorcycles. Wonder if he knows what he is talking about.

I've got nearly five minutes to gab with you before the rest of them come

121. A major temple of the Buddhist True Pure Land sect (Jodo Shinshu).

trooping in. That little girl who is studying to become a nun came to my place yesterday and wanted me to teach her English. I couldn't turn her down. Now I am going to teach her on Tues. and Fri. She is the sweetest little thing, and doesn't look the twenty or twenty-one that she is. She is at the St. Francis church.

My gosh, Kay, that letter of mine to the Army Postal Officer caused more furor than I'd even hoped! Babs just came up and said that they wrote to Capt. Fitzgerald of [the] PO here asking him if he approved of Jap-Americans writing and using the APO and he did approve it, and so sent the approval up. Now all they have to do is to act on it, and we can use the APO! Now isn't that wonderful? And all on account of my little letter! Honestly, you ought to see me now, I'm beaming so much that it puts the sun to shame! Then I was so happy and excited over it that I spilled it to Father Dunn, and he said he knew all about it, and that is why they were investigating me. And the Adjutant General was talking about me, saying that it's not everyone who can write like that. Father Dunn said that a girl writing to GHQ surprised them so much that they just had to give in. Wow! I feel famous overnight! Listen, Kay, the moral is that there is much power in the pen, and it is up to us to wield it. Say, it is waking me up to some of the possibilities hidden in our pens. We can move the world with our pens. Isn't that something? Let's wake up out of our listlessness and shout to the world!

Well, I was so happy over all this that I just had to tell you. Now I can write to the States! That will be wonderful. And you can write to your sis. O, boy, I surely am glad! Well, I'll get back to my stencil-cutting. Just wanted to let you know, for I couldn't contain such tremendous news all by myself.

Goodbye, my dear. Say, did you phone up the consul and ask him when we have our appointment? I hope the censors haven't got all the letters I wrote to you about that in.

Kyoto, August 7, 1946

Dearest Kay,

I wonder what is the matter. I changed the ribbon of this typewriter, yet it doesn't type right. There, that's much better. Larry fixed it for me. And he also got an empty room for me where I could type. You know, he's really thoughtful and helpful to me. I'll miss him when we move to Station Hotel. I told Chappy that I didn't want to pay for two weeks' food when I wasn't here, and he said to go see Major Bogard about it. So I'll do that, and if I don't have to pay, I might leave around Thurs. That will give me two days to settle down.

I was developing the worst mood up in my room, with the femmes chattering around up there, but now that I have my coveted privacy, I don't mind it so much. Funny how much difference it makes when I have a room to myself. Babs is just swell, but the idea that she is sharing the room somehow inhibits me. And I like this room because it is so bare. The desk has nothing on it except a lamp and my typewriter. While our desk upstairs has a million bottles and boxes and mirrors and junk on it. I hate all that clutter, and if it were mine, I'd put it all away.

I brought home the slang.[122] Out of meanness, I hope Sr. comes and finds me not in the room. The joke will be on him. How I hated it last night when I wanted to come home, but knew that he was here, and if I did come home he'd talk to me until way late. So I drove another round with Russ. Which is really a waste of time. I guess I am a hermit at heart, and at present I am at the height of my anti-social feelings. Well, I think I'll cut out my nonsense and get down to work [on the book]. Tonight I was feeling so rotten that I knew that if I had anything to drink, I'd go to it, but I satisfied myself with cigarettes.

There, that's a good night's work. How's this for Chapter 11? Use the other three pages I formerly sent you about Yoshiko for the first three pages. I'm rather proud of ourselves. Gee, Kay, you must have worked a lot on it. Now, if I could get the other two chapters off we'd have a book. Let's get it out, anyway. It's driving me nuts. When I once get started on it, it is fascinating. I want to get it off my mind before I travel, too. You know what, I'm going to ask around and see if I can't find a publisher in Kyoto because it is too much bother to take it to Osaka. I bet a book like this will sell like hotcakes. Lots of people want them now. And we needn't put in all that stale list. Kay, you're a genius for making up those chapters, and for getting all the ideas as you did. Do you have time to type this out in a uniform way? All the details count, you know. You must not expect the publishers to add or detract anything. I know I still have a lot of mistakes on there. I'll leave it up to you to type out in final form. Double space, I think. In fact, I know, for I used to double space for Natori.[123] Well, it's nearly eleven. Enjoy the satisfaction of a job well done, our professor used to say. And I am now. Good night.

Kyoto, August 7, 1946

Dearest Kay,

Do you know that Johnny, Francis Horner's friend, was a father? He went home yesterday. And I never even thought he was married? You never can tell,

122. Mary and Kay had begun working on the book of American slang they discussed when Kay was in Kyoto during April. They sent chapters back and forth for additions and comments.

123. Mary had translated an elementary Japanese history textbook and the folktale "Kachi Kachi Yama" for the professor.

can you? And then, was I surprised yesterday when who should I see outside of Daiken but Scotty himself! Didn't talk long. He said that Gene was married at one time and had one child. I wonder just how much of what Scotty says is true. Now he's got me wondering again. But then, I don't care. It's just that I hate to think that he ever lied to me. Scotty said he didn't know if they'd count Gene a father or not, because they were separated.

Went and got a permanent yesterday afternoon. They set my hair in a hurry because I would be late for supper. It looked so silly, and the ammonia smell in my hair was so disagreeable that I washed my hair and took it all out. This morning my hair looks just a fuzz, and I don't like it at all. I knew that I shouldn't have told them not to set my hair because I wanted to wash it out, but I was afraid to tell them. Even yet I am afraid of the Japs. I'll never lose that as long as I am here, either. Never will I feel free with them. Forever must I "enryo" and I don't like it.

Then all of a sudden it started to rain cats and dogs. But I went to practice anyway. Then rode with Russ, and wanted to get off, but I saw Sr. at the door, and I didn't want to be bored by him until eleven or twelve, so I kept on riding, even if I didn't want to. I hate it when my freedom is taken away like that. I hate the way Sr. stays until so late when I am so sleepy. But then, when he does come, I rather like him and am interested in what he has to say. O, well, I'm just letting things slide.

Did you see that picture in *Life* about the Warrens? If not, I am enclosing it. I'm enclosing it anyway. I thought of you when I saw it. It was in an article about Congregationalists. I liked it because it said that they fought against racial discrimination, and showed pictures of Negro members.

You ought to see that museum in Osaka now, how they've got barbed wire all over the place. Rolls and rolls of it. There's only [one] place even a flea could slip in, and that is the entrance gate on the side and in front. When I went up to the old rooms upstairs where we spent so much memorable time, old memories kept crowding back, and all I could do was just sit and sigh.[124] Old memories of the people who have been up there, of the fun we used to have, of how we used to be "caught" by the old grandma, of having to bow and bow and how we hated it! O, by the way, did I tell you that the bride is going to have another baby? By the looks of it, it seems like the stork is nigh. When I slept there I was nearly eaten up by mosquitoes. Our hotel is heavenly to be so free of insects. When I read of how you are bothered by fleas and mosquitoes, I feel for you. How glad I am that I am now rid of those enemies of mankind!

124. Mary is referring to the rooms she and Kay had rented together before she moved to the army's billets for foreign nationals.

Guess who is now waiting to see Father Dunn? None other than Lipstick. He said a few words to me, then quietly sat himself down. Somehow, when I see him, I can't help but chuckle inside of me for I recall how you threw him over flat. Ho, ho, good for him!

Kyoto, August 7, 1946

Dearest Miye,

Hooray! I'm getting results! Did I ever tell you about the letter that I wrote to the Army Postal Officer in Tokyo? Well, I was so darned disappointed and disgruntled over us not being permitted to use the APO that I roused myself out of my usual lethargy and up and wrote a letter, saying just what I thought, and using all the rhetoric and argumentation that I have ever learned. Over a week passed, but no answer did I get. Well, you know, Miye, mail from you and my family means a great deal to me. So I copied the letter and sent it to them again, with another letter. I made three or four copies, for I was determined to send up a letter every week, enclosing the former letters, until I got an answer of some sort.

Then, yesterday Babs came up all excited. She was smiling all over and raising her arms and said, "We might be able to use the APO! And all on account of your letter!" Gee, was I surprised! Then she went on to explain that her Capt., the APO officer here, received a communication from GHQ with my letter enclosed as reference, and asking him if he approved of us using the APO. He did, and sent it up. Now all they have to do is act upon it, and we have the long-denied privilege. And Babs kept repeating, "And all on account of your letter. If you read that letter, you couldn't help but sympathize." Well, she was putting it on thick, but I was so happy over it that I couldn't help but beam all over. I was so happy over it that I even told Father Dunn, and he said that he knew all about it. That the AG was surprised that someone here, especially a GIRL had been able to get GHQ to do anything. Father said that GHQ was probably so surprised to hear from a girl that they couldn't help but give in. And Babs said that me saying I worked in the Chaplains' section helped. I never thought of it that way. But anyway, isn't that something? Hereafter, when I find something that I think should be done, I am going to put it into words, and send it up to the highest headquarters. If we just grumble around here among the lower people, it doesn't do any good.

But what a lesson I learned! There is power in our pens. Perhaps we can help to correct some of the many wrongs about us. It is a responsibility of us who have had the privilege of schooling. And if we don't write for Japan, who will? O, if only I could really write and get something done! But this little victory is very encouraging. And just think—perhaps I can be able to write to you after all! We are in the right, and the right should win!

But now that my humble letter has brought results, I won't need the many copies I have made. I'll submit one to you. I really didn't put much thought into it, just put down on paper what had been smoldering in me for a long, long time.

Today in *Stars and Stripes* was a gripe letter from some T/5 right here in Kyoto, saying that he approved of the prohibition of dates (Japanese) at the Army Theater, and further, he stated that he believed foreign nationals should be barred. Of all the nerve! Why should he be so narrow-minded? I felt at first like writing a reply. But is there any use? I don't know; such narrow-mindedness is so distasteful that I don't even feel like answering him. That theater is always only about half full. And soldiers do crave feminine companionship, especially with girls who can speak their language. Besides, we are so few—what difference does it make? Is it entirely our fault that we are over here? He implied that foreign nationals were all for Japan during the war, then as soon as the war was ended, and the occupation started, they all climbed on the Allied bandwagon. Does he have any basis for his sweeping statements? Foreigners, as a rule, were looked upon with suspicion and dislike over here during the war. Why, many of them were interned and restricted in freedom. Besides, those who are working for the Army now are those who have been cleared, for the CIC has investigated our pasts and those who were engaged in any wartime activities have been weeded out. It is only those who are employed by the army who are allowed to go to the army theaters. What would the army do without the foreign nationals? They could get along in their bungling fashion, yet, any disinterested onlooker would immediately say that we, with our knowledge of both languages as well as the customs of both lands, are of the greatest help in [making] the occupation run smoothly. The language barrier is nothing to be taken lightly. And just how much Japanese do the GI Nisei know? I think you know as well as I that it is not much.

Kyoto, August 9, 1946

Dearest Miye,

Sr. says that he saw an ad on the inside cover of the May *Esquire* for the Parker fountain pen saying that there will be more pens coming. That means at that time they were few and hard to get. In spite of that, you succeeded in getting him a wonderful Parker. From the basement of his heart he thanks you. He came up this morning to get the *Latin American Civilization* and was so happy over it. He couldn't believe that it was only $4.50, and said that someone must have contributed towards it, and sure enough, it was the Rockefeller foundation or something like that. He said that he would write up something about it and send it to the *Nippon Times*, for people in Japan are interested in Latin America.

Sr. marvelled over the super purse you sent me, too. He had to look in all the compartments, and he advised me not to use that mirror since it has raw edges, and when I stick my hand into my purse, I might cut myself. I told him that I do look before I thrust my hand into my purse, and I like the mirror and I shall continue to use it. He could only look at me dumbfounded.

O, Miye, I am so happy! I get to have a room all to myself at the Station Hotel! Now I'm glad we are moving, and hope that this good situation will continue. Larry kind of managed for me, too, for he said that at first they had me in with someone I didn't even know. I had told him that he ought to put the perverse old maids in separate rooms. He followed the advice.

Amy in IG now has a civil service job. She had to go to Yokohama to see about it. She has her same old position, only it is called different and she gets much more pay and lots more privileges. Babs said that she can get things because her bosom friend is secretary to Gen. Woodruff, the CO of I Corps. But she said that perhaps I could get the same thing if I asked Father Dunn, for Catholic chaplains have influence in the army and he is so nice to me. Gee, I hope so. I would be content to stay right here, working for the chaplains. They are all wonderful people. And people who work for them are nice, too. That doesn't include me, for I just happened to stumble onto them.

Kyoto, August 10, 1946

Dearest Kay,

I don't know what's come over me, but I just don't get the consolation in writing to you that I used to. Even getting such wonderful letters from you doesn't arouse me. Stubborn thing I am. I guess I was hurt because I'd be so faithful in writing to you every day, and it just made me sore because I'd get your whole week's worth at once. Or what is it? Is it because I am just about to travel, and have a lot of things on my mind? Or am I becoming stale from staying in all week? Perhaps I need new and stimulating company. Sr. is nice, but as you say, I get tired of his talking. And I only wish that he'd go home so I could go to bed. Homer Clark, too. He aggravated me today because I was so busy and he stood there wanting me to translate a letter for him. What do I care about his love affairs? He's not much fun to talk to. So full of his own ideas and his own importance. I guess I've got an anti-social spell. Woe is me when that even extends to my letter loves. Haven't written to even Miye. O, well, this also is a stage which I will pass.

And I am so sore all over. Wonder if this is how rheumatic old women feel. Moving this Tuesday is on my mind. I feel like moving it all piece by piece. I hate to move with the crowd, as I hate to do anything with all the others. It will be so much a waste of time, just waiting around and everyone will try to get their junk in first, and all the bother. Gosh, I hate it. Just as I hate to eat when everyone is in the dining room. Can't have any peace of mind. As you said, I hate to have people around even if I don't talk to them. So I wait until late when no one is around and I can think my own thoughts. What was that that your Tony said—that people would get up and dissolve—no that wasn't the word—disturb was it—no it wasn't that either—his thoughts. Anyway, I liked his letter definitely. Although he seemed like a dangerous romantic soul. He's definitely infatuated with you, too. Aren't you flattered? Perhaps I'll hike on up to Daiken and type out his letter. It is so ethereal, and so different. I am very much impressed with it.

One of the girls said that there's ice cream AND cake tonight! On second thought, I guess I can write to you after all. Now that I have a typewriter at the tips of my fingers, I can rattle off to you. So the world is right side up after all. The last thread is when I will be unable to commune with you.

Say, Homer Clark said that you quit the Club. But I don't understand if you did or not. I don't like you working there. How do you manage it? How can you live so intensely? Ah, me, down here in peace and quiet can't understand how you can work at TWO places, go boating and motor cycling, and write and talk and I don't know what else. Let's see—I had an idea. It's flown now. Darn it, it was important, too. O, I know. I'm glad you liked the slacks. I'll send up the skirt and other skirts too. Glad to get rid of them. I feel like throwing all my junk overboard. And I've got to lug your two boxes around too. GRRRRR. Good thing it's you that my soul lovest, or otherwise I would really throw them overboard. And I'm so sad that you want to wear nice new clothes but haven't any. It is wonderful to have new clothes to flash off to other femmes. The cat in me just purrs so contentedly!

Today when I was going home, Father Gefell asked me if he'd see me next Sunday at 10:30, and I couldn't refuse him, although I'd rather go to Protestant services. As long as I'm working for two Catholic chaplains, I might as well go to Catholic church. It is nice, though. Maybe I'll be in a nice gloomy mood for it too. We're having storms every afternoon recently. And it passes over in an hour. Maybe I'd really better go. It is 5:30. I'll write again. I hated sending out a one-page letter to you today. I only wanted you to know that I was going up North this Thursday. I hope I informed you. It looks like Father Dunn has managed to get it fixed up so that I won't have to pay for the meals during the two weeks that I am gone.

Today at school I was so darned sleepy that I could hardly keep my eyelids from sticking together. And my piano lesson was only about half an hour long. I don't know, I am rather disappointed in Mrs. Hoshina. O, well, after all, she is much better than most Japs, and females. And then, when I came back to the hotel, Larry was in trouble because he couldn't write a recommendation. And Shirley couldn't help him either. Not bragging, but Kay, I betcha there aren't many people our age who can write like us. I remember when I first began writing for Mr. Natori, I had the hardest time forming sentences and paragraphs. Now it comes like second nature. We are rare, Kay. And don't let anyone tell you different.

No one praises us so we will have to praise ourselves. Although Al does tell me lots of flattering things. He tells me of the GIs who have said that I am intelligent, and it surprises me. Well, it's not getting me anyplace. Or will it? Writing like this, it makes me mad because we haven't got our slang book out yet, so I think I'll write up Chapter Three tonight. That will be something. Then let's us work on something else. We won't be nothings.

You know, at supper tonight I was eating all by myself, when the Chinese boy Wong came along. He's the one who used to ask me about American slang at times. Well, he said in course of conversation that he is going to Tokyo next Tuesday and I said that I was going to go to Akita next Thursday. It so happens that he was in Akita for three years during the war. And he is going to Akita on Friday! Well, he told me how to go—a quicker way than by going through Tokyo. Said that if I have travel orders I can go on Jap cars, but I get a special seat on the second class. Isn't that wonderful? He'll be in Akita for four or five days, just when I'll be at Teruko's. What a fine coincidence! Now, I have to go see what time the trains connect and stuff. Gee, I'm all excited.

There's no one at the piano in the lobby now, so I think I'll go bang on it for a while.

[Later]. I was playing on it when a lot of people came around, so here I yam back to you. My equilibrium has been broken and I feel all shattered again. It must be fun riding around on a motorcycle, although it must be very tiring. And it will be fun for you all to get together. Be sure to write to me all about it. It would be interesting to see what kind of boyfriends the girls have now. Personally, I am content to be away from them all. I have my own little world, and am perfectly content with it.

Did you see in *S & S* today about the Kyoto GI who got a life sentence for "rape and sodomy" of a thirteen-year-old girl? He was a Pfc in the twenty-first car company, the same company that Murphy is in. I had to look up sodomy in the dictionary. Also, I avidly read that article about the churches lamenting the breakdown of morals in the Philippines, but that most of the girls were forced to "shack up" with soldiers because of economic reasons. And, changing the subject, don't let little Freddie get you all ruffled up. I'm sure he doesn't know how he is hurting your delicate feelings. After all, he belongs to the egotistical Male gender.

Kyoto, August 11, 1946

Dearest Kay,

There, I've finished the story part of Chapter Three. And I'm getting so much done! I looked over the whole list and am sorting it all out. Want to add more to the three chapters, just the list. And I was thinking of making a Chapter IV for underworld slang, with a story, but don't know how it will materialize. This morning I got up and worked on the thing until breakfast down in the office (hotel), then after breakfast I got Larry's typewriter and did the rest in my special private room. It is ten, so I stopped to write to you. Then I am going to church.

It surely feels good to get it done. I've been haunted with the thing for months. Now all you have to do is type it all out in final form (double space, I think) and we can send it on to Little Boy Blue with our compliments. Won't that be wonderful if we actually get a Mary and Kay book out? It is worthwhile, too. And at long last we are beginning to express ourselves. I feel so superior that we are doing something when the others are only foolishly playing. There is real satisfaction in this. I don't feel so worthless now.

I might as well quit my gloating. I hope Father Dunn gives the sermon this morning. I've never heard him speak. Listen, my dear, I have just about decided to leave Thurs. night. That will mean that I'll reach Tokyo around eight Friday morning if everything goes right. Then I have to hurry to Ueno to catch the train going North. I haven't looked up the connections to Akita yet. Guess I ought to do that today. I did find out that I'd have to pay for my way if I went direct to Akita, so I'm going the skinflint way. Besides, the other way I would have to ride the crowded Jap cars. That RTO surely is cold. I hate to ask them anything. Of course the Japs are cold and snotty too, but I am used to that from the Japs. I guess I am expecting too much when I want the Americans to be nicer than the Japs. If I expected the Americans to be as rough and impolite as the Japs, I wouldn't be doomed to disappointment.

It's going on to fifteen after ten, and I don't want to be late, so here goes off my nice fat letter. I hope you have got my two other chapters.

Kyoto, August 12, 1946

Dearest Miye,

I feel all keyed up again. Guess it's because I am looking forward so much to the trip and to moving to the Station Hotel. Last night, Miye, it was really so wonderful! I felt so close to you! You see, I went for a rendezvous with the River Kamogawa again. The moon was so lovely that I could not resist the temptation. It lured me out. Besides, I was tired of staying in all day. Out I went on the old course, along the Sanjo St. to the ancient bridge, then out to my little Niagara falls. It was all so lovely it took my breath away. And I thought of you. You're a part of me, Miye, and you always will be.

This morning[125] I was talking to Ram, the Indian who works for the Chaplain section, and he was giving me a piece of his mind. He said that if in India a member of the occupation army did what some of the GIs are doing here, they would hang him. I suppose he is referring to cases like attack and rape and robbery. Ram said that the Europeans have become great from exploiting the East and now they treat them like dirt. One time he actually saw a French cop strike an Indian officer, and the officer could do nothing, just because his skin was dark. And it wasn't his fault, either. O, Ram was mad about the injustice of it all. What started him off was that he said he could eat his lunch at the museum (I Corps co.), but he didn't want to because they didn't treat him right. And now, he can't eat just one meal at our hotel and pay just for that one meal. No—they have a new ruling out now that everyone must pay for three meals regardless of how many he eats. That is not right. In Osaka they kicked, and so they are writing up to Eighth Army about it. They ought to do that in Kyoto, too. So I told Ram, and he said he'd see the Maj. in charge of us and give him a piece of his mind. "The Americans here are not what they represent," said Ram. I fully sympathized with him.

August 14. Tuesday morning and I am nearly through packing. I have decided to leave Thursday morning, then that means that I will reach Tokyo Thursday night and Akita Friday afternoon at two. It's a long trip, but worth it I am sure. Tomorrow is VJ day [the 15th in Japan but the 14th in the United States] and a holiday, so I can get settled at the Station Hotel. I've got a busy day ahead of me—typing, filing, getting my travel orders. And moving. I'm going to have breakfast as soon as the bell rings, then hurry to work. Guess I won't have time to write to you for a while. They are cleaning the halls, and it

125. August 12 is an inferred date for this interesting comment Mary added to her letter of August 9 under the impossible date of "Monday 19 August." From the second paragraph of that addition (omitted), it is clear she was writing on a Monday, but she also goes on to tell Miye she wants to get her work on the slang book done before she travels—which is to say, beginning on August 14. She was in Akita on the 19th.

is dusty, making me sneeze. Sr. is really kind in helping me move. You should have seen all the boxes he took to the hotel for me! It is just simply wonderful. He came over last night and we went for a walk. I didn't get the thrill from the river in the moonlight as I did when I went alone last night though. I wonder why? And yet, if I were with you or Kay, I know I would have enjoyed the beauty of it all just as much if not more than if I were by myself.

Miye, dear, I was so disappointed in Chappy yesterday. I'm afraid that I have been fooled by him, too. I thought that he was sincere and honest, but I am afraid that I am wrong. It's hard to find a GI who is really sincere. Or is it that sincere GIs do not have anything to do with girls? I hope that is the answer, for I am disillusioned if all of them are like the ones I have met thus far. But I should not be harsh on them. Take the usual run of people—you find very few really sincere, regardless of race, creed, color. But it is so disappointing when you [believe] in someone and find out that he is not what you had hoped. And then we got to talking and [Chappy] said that I ought to stick to Kaneda, the Korean, for he is rolling in money now. I said I would not go with anyone for any money if I didn't like him. He says I am foolish, for I am not going to be here all my life, and when I go back to America, I can just throw the Korean overboard, and have a nice fat bank book to boot. I said I do not sell myself, and what does he think I am—a whore? He pricked up his ears at that, and says, "What's that you said?" He continues, he knows lots of such women who have married rich men, and their husbands never found out. He must think that money means everything. What do I care for money? Just so I have enough to get along in comfort, I do not care for more. I told him that perhaps those women have different standards and have had different upbringing and so they could do it. Let them do it if they want to, but as for me, well, no money is worth it. "The Americans here are thinking of how to make money," said Kay's friend, and how true it is! Money is the idol of most Americans. But it is not mine.

August 15. One year since the victory of the Americans, so we are taking the day off. Yesterday, did we have to work, moving! Chaplain Newby, the Protestant chaplain I think a lot of, lent me his jeep, so Babs and I moved with it. That surely helped out a lot. They did have two big 6 × 6's for us, but you know how it is when lots of girls are trying to move all at once. It was so much more convenient to have the jeep. The poor driver had to wait out in the sun for the longest time, and I didn't know what to do for the poor guy. I kept saying that we thank him and we must have caused him a lot of trouble, and he says, "It was the chaplain's idea." I feel sorry for the drivers at times. The ones who drive the sedans for some of the colonels don't get in until four in the morning, getting them home from parties, I hear. What a caste system!

I must pack yet. And I want to recuperate from the moving. We used to work a lot, didn't we? I know your family did. And I did, too, when I felt like it. I'm glad to hear that you quit your job. It must have been too much for you. Now you can be a full-time wife for your Nick. I can't wait till I see Teruko! One of my Joshi Dai classmates was working at the Station Hotel, but she quit suddenly last night. I wonder why. I am worried about her. I wonder if it was humiliating for her to have to serve me. I never knew that she served. I thought she was only an interpreter, and supervised the other girls, and was surprised when she was serving at the tables. That should not make any difference to her—it is only the turn of fortune that has put me on the other side of the fence, for the time being. I have served that Mrs. Korb and others of her clique—I have served that horrible Mrs. Sakai and her clique—and I thought, in fact, I knew that I was just as good if not better than they.

Yokote [Akita], August 19, 1946

Dearest Kay,

I feel like I've been away from you and civilization for ages. A change does do me good, though, for I need something to jar me out of my smugness.

At last Teruko and I have a little time to call our own! The maid finally came back this evening. Until now Teruko, her husband, and I had cleaned house, done the washing, took care of the baby, and the house was a big mess. Teruko would get all tired and bothered and she'd scold like any overworked Japanese mother. So I couldn't just sit and write while she was doing the housework. It was awful the first few days, for I was all tired out from the trip and I felt not the least like even lifting a finger. But thank God I'm back to normal now.

All except for the fleas! Fleas bother me at night—my body is speckled with aftermaths of their feasting. How thankful I am that I don't have to live in Jap fashion anymore!

Listen, Kay, if you give me your word of honor that you'll return them, I'll send you the carbon copies of my letters to Miye.

I just don't feel so much like writing anymore. I'll see you on the twenty-seventh. I haven't seen my Chinese boy who came to Akita. I'll be leaving for Yonezawa this Friday.

It's only eight, but I feel like going to bed already. If only I had a typewriter, I'd write volumes to you, but since I have to write, I'll quit with this.

Yokote, August 21, 1946

Dearest Kay,

Last night I had a dream about Dr. Simms—that he sent Emma some mail-order catalogs, so I went to APO 301 and sent them to her. It was all mixed up. Then I awoke. Wonder how Dr. Simms is? You know, Kay, I believe that it was worth being in Wakayama if only for having met him. It's so hard to find anyone as sincere and worthy as he. I do hope we can write to him soon. Perhaps by the time I return to Kyoto we might be allowed to use the APO.

Only two more days here—no, only today and tomorrow, and the day after that I'll be on my merry way again. I suddenly realized that I'd have to be in Yonezawa three days, which is too long to mooch off my stingy relatives. Maybe I might go to Tokyo—I'll see how it is.

I'm certainly glad I'll be seeing you again soon, anyhow. And I'm so homesick for Kyoto! I miss Sr. and my cozy office with Al and Father Dunn. And my little room with all its Western conveniences.

These flea bites—I must have a hundred on me. Well, I've had it worse. Only hope that I won't carry a family back to Kyoto where they can grow fruitful and multiply. I shouldn't, since I'll be in Tokyo on the way.

Today Teruko and I are going to the city of Akita. They have not come down from their bedroom upstairs yet. I don't see how Teruko stands this life—and she hates to be inhibited even more than I. I often wonder if she regrets having married. I don't think so. They get along well, and think the world of their baby. Besides, they won't live out in the country like this for long.

I'm getting hungry, too. First time I've felt hungry since coming here. The day before yesterday Teruko cooked *mochigome* by mistake; so we had to eat that yesterday too.[126] I love the fresh tomatoes, apples, and watermelon I feast on here. Otherwise, I'm getting tired of Jap food.

Yesterday I sewed all day. It took me over half a day to make Mr. Odashima's shirt. Then I mended another shirt and two of my slips. I brought a skirt of mine to sew, but absent-mindedly left part of it home. Now I'll have to finish it by hand.

It seems like they've gotten up. We won't make the first train as Teruko said, though. A baby surely is a lot of bother. They talk as if they're not going to have any more.

I'll quit here so I can get this sent off today. If only I had my typewriter! When I get rich, that's the first thing I'm going to buy and I'll carry it all over with me.

126. Usually the Japanese eat *mochigome* (glutinous rice) only on special occasions, such as at New Year's, when it is pounded into cakes.

Yonezawa, August 26, 1946

Dear Miye,

It seems so long since I've communed with you! I just haven't been in the mood. Let's see—on Friday, that's the twenty-third, I left Teruko and came to Yonezawa. Came on GI coach which is hitched on the regular Jap train. There was only one GI on, and he got off at Yamagata. We had a little chat. He was a good boy. Said there were only forty men in the MG at Akita and they have it very nice. I left Yokote at eight in the morning and reached Yonezawa around two in the afternoon. Teruko ordered a "*Koseisha*" for me to ride from their home to the station. It is a cute little thing—a box built into a bicycle, and someone pumps the bicycle and off you go. At Yonezawa I was surprised to find all of my cousin's kids—three of them waiting for me at the station.[127] They were sun-tanned and healthy looking.

So I've been in Yonezawa ever since. I've been feeling so tired, though. I guess the soft life I'm leading is weakening me. God, I thank my lucky stars I no longer have to live like these people—eating rice, sleeping on the floor, being bothered by fleas, flies, mosquitoes. I'm glad I'm leaving today. Guess I won't be able to write anymore until I'm back again in Kyoto. I'm taking the train at nine tonight and will reach Tokyo at seven in the morning.

They've made drastic changes in the laws of Japan now, and I'm certainly glad to see the women being recognized. Until now an only daughter could not marry into another family. She had to have a husband come into her's, so that the family line could be never-ending.[128] All that is gone. Upon divorce, a man has to support his former wife. And extramarital relations is good reason for a woman to divorce her husband. Such ideas are revolutionary. Until now the woman had nothing at all to say in matters of divorce. She could be put away with a word, but never could she divorce her husband. The law did not recognize as wrong any extramarital relations of the husband. Now, the possessions of husband and wife are held jointly—formerly, everything belonged to the man. I'm certainly glad to see the arrogant Jap male knocked down a step or so! . . .

Kyoto, August 30, 1946

Dearest Miye,

I've been wanting to write to you, but have just not had the time at all. You see, I returned to Kyoto yesterday morning, and ever since I have been

127. Tomi-san's husband had died during the war, and she moved her family into Mary's grandfather's house.

128. She means that if a family did not have any sons, the oldest daughter could not take the surname of her husband when she married. He had to take her family name so it would be carried on.

writing bread-and-butter letters, washing up, fixing up the junk I brought with me, and have not had time to do what I really want.

It's wonderful to be back in Kyoto! First of all, I must tell you the good news—my registration is over with, and my papers will come through in two or three months, and I can go home anytime after that. That is, if everything goes as it should. Look, Miye, I can hardly believe that my dreams are about to come true! And sooner than I dared expect, too! They asked me if I wanted to go back next month, can you imagine! It took my breath away. I do want to go as soon as I can, yet common sense tells me I should stay for at least half a year after I get my papers in order to not go back broke. O, the whole country will be mine after I have a War Department civil service job! And as soon as I get my papers, I can write as much as I want! So it won't be long now.

The latest report is that all men with eighteen months will be home in ten days. For me, all I care about is Al and Russ. And a few others, I will miss a little, but not much. Anyway, Sr. is wonderful again, and so I am not concerned how many GIs come or go. He said that he missed me while I was gone, and now that we both live at the Station Hotel, we can see a lot of each other.

Kyoto, August 30, 1946

Dearest Miye,

Miye, I can [really] write to you now! Happy day. At long last my fondest hope has come true. You can address me [at] the Chaplains' section like you used to do. And all because of my letter, too. If it hadn't been for that, I would have to moan around and wait until my papers came through. Goody, goody, I haven't heard such good news for a long time. And it makes it worth much more when I flatter myself in thinking that I was instrumental in bringing about this change.

Here I am so involved in myself that I forgot to thank you for all the wonderful things. The shoes are just simply perfect, and just what I wanted and needed. And so many blouses! It was so sweet of you to put in the candy, too. What shall I do? I am overwhelmed with your generosity. It came just after I left Kyoto. I had told Sr. to go up and see if there were any packages from you. He did and can you imagine—he didn't even open it! When they might have been his beloved books! That man surely has had strict upbringing, and he sticks to it, too.

The only catch about us sending mail is that we don't have the right kind of money to buy stamps with. Maybe I can manage to beg someone for them, but would you enclose some when you write? I hate to always have to beg you, but I'd much rather beg you than anyone else. I know I've told you before, but it makes me think of that article about the occupation in France, how the French found out that GIs feed starving women, but for a price. Yes, that is true of the GIs anyplace. There are a few who do things for you just out of the kindness of their hearts—like Al and the chaplains—but they are the very few and far between. And I guess I am warped, but I do hate to ask them for anything.

I'm so happy that I can write to you, to my family and friends. Of course, it really didn't make so much difference between us, since I wrote to you and kept the letters, but I do miss the frequent inspiration I used to receive from you. And now I can write to Dr. Simms too. Before, I'd limit myself only to you and the family, but now I have an unlimited field.

Monday is a holiday. Father Dunn asked me if I knew of any place where he could drive—preferably hot springs—and stay overnight. I said when we were in Wakayama, my girlfriend and I (Kay) thought of going to some hot springs over there, but it never did materialize. He said that he and the driver could take us this time. How I wish that Kay were here! And I'd feel so safe with Father. I feel safe with Sr., too. He's surely got high moral standards, and lives up to them.

Today I brought up a suitcase because I wanted to get it fixed. The store is across the street from Daiken, and wasn't open when I came. So I took it up to the office. On the way home, I took out the suitcase, and the MP at the foot of the elevator called after me. I nonchalantly opened it in his face, and he went away sheepishly upon finding (to his disappointment) that I hadn't smuggled papers and goods in there. Someone who was at the information desk laughed outright, and I couldn't help but laugh, too. I thought it was a good joke on these smug, self-righteous MPs.

I'd like to rattle off like this to you forever, but I must write to others yet, so I'll be good and quit for now.

Kyoto, September 3, 1946

Dearest Kay,

I've been feeling just simply rotten, due to a cold I must have gotten during the trip, and then further amplified by little RRH.[129] So I am way down in the dumps and woe is me.

Sr. blew his top last night. It's a long story, but I don't feel like writing, so I'll give you the skeleton of the thing. You see, on Sunday, I happened to come home in the afternoon and saw a poor little filthy girl lying on the sidewalk. I looked at her, then went on up to my room. But I couldn't get her off my mind. Especially after hearing a sermon about the Good Samaritan. On the

129. Little Red Riding Hood, Mary and Kay's name for their menstrual period.

impulse of the moment, I brought her up to my room, let her use my bathroom to bathe and wash her hair, then put her in bed, after giving her what food I had. Then I washed her smelling, filthy clothes. Well, Babs came to my room and saw her and wondered what I was going to do with her. I didn't know, either. I sewed up my old slip and panties and dress to fit her. At supper time I happened to sit with Wong, and told him the whole story. He wanted to know what kind of a girl she was, where she'd been staying, and where her parents were. Said that he had experience with those kind of people, and if he could talk to her, he would find out what she was like. So I asked him to rescue me and talk to her, in my room. He did very obligingly. And he took her to her relatives. That was a relief, and he was very gentle with her. He told me that she had a skin disease, and for me to change my sheets. So I had a time, washing and scrubbing everything that she touched.

The next day, I nonchalantly told Sr. the story. He was so angry when I told him that Wong had come to my room that he didn't know what to do. I thought it was so silly of him—for Wong only came because of the little girl, he only stayed a few minutes, and he was very kind about it all. Sr. says he didn't know why I washed the sheets, either. Isn't he awful? But I didn't care—I guess he is afraid that he is going to lose me again, and that causes him to blow his top like that. He'll come back, I know he will, and it doesn't bother me. Only it's amazing how narrow-minded he can be.

Gomis left this morning. How is Babs going to take it? Her outward appearance is brave, and she is taking it very well, but I know her heart must be bleeding. Poor thing!!! I told Sr. that Babs had told me Gomis had told her that he was coming back. Sr. said that there is no possibility of that at all. Once he is gone, he is gone forever.

Al says I can go now. Goodbye, my darlink. Hope I hear from you. I betcha it's because you don't know my address. All you need is Kyoto, Station Hotel.

Kyoto, September 5, 1946

Dearest Kay,

At last I am getting down to my former routine. Still have this wretched cold and have to cough something embarrassing. Think I'll type out *Ichiro*.[130] Say, I'm so darned tired of the whole business—let's get it off! What if it is only three chapters? I don't want to have it hanging over my head any longer. Did you type out the other chapters? If so, did you send them to LBB [Little Boy Blue]? I wonder what's happened to you anyhow, that I don't hear a thing?

130. Mary and Kay playfully used Ichiro, the name commonly given to the first-born son in a Japanese family, for their first joint venture in writing.

I've quite decided to work a year and get a little bank account before returning. Father Dunn was saying that he might go home anytime now. I don't know what I'll do after he goes. I'll have no one to look out for my interests anymore. He really has been so kind towards us that we'll miss him loads.

O, by the way, it's only us foreign nationals in Kyoto who can use the APO. I'm so sorry that you cannot! It's because our postal officer worked so hard for us that we can, and it's up to the various postal officers in other localities.

Whew! I did a lot of work this afternoon. And [*Ichiro*] goes wandering back to you. He's in final form except for the list I want to tack on back. And how do you like my preaching chapter? These stupid Nips make me so mad, and yet in a way I have compassion on them for they know not what they are doing. It was written off on the spur of the moment, and if you want to add or subtract anything, go right ahead. It is all rather sweet and idealistic, I know, but I don't think that will hurt anything.

Must hurry back to the hotel or I won't make it in time for supper.

Kyoto, September 5, 1946

Dearest Miye,

I wonder if this bulky map of Kyoto will go for six cents anyway? If not, I'll take it out and wait until your stamps come to the rescue. Sr. has a lovely set of china he wants you to have. Honestly, I sure do like it! It is a tea set, and a kind of bulky chinaware. I don't know what you call it—it looks like it is made of clay, and yet, there is a kind of simple beauty and dignity in it. I'm sure that you will like it. Now I don't know how I'll ever get it sent off to you. After I am an American[131] perhaps I can get it packed properly and sent off. It would be a pity if any of the pieces broke. It is made by Serra, a Spanish artist who lives close to Babs in Kobe—the foreign settlement. The china has "Serra" written on them—no, not written—it is [scribed] in. They are a gray-purplish-bluish color, and sturdy-looking. Gee, Miye, I'm so glad that Sr. got something for you!

I asked his advice last night, and he said it would be wiser for me to stay and work for a year and to get as much out of the occupation as I could. Of course that is the sensible thing to do. A little bank account will not hurt me at all. I really hate to go back penniless, especially when I could earn some money if I only stick it out here for a while. That will make it that much longer before I see you, but if I've stood it for all this time, one more year shouldn't make too much difference. Besides, I can correspond with you, which is the most important thing.

131. That is, after the reinstatement of her citizenship.

Sr. was telling me last night of how he had spent all day trying to get some penicillin for a Jap student of his, whose father was dying of septicemia, or some kind of blood poisoning. He went to Dr. Tai, who is working for the army, at the Kyoto prefectural office, only to be told that he had 200 bottles of the precious penicillin, but that it was to be used only for cases of VD among female Japanese. So Sr. tried to get some from the Japanese. After running around to various research centers, he discovered that the Japanese have not succeeded in making it yet. But Sr. said it was sad how the head of a family dies for the lack of the precious medicine which the army provides for the worthless whores. But it isn't for the prostitutes—it is for the GIs who will become infected. But that's the way it is.

Now the next thing for me to get all excited about is how to get a civil service job. Think I'll go down and see someone while I'm thinking about it.

September 6. Haven't had time to write at all, but I think I'll send this out. Air mail is going to be five cents after October 1. You know, Miye, I am so happy now, working for the chaplains who are so nice to me, and being at the hotel with my own room, and having Sr. for a friend. My little world is as near to perfection as it could be in Japan.

How's Little Mary? I never imagined that having a baby was so much trouble and work.

Going down to the Post Office now. The International Postal system is going to start from September 10, it was announced in the paper today. But we can continue to use the APO.

Kyoto, September 8, 1946

Dearest Miye,

Why do I feel so dead this morning? It is a grey Sunday, nearly eight in the morning. Guess I'll go to Protestant service this morning. I want to hear Chaplain Ogborne, the big, good-natured man, speak. I'll wear my new dress to boost up my morale. I haven't worn your lovely blouses or shoes yet—I'm carefully saving them. And, in a way, they seem too precious to wear.

There's something being done about an orphanage. Chaplain Ogborne had a writeup about some men of the *Gospel Hour* being interviewed in sponsoring an orphanage, and it had to go to the Corps Chaplain (Father Dunn) for approval. Father Dunn said that the army was not allowed to procure any buildings which [were] not for army use. And [as he put it] these GIs had gone ahead without letting the chaplains know about it, which was impudent of them. He didn't say that exactly, but that's the impression I received. Let's see—I ought to get it to you straight. Some GIs, in cooperation with Japanese

Christians, led by a Rev. Shiozuka, procured a building for lease of ten years to be used as an orphanage for war orphans. Shiozuka wants to make that his life work, and he agreed to clothe, feed, and house the orphans found around the station and on the streets. Well, I thought that was a very good idea, and was disappointed with the rather cool answer from the Corps Chaplain. Then I spoke to Chap. Ogborne about it, and he said that there's a right way and a wrong way in getting this orphanage started. Now, I wonder about Chap. Ogborne. I said it was a very worthwhile idea, and he agreed solemnly that it was very worthwhile.

Wonder if the end justifies the means anyway? I know that there is a lot of illegal procuring being done only for selfish reasons. Is it wrong to procure anything for such a great cause? For instance, officers procure private homes in which to live with Jap mistresses. And if a bunch of Christian GIs try to do good by having compassion on the homeless waifs, they are censured. As for me, I am all for it. If you wait for channels, you can't get anything done. And this work is vital, and cannot wait. It is getting cool already. They should have the orphanage started before the cold winter. Now these poor children can sleep out in the streets without freezing to death, but later on, I know that if they do that, they will be found lifeless in the morning.

I was wondering who this Mr. Shiozuka was, when I happened to bump into him. He is working at the desk of the Kyoto Hotel. He has come to our office before to talk to Chaplain McCandless. He really looks like a Christian, too. His eyes are so kindly, he looks like joy is abounding in his heart, and still, you are inspired with confidence and trust in the little man. As I remember, he is a repatriate from Manchuria. He said that he hated to leave his congregation in Manchuria. Yes, he is the ideal man to start and run an orphanage. I said, "I don't think the army will help you." He answered that they would, maybe not openly, but they would anyway. I told him that if there's anything I could possibly do, I should be very glad to. Hope he comes up to the office to talk to me about it.

You know, last Sunday when I brought in that little filthy girl to give her a bath, some clean clothes, and food, what you said kept running through my head, "You would do it."[132] But, Miye, I am not qualified to. If I had the confidence that I could see it through, I would throw everything else to the winds and pour myself into the work. But you don't know the Japanese. I could never influence them or get their cooperation. And I wouldn't know the first thing about running an institution like that. It takes someone like Mrs. Uyeda of Akita, or Rev. Shiozuka. They are native Japanese and know how to handle

132. Miye by now had all of the letters Mary had held onto during the clampdown on APO mail. This was in response to Mary's letter of July 30 mulling over the possibility of working to establish an orphanage in Japan.

any problems. I would only bungle it, for I know the Japanese enough to realize that they would never accept me.

I have been wanting to write about Mrs. Uyeda. She is an outstanding Japanese woman—aggressive, energetic, and willing to fight for what is right. Really, I never knew that it was possible that such a gem could be found among these passive, mild Japanese women. Teruko thinks the world of her.

When we went to Akita, we looked her up. Her home is quite messy, and there is an informal air about the place. I was impressed with her children—how they seemed so uninhibited and free. And Mrs. Uyeda jabbered away at us in her high voice, so that I didn't have a good impression of her at first. But as she talked on, I could not help but admire her. Perhaps one of the stories she told us would be the best way of showing her character.

One day all of the housewives of the neighborhood were lining up for fish. Mrs. Uyeda was lined up, too. Then two young, smartly dressed women stepped in front of her. She didn't like that! She told them that she distinctly remembered that she was in back of another woman, and weren't they ashamed to step in front of her like that when there were many others who had been waiting in line for hours. They insisted that they had been there before, and that was their place. But Mrs. Uyeda said that she was certain that she was in back of the woman ahead of her. Finally, that woman couldn't stand it any longer, and said that she had saved a place for them. But Mrs. Uyeda had told these two women off to such an extent that they quietly slipped away.

After they had been waiting for over two hours, the fish market owner came out with a stick, placed it right in back of Mrs. Uyeda and declared that only the women who were in front of that could get fish that day. There was a long line in back. These women who could not get fish were very disappointed, but many thought it couldn't be helped, so left. However, some of them just couldn't give up. They had waited so long already, and they were planning on having fish for supper. Well, Mrs. Uyeda placed that stick in back of the women who were in line, including all the women who were still there. They were all able to buy fish. These women bowed and thanked Mrs. Uyeda profusely for her boldness. She told them not to say anything or the owner might suspect something. That's an example of how the merchants operate. They say that they sell on the black market and make huge profits.

Something like this wouldn't be so extraordinary for Americans, but for the passive Japanese woman, it is revolutionary. She has her own ideas, and she carries them out. She is so progressive, and her ideas coincide with Teruko and mine.

Mrs. Uyeda had all her plans for the orphanage she wanted to build. She wanted it to be run by women, just to show the Japanese that women can do something. She said that in the orphanages in Tokyo there is much dishonesty going on. The princes and princesses send cakes to the orphans, and the directors sell [them] on the black market. Their sugar rations are never used for the orphans. According to Mrs. Uyeda, the main trouble with orphanages up to now is that those who work in them are not paid any salaries. Theoretically, they were volunteers. So they would always be on the lookout for ways to make money illegally, at the expense of the helpless orphans.

She wants to build a house for them out in the country so the children can grow their own food. Akita is known for [its] delicious rice, so the homeless children are flocking there. Now they rob, pickpocket—anything to keep body and soul together. She would like to have the army procure a house for them.

Fr. Dunn let me bring home this typewriter over the weekend. I am going to the show with Sr. Goodbye for now.

Kyoto, September 10, 1946

Dearest Miye,

Thank you ever so much for the package! It was so embarrassing, how it came. You see, I wasn't here to catch it, and so Father Dunn got it, thinking it was for a missionary priest here in Kyoto. He took it to him unopened, asked the priest, who said, yes, he knew someone in California, and it was candy. So at the table, where a lot of priests were gathered, they opened up your package, only to find the lacy underwear come out! Father Dunn was telling me about it this morning, and he said that there was lace all over! Anyway, thanks a lot. It won't have to happen like that again since I can get my own mail.

And I think perhaps I might get a new job. I talked to the CI&E man in MG yesterday, and he said that they have a position as librarian open. Whenever replacements come for the Chaplain section, I think I can get off. I'd much rather be working with books. But don't know for sure yet. Then, he said that after I get my papers, I could work for the Federal government as librarian. If that is true, it would be perfect. But I realize now that it is a great drawback if I do not have any degrees. If I did, I could get very good positions here in education. That's what I am most interested in, I have found out.

Well, I'll get this off and get back to work. Thank you again.

Kyoto, September 11, 1946

Dearest Miye,

Dear, dear Teruko, I wonder what has happened? She wrote me a letter, which I received last night, saying that something tragic has happened to her, she had lost grasp of herself, and everyone was making fun of her. And that my case, and the time I discovered that I was no longer wanted, was as nothing compared to her. It must be that her husband has "put her away." How dare he! For heaven's sakes—and I thought all was going well. Was the difference in age too much? I couldn't understand all of Teruko's letter—she must have been confused in mind. Besides, my reading of Japanese is not too excellent. But she said something about that she knows how that woman in *Goodbye Mr. Chips* felt. What was that? All I remember about Mr. Chips was that he fell in love with a young woman—much younger than himself, and they lived happily. But Mr. Odashima, Teruko's husband, must be no good. After Teruko trusted in him so much, too! How tragic, and when there is a child, too! They both loved their baby so much! I can't believe it! T. said that she would send me her diary and another letter soon. What could have happened?

And Teruko repeatedly asked me to befriend Etsuko, our classmate who is now in Kyoto, and to save her. Yes, I am afraid that Etsuko has chosen the wrong friends, and she is going down and down. I can see it in her flippancy. But can I—shall I—save her? I don't know. As the Doctor (Freddie's friend) told Kay, it is not the prostitutes of Japan which are important, and which are so influential in re-making Japan—no, it is the women of the higher classes. And any woman who went to Joshi Dai is definitely of the higher class—in money and family background. They make up many of the intellectual women of Japan. And look at my classmates. How are they taking the occupation? Is Etsuko a typical example? I hope not! Yet, Etsuko was one of the outstanding students—she was studious, energetic, intelligent.

Yet I cannot blame Etsuko, or any Japanese girl for going astray. I know how awful it is when you are hungry and can't get the very necessities of life—soap, decent clothing, food. When a woman wants so much, and someone is generous with those things which she has gone for so long without, the temptation is great. I do not want to censure them. I am not in a position to. I felt that I have less sympathy for girls who go astray only for the extra money or just for fun. It is easy to be secure, and to have all that you need, then point the finger of blame on those who sell themselves for the very things that one has. I don't know—it is all so involved.

But to get back to Teruko. I love Teruko. She is the only really true Japanese friend that I have found. She has high ideals. Among all our class, she only could thrill to Milton, to poetry, to the skies with their jeweled stars, with me. Dear Teruko—how wonderful it was to get away from the Joshi Dai dormitory, and to go out under the stars, to gaze and gaze and to just unburden ourselves! We were young then. Now, Teruko has taken on the burdens of wifehood and motherhood. She has become skinnier and paler. Her rosy cheeks have lost their bloom. Yes, I am afraid tht she has suffered. How can a man be so heartless? I knew that he was going with other women, and when I discovered that, it was a great shock. Can't he ever be true to one? Teruko told me, before she married, that she knew that he was a Casanova, and that it was like an incurable disease with him. But she believed that if she trusted in him, he would always return to her. Has she been rudely awakened from her rosy dreams?

Miye, at least, I hope and believe that you will make a success of your marriage! It is so tragic how marriages often break up after only a year or so. Sr. has been reading some book about marriage, and he said that it is proven statistically that those who have known each other longer before getting married have more chance of success than those who marry after only a short friendship. I think that is very true. Although there may be exceptions. He is a Catholic, and you know how strict the Catholics are supposed to be about things like that. He said that in Spain a man and woman must be friends for a long time, and be very sure that they will make a success of marriage before they take the step, for there can be no divorce.

I told Sr. that the women of Japan ought to have much freedom now that they are given new rights and privileges. He said that it would make no difference whatsoever since Japanese do things, not by law, but according to custom. And he further went on that the laws of Japan are splendid, and that there was no need at all for making a new constitution. During the Meiji period, scholars came from Europe to make a constitution, and laws for the country. According to a law, a girl can marry of her own free will when she is twenty-five. Yet, is that ever done? No. Custom dictates differently, and according to custom go the Japanese. It was interesting to hear Sr. talk about those things because he is an LLD and has studied such subjects. I know that what he says is true, and the result of much study.

Sr. surely is moody. At times he is way up in the clouds, and at times he is way down in the dumps. At times he is energetic and talkative, and at other times he says nothing. How strange he is! I never know what to expect.

Nearly all the GIs we have been with in Kyoto are leaving now. Al, poor kid, is in the hospital with an in-grown toenail—or should I say WAS, for he had it operated on. He is supposed to go home in a couple of days. He says he is praying as never before that he will be able to go with the other 20-month men. I hope so too. He is really one GI I have become very fond of, and someone I shall remember forever. I've never gone with him, either. Just seeing him around the office, and talking to him I have grown to know him like a classmate or someone like that. We'll really miss him when he goes.

This is my last envelope. But I'll find some way to get some more. I love to write to you, Miye. It makes me so happy that we can use the APO. O, I forgot

—I was going to write to the Army Postal Officer and thank him. I don't want to be like the lepers that Christ healed and they didn't come to thank him.[133]

I like this Uneno-san whom I am teaching. She is very sweet and ambitious. I do wish that I had some books for her to study. I am wearing your slip already, Miye. It is perfect! It is nice and durable, and fits perfectly. I showed [it] off to Amy and Peggy, the two Nisei girls who have civil service jobs, last night. They surely envied me.

Kyoto, September 12, 1946

Dearest Kay,

At last a letter from you! And congratulations on that word of advice. I liked the way you fixed it up, even if I was exasperated with the errors and general sloppiness of expression and grammar. But it showed originality and humor, which was definitely lacking in mine. I just rattled off what was on my mind at the moment, thinking I'd fix it up later, but later came and I was unable to do anything with it. I guess it is your touch that it needed. I'll do it over and send it off to you if I can.

Al is going home tonight. Dear, sweet Al—so sensitive, so sweet and sincere, so temperamental and romantic—how I'll miss him! And yet, I feel like he'll really be a friend forever. He touches your heart and how it hurts when he leaves!

Which makes me think—perhaps friendship is the most beautiful thing in the world. It really is beautiful, isn't it? Somehow—perhaps I have never experienced the real thing, but it seems like love leaves a bad taste in one's mouth. Love—what is it anyhow? Al was never a lover—only a friend, yet I really miss him more than any "lover" I have known. That is quite a broad statement. Perhaps it is not altogether true, but its effect is good. But look, like Miye and you and I. Isn't it perfectly wonderful? Miye, after all these years, so true to me. And your girlfriend in the States, too. Whereas a lover, if you break up, that is absolutely the end. Yes, as you say, we look for stability in this ever-changing world, and perhaps that is why friendship is so valuable.

What was that you wanted my opinion on? Something about the morals of the Japanese being due to their low standard of living. It is hard to answer that. You cannot say definitely yes or no. I would say that their low standard of living contributed towards their low moral standard, but I wouldn't say it was due to it. Where is your letter—I'll get the question straight. There, I'll answer your questions in order: Just because the living standards are lower

133. According to Luke 17: 12–19, Jesus healed ten lepers but only one, a Samaritan, thanked him.

than America, the moral standards should NOT be lower! That is, speaking from an idealistic viewpoint. Yet, in actuality, I am afraid that because the living standards are lower, the moral standards are lower. The living standard does NOT have everything to do with the way the Japs are. Look at those rich Japs—are their morals any higher? On the contrary, the richer Japs have the means and money to indulge in immoral pleasures. And, many of the rich Japs made their fortunes by disregarding moral principles. The smallness of mind is NOT caused solely from the difficulty of gaining their bread and butter. It is hard to say that any one factor is the only factor in causing a certain result. There, are you satisfied? Someday when I have time, I'll expound on this.

Anyway, my dear, it is satisfying to read that you are arguing about such subjects. How much better are your letters now than the time you were working for the officers' club! And you'd write about the exotic women and the officers' private lives. That stuff is intriguing, but it gets to be very distasteful. I am glad that you are in [a] much better atmosphere now.

Don't tell anybody, but I think Sr. is very fond of me. Last night we had another fight. You see, it is all because he is so possessive and jealous. Just as Babs said. Only, this time it is rather flattering, for I like Sr. and would not leave him for anyone. I'll tell you what happened. I saw Larry [this] afternoon on the bus, and asked him if he was going to the Gospel Hour that night. He said yes. After supper, I had a stomachache, so told Sr. that I didn't want to go to the movies with him. I really didn't feel like going anyplace. Well, right after he left for the movies, Larry phoned and wanted to know if I was going. On the impulse of the moment, I said yes, and I'd try to catch the seven o'clock bus. There was Sr. on that very bus! He got off at the theater, and told me to get off too. How could I when I'd told Larry that I was going with him? Besides, I don't care to go to movies, but I did want to go to the Gospel Hour. So we went on. I enjoyed the Gospel Hour. Hereafter, I want to go regularly. Chaplain Ogborne spoke about prayer, and I was really inspired. You know, Kay, I believe there is something to Christianity after all. And I cannot understand the Catholic religion, but when I go to Protestant service, I can understand what they are saying, and it is gratifying. I love to sing those old hymns I used to know, too.

Well, after the service, Larry and I and another girl were running for the bus when I hear Sr. call me. Was I surprised! He was so mad at me, for he said that I refused to go with him, then went with another man. But Larry is so young and harmless, and I think of him as a brother. He is really sincere and nice, too. Well, he made a lot of false accusations and I got sore, for it wasn't true. I said that if he wanted to own me, I didn't want to be owned, besides, what right has he to order me around? Just think, Kay, he had been standing outside of that chapel all the time! After we got to the hotel, Babs wanted to know what happened, so I told her. Then the phone rang, it was Sr., and later he came. Yes, he comes back. Afterwards, I told him I was sorry, and so everybody's happy again.

Well, I must get to work. Only, your letter was so refreshing that I couldn't help but write back right away. And I'm glad that you gave me your ARC address. O, by the way, I went down to see about my prospective job again, and it sounds very promising. I want to take it as soon as a replacement comes into the office. Mr. Anderson, the person in charge of CI&E, is a wonderful person. He was connected with Stanford University in California, and before that he was teaching in Japan for ten years. He said that he would, after I got my papers, try to get me on as a librarian for the State Department; as I told Al, I am extra in this office—anyone could do this typing work—but at the library, I could put everything I have into the work, and I could be of help to many people, I am sure. I love to work with books, anyway. This is a fine opportunity, I think. And Mr. A. is very understanding. He said that this job would only be a stepping stone to better positions. So that even if I got back to the States, I might be able to get a job there. Well, I must think of the future too.

You know, I think I'll tread the straight and narrow path hereafter. I've had enough of running around. But then, after all, that was a period of transition, and we didn't know what was what. Besides, it is so hard to stay at home when you have no spot you can call your own. But now that I have a room to myself, and I am settled in so well, I can be very conventional, go to church, and be in early every night. It's funny—I don't even care to go to the movies anymore. Sr. doesn't have this inner tranquility at all. That is why he is drinking lots of beer, and he is going to movies when he knows that they are stupid. Wonder what is the matter with him? Anyway, my heart goes out to him in sympathy. Maybe it is because his future is so bleak, for he says that there is no way for him to get out of this country. That must be awful.

I think, though, that this experience has made me very lenient towards those who do not tread the narrow way. If you are well set up, with home and security, it is easy to blame others for going astray. Yet, if you are alone and insecure and friendless, and have no place to call your home, it is only natural to try to find happiness and even momentary pleasure elsewhere, or wherever you can find it. So I don't blame girls for going astray. Well, I try not to believe the wild stories that fly around about the girls here anyway. Who knows how much truth there is in rumors? I don't want people to believe the wild rumors that go around about me, that is why I try not to believe stories about others.

My, where did I get all this self-righteousness? I'll be a full-fledged preacher if I keep this up.

This Gospel Hour is really amazing. GIs run the show. They lead the singing, they give prayers and testimonies, and it is marvelous. It is what do you say—heartwarming? or consoling—to find that there are good boys like that among these rowdy GIs. Chaplain Ogborne said there is some civilian worker in Tokyo who is interested in nondenominational help for the Japanese, and that it is he whom we should contact about the orphanage. The Rev. Shiozuka said that all the Jap preachers are too involved in their own troubles to care about any less fortunate. So the best thing, I think, is to get help from the churches back in the States. I am sure that many churches would be very willing to help out in such a worthy cause.

Well, I must be going. I am not hungry at all. Father Dunn brought us up some ice cream today. At times Chaplain Ogborne brings us up ice cream. I bet there aren't many girls who get treated as well as we do!

I think I'll copy that poem about "Some Days Must Be Dark and Dreary"[134] and send it to Al. He gets the moody spells so often that I feel sorry for him. Remember when we used to read that and how we loved it?

Kyoto, [September 12,] 1946

Dearest Miye,

Al, our chief clerk, left tonight. We went to see him off. And it made me think—when will that blessed day come when I can again return to you, to my family, to the country of my own. Yes, when will that be? O, I do want to go back! I am tired of struggling, of working by myself, of being alone. Of seeing misery all around me, of seeing signs of stupidity and cowardice in the Japanese—those people who are my own, and yet they are not. As I write on the typewriter on my desk, I can gaze at the pictures on the wall before me—pictures of the people who really count in my life: Mother, Father, you and Nick, Kay, Teruko, Emma, George, Blanche. When can I return to them?

And Al is going home. To Idaho. Dear, sentimental, moody Al! He is so lovable! I mussed his hair for the last time tonight. You can't believe that he won't be there from tomorrow. What was that line—"Parting is all we know of heaven and all we know of Hell"—or something like that.[135] Dear Al, God be with you! A devout Catholic he is, yet he doesn't have the peace of mind, the inner joy that real Christians should have. What I have observed of Catholics and Protestants in the army has definitely prejudiced me in favor of the latter. There was one Protestant boy I knew who went home this evening too. He gave a testimony at the Gospel Hour last Wednesday. There were four little Japanese girls to see him off, and they sang a song for them. And Tommy,

134. "Into each life some rain must fall,/Some days must be dark and dreary." From "The Rainy Day," by Henry Wordsworth Longfellow (1807–82).

135. "Parting is all we know of heaven,/And all we need of hell." From "Parting," by Emily Dickinson (1830–86).

as his name was, looked so happy when they sang for him! He had probably taught them Sunday School lessons or something. Protestant boys get out among the Japanese and do their best to help them. Catholics never do anything like that. I do believe that the Protestants are nearer the teachings of the Great Master.

Received a letter from Mother today. Hope I hear from you soon. It is about time, for it is nearly two weeks since I let you know. Miye, I wore your brown shoes today, and they are simply wonderful! The international post office is open now, and you can send parcels to Japan. Also postcards. I have never heard from your relatives, or from Alice. You might try writing.

"Is it not to deal thy bread to the hungry, and that thou bring the poor that are cast out to thy house? When thou seest the naked, that thou cover him and that thou hide not thyself from thine own flesh?"[136] Isaiah preached practical Christianity. You know, Miye, I am again becoming interested in the church. The church is one influential organ for doing good. And there is really a difference between Christian GIs and non-Christian. I do admire the chaplains, though.

Hope we get some replacements soon. I want to get started on that library. Although I hate to leave the chaplains. They have been so kind to me. Say, when is Nobu[137] coming over? I certainly want to see her! I must be getting old, I ache all over today. Wish I could take a bath. There's no hot water now. Last night I left the faucet for the hot water on, and got up at three in the morning and took a bath. Think I'll go to bed with the faucet on again.

And your chocolates are so wonderful! When I first got them, I was craving candy so much that I gobbled down about three or four, but now I've got them put away to munch at leisure. I hope you don't mind, Miye, but I must confess that I gave about a third of the box to Toshiko, the girl whom I teach English to, and who is studying to become a nun. I showed your picture on the wall to her, and said they were from you. She said that she divided them with her family, and they hadn't had chocolates for a very long time. You can be assured that they were well appreciated. It makes me mad that women of the street probably get chocolate from GIs but nice girls like her can't get any! So I'm administering justice in a small way, thanks to you. I know I shouldn't give away what was given to me, but it was only part, and I don't think you would mind. I promise I'll eat the rest myself.

Bottom of the page already. I'll send this off tomorrow.

136. Isa. 58:7.

137. Miye's younger sister, whose husband was in the army. They went to Japan after Mary had gone home.

Kyoto, September 13, 1946

Dearest Kay,

These people who are so important in their own eyes make me laugh! Babs thinks they are ridiculous, too. I guess that is why she is always saying that Peggy is SO important, and last night she said that Connie—that woman we both don't like—thinks she is so important, and she thinks the rest of us are small fry. That surely is true, and I rejoiced secretly, for I thought Babs liked that woman since she used to talk to her quite often. But now I see that our first impression must have been correct.

This morning the little Rev. Shiozuka, who wants to start an orphanage, came in to see Chaplain Ogborne. I kind of interpreted for him. I say "kind of" because he can understand nearly everything. And in the course of the conversation, we arranged to teach each other—he is going to teach me Japanese, and I will teach him English pronunciation. Every day except the days I have to be CQ.[138] Now, I am so happy over it. He said that he would try to get some literature for me to study.

My little would-be nun came to the hotel for her lesson yesterday evening. She comes two evenings a week, and I plan to take Spanish two times a week, in the evening. Wednesday I'll either go to the Gospel Hour or out with Sr. and Sunday too. So that keeps me well occupied, and in a way that I want to be.

How come Hisako has a second lieutenant rating? What is she, anyhow? That's quite high, you know. She must get plenty. I wonder what CAF [civilian affairs] rating that is? I've been trying to find out Peggy's and Amy's CAF rating, but they refuse to tell me, so I let it go, for I don't care so much. I told Babs, and she said that they wanted to know what CAF rating the former WAC who works in the MG base has. What hens—keeping their own rating secret and trying to find out that of others. Boy, just for spite, I hope I can get a position that will outrank them! And now that I want to get that job as librarian, I asked Mr. Anderson to ask for a salary of ¥2,100 for me. I think I deserve that if even dumb stenos like Connie are getting 2,000. And won't I feel superior if I do get it! If I don't get it, maybe I won't change jobs, since the chaplains are so nice. And Father Dunn doesn't like it because I am going to quit them. Although he was very understanding about it and said that he wouldn't stand in the way of my getting a better position. I was afraid that Mr. Anderson would take it wrong when I asked for so much, but he smiled and said that we all want to get ahead. Really, I have a very good impression of him. The Nisei boy who works for him—Ken Ishida—said that he is very nice, and so did Hauchecorne. Ken is a graduate of Ueno Music Academy, and practices the piano at school quite often. He can play very well.

138. Chief of Quarters. Here the person in Mary's office assigned to keep the doors open from the end of the workday at 1:30 until 4:30.

Your letters with the retyped "Word of Advice" came today. Thank you very much, and you did a good job of it.

It is Friday already. This weekend I want to type a lot. Did you see where international mail is allowed now? I'm going to ask my mom to send some food to Rev. Ito and some other people who have been kind to me. We can send postcards only. Can't you use the APO yet? You know, Kay, I feel so proud of myself because I wrote up to the Theater Postal Officer in GHQ thanking him for helping us. It was a short note, but it made me feel good to thank him. O, and I must write to Mr. Brody too. Guess I'll do it this weekend maybe.

Kyoto, September 14, 1946

Dearest Miye,

Miye, I feel so sad! Should I unburden myself to you? Yes, I must. "I cannot bear my burdens alone."[139] It's Sr., Miye. I do like him a lot. And today, after he drank a lot of beer, he told me what he thought. I wonder if I have lost Sr. I'll tell you everything frankly. You see, the night before last, he came to my room, and stayed until very late. In the course of the evening, he began begging for me. I kept on refusing him. He said later that he would never forget that. He said, "My flesh called to your flesh, and you refused." And that he would never forget, and that he would despise me forever for that. Is that right? Back in Osaka, Father Wolber told Kay and me that if a man did not respect us enough to enjoy our company without asking for pleasures of the flesh, he was not [worth] spending your time. And that our answer should always be NO until we had a ring on our finger. But look at the result. I like and admire Sr. more than any man I have ever met.

Or was I disillusioned? Is Sr. really not the splendid man I had built him up to be? I cannot stand for that dream to fade away too. If he really isn't all that I thought he was, better it is that I faced reality right now. But he said that he would be a sincere friend forever. Well, I ran out on him when I went with Russ instead of him. Now it is his turn to hurt me. I must bear the result of my carelessness.

It hurts, though. It always hurts when a woman thinks she has lost her man. Will he come back this time? Deep down, I believe he will. He has always so far. But then, we have never gone as far as we have. However, I am determined to keep our relationship clean. And if he doesn't like it, it is better if we broke up right now.

And Sr. is going to quit working for the army. That means that he won't

139. "I must tell Jesus all of my troubles/I cannot bear my burdens alone." From a Baptist hymn by Elisha Hoffman (1838–1919) sung in the Holiness church.

stay at the hotel anymore. I won't have any friend here at all. None with whom I am intimate. And I don't want to make any more GI friends. The very thought is distasteful. I'll go back in my little hole, and not go with anyone.

I knew it was too good to last. It's been so wonderful to be sure of Sr. To always eat with him, to always depend on him to go to the show when I wanted to, to talk with at night.

He made me cry today with all his accusations. It made me mad because I was doing right as I saw it, and he had no reason to blame me. And I thought, I am so alone—so alone out in a foreign country. I am tired of it all. Why must I struggle so? Now, if I didn't have any sense of right, it would be so easy to get along now. But I can't deny—my strict upbringing has molded me.

Dearest Miye, it is wonderful to know that you are always my true, true friend, and I can always turn to you. Really, you don't know how much consolation it is to be able to unburden myself to you. And our background has been so alike—I am sure that we understand each other perfectly. And I'm so glad for you that you are happily married and expecting a child to bless your home.

It has been raining for the last couple of days, and my mood has been as grey as the skies. It is very depressing weather, with the sultry heat, the continual rain. It makes one very tired, too. I thought it was myself only until Cecilia said that she was terribly tired last night. And the soldiers going home has not added any cheerfulness to our moods. Al is now gone. The old familiar faces have disappeared. I hate it because it reminds me clearly of the transitoriness of life. Here today and gone tomorrow are all these GIs. And then there are stories of the girls left behind. Somehow, it insults my sense of justice.

I don't have an appetite, but I guess I'd better eat. And everyone will ask me where Sr. is. He wanted to eat by himself tonight. And then he is going out. By himself. O, well, I'll stay home and write. I am definitely in [a] sad and writing mood. If I don't write, I feel that I will burst. I want to write and write and write. Maybe I'll be a little appeased then.

I'd like to fill out this page before I go down to supper. I can hear the women stamping back and forth in the halls, making a racket. You know, Miye, I do like Larry. He's really nice. Wonder if you know who I am talking about? He used to work at the desk of the Chuo Hotel, is Chinese, around twenty years old. Very sincere and thoughtful, and yet, friendly and kind. He looks young and manly. Today, I went to take a piano lesson and after I finished, he came. He is the only faithful one who comes regularly for lessons. I'm glad that he comes, too, because he said that it was a good way to spend his time, in practising. And I told him about it in the first place. Now he is working for the MPs. While I was in Akita, he transferred to his present position, and he wrote me two letters informing me. His English needs much correction; yet what he says is interesting and has something to it. It's a pity that he cannot write better. I'd like to teach someone like that. He can speak English well, but when it comes to writing it, he's not so good.

My little Uneno-san, the girl student, writes me a composition every time she comes. I felt quite important correcting her composition. She is very intelligent, and ambitious. She wrote a composition about Father Gefell, but it was all scattered in thought. So I explained to her that it should be more connected in thought. The next time, she corrected it, and it was very well written. Yes, it is gratifying to teach her.

September 15. There, I feel much better with the new day. You know, Miye, if it's one thing I learned from being in Japan for all this time, it's that I found confidence in myself, and that come whatever may, I'll live through it. It's really strange, what the human body can stand. And you always live through it, which is the marvelous thing. So if sorrows come and go, I know at the time I am deepest in grief that that grief too is passing; the next day, or the next week, I will forget about it. Life must go on. I forget just why. Remember that line? I remember that it was when we were going to high school, and I loved that poem, and how happy and thrilled I was when you, too, loved that poem equally! I think that was one of the happiest moments in my life when I discovered that you had a soul I could commune with.

Last night, after supper, I wrote a little to Kay, then I washed my hair, put it up, took a luxurious bath, washed my clothes, and it was nine o'clock before I knew it. Maybe that is one consolation for being a woman. If I am disturbed mentally or emotionally, I can wash or sew or do something or other to occupy myself, then I go to sleep and forget about it. Thank God I have a room to be myself in without having to "enryo" to anyone!

I awoke up at five o'clock this morning. It was still dark outside, and I could barely make out the stooping figures of the men wandering listlessly about the station. Always when I awaken in the night I hear the people wandering outside my window. Wonder what they are doing—these homeless people who gather about the station?

Here it is afternoon already. The weekend flies altogether too quickly. Went to church this morning. The dedication was at nine. That is, of the I Corps Chapel. The commanding general made a speech, but it was broadcast, and we could not hear a word. Then the service was at 10:30. I went upstairs and wrote on the back of the program to my mom. After the service, while waiting for the bus, I talked to the many shoeshine boys that gathered around the GIs waiting for the bus. It was surprising that they make up to fifty yen a day! That's more than I get in cash. Besides, they get gum, candy, donuts, etc. They are among the high-salaried personnel of Japan.

Your white blouse is so sweet. I just love it. Wore the one with lace trimmings today, for the dedication. I surely do love it, and especially when I think it is from you, it makes me feel like you are really close to me.

Kyoto, September 14, 1946

Dearest Kay,

Hauchecorne said that you are a strange girl. He further said that you are hard to understand. I said that you are intelligent and have talent, and he was more than willing to agree. Asked what you are doing, and I said that you are going to school and that it was admirable of you to see it through. He agreed very readily on that too. It all started when I told him that you mentioned him in your letter.

Now, my dear Kay, I feel like you. Only not to the extreme, like you. I, too, want to shout Damn Damn Damn a thousand times. Yes, and I'd like to act crazy, but luckily, I have my refuge in my comfortable room, and instead, I am pouring forth my heart to you. Kay, what are we? What are we here for? Why did we stay in Japan and what are we staying for? For I must admit that there is a kind of charm in this place, keeping me. I cannot tear myself away. O, but I must, and I will!

At the office, I went and took a poem to Amy, and she gave me back my copy of the APO letter. She praised me to the skies about it. Said that it even went to the commanding general of I Corps. I never knew that. But I must not live on past glories. I just wanted to gloat a little teeny wee bit more about it, is all.

Can you use the APO? Ever since that letter pulled the trick, I have thought of befriending some other causes, like about foreign nationals riding GI cars (we got kicked off last Sat.) and some other things, but I really don't care so much about what happens. This orphanage, though, is something I want to write about. You know that it takes quite a bit to rouse me out of my lethargy.

I was sorry to hear about Patricia. Did you read that article in *Reader's Digest* about marriages in the US and how so many of them ended in failure? It certainly is a pity. And that is why, before I get married, I want to be very very sure. You speak lightly about Sr. and I, but I really wonder. For one thing, and this is very important, the religions we were brought up on are different. There is certainly a lot of difference between the Catholic and Protestant religions. And frankly, I do not like the Catholic at all. I have tried it a little—I mean, going to church and seeing the Catholics around me, and I find that I like Protestants much better. Another thing, Sr. will be in Japan for quite a while yet, I think. I do not want to stay in this country for any man! I'd rather be an old maid back in the States. I wonder why—is it because I am rather sure of Sr.—that I do not dread at all being an old maid, nor do I feel lonely. Guess after I pass my thirties, I will become lonely, as I have been told. Ah, well, much of it is fate, as you said. So why worry about it?

Wish I'd hear from Miye. It's two weeks now since I wrote to her letting her know that I could receive mail from her. Even if it's only a line, I want to hear from her. At least, her life has something stable about it. And it is so wonderful that she is happily married.

By the way, did you see that poster about Nisei? Quite good. At last we are getting publicity. It was posted at the school. There were four pictures—one of the homes being burned down and the Japs forcibly evicted from their homes on the coast, another about the raids upon them by foolish terrorists, another about them fighting in Italy, another about what is the future—I forgot what this one was about. And on the side, it had a large picture of a Nisei soldier, with helmet on. Sr. said that he has that poster. He's wonderful.

Today I bumped into so many nice colonels. That IG Col. Walker is very nice, really. He always greets me warmly, although he never talks to me much. And that finance colonel, Col. Delihant, asked me if I had my papers yet, and he told me to work here, for it is good money. And he advised me to get away from the coast—back in Chicago there are many Nisei and they are getting along fine. He has grey hair, and he is really fatherly. Well, I guess that's about all. At least, even if the GIs I know are leaving Daiken, most of the officers will stay. I don't know many, but those I do know are quite nice. Col. Delihant goes to Catholic church.

My shoulders are beginning to ache from typing. Hauchecorne wanted me to go to the show with him. It was a temptation, for I wanted to show Alvarez, but I resisted. O, that's right, I haven't told you what happened, did I? Well, night before last, after we had the fight about Larry going with me to the Gospel Hour, Sr. came to my room, and we made up. Then Sr. began begging for me. I firmly refused. Well, after all his fine preaching about the evils of premarital relations and stuff, why should he scold me if I did what I thought was right? I think what makes him mad is that he lost his control, and begged, and I did not equally lose my head. He was rubbing it in so much this afternoon that it made me cry. I felt so alone and pitied myself. I don't know what to do. I don't want to lose him. I do admire him more than any man I have met yet. [But] I want to keep our relations clean. Especially when I know that the whole hotel probably thinks we are the same as married, the way he spends so much time in my room. What do I care what they say, so long as it isn't true? They always want to tell stories, anyway. They judge others by themselves. Just like the stories you say they spread about you. Don't let them bother you. Wouldn't you rather have it that way than to be so insipid and insignificant that no one talks about you? And as long as they are not true—those fine rumors, why should it bother you? That's what I think.

I was thinking that I am beginning to understand why you and Marie stand up for each other so much, and attack the men who do you wrong. I think it is very American. Stanley Dresser was telling us that he talked to a GI, and this GI said that the girls here are tamer than back in the States. By that, he meant that back in the States, if a man did wrong to a girl, her friends would get together and go to his home, tell his mother, and get revenge in some way. Well, I suddenly realized that that is what you and Marie were doing for each other. When I was back in the States, I never did go out with boys, so I was away from all this social life. But you must have learned this from your friends. I think it is a very good idea. Only I had never heard of it, so was reluctant to butt into another person's affair.

Remember Carol? Well, she was going VERY steady with an MP who promised he'd take a civil service job to be with her longer. I hear that even his mother wrote to her, so she was quite confident of marrying him. He left the other night to be discharged in Yokohama, supposedly. He was supposed to phone her from Yokohama. But did he? Not a word. She's afraid that he took the boat for home. And he did do that in Manila. Well, there's one girl left flat. Poor modern Madam Butterfly!

And Kaz, the girl who was going steady with the Nisei GI, is expecting the stork. And they won't let him marry her. Amy said that she admires her for not being ashamed of herself at all. And she further stated that she is brave, for not every girl could go through with it like she is. I told that to Sr., and he said that she is not brave—perhaps it was accidental, and some contraceptive did not work. What two entirely different attitudes. Anyway, it is true, as Sr. said, that society does not accept natural children, and they will have to suffer.

Sr. said today that he is going to quit his army job because: 1. He doesn't have time to read what he wants to, 2. He gets the foreign national ration, which is sufficient, [and] 3. He doesn't have many soldier students. I'll surely miss him if he does quit. Why doesn't he read at the hotel? I know, he doesn't have that peace of mind here, with all the stimuli. Well, he told me that what he [said to] me this afternoon was what five bottles of beer said, not Sr.

Think I'll go to sleep. I am getting tired of typing. I love my desk in my room, for I have all the people I love on the wall in front of me, and my thoughts are pleasant when I see them. I sent you a card today. Hope you got it. In case you never [do], I'll repeat: the damn censors got into your week's worth of letters from August 31 to September 9. So that I just received it today. And why is it that they censor your mom's letters always? I can't understand. Good night.

Kyoto, September 18, 1946

Dearest Miye,

Now I don't know how many times I have re-read your letter! It's so wonderful to hear from you that I really value your letters. And with every reading, I get a chuckle.

It seems so strange that the same old teachers are at JC. Some how, my life is so full of transitions that it seems queer that some places are stable and the same as when I left them. And whatever happened to Pop Knorr?[140] He liked you a lot. It's funny—I dreamt about John Knorr the other night. I guess it's because you wrote about him, long ago. And I'd like to know what happened to Bea Login too. You know, I have a hunch she just ordinarily got married. Or I wonder. She's a character I'll never forget. And she and that Kinkenhammer—they used to get together and smoke, and I thought they were so Bohemian! But Bea was really an intellectual genius—no, maybe that is too strong.

Your comments on Teruko were so accurate that it surprised me! She really is beautiful. You ought to see her—she has the beautiful, fine Akita complexion. It's just lovely—such fine skin, and so white and spotless. She used to have apple red rosy cheeks in school. She still has red cheeks, but they are not as rosy as they used to be. And she takes big strides and swings her arms, and she talks in a loud voice. As you said, she is far from the typical passive Japanese maiden. That's why I love her so. Wish I'd hear from her. I want to know what happened.

The other night, Etsuko came to my room saying that her girlfriend had a fight with her GI boyfriend, and she was downstairs crying. She wanted me to write out for her words to the effect that she didn't want to part like that—that she wanted to be friends to the last. I did it for her, and she disappeared quickly. Later, I told Sr. and he said that most probably it was she and not her girlfriend who was in distress. I am so naive—it didn't even occur to me! Sr. said that Etsuko was going towards the bad. It's really too bad.

Your speaking of Nick's pink pants made me think of Al. One day he appeared at the office with his pink pants and we surely teased him! After that, he wouldn't wear them. Dear Al, I wonder where he is?

140. A bacteriology professor and student counselor at MJC, who had helped Japanese Americans when they were sent to camp. He was dismissed during the war when enrollment went down. His son John, mentioned below, was a classmate and friend of Miye's.

Poor Kay, I feel sorry for her. Sr. said that a boy with the family background that Kay has would likely commit crimes (he's studied criminology). The wicked man her papa is—going with other women when he has a wife. We were lucky, weren't we, Miye, to have such God-fearing mothers and fathers?

Kyoto, September 22, 1946

Dearest Kay,

If you ever see *Enough Rope* by Dorothy Parker around, be sure to get it because I am sure that you will like it. If you can't get it, I'll send you mine, for I think you can appreciate it better than I. Her poetry reminds me of you.

Well, my dearest, I haven't written or received letters for three whole days now, and it seems like I have forgotten how. These last days have been hectic, for I have been so busy with Father Dunn's work that I haven't had time to do anything of my own. But then, it was voluntary labor so I didn't mind. Besides, it was for HIM, so I didn't mind more. At last, I have finished the typing that I could do now. Even came up to the office on Sunday morning to do it, too. I came at eight and expected to be at it until time for church, but surprisingly, I finished quickly, so I have time to write to you. Also, I am pasting pictures in his album, which takes whatever other time I may have.

Enough of my woes. How are you? Wonder if you're still going with Hisako. And I wonder if time is healing some of the wound Norman left Marie with. I wonder what life has for you two up in Tokyo. This is nearly the end of September already. Maybe I'd better start sending my letters to that grouchy uncle of Marie's place. Yes, I think I shall, for if the snoopers get their stinking noses into these letters, they won't reach you until a month from now.

I hate to leave the chaplains, I really do. And Father Dunn keeps rubbing it in that I am quitting them. However, opportunity knocks, and I am answering. Hope that position is better. I'm starting from tomorrow at CI&E. I'll have to associate with Japs all the time, but now I'll have the upper hand since I am employed by the great white conquerors.

And it's nearly a month since our interview. Hope we don't have to wait much more for results. I can't wait until I get a civil service job. I want to get a CAF rating as hi as an officer's because I want to get better than Amy and Peggy. Besides, why shouldn't I get that hi? But in a way, I don't want it because then I'll have to go to the Kyoto Hotel to live. That might be more interesting. But then, I'll be away from Sr. That's the only drawback.

If I do get higher rating than those girls, boy will I be happy! I'll stick up my nose at them! And now, they go strutting around in all their self-importance. Especially that old gal we both don't like. I'd like to show them a thing or two! And then, when I do get CAF, I'll be able to get quarters if I go up to Tokyo to visit! Won't that be wonderful? I could fly up there for weekends.

My, how I count my chickens before they are hatched!

I must write to Miye and Mama and the rest of the family to let them know I am transferring.

Sr. went home last night.[141] He has to attend a wedding this Sunday. He's going to take me to the USO show tonight. I haven't been to a show for over two weeks, I think. This afternoon, Mr. Frank and Jerry, who works in Chief of Staff, are going to give a twin piano recital. I'm looking forward to it.

I love this chaplains' office, and how I hate to leave it! But then, if a new Corps Chaplain comes in here, I guess I won't feel at home like I do now. I want to type out the rest of the things for Father Dunn, too. It will take me at least two weeks. But I'd be glad to do it for him.

Kyoto, September 22, 1946

Dearest Miye,

Tomorrow I am transferring. So if you'll address me to MG instead of Chaplain section, I'll get the letters directly. You can be sure, though, that I'll be running up to the eighth floor to the Chaplains' Office to see if I got any mail.

At last I have finished typing out the grave registration for Father Dunn! I even came up to the office on this Sunday morning to finish it. I finished quicker than I'd thought it would take, so I finally have time to write to you. You know, when I type all day long, I just cannot make myself sit down to a typewriter to write to you. And it is too much work to write by hand. You ought to see me now—I can type pretty fast. I think I can type faster than I can write.

My brother George wrote to me a few days ago and told me to come home as soon as possible. That's sweet of him to say that. But I guess I'll sweat it out. I want to get some PX souvenirs and stuff before I make my trek homeward. I'd like to get presents, but now if I have to buy them out in Japanese stores, they are priced so high that I cannot afford them. While, at the PXs they have nice things priced very reasonably.

I'm going to church in ten minutes. A change will do me good. All work and no play is making me very dull. After noon I plan to go to the twin piano recital by Mr. Frank (the Jewish piano teacher at the Army School) and Jerry (Al's friend). I am going with Amy and Peggy. I like them better than the other girls at the hotel, except for Babs. Even if they are so self-important. I "OH"

141. He had a house in Nara.

and "AH" at them, while underneath I am chuckling. And then, tonight, Sr. is going to take me to the USO show. I did want to go to the movies the other night, but resisted the temptation, for I would have to go with someone else, and I didn't want to withstand the onslaught of Sr.'s sarcasm afterwards. So I haven't been to the show for two weeks or so. They don't show many good pictures now anyway. Besides, my student comes two evenings a week, which keeps me quite occupied.

This morning some important personage came into Kyoto, so they had all the MPs standing at attention, the band playing, and all the traffic stopped in front of the Kyoto Station. It all seemed so childish and silly. I had to laugh. I wonder if that important personage gets a satisfaction out of having all the MPs out there standing at attention, and even a band to toot for him! And then, when he went down the street, the sirens rang, and MPs cleared the way. Children love to play at things like that, but it is funny that so-called adults love it too.

Sr. got an easy book of English, and I am helping his English pronunciation. He knows lots of words which I have to look up in the dictionary, but his pronunciation is enough to make me tear my hair. But he's very willing to learn. It is a pity that he cannot pronounce better. He's much improved since the first time I saw him, though. He said himself that at first he couldn't understand English as it was spoken at all, but now he can understand everything.

Kyoto, September 24, 1946

Dearest Kay,

I must thank you for all the beautiful white paper. It did get a little mussed up, but it will do. And your comments about me not working on the book made me sore. Listen, my dearest, I've been working my fingers to the bone, and I don't go gallivanting all over the country into cabarets like you. At night I am so tired that all I can do is plop into bed. Either that, or I have to teach. And when you get after me, I get all ruffled up, and my feathers aren't so soft, either.

Let's quit the nonsense, and let me tell you something more important that happened to me. Well, you see, my darling, I was talking to the man who started this Krueger foundation, for he was at our [CI&E] library looking it over. During the course of the conversation, he brought up the idea that if we could translate Emily Post's *Etiquette* it would sell like hot cakes, and enough money could be made to keep up the foundation without asking for donations. Then I brought up about slang, and he said that was much needed. I further timidly put in that a friend and I have a book of slang all ready for publication, but don't know where to publish it. It so happens that the head of

"Fusan-bo" Publishers is a friend of this man, and he is going to see him soon. He said that he would ask about it. Now, won't that be better than bothering Kimi-chan when she is so busy? It's better if we do it by ourselves, too. Only I don't know how much to rely on this person. He's been to America and he seems to be quite wealthy, so I think he is different from most of the Japs. Now, I have incentive to get on with the list.

Besides, I finally finished Father Dunn's photo album this morning. Now I have nothing to do at home—I mean in the way of other people's work. If I'm not too tired out tonight, I'll work on the slang.

The mail surely is snafu now. No one in the chaplains' got any mail today. And I haven't gotten any mail for nearly a week now. I know Miye would not fail to write for such a long time, or my mama either.

All this morning I was running around trying to collect things for the library. The GI who works in CI&E is quite a different person—you know, in our way of different. He was born in England, I think, was raised in Germany, and went to America in 1941. He really worked hard for the library. And he said that it would be a good idea to write to the State Library and various medical associations and things to get more books. I am so enthused about it all. And you know, I love to have a cause to work for and to write about. He said that the State Dept. has a library in each of around fifty countries. There's one in Tokyo now, and Kyoto is going to be the FIRST branch library. That's where yours truly wants to come in. It would be ideal to be a librarian for the State Department—even in a branch way out in Kyoto. And, today, that man said that several men in the Sixth Army contributed books before they went back to the States, so that they have around 3,000. I was getting rather disappointed with only the Armed Forces Editions we have. But that is only the start!!!

[Later.] Sr. says he is not too pro-American. It was certainly funny when he came out with that! You see, last night he got started on the Latin Americas and the U.S. He told me how the U.S. took over Panama, calling it a republic only to build a canal there. There used to be a small country there that refused to let the U.S. build a canal. Therefore, the U.S. loaded some guns and ammunition on some ships, went to the place and handed the natives some guns, then the next thing they knew they were said to have caused a revolution, and Washington recognized them as an independent country which would permit the U.S. to build the canal.

He says half of America—Florida, California, New Mexico, Texas, etc.—was taken from Mexico. I said, the people wanted to be a part of the U.S. He replied, "So did the people of Korea want to be a part of Japan. The victor explains the victory." He further said that in Central and South America, if you say you are Spanish, the people welcome you and say that some distant relative is Spanish, or that some ancestor was Spanish. But contrast that with India, or Java, or any place where the British and Dutch conquered. There they curse the conquerors. Well, I guess there's something to what he says. And after saying all that against America, about the Big Stick policy and Dollar Imperialism, he comes out with "I am not TOO pro-American." I had to howl at that.

Rev. Shiozuka came just now and I helped him with English reading. He is such a quiet, peaceful little man. But, just as he said, it is extraordinary for a man of his age to like to study. That is very true, for the Japanese, after they get out of school do not study at all. Sr. was saying that the profs who teach in the same school as he do not study at all either.

I must get back to work. Tonight my little Uneno-san is coming.

Kyoto, September 25, 1946

Dearest Miye,

For the first time in my life I have bright red finger nails, and I keep looking at them, for it seems like they are someone else's nails—mine never did look like this. But the eternal feminine in me is so pleased—it is almost funny. You see, last night I was so tired that I was not ambitious enough to do anything, so I wandered to Babs' room and took a bath. When I came out, she was no longer in the room, so I went to the only other room where I go to, and that is the abode of the important Peggy and Amy. Amy was painting her nails, and she insisted that I do mine, so I did. They have only two colors at the PX, so all those fortunate enough to get them get only those two colors. As they were saying, all the Mary Janes and Lulus have the same color of painted nails. You see, we're not allowed to buy there, but only those who have friends can get them. Of course, I am outside that picked circle. Peggy and Amy being civil service, can get it.

I am so enthused about the library. What I like the most, I guess, is that I am more or less my own boss. So I'm working away at it very hard. Besides, I like the job itself. It is not routine like typing. We have only Armed Service Editions—several hundreds—now, but we'll get more in. And it will be a branch of the State Department Library, and won't that be something? My ego is satisfied, too, because I get more salary (I hope) than any other foreign national here. I ought to get more than any typist and steno, don't you agree? Amy said it is not good to skip around to many sections, but I think that is the only way to find the work I really like. If I'd found interesting and worthwhile work at the very first, I would never have budged. But who wants to be a stupid typist all one's life?

Babs said to me last night, "Do you really think Sr. is in love with you?"

I don't know. She said to watch out, for he might catch me, and who would want to marry someone like that? He has the biggest beer belly, and his stoutness is not evenly distributed. I don't think anything of it, for I am going back to the States, and he is a good friend is all. He came last night, and left in bad humor. I think it was because I didn't have any tea or anything to eat for the poor man. Now that I don't work in Daiken, no one gives me ice cream, so I am hungry for the meals, and eat every scrap. I had a *Reader's Digest* written in Spanish, and he forgot to take it. He's surely moody anyhow. He was sore too because I don't go to Spanish lessons. I simply don't have time.

Haven't heard from the States for going on five days, and from you for over a week. No one in our section has had mail, so it must be the mail is snafu. Well, I must go to breakfast. I was going to write only a short note to you anyhow. After I once get settled in the library, I hope to have plenty of time. It is going to open on the first of October.

Kyoto, September 26, 1946

Dearest Kay,

I'll fool those censors and make two carbon copies, and send you up two letters. To both places. Now first of all I'll answer your questions: Yes, by all means get Mr. Y to publish it. And do include Kimi-chan and Mr. Y in the preface. Now, what else did you want to know? I forgot, so it must not be important. And I do want to work on *Ichiro*'s list, but I haven't had time at all. You with nothing to do—why don't you make the list yourself instead of whiling away the time? I am just going dizzy with things to do. Why, I even work on the books of the library in my dreams. But I feel quite energetic today. And tonight, I'll have to spend the whole evening with my student. Last night I went to bed early for I was so tired. I've given up my piano and Spanish, I never go to movies, and I do not have time at all to be working on *Ichiro*. Now, you'd better not ever get after me again, or I'll give you more of my troubles!

Today, I feel very happy. Had a lovely morning. Got up at five and copied out the twenty-third Psalm for my student, and also got a list of colors, and their meanings in English, you know, like I feel *blue*. Then I wrote to my mama and to Miye and I was going to write to you, but it was 6:30 by that time, and I wanted to get down to breakfast, then to work on the seven o'clock bus. It is wonderful to have interesting work like this. I feel so important! I can get typists to do the typing for me, too. Now, isn't that something? And we've been having such a hard time getting mops, soap, brushes, etc. for cleaning that I just picked myself up and marched in on the people who are in charge of those things. If you try to go through channels, it takes weeks. And I succeeded, which made me very happy. Then I saw Father Dunn and Cecilia.

Father Dunn always welcomes me. I love that Chaplains' Office, and go up every morning. Mr. Anderson asked me to go over the books and to screen them. I have to decide whether a book is good for the ignorant Japs or not. Another reason to make me feel important, and Father Dunn said Col. Delihant of Finance said I couldn't get a CAF job from CI&E. I explained to him who Mr. Anderson was, and what he had promised me. But anyway, it feels good to know that some people are concerned over what happened to you.

Enough of my bragging about my importance. Did I tell you that Amy has a rating of four and Peggy, being the important Secretary to the General, gets a rating of six? That's pretty high. And Carol's boyfriend has been true to her. He got a civil service job and he phoned from Yokohama.

Kyoto, September 27, 1946

Dearest Kay,

ALL RIGHT, I promise you faithfully that I will at least get started on that list tonight, even if it kills me. And I intensely dislike that remark you made "Why don't you work after hours? I do." Listen, my dearest, would it interest you to know that I work until 5:30 or six, and only go home then for I would miss supper? If I was only working until one as in my days of leisure, you might have reason to give me some of your pert remarks, but not now!!!

We're getting the library sign painted up today, and I feel more important than ever. The only thing is I wish you were here to build me up, and I could look demure and modest and pretend that it is nothing. Humph—I guess I have come up a degree from these females who are tied to their desks and hours. I have time pretty much my own, and I can do as I want to. Which is really wonderful.

As for your dear mama, you poor thing. I don't know what to say. She is really so skinny and hesitant and pitiful, and here we are with good food and we can act as crazy as we want to without caring what the Japs say. Poor thing. Yet, as you say, perhaps she would be dissatisfied wherever she is. 'Tis a pity, really. And you do your best, I know you do, to satisfy her. But you have a right to live your own life. What a problem. I hope that your sis will send her things, now that we can use international mail. Have you tried it, or can you use the APO?

Here I am so free from all dependent trouble. I don't think it would be half as bad having to worry about your husband or kids as it would be to worry about your parents. Because, in a way, you are responsible for the former, but who can choose his parents? That is where injustice begins.

Kyoto, September 28, 1946

Dearest Kay,

I received three wonderful letters today, and I was too happy for words. From my ma, my Blanche, and my high school/JC girlfriend. My mom said that Blanche entered Boston College,[142] so I was glad for her. I was afraid that she wouldn't be accepted. Especially after what the Doctor said (by the way, do you ever see him? What is his address? I'd like to keep up a correspondence with him) about the difficulty of getting into Eastern medical schools if your parents and grandparents hadn't been doctors. Did you see that article in the paper about no more WD [War Department] civilian jobs over here? I didn't but Sr. did, and he said that maybe it's a good thing I did go to the library. If I should get a job there on the federal payroll, it would be for the State Department. We're getting the library fixed up just fine. The books—330—came from Doshisha [University], which composed the Krueger Library books. I mean the original ones. We had about ten laborers in today scrubbing the floors. A press photographer from a Kyoto hometown newspaper was in this morning and took my picture. There was an article about the library in the *Kyoto Miyako Paper* this morning. And Mr. Namba, professor at Doshisha, said that that was all that the mayor and high officials of Kyoto talk about now. Isn't that something? Most of the Japanese (and I want to spell out that) who come to the library, and who are in the Krueger foundation are well educated and can speak English well. This Mr. Osawa who is president, is the head of Toho Films.[143]

Wonder why I don't hear from Miye, though. I'd enclose Emma's letter except that the buttinskys might find it interesting. There was so much I wanted to tell you, but it has all slipped my mind. O, I know—I despise that Lt. Lane who is in charge of the MG typists. He refused to type out the cards for the library. I was rather upset about it, and talked to Mr. Weil (another civilian in CI&E) who only answered with a smile, "There are other men besides Lt. Lane." All the CI&E people dislike that Lt. Lane. And Mr. Weil goes to Col. Partridge, the head of MG, and the Col. said that he would get one of the typists assigned to do our work next week. Ha, ha—we'll see who gets the last laff, Lt. Lane! Mr. Weil said that the Col. is all for the library. It is really a good thing, and any decent-thinking person would approve of it.

As you can see, I am so enthused about the library that I live and sleep in it. Father Dunn came to see me there today, and I was so flattered! When I went to the chaplains' this morning, he wasn't in, and I felt so lonely. Went again in the afternoon just to see him, and was sorely disappointed again.

142. Mary was mistaken; it was Boston University.

143. During the war, the Japanese government consolidated the film industry into three large studios, Toho, Shochiku, and Daiei. Toho was the largest of these conglomerates.

And so I was just thrilled when he came. If he weren't a priest, I am sure that I would fall for him.

Hope I can finish the list tonight. Then I can take deep breaths again. God got mixed up on his marble cake, and had two straight days of chocolate. Isn't that cute? God mixing his cake, and we are the little ants that are crawling around, thinking we are so important.

Here it is nearly eight already. Sr. is mad at me because I ate with Hauchecorne. Can you beat that? He asked me to go to the USO show with him tonight, but after my "unfaithfulness" he would not stoop to escort such a wanton female.

[Later.] I am so proud of us that if I had on my buttoned-up blouse, I'm sure all the buttons would pop.[144] Just think—we have 45 pages now!!! And I'll get at least five more pages for the list at the end of *Ichiro*, so we'll have at least fifty pages. Yes, just as you said, I leaf through and fondle the pages just as a miser does his gold. It's surely a satisfaction to actually see it form. Kay, Dearest, forgive me for being so aloof about it at times. Now I know why you kept harping at me. If only I had gotten to work on it sooner! But you know stubborn me. Unless I generate enough energy slowly and surely, I absolutely refuse to do anything like that. Well, I'm going full blast now. I'm glad that Sr. got mad at me and I didn't have to go to the show. I would have missed out on a whole evening's work. One thing I must do is get that book [from which] I got some of the GI slang. And listen, Kay, won't we be sued if we use the Thesaurus and other books without permission? Aren't the Americans strict about that? Let's find out. But we did not copy them word for word. Only got the ideas, and everyone does that. But I was thinking that if we mentioned the books, we would have to get permission first. Whereas, if we kept quiet about it, no one would know the difference. What do you think? And you're not going to put two poems in, are you? I like the second better. How about putting in "WE hope we've helped" at the end of the second? Or does it fit?

I *would* finish when you are no longer working, probably. But let's you get ahold of a typewriter and finish it up, huh? I hope your ambitious spell lasts longer than mine usually does. Well, we've worked plenty hard on it, and I am right proud of it. The bright ideas are all yours, and most of the stories. But isn't it marvelous how, like a snowball, it had its humble beginnings and then rolled from you to me until it became one great big snowball? (All it needs are its finishing pats).

So I'll drop off now to sweet dreams. It's worth sending you two different copies of this!

144. Mary was happy that the book was on its way to completion.

O, dear, how can I let all this remaining space go to waste? I cannot. You know, I was thinking that we could make a very interesting book about how we first saw the occupation in Wakayama. Remember our very first time when we saw the sailors, and then how we moved to Kainan and our lovely autumn walks—that time we tried to hitch a ride, but couldn't—that man with hard, hateful eyes you saw—that time the streetcar broke down and I got a ride with a bunch of drunken GIs who treated me with the utmost Southern hospitality—[that] *Ojiisan* [elderly man], and how we admired and loved him, good Mr. Chips, Dr. Simms—and the first time we ever saw K rations—that time we watched the world go by in front and got gifts from heaven—how Gene laughed and yowled and barked and sang and yodeled for us—how we ate boiled sweet potatoes at my cousins'—the mellow, calm days of Kainan when we felt first the thrill of liberation and freedom, etc., etc. I love those first days, and let's make a little book about it. Put in the dream and loveliness of those early days. Wouldn't that be wonderful? And let's get it published in America. I'm sure that something like that would help understanding. And wouldn't it be wonderful to get something actually published? What wild dreams—when writers have written thousands and thousands of pages, which were rejected before anything was published. But I think our case is different. People in the US want to know about Japan now, and there aren't many who can write about it. So let's, huh?

Kyoto, September 28, 1946

Dearest Miye,

Now I really can't keep the lid on. I'm just bubbling over with so much, yet nothing really of importance. Only, to me, everything that is happening is of the utmost importance. Most of all, I love my work now. It is something that I love to do, and I can put myself into it. Not that it's so much—it's really simple, straightening out books, sorting them out, getting the library presentable, but I love to have freedom and I love to use my own judgment.

Where shall I start? Today has been quite normal, but very satisfying. One hi spot was when I went to the Chaplains' Office, and found THREE letters for me. From Emma, Mama, and Thelma Christiansen. All wonderful letters. To have heard from you TOO would have made me burst with happiness. As it was, I was so happy the rest of the day that I was grinning all by myself. Wonder if Little Mary is bothering you? Or maybe you went to Modesto, as you said you would and that is the reason. I hope Little Mary won't be a problem child like yours truly. I hear that Blanche got into Boston College, so I was glad for her. And mother seemed so satisfied with having Blanche staying with them. And Emma sent a picture of her Emma Lee,[145] and she certainly is growing up. It will be so much fun being old Aunt Mary to them! I'll have to get me a cottage, cat and knitting to fit into the picture.

This afternoon Father Dunn came to see me at the library, and was I thrilled! When I went to the office this morning, he wasn't in, so I went back in the afternoon, but still he wasn't there. Surely was disappointed. He's like an uncle or something, for I can tell him everything, and I joke around with him and have lots of fun. He's stubborn and set in his ideas, but I'd forgive him anything. He looked the library over, then said that if he were running it, he wouldn't even open it, for it is communistic. If anyone else dared say anything so narrow-minded, boy would I be mad! But I know that Father Dunn exaggerates, and he has some kind of complex against anything that smells faintly of communism, so I merely laugh and pass it over as one of his whims. I really do miss him when I don't see him, though. What will I do when he goes home?

My bubbling over has fizzled down awfully fast, and I am left dry now. I guess I can write more when I am disconsolate and bored. Now that I am so interested in my work and doing things, I can't sit down and write. Besides, I'm half expecting Sr. to come anytime. He's so silly. Today, before supper he came to my room, then said he'd see me at suppertime. I went down before he did, and sat down with Babs, Hauchecorne and some girls. Well, Sr. comes in and avoids me. And he stalks out like he has been insulted. He doesn't like it because I talk to Hauchecorne, the Frenchman. And I don't care a thing about H, but it's just that he is somewhat of a Bohemian, loves to talk, and he says interesting things. It was through him that I found out about the CI&E. We (Sr. and I) were going to go to the USO show tonight, but now I wonder. O, well, if he doesn't come, I'll answer the letters I received today.

And Mother said that she would send food to relatives and Ito-sensei, which made me very happy. Those people will be overjoyed to receive them. Gosh, my back aches, and I don't want to type anymore. When Sr. doesn't come, I do miss him, only I won't admit it.

Kyoto, September 29, 1946

Dearest Kay,

Here I start with "Dearest Kay" again. It is Sunday morning, and I got a spurt of ambition and got up at 5:30 and have been working ever since. I finished the list as far and including the Underworld terms. Note that on page 13 I have words that should follow page six. And it seems to me that I have repeated quite a few of the words, so if you see any, please cross them off. Other-

145. Emma and Hilo Himeno's only child.

wise, it won't hurt if they are repeated, for they are in special places. There, what a load off my mind. I could die now in peace. No I couldn't! I WILL get back to the States first!! Besides, I am beginning to think about our next MARY AND KAY book. You know, it feels so good to get something concrete done like this! It makes you feel that you are not living in vain, and you get that inflated feeling that you are worth something—and more than the other vain females, no? So I guess it all is fundamentally egoism. But then, our book is wonderful, and I am not ashamed to show anybody. I am really proud of it.

Twenty to eight now. Even on Sunday I shall go to my beloved library. That is why I woke up in the first place. I began thinking of all the things that had to be done yet. You have no idea, Kay, we have thousands of copies of some magazines. It is all so uneven—some issues we have thousands of copies and don't know where to store them, and some issues we have only a few copies, and not even one to store. And I have to have everything possible done before the opening. Yes, it's a lot of work.

Guess I'll have to put another stamp on the envelope since it will be so fat. Only today and tomorrow before the opening ceremony of the library! And millions of things to be done! I like this Nisei boy who is working with me, Ken Ishida. He writes English very well, too. He bosses the Jap laborers around, so saves me the trouble. And he looks after so many details. And he is so impersonal, and he is as enthused as I about the library.

Kyoto, September 29, 1946

Dearest Miye,

Well, my darlink, I have crashed the local paper with a picture. Ain't that something? Only that poor photographer must have been confused with my jabbering of English and forgot to get my name. I only wanted to get the paper to be able to send it to my mom. You'd make such a fuss about it that it would embarrass me. But when I saw that the picture was quite big, it surprised me, and on the spot I bought all the copies that the woman squatting on the sidewalk had left, which was seven copies.

Worked in the library this morning. After ten, I was going to go to wash my hands and then go to church, but the janitor had the linoleum soaking wet, and I slipped and dirtied all the clothes I was wearing. If I went back to the hotel and changed, I would be late for church, so I decided to stay until noon.

Afternoon. Sr. and I surely had a bout! Boy, you know how stubborn I am, and he has such a hot temper that when we have disagreements, everything is flying. Now that I look back over it, it seems so childish and not worth telling you. It makes me mad because he won't let me even talk to any boy. I can't resist the temptation to tell you about it. Afternoon, he came to my room and was talking when the phone rang. It was Larry, and he said that he would like to talk to me. He doesn't live here, [and] I hadn't seen him for quite a while, so I thought I'd go down to the lobby to see him. Sr. was looking daggers at me, and the devil in me got the upper hand, and I merely started putting on my shoes (I wear slippers in my room) to go out. Sr. was demanding to know who it was who phoned. I said it was none of his business. That was like setting a match to a bomb! He accused me of having a date with someone else, and boy was he sore! I didn't want him bossing me around. Well, we were both excited and it took several hours to cool us down. But we did. And I went to Heian Shrine with him. It was really peaceful and beautiful there. Went shopping after that. I got some tea for you and will send it to you as soon as I find a can to put it in.

That book by Kay and me is nearly done. All it needs is some more retyping, I suppose. Sr. looked over the first part and criticized it. His criticism is good, though, and I appreciate it.

I'm awfully tired. Think I'll take a bath and go to bed early.

Kyoto, October 1, 1946

Dearest Miye,

Again and again, thank God for a true friend like you! Miye, I love you with all my heart. I always have and I always shall. You don't know how much it means to me to know that no matter what, I can depend upon you. I know that you will understand me. I always think this, yet never get around to telling you. Kind of take it for granted that you know, I guess.

I've been rather down in the dumps. Your letters were so wonderful that I received yesterday. Last night I was supposed to go to Jerry's concert, but I was so tired that I just couldn't make myself go. So I stayed in bed and read your letters again. And the greatest longing to go home came over me. Why am I staying here—a foreign land where I do not belong? I hate this feeling of instability and insecurity that is ours. We foreign nationals are at the mercy of anyone who happens to have the power over us. We work for the army but we have to abide by Japanese regulations. Sr. was saying that they tax us half of our income. And someone else said that soon the yen will change again, and what we have will be almost valueless. Kicked around by the Americans on one hand, and bled by the Japs on the other. Boo hoo, I was certainly feeling sorry for myself. And if I'm going to work, why not work among people who have been brought up, more or less, upon the same ideals and principles? Your reaction to my letters is what brought up so clearly to me the abnormal circumstances we are in now. The Japanese have very little moral sense. And as far as sexual morality is concerned, they have so little it is pitiful. If I stay here too long, my ideas will be influenced by theirs. I see some of it already. Once upon a time, I know that I thought just like you and was disgusted by the idea of a man having relations with any other woman but his wife. But the Japanese man thinks it is only normal. Yes, and poor, poor Teruko. It is unfair and cruel and unjust! She, if any woman, deserves a happy home life and love. Why can men be so cruel? O, it burns me up, too. And to think that is the unhappy fate of so many women in Japan is so depressing!

I wanna go home! O, that wave of homesickness is on me again. What do I care about this God-forsaken country? I want to go back to stability, and to people I know love me. I am tired of being alone and lonely. George told me to come home. Emma said can't I go home for a year, then come out again for a job? Mother told me to stay here for a while. But I can influence her to thinking different. And yesterday, I read over the folder Mr. Anderson had about the library. And it seems that the possibility of me getting a State Department job is very slim. Besides, there was an American woman around before, and if anyone gets it, she will. If that happens, boy, I'm going! Maybe I made a mistake. Maybe I should have stayed with the chaplains. And Father Dunn isn't here now. He is so fatherly to me, I really miss him when he isn't around. Maybe that has helped me to feel so blue. He's going home, too, then I'll have no one to befriend me among our conquerors.

Just had breakfast and feel better. As I was entering the dining room, Sr. came out and said he is going to take the seven o'clock bus. Well, that leaves me alone to commune with you. So I don't care. Sat with Peggy and another girl named Violet. When they asked me how I was, I said I was down in the dumps and wanted to go home. Violet said she went for her appointment in July, but she hasn't got her papers yet. She's a repatriate. Her folks are in Kyoto, and she said that she has to take care of them. So in comparison, I am lucky to have my folks back in the States. I'll have someplace to go. Of course, I know I could mooch on you, but if my parents were over here, I would be obligated to take care of them. And the food situation is so bad that if someone doesn't help, the people will starve. Violet said that her father used to love to drink milk, but he never gets it and so is thin. These repatriates—I bet they are certainly sorry they decided as they did.

Like the Yamadas, who used to live in Baldwin Park and returned to Japan just before the war. When I visited them on my last trip to Tokyo, Mr. and Mrs. Yamada were rationalizing, I know. They said that there would be good jobs for Nisei in Japan soon, that the Americans would never treat Japanese like equals, etc. But their family is rather pitiful now. Poor Youkiye came back from Manchuria without anything. She and her sister had to leave all their clothes and worldly wealth there. And now, when I gave them a few things that I had asked them to keep for me during the air raids, they were so thankful! The tables certainly are turned now. Before, they had lots of goods and clothes, and they used to give things away right and left. Mrs. Yamada was so generous with everything, and Masako used to warn her that she would regret it later. I guess she has found out now. You know, being in America makes me generous. When I first came from America, I used to give away things, thinking nothing of it. But not now! I think and weigh things before giving. You learn to be this way in a poor country where every little stitch of clothing is valued. And if you do give anything, they expect more and are not thankful for what you do give them. I don't like the whole business. Japanese give for the sake of receiving. Like that stingy Mrs. Sakai used to say, she hates to get things because she has to give something more valuable in return. But she never does that, you can bet your boots. Stingy old witch! She used to get after me for washing out pans that she had made *o-mi-otsuke* [bean-paste soup] in because she said there was a little left sticking in the pan, and it was not necessary to wash it off, for she could cook something else in that same dirty pan and thus save the precious nourishment sticking to the sides. Have you heard the like? And she was that way about everything. Like, after taking out the rice, every little grain, from the *okama* [pot], she would put water in it and boil it and make me drink the faintly whitish water, saying that it contained precious nourishment. O, it's funny how she used to be. But at the time, it was tragic.

I'll cut out this crying on your shoulder. But it makes me mad because Sr. doesn't understand when I sleep so much and get so tired out. I didn't used to be this way. It's during the war that I did break down from undernourishment, worry and overwork. And can you imagine—at school I used to be classed among the weaker girls who couldn't do much. To look at me so robust and fat now, you'd never imagine that I was skinny and nervous. I can't believe it myself. But I have learned to be careful of my health after that. I never overdo myself, for I know I can't take it. Consequently, he usually finds me in bed and makes fun of me. It makes me furious, but I'm not going to cry on his shoulder and tell him of it. It's only to you that I tell these things, for I hate people to go around asking for pity. And I'm not asking you for it, it only helps to [tell my feelings to] someone I know who understands.

Today we have the opening ceremony of the library. At last the day has come. Yesterday a boy came who is going to work there. And I'm trying to get my classmate Etsuko in. I'm sure it would be much better for her than working among the GIs in the ice-cream bar. Teruko asked me to take care of her. I don't know, Miye, I do admire how you and Nick both think it is so wrong for a girl to "sell herself." If it weren't for people who think like you, decent society would break down. Nick must be wonderful. And I don't think it is a Christ-like attitude that many of these people have at all. Was it Honen Shonin[146] who used to forgive everything? I forget now, but I did not admire it much. But it's hard to make generalizations. Now I take the attitude, "well, it's their business." And two wrongs don't make a right. If society is wrong in permitting conditions which lead to women selling themselves, it is still wrong of them to do it. But I think that many of these street girls do it just for the fun, without the necessity. Or maybe, necessity forces them into it, then they cannot be redeemed. 'Tis a pity. And I don't know how much truth there is to the story of Mrs. H.'s that girls of good families are becoming mistresses of the officers. I don't know, I'm rather sick of the whole business, and avoid everything—gossip about such topics. The less said about it the better. I guess I'm really not a social worker at heart, for I become interested in the unfortunate only in spurts.

Gosh, I guess I'd better get going. It is nearly fifteen to eight. I'll catch the eight o'clock bus. I dislike this Station Hotel now. The trains are always coming or going, and the smoke all comes into the rooms. And the noise and racket and dirt are not healthful.

I certainly laughed at your sending me all those "Women Wanted" ads! And I showed Sr., saying, "Miye *wa kawaii desho*?" ["Isn't Miye cute?"] He thought it was cute, too. And did I tell you that I went shopping with Sr. last Sunday after we went to the Heian Shrine? I borrowed some money from him to buy some tea for you, then tried to pay him back that night, but he said that if it's for you, he wants to give it to you. We had some that night, and I liked it. Wonder if you care for Japanese tea? If not, you might give some to friends. Your Nick might like it. I wanted to send it yesterday, but only had air mail stamps, and not enough to send it air mail. I'll get someone to trade the air mail stamps for some ordinary ones. Want to do it today, but don't know if I'll have time. It's so much fun sending things. I just love to do it. I love to give people I love things.

Well, I know I'd better be going now. You know, I've got an idea. Hereafter, I think I'll visit some place in Kyoto on Sundays, then write up on it, just my personal impressions. Then I'll make a scrap book. Won't that be something?

Kyoto, October 4, 1946

Dearest Miye,

Happy, happy day! I heard from the consulate today informing me that my citizenship has been reinstated! O, now all my worries are gone. They can't

146. Also known as Genku (1133–1212), the founder of the Jodo sect of Buddhism. He taught that salvation could be achieved by continuously invoking the name of the Amida Buddha.

kick me around any more like a stateless foreign national. Miye, I'm so happy that I can't wipe that grin off my face. Goody, goody! Now I have no worries at all about going home. Just think—I'll actually be seeing you FACE TO FACE soon! O, what a relief. Guess my mama's prayers have been answered.

Here it is evening. I wrote the above off just after I got home at lunch time, then had to dash off again. Just phoned Father Dunn up and told him the good news. He did worry a lot for me I am sure. And if it hadn't been for him I wouldn't have had that letter from Emma, which must have made a lot of difference. I certainly got it [the reinstatement] quickly—only a month and a week. Hope Kay has hers too.

Got your letter with parents' picture. Your pop surely has aged, but your mother looks as young as when I knew her. Your pop reminds me of many old men in Japan. You made me laugh when you said that he keeps his teeth in a jar.

Gosh, Miye, what shall I do? Should I go home as soon as possible? I'd like to get on the next boat and forget this cruel land in which I have suffered so much. Gosh, I can't believe that it is actually possible! What to do? But wouldn't it be cowardly to leave now? And now that I have interesting work, perhaps I should stay awhile. For heaven's sake, I don't know what to do! But it just sends shivers all over me to think that my dreams will actually come true, and I will be able to see my loved ones again!!

The library is going on so-so. Still have a lot to do, but now I do not feel as confused as the first day. Made out attendance reports for yesterday and today. 150 yesterday, and 135 today. We're going to get the furniture painted, so we're having the library closed Sat afternoon and Sunday. So I'll get caught up on my typing, I hope. Mr. Anderson didn't seem to have any ideas about me getting a civil service job. He's rather indifferent to my personal problems, in contrast to Father Dunn who was always so willing to help me. Little Boy Blue was in Kyoto today to see me. He came to the library but I could not talk to him hardly at all because I was so busy. He said that he read in the paper about me, and "*Taishita mon da na!*" ["How wonderful!"] says he. It made me laugh. O, and a newspaper man from the local paper wants me to write an article for him. I'm getting famous overnight. And I'm meeting a lot of interesting people. The kind of people I want to know. So life is smiling on me now. And with my citizenship, I feel wonderful.

My letter-writing *jidai* [era] is gone for the present. I live solely for the library now. O, but I love it, having some work that I can put everything I've got into.

Kyoto, October 6, 1946

Dearest Kay,

Once I asked you to destroy some things for me and you refused. Therefore I am not writing any more than one page to you at a time until you do as I have requested. So there! And you can just quit your old bitching, too, because it won't do you one bit of good.

I'll soften and not double space in between, for you know how stubborn I can be, and if I have said the above, I'll stick to it through hell and heaven—well, I'm not in too good humor now, although I do feel a glow of satisfaction, for I have spent all day in writing up one measly article for the *Kyoto Shimbun*. Finally got it done, and it's only two pages long. It made me sore because it took me so long to write it, and look, when I rattle off to you, two pages is nothing. O, well, I guess it does me good to think once in a while. But then, they're going to translate it, and I betcha they'll lose all the points when they get their Jap translators at it. But then, I can't write Jap well, so I'm going to stick to my English. Afterwards, I thought of sending it to *Nippon Times* in Tokyo because it does say a lot of things worthwhile, even if I do say so myself, only I don't think they'd be interested in my little Kyoto and my even littler library. Sr. helped me get ideas for it. He surely is helpful and clever, too. Went this morning to Daiken and looked in the encyclopedia, and he got out a *Nippon Times* editorial about the need for more libraries for me. He is interested in the library too, but he won't admit it. And you disappoint me—you don't even mention it! When I'm so proud of myself for it, too!

Heard from Blanche today. That squirt kid sister of mine was offered the assistantship in Psychology, or something! And that is in Boston University! Wow! I'm glad for her, but it makes me feel again like I'm the miserable failure of the family. That's what Sr. said when I told him about Blanche, and I answered, "*Nihon ni shichi nen mo kabi haete ita kara.*"[147] He didn't say anything to that.

Today, when I was hunting for inspiration to write my article, I came across Milton's essay (or speech it was) on censorship, and I was so in accord with all he said that I read it all. It certainly is true, and I'd like to show it to whoever is responsible for the dirty censors getting into our mail!

It seems that you haven't gotten your citizenship papers yet. It's probably because you had that mix-up about your passport being taken away, etc. Hope you'll get it soon.

There, I certainly got a lot done tonight. I fixed all my letter files, for over a month ago. It certainly feels good to get a lot of things off my mind. That article had been on my mind since Friday, when [the editor] told me to write

147. "From rotting in Japan for seven years."

for his paper. And those letters had been there since a month ago. Well, now I can breathe freely. It certainly feels good to be caught up. And that library is launched on its way. Soon we might have more people working. My ironing is almost all caught up. Whew! It's nearly ten, so I'd better say goodnight.

Kyoto, October 9, 1946

Dearest Miye,

Your letter with all the stamps came just in time, for I had used my last ones, trading them with ordinary stamps to send off the tea. I'm sorry I didn't have enough stamps to send the tea [first] class, so I had to send it third. That's a load off my mind, though. And as usual, Father Dunn came to the rescue. He's the only army personnel I can ask without hesitancy to do things for me. It's too much mathematical work to find out how much it costs a pound. In the first place, they use a different system of weighing—not in ounces and pounds—and in the second place, there is no set rate of exchange for yen into dollars, except for military personnel. So let's forget it all. Besides, it's a gift from Sr. So I hope you think of the excitable Spanish Doctor of Law when you drink it.

Sr. was unusually calm last night. Said he was tired out. Yes, I'm lucky to have a friend like him. He's never touched that subject after that one time, and it is wonderful to be just friends. Miye, my dear, I do want to go home awfully badly. I heard from one of the girls that there is going to be a boat in December, and it is easy to get passage, just so you have someone pay for you. Wouldn't it be perfect if I could get home by Christmas? O, it makes tears come to my eyes for the sheer ecstasy of even thinking it is possible! And I am so disappointed in Mr. Anderson. And his vain promises. Father Dunn was peeved about it, too for I tell him everything. He promised me that I could get a raise in salary—well, I did, but not what he promised. And in the second place, he said that I could be the CIE librarian, or if that was impossible, I could get a job from the I Corps in civil service. And now that I have my papers, he is so slow about taking care of my affairs. I know that he is very busy and has no time, but after all, my whole future is involved. I left a very good job with the chaplains to come and start their library. And how do they treat me? When I asked a certain captain in charge of civil service about it, he stated that Mr. Anderson had no right to make such promises. Gullible Mary, all over again. I guess I was too well protected and cared for by Father Dunn. None of the other officers are like him. I'm certainly learning that out the hard way. But it's wonderful how he still cares for me, and is concerned over my welfare. Good Father Dunn! May he get his just reward in heaven!

Well, I've been wanting to let off steam about my little problems, and now that it is all out, I feel much better. Note the picture enclosed. The girl on the left, sitting down, is Etsuko Onishi. And she is going to start working at the library tomorrow, I think. I'm happy that she was able to get in. The girl standing is not working in the library, but she belongs to some society and helped out with the opening ceremony.

This CIE-Krueger library has been one of the biggest items in the Kyoto news—nay, in Western Japan, for the past two weeks. You see, Miye, there are very few libraries in Japan, and as Sr. says, the Japanese have mistaken the word "museum" for "library." If a book ever finds its way into a so-called library in Japan, it never leaves that nook. They put away books, they do not circulate them. And the Japanese people love to read, and as a whole, are very well read. Before the war, they could buy for only ten or twenty-five sen paper editions of all great works, modern and past, as well as their best sellers. Now there is nothing like that. Books are expensive and hard to get. Listen, Miye, in case I do get back to America soon, would you mind if I donated these good books you so kindly sent to me to the library? We need books very badly, and I'm sure that many hundreds of people would be benefited.

The library is going pretty much as it should, so I am going to start doing things, such as practicing piano again, and writing letters. Guess who I should hear from yesterday but Thelma Christiansen's sister, Hulda. She is in the Philippines, and said she is coming to Japan for a ten-day vacation, and that she'd like to look me up. It would be so much fun to see her! The big Swede. And I hear from Thelma once in a while. She is teaching, and running their farm in Modesto while her mother and brother are visiting the old country (Denmark). Thelma is going to study at Chicago for her master's in Religious Education. Anyway, I was rather pleased to find out how my old hi-school and JC friend was getting along. She wanted to know about the "Japanese friends in JC" too. I must write her. Now that I am rich in stamps, thanks to you, I guess I shall. I should save your stamps to write to you, shouldn't I? But I know you won't mind. I'll never run out of stamps to write to you, for I'll beg, borrow or steal them only if I don't have enough to write to you. The others can wait.

If Mr. A. hasn't found out by this morning about my civil service, I'm afraid I cannot look calm and unperturbed any longer. You made me laugh when you said that I must look "Calm and undisturbed" when Sr. raves around. My dear, let me congratulate you upon your understanding and insight. Because I am sure that I do just that. It is so silly, how excited he gets about some things, and I only say, "Calm yourself, Sr." He stops his ranting and waving of arms to look at me in disbelief and wonder. "How can she be so undisturbed when this matter, of the greatest importance, is tearing my soul?" thinks he. Or at other times, when he gets mad at me for something equally trivial, like talking to a boy (Larry or Hauchecorne or somebody equally innocent), I only laugh at him. And that makes him madder than ever. It's really funny how angry he can get! What a moody guy!

They've built a new I Corps library for military personnel, and so Sr. and I went to look at it the other evening. It is beautiful, and such bright and sufficient lighting that it made me just stand in awe at the whole thing. I went with the intention of getting mad because I had heard that it was so nice, since I thought if the army could do that much for the GIs, they ought to be able to do much more for our library for the Japanese. But after I went, I was so awed with the beauty, light, and cleanliness of the place that it left no room to be angry. And, wonder of wonders, they allow us poor foreign nationals to come in, and to even check out books! It is unbelievable. The librarian was quite nice, too, so I didn't feel like letting out any righteous wrath.

Dear me, it is ten to eight, so I must be getting along. Must catch the eight o'clock bus. The future is so bright when I think I might be going home soon! Just think—I'll be seeing you soon, MAYBE!!!

Kyoto, October 9, 1946

Dearest Miye,

Boy o boy was I mad today! You know, Miye, they've played a dirty trick on me. Father Dunn was sore about it, and that is what got me started. He talked to me this morning, and made it plain that he had let me be transferred only because the librarianship sounded more promising, and he felt that he could not hold me back with a clear conscience. They were very busy at the chaplains' then, too, but he let me go. And what does Mr. Anderson do but go back on his promises. Father Dunn said that he took advantage not only of me, but of the Chaplains' section. Father Dunn told him that I had been offered better salary and the promise of a CAF rating, which he could not give me at the Chaplains' Office, so he let me go. Now, after I am gone, what happens? I get my citizenship. I asked Mr. Anderson to see about a civil service job. He says there are two possibilities—a civil service in the CI&E section or in the State Department in the library. He kept putting off seeing about the former. Last night, after I had begged and begged him over and over about it, he did get around to it. And this morning he told me that lots of Nisei had applied recently, so that there were very few chances of me getting a job there. Furthermore, I could not work in the CI&E since they were all filled up, and consequently I could not work in the beloved library. Well, he said he'd find out about the State Department. He did. The man in charge, at Tokyo, stated that they would have only two positions open—chief and assistant librarians—and both had to have library experience and schooling. I have had neither. So I am left flat.

Now, what Mr. Anderson should have done was to find out about it before he had me transferred, instead of giving me vain promises. O, I thought of that and it rankled in my mind so much that I determined to see the MG colonel about it. I went to MG and asked the Nisei receptionist how I could see the colonel, and he popped open his eyes, and asked, "THE Colonel?" I said yes. He told me how to go, but warned me that I would have to go through channels. That kind of scared me, but I wasn't going to back out at that stage of the game. There, when I entered the office, the Nisei girl, the secretary was not in, and only one officer was standing with his back to the door. I boldly walked in with an "Excuse me." It was not the high-up colonel, but the major. He said that the colonel was down in Kyushu. But I had to tell him my piece. Honestly, I was so wrought up about it all that I thought I'd break down and cry like an emotional female, but I did get through with it even if my voice quivered and my lips would not do my bidding. He was very nice about it, and said he would talk to the colonel about it. After all, the library is important, and I am confident that I could do some good here. But what burns me up is the way Mr. A. has let me down! Boy, I still haven't gotten over it.

I am really tired out, but I am so mad I can't see straight. After lunch I usually rest a while, but today, I hurried right off to see the colonel. I would have gone to the general himself if it would have done any good. Come to think of it, guess I should have gone in to see the Chief of Staff. I don't care if nothing comes of it—it is not right, and I want them to know my side of the story. In fact, maybe I'll go home because I am so disgusted with it all.

Kyoto, October 10, 1946

Dear Kay,

Last night I told Sr. all about what had happened, and he listened very patiently and sympathetically. He commented quietly that perhaps his getting angry about injustices had infiltrated into me. Well, perhaps he is right. I know that during the war years in Japan, I would never have stood up for my rights, but would have let them run all over me like a passive woman that the Japanese woman is. But with our "liberators" I have re-learned to stand up for my rights, and when injustice is done, boy it gets me sore.

And last night I heard that we might not be allowed to use the APO anymore. Of all the fickle people! First they say we can, then they clamp down, and then they say we can again and now I wouldn't be much surprised if they went back on their word again. No wonder GIs in the army become cynical of army promises. So I'd better write while I can. They say that hereafter only War Dept. civilian employees can use the APO. That made me want to go home more than ever. This morning I talked to several girls about getting passage home. They said there's a boat in December, then none until March. Well, if I'm going home, I surely want to make the December one. And they said that we have to go to Yokohama and fill out a lot of forms. If it weren't for all this dilly-dallying about my civil service, I could have gone to see about it a week ago. Was I a fool for quitting the chaplains? I gained a lot of experience, but at what cost? No, I do not regret it. As Ralph Miller (the GI who was in our section) said, if you work for the army it doesn't do any good, but he worked hard for the library because it is for the Japanese people. No, even if I did sacrifice my time and labor, it is worth it. Every day when the people come in and enjoy seeing the many magazines, I know that my labor has not been in vain. So what are trivial personal matters?

Now people are starting to come to work. I came to the office early because I must bring in a girl to be interviewed by Mr. Anderson. The way these Japanese run things is awful. This Krueger foundation is the slowest acting thing I have ever seen. If we had left it up to them, the library would not be open yet. And even now, they have not paid the students who are working part time there. And they've been working for a month. And they tell this Mr. Tsujii who is working in the library to get things, and don't even give him the money to get [them]. I'd like to kick the whole bunch out and let the army run it. In theory the Krueger foundation is running the thing, but in practice we are. When I think of all the little complications that arise, I want to forget it all and go home.

And you know what! Sr. is saying that he wants to go to America! Isn't that wonderful? He is wasting his talents over here. He ought to be a prof in some university. Then he could be with people like himself. Here no one appreciates him—except me, of course! Babs was saying that he is [talking about] it because I am [thinking] about going home, and he said that he is going to [make] me—his housekeeper. Well, he ought to go to the States. He has degrees from good universities; he's been teaching Spanish for eleven years. Guess it's time to stop, so I'll leave you.

Tokyo, October 15, 1946

Dearest Miye,

Miye, me darlink, I'M GOING HOME!! Ain't that superb? O, I'm so happy over it that I don't know what to do. I came up to Tokyo today to see about it. I'm having my rich brother pay for the boat trip. They have to contact him and have him make the deposit with the company in San Francisco. Then, all I have to do is sign for a passport and go on the next boat. I heard that there might be one in November. Officially, they do not know when the next one will be, but unofficially that is what I done heard. Miye, my dearest, are you going to be out to welcome me home with bells and banners? So long ago you saw me off. So very very long ago. And at last you might see me come in. Happy day. O, Miye, I am a lucky woman!

Received two of your letters yesterday. It was a relief to hear from you since there are rumors that we cannot use the APO anymore. Isn't that the army though? Making a decision one time, then breaking it the next day. Won't I be glad when I am out of this country! If we don't have someone pay for our passage, we cannot go. You know, Miye, I'll have to come home like a penniless repatriate. But I don't care.

Thanks for the stamps. I am getting low on stamps again. Wonder if I told you that I sent off your tea, thanks to Father Dunn? God bless him. He and Sr. and Kay. Sr. came to the station to see me off. Warn't that sweet of him? He is so sweet to me now, now that he is about to lose me. And do you know that he can leave Japan any time he wants to? He refuses to come until there is a job for him over there, though. He is a wonderful Spanish teacher. He has a long list of qualifications. After I get back, I'm going to see if I can't find a position for him in some university. It is a pity to see such talent going to waste here. He is not happy in this country, either.

I love to hear everything about Little Mary. It seems like it is going to be mine. So keep on writing all the details. It must be a wonderful experience. And is it actually only 4½ months more now? That is very soon. Just think, Miye, maybe I can wash her diapers for you!

I'm leaving for Kyoto on the night train. It *would* rain today. And I wasn't prepared for it, either. Surely got soaking wet, but it was for the sake of getting back home, so I didn't mind at all. Right now I am at an ARC office. Kay's friend. Couldn't see Kay today. Couldn't get in touch with her. And since it was raining, I didn't want to go to her place, not knowing whether she would be home or not. Before I leave this country, I'm going to spend about a week in Tokyo if possible.

I might break off right in the middle of a sentence, for Violet might come back any time. You see, she went to eat, and I am waiting for her to come back. Then I'm going to the Marunouchi Hotel to see a friend. The Marunouchi Hotel is for foreign nationals. Everyone has to get out by the 20th, and many of them have no place to go. More unreasonable things.

Last Sunday afternoon, I went [with] Sr. to his home. He has a lot of Japanese staying there. Has he got a lot of books! I'd like to live by him in the States to be able to see his books on Japan. He has quite a complete collection of books on Japan, and the history of Christianity in Japan. He showed me the books that he had written. But those people who stay in his home do not appreciate him, and it makes me sore. No wonder he gets distemper every time he goes home. It's hard to live with Japanese. There are so few who can understand foreigners.

And how the people stare at him on the streetcar! I, being with him, shared the gaping. They all gape at us in blank stupidity. It is something terrible, as Sr. says. Why do they stare like that? If Sr. sits in the middle, those to the right, left, and middle [all] turn to stare. Eyes to the left of him, eyes to the right of him, into the valley of stares goes Sr. wherever he [goes]. Whew! Even I who am so nonki felt discomfiture at all the stares. People stretch their necks to stare, and keep their poor necks stretched. Sr. said that many people forget to change cars where they are supposed to because they are lost in staring at him. He had to laugh at their stupidity. And I shared it, and I know they were wondering what I was—with the face of a Japanese, but talking a foreign language and with a foreigner. He said that before the war, the Japanese had it fixed in their mentality that every foreigner was an Englishman. During the war, every foreigner was a German. And now, every foreigner is an American. He insists that he is Spanish, but to no avail. If once a Japanese gets a notion fixed in his head, nothing can uproot that idea.

I have a lot of fun with him because everything he says interests me. We are interested in about the same things. My JC record came the other day, since I had requested it for in case I got a civil service job. I showed it to Sr. only and he was so surprised at it. It helped my vanity to hear him being so proud of me. Now he doesn't lose his temper at all. Well, I don't have anything to do with any other men or boys, so I guess he is satisfied. He doesn't like me to even say hello to anyone else. That's what you call Spanish possessiveness.

The Ginza in Tokyo surely is building up. It gives the illusion of prewar in some places. Most of the bombed and vacant lots are gone and in their place are one-story stores. Quite neat, too. Most of them cater to the occupation. Souvenirs mostly. I walked down the street with my eyes open in wonder.

Here's Violet, so I'm going. It's been so nice talking to you. Goodbye. Just think, in a few more months I'll see you!

Tokyo, October 15, 1946

Dear Kay,

This morning just after I got out of Tokyo Station I bumped into Kimi-chan and Kiriyama-san. Kimiko told me to go while the going was good. I meant to see her this aft, but just didn't make it. And at Radio Tokyo I saw Hasegawa-sensei, senior. She is married, but working in some division up there. Her sister returned from China. After that, none other should I meet but—what was his name—that cracked teacher we had in *tokusetsu-ka*[148]—was it Ishihata? Had cobwebs on his sleeve, and his poor coat looked dirty and well worn. Said he has quit school and is working for something or other—was it *Okurasho* [the Finance Ministry]? Here they brought some coffee. It's wonderful to have this refuge in all this cold and rain. It's all due to you, too. But gosh, I wish I could see you!

Haven't you gotten your citizenship cleared yet? Say, isn't this place swanky? They have even a girl in the washroom hand you a towel. And hot running water. Such a luxury! Wonder where Midori is? I hadn't thought to ask Violet. It might be kind of fun to see Kona. At least, that will be one place to keep warm until the train comes in.

O, and I brought up a dictionary for you too. Well, I'll send it to you. Tried to get you at the Park Hotel, but the woman who answered said it wasn't the number. Everything went wrong today. Rain—and then, not being able to see you.

I'll get back and work on the book. Before I leave, I want to get that off my mind. Well, so long. And hereafter, I think I'll have time to write more.

Kyoto, October 16, 1946

Dearest Kay,

They've gone and done it! Namely, they have put someone else into my sacred domain—a foreigner is polluting my sacred soil! It isn't right, and I'll make a fuss about it, just see if I don't. They're supposed to double us up according to the length of our service. Well, I've been working with I Corps since last October. Practically a year. How many are there who have been working that long? Not many. And look at those who have just come in and have rooms to themselves. Well, they can't push me around and not hear any roars and kicks. I'll go and tell Capt. Sawbridge, who is in charge of the hotel tomorrow. And if he doesn't pay any attention, I'll go to Col. Broderick. I'm not afraid to go to IG or to the general himself. Doggone it, it makes me sore! And you know how I covet my privacy. I can't think when someone else is in the room. Besides, look, I am an American citizen. Why should they give preference to a foreign national or a Japanese? Isn't the US Army supposed to defend the American citizen? But look what they are doing—people working in the very same place, under same circumstances, and they should give preference to American citizens. But no, they give preference to those who brown nose some officer. And my room is extra small since they have a closet built there. My bathroom water doesn't run like the other rooms so that it takes

148. The special preparatory class for foreigners at Joshi Dai.

hours to fill up the tub even for a few inches. How can we keep clean under such circumstances? And the bathtub is too small for two to go in at the same time—besides, who wants to do that? And I guess I should be of a higher category than the typists, stenos and secretaries that the other girls are! Boy o boy, they'll hear about this!

I wonder who is at the bottom of all this, anyhow. Probably that skunk Brian Gorrez. He is a skunk and he sure stinks. I tried to get Capt. Sawbridge all afternoon, but couldn't. Good thing I never, for tomorrow I'll be madder. I never knew that sweet little roommate of mine would be in tonight already. And here she came at seven, just when Sr. was starting [to tell] me things. Does that make me sore! I'm getting sorer and sorer and had to let off some steam someplace, so I picked on poor you.

Sr. is mad about it too. Said old Gorrez is doing that because I am friendly with him. He told me to raise the roof about it, and I certainly will! Just the other day, Ram, the Indian who works for the chaplains, said, "There is no justice." I did not exactly agree with them then. But when I see it actually happening to me, well, it hits home. If I were still working for the chaplains, I could get Father Dunn to say something for me. But I'll try to fight my own battles. That Mr. Anderson would not lift his little finger if it would involve him with any officers.

Gee, I love this typewriter. Sr. came to run off some mimeographs, so I tagged along to school since I am too mad to go peacefully to sleep. Wish I could talk to Capt. Sawbridge right now. That's an idea—think I'll try calling him up—I couldn't get him. So I'll have that seething in me all night. And my feathers aren't so soft when they are all ruffled up, either, my dear. I'm like a porcupine now.

Kyoto, October 18, 1946

Dearest Kay,

It makes me so mad because I don't seem to have any time to myself at all anymore! And today I am so tired out from my trip to Tokyo—my back aches, my eyes are runny and I am in *muy mal* humor. Took it out on the janitor this morning. He surely made me mad with his slip-shod cleaning. After nearly two hours the water from his mopping the floor did not dry up, so I told him to do it all over again. Then, too, I read the two articles in *Comment and Query* written by Nisei veterans, against the newly reinstated "pseudo-Americans," as they termed them. Surely, you must have read them. I never knew anything about it, but Sr. told me and brought the paper to me. It referred to another letter by a Nisei veteran, so Ken Ishida looked that up. The first letter was quite fairly written, and I couldn't help but sympathize with him. But the second letter burned me up. And it makes me mad, because I haven't had time to write a reply to it. But I will, and I won't be a coward like the other two and leave my name withheld.

Besides, I can't even write to you [direct]. And I'm not getting any letters from the States, either. I am disgusted with the library, and don't even think about improving it. Anyway, my back surely does ache, and literally too. And I don't have time to type out our book, and I know that you are waiting impatiently for it. And it makes me sore that the censors held up the mail. O, I could go on like this forever, so I'd better stop right here.

I'm enclosing a carbon copy of what I typed. I sent the original a few days ago. One thing I like, though, is that I have a typewriter at work with the small type. And tonight I have to teach the little girl, when I do so want to go to bed and forget everything. I was feeling so sorry for myself that I was nearly in tears when I started to tell Sr. And two men, librarians, came down from Tokyo and one of them said that the first impression he gets from our library is that it is cold and undecorated. I tried to look at his remarks objectively, but I did feel bad because I have tried to get it fixed up, but you know how the Japs are—promising to get things, and those promises never materialize. And at first, they publicized this library so much in the papers, but now they [don't even say a word]. What else? O, I wonder if I told you? The sukiyaki party we had on the night of the opening ceremony cost 8,000 yen, not including the sake and rice which were contributed. Now if that isn't a fine thing to do—charge the Krueger foundation 8,000 yen for a party when they are so stingy about buying books, lights, or desks, or tables or chairs. That is the limit!

Guess that is really about all. Anyway, I got a letter [off] to you. And I'll be thinking about my reply. Doggone, it made me mad last night because we went to see *Going My Way*[149] at the Jap movie house, and the girls Sr. and I went with wanted to see it all over again. It was torture sitting through it the second time. I hate to see pictures over again. Well, I'll go home and nurse my poor wounds. In this mood I could write to you endlessly.

Hope I hear from you one of these days. I'm still griping because I didn't get to see you when I went to Tokyo. I love you. I love you.

[P.S.] Sent your dictionary today.

Kyoto, October 19, 1946

Dearest Miye,

All day yesterday I was so peeved and dissatisfied about the letters some Nisei veterans had written to the gripes column of *Stars and Stripes*. It made

149. An Academy Award–winning movie of 1944 starring Bing Crosby and Barry Fitzgerald.

me so sad that they should be so narrow-minded. And that they should censure us Nisei who remained in Japan from before the war. Yes, I see their point. They fought for America, and now, when they get discharged, they cannot get WD civilian positions because some Nisei who have been in Japan and not even fought for America has beaten them to it. But they made such broad accusations. And should our Nisei problems be brought up to the light of the army newspaper, which has circulation in all the Pacific area? Why should we be fighting among ourselves? We have our hands full in fighting the prejudice against us from the outside. We ought to stick together, at least. These veterans are wonderful, I know, and I do want to give all due honor to them. But they fail to understand the circumstances we [faced] in Japan. Besides, [one] said that many who had contributed towards the war effort in Japan were now enjoying all the privileges of American citizenship. Doesn't he know that if there is any doubt at all that any of us helped the Japanese during the war, we would not be reinstated? And is it easy to get reinstated when we have to wait for half a year or more before we can even get our appointment, then for anywhere from a month to a year or more before we receive a definite answer? No, if you think that we had control over the events which caught us by surprise, and that many of us are rightful citizens, they should speed it up. And now, they are not even taking any Nisei for appointments. I was lucky, compared to many others.

So I felt bad all day yesterday, mulling over that. And I did want to put in my two cents worth. Finally wrote out something last night, then felt much better. Just typed it out this morning. Sr. said that it would be wiser not to put it in, for the less said about the Nisei problem—such a delicate subject—the better. He certainly is wonderful. [It was he] who first brought the letters to my attention. And he showed me an article in "Tips" about the Nisei. A very good article, too. I was feeling so sorry for us poor Nisei, and he looked so sympathetic. He surely hates all racial discrimination and prejudice.

Of course, I had to make you a carbon copy too. I did want to write a lot more, but the space we can take up is limited.

Feel like I haven't heard from you for ages. Hope George hurries up and pays for my way home. Everyone envies me when I say that I am going to take the next boat home. It is like a dream, and I am so happy over it.

Kyoto, October 20, 1946

Dearest Blanche,

As I wrote in Mother's letter, I dreamt last night that I was at home, and when I woke up I was confused and didn't know where I was. And how disappointed I was when I found that I was still in Kyoto, in my room. In a month or so that dream will come true, I hope.

So it is not necessary to send me anything. I only requested those things because I thought I might stay here longer. The only thing I need now is stamps. I asked Emma to send me some, both airmail and the ordinary but she hasn't sent them yet. I think there is something wrong with the mail, for I haven't received a letter from the States for the longest time.

Wonder if you ever got the tea I sent you? I'll get some when I'm going home. The only problem facing me is getting cans to put the tea in.

It's Sunday, but I've come to work at the library. I'll take time off to go to church if I can. It's a lovely autumn day. This evening, the boy and girl who work here have invited me to their home to a sukiyaki party. I kind of hate to eat their food when they are so badly off, but it will be nice to be with them. O, Mr. Nagata asked me for some safety pins for diapers, so if you can, would you please slip in a half dozen or so of big safety pins—or in Mother's next letter? Their eldest son came home from Manchuria,[150] and he has a baby and they have a hard time with the weak Japanese safety pins.

Rev. Ito was down in Kyoto for some kind of Christian conference. When I told him about you sending him things, he surely was happy. He is looking quite healthy now. Only his hand is still rheumatic, I think.

I hope that you are getting along fine. It won't be too long before I'll see you. I'll let you know by cable when it is definite when I'm sailing.

Kyoto, October 22, 1946

Dearest Kay,

Fool, here I let a Jap use the telephone here in the library and he shouts over it, disturbing what little peace there is here. I think hereafter I won't let anyone use the phone. Boy, am I irritable nowadays. Don't know why, but I've been feeling like an old witch, and I'm sure that I must act and talk like one too.

Received a letter from you yesterday, which made me a little happy. Now today when I get nothing, I am in *muy mal* humor. Guess I'm still down low in de dumps. It makes me so mad every time I think about having to teach that girl tonight. Really, I never have any time to myself and I am sore as heck about it. This morning I went to Tenri Gaigo library in Nara with Sr. It was rather interesting, but it wasted my whole morning. And this afternoon I didn't want to go to work. The attendance is falling down at the library but I don't much care. Don't care about anything anymore.

Did I ever tell you that the gal was kicked out of my room? Wonder if I ever wrote to you about it? You see, I went to see Capt. Sawbridge who

150. By the end of 1946, some 3,000,000 Japanese nationals had been repatriated from Manchuria.

is in charge of the hotels. He was surprised that someone had been put in my room. He immediately phoned up the Station Hotel and demanded who gave the orders for her to be there. And he said that she shouldn't have been allowed to stay at the hotel yet, and not in my room at any rate. It's that dirty Gorrez who put her in there, I'm sure. Just because I go with Sr.

I'm certainly glad that I am leaving this country. The sooner I am out of here the better. As I've said before, the only regret is that I am leaving you and Sr. Everything has just made me sick and tired of it all. Maybe Father Dunn spoiled me up in the chaplains', for after I left that comfortable office, I have never had the former tranquility of mind. Besides, when they forbid us to go to the theater or to use the APO that is the limit. They push us around and I am good and tired of being pushed around.

Yesterday I met a wonderful American woman. She reminded me of Mrs. Iwamoto. She is going to teach at Doshisha. A good Christian woman who has lofty ideals, and she is so warm and kind, it does one good to see that there are American women like her left. You know, you forget it when you see these brazen super-super ARC women and nurses and dependents. She said that she worked hard for the Japanese back in America all during the war, especially for the internees. And she said she would give me a letter to men in the US like those in charge of the Oriental section of the Congressional Library. She said I would have good chances of employment. She certainly raised my hopes, for I have no idea what I could do after I once get back. I'd like to go to school, but I wouldn't have the money. And, I think it is very true what she said (and Sr. said the same thing) that the sooner I got back, the better chances I would have of employment. Kay, I hope your father is rolling in money again soon so that you can get back to the States.

Kyoto, October 24, 1946

Dearest Miye,

Yesterday a blue envelope came for me, and I was so thrilled, for I thought it was you, but it was from my brother George. It was good to hear from him, though, after I got over the disappointment of it not being you. Then I thought that I had neglected writing to you. Now I am not in [a] writing mood for I have so many things to do. I guess one must have a reasonable amount of leisure to write. Like when I used to be a leisurely typist.

I began looking at the Nisei around me at the hotel, and now that I know that I am going home, I feel benevolent towards them. As usual, it is only those who are loud and disorderly who attract attention. Among those, there are many who are pitiful to observe. Those poor girls whose parents have come over here are forced by circumstances to stay here, being misfits, all their lives. They cannot leave their parents who are so dependent upon them now. Sr. said that he felt sorry for the girl who ate at the same table with us last night. After dinner, she confided to him that she had only had grammar school education in the States and that she wanted to study more English. These poor girls who have come over here so young that they cannot act for themselves! When I want something now, I try my darndest to get it, but these other girls do not have the self-confidence to go after anything. It is really pitiful.

This morning Mr. Textor came in with a big package of rosy big apples and said that they were from Nagano *ken* [prefecture], and he gave us each one in the office. It is such a big red apple all shining! Last night, Sr. and I went to the stores around the hotel to get some fruit, but they are so expensive that we gave it up. Went to the USO show last night. We get to go to only the USO shows—no movies, since everyone has to pay and we don't have the right kind of money.

I'll write again if I find time. If not, I'll close here with my love.

Below is a letter I received from our "Little Boy Blue":

Dear Mary,

I surely received magazines and your draft of slang-book some time before. Thank you very very much and I am sorry that I didn't write back to you right away. Due to the pressure of business and affaires private or official, I can hardly have a leisure time these days. A poor man has no leisure time, as they say. I am always poor and I fear I shall be forever. But I give up to be a rich person. I don't care for a worldly richness. Glancing at the world, the street crowded with so many scum of people I once became disgusted with living and even now the feeling haunts me. But I don't envy such superfluous company. I only regret for such a state of society as now. What a great contradiction it is that the most faithful conscientious are the most unblessed and forlorn. It's no use complaining about it. I wish I could only be rich in mind.

As to slang-book, I will try to make it public as early as possible. Now I am reading it. Really it came out fine, wonderfully fine. Shortly I will show it to a certain professor of university who is an authority in the line. When I saw your name in the paper I was really glad and told it to mother and sister. I put away that paper to show you some day.

I want to go to Kyoto to see you but now I can't tell when. Are you busy yet? Take good care of your health. Let me close here. I will write again.

I want to hear from you again.

So long,
T. Sawa, Your LBB

Isn't that sweet? He lives in Osaka. The last time he came to see me at the library he was so skinny, when he used to be nice and plump before. I'm afraid that he is undernourished. And I was sorry that I was unable to talk to him as I wanted to before, since I was so busy.

So I'll really close this time.

Kyoto, October 25, 1946

Dear Miye,

Not only did my article about the library come out in *Nippon Times*, but my answer to the Nisei veterans came out in the *Stars and Stripes*, and now I really feel famous. I was more glad about the letter, for Sr. didn't think much of it, but said I might send it in. And he said that they would never print it. Kay was all indignant about the Nisei veterans' statements, and asked me to write, saying that she did. I was glad, for her sake, that my letter was printed, for she said that between the both of us, one of our letters ought to be printed.

The chaplains' section was all enthused about my articles, so that satisfied my vanity. And Sr. noticing it. That's about all I care about, really. It was so funny, when I went up there this afternoon, Chaplain Ogborne comes up and says, "Here's our author, can I touch you?" But he complimented me on it, and said I ought to take up writing when I get back. That's easier said than done, Dear chaplain. And it's only when I get good and mad about something that I like to write and get it out of my system.

Enough of such self-worship. My papa wrote to me today. That's about the third letter I've had from him in all my life, and it flattered me. (Mr. Anderson is on the phone now, probably the colonel—I hope—and they are discussing the library. No, it must be Tokyo. They mentioned my article. If it has anything to do with creating interest in the library, I'll be satisfied. They're talking about procuring the thing. It ought to be run by the army, then we can improve it and keep on expanding it.)

Sr. was angry at my impetuousness in drawing out my money from the bank. He says I am an infant in economic matters. Which is very true—I've never had enough money to concern myself about it. He's a good consultant, even if he does scold me, but I only laugh it off.

[The text of Mary's letter as it appeared in the "Comment and Query" column of Pacific Stars and Stripes, *Oct. 25, 1946, p. 3:]*

A Statement to Charges

Our admiration and respect go to the Nisei veterans who, as General Joseph Stilwell, one [of] their commanders, aptly said, "bought an awful big hunk of America with their blood." Yet, the letters by the Nisei veterans have made me wonder what they really fought for. Was it for American tolerance and fair play? They now are doing the very thing which has victimized so many minorities in the past—namely, making generalizations from insufficient information.

I believe that the Niseis definitely have NOT amalgamated themselves with the Japanese. Any Japanese will tell you that he can distinguish a Nisei from his countrymen. During the war, we were looked upon with suspicion and contempt because of our American ways. The police and kempeitai were on our tracks, and Nisei girls were slapped by ultra-nationalistic Japanese men because they read English books or spoke English. And have we ever really been congenial with the Japanese? No. Sad years of experience in trying to understand and to harmonize with them have only emphasized the fact that we are basically different.

Not only Niseis, but many servicemen have realized what home meant only when they first left it. To the Nisei veteran's question of whether we reinstated Americans can appreciate the meaning of American citizenship, I can answer a definite yes. Having witnessed the disastrous effects of militarism and a life inhibited by old customs, we realize the privileges and responsibilities of being Americans.

Of course, there are always a few—and those few are the very ones who can draw the most attention—whose actions are disgusting. But should all of us Niseis be judged by them? Let us not make generalities from a few shameful examples.

Mary Kimoto
Kyoto, Honshu

[Extracts from Mary's letter to the Nippon Times, *Oct. 25, 1946:]*

To the Editor:

The CIE-Krueger Library was opened for the Japanese public on October 3, 1946, under the joint auspices of the CI&E Corps in Kyoto and the Krueger Foundation. It consists of many recent American magazines donated by various organizations and also books donated by former Sixth Army agencies. The library is located in a busy section of Kyoto.

The CIE-Krueger Library is an attempt to meet the urgent need for a readily accessible library for the general public. It provides recent reading material from abroad which the Japanese have not had since before the war. It is not a reference library. . . . Our library is planned to give freedom for browsing and reading.

We want the Japanese people to renew their contacts with the outside world, the contacts which were abruptly broken by six years of useless and devastating war. . . . At present we have available reading materials from America only, but in the near future we hope to have reading materials from all parts of the world, thus making a United Nations library.

And through renewing contact with the world by means of modern literature, people will gain knowledge and truth, thereby laying the foundation for rebuilding a new and peaceful Japan. All thoughtful Americans, and especially those who are members of the occupation, realize that the Japanese themselves must be the ones to reconstruct their war-torn country. And the foundation must be built by the people—these very people who have been bound by fetters of ignorance, according to the dictates of the few in power. . . .

John Milton, recognized as one of the greatest figures in English literature, said "who ever knew Truth put to the worse in a free and open encounter?" Until now, the truth has not been presented to the Japanese "in a free and open encounter." Those in power swayed the masses from one extreme to the other through their arbitrary dictatorial powers. . . .

To cite my own personal observations about the libraries of Japan, when I came to this country as a student over seven years ago, I was shocked at the lack of public libraries here. At the National Library in Ueno, Tokyo, I was surprised and pleased to find that there were many valuable books, but it exhausted my patience to have to wait for hours before I could see them. . . . As the U.S. Education Mission to Japan stated, more libraries are much needed in Japan. The CIE-Krueger Library is a step towards fulfilling this immediate need.

It is encouraging to see a daily average of 150 people come to our library, which has been open for over a week. I am happy to see their general good behavior and their enthusiasm over the new reading materials. As a rule, the Japanese are avid readers and intelligent, and, after the intellectual famine they have suffered, are eager to learn more about the world about them. If Japan is to become a country "of the people, by the people, and for the people," as Lincoln said, the people must learn to think for themselves, and gaining true knowledge is the fundamental to attain this aim.

Mary Kimoto

Kyoto, October 27, 1946

Dearest Kay,

For once your letters came within only a couple of days, and I still can't get over the marvel of it. Those damned censors surely do make it miserable for us. Wouldn't life be much better without them?

About our book. If it is going to have to sell at twenty yen, I agree with you that it isn't worth it. As usual, I told Sr. my troubles, and he suggested that we get it published through the Krueger Library in some way. He told me the first thing to do is get it in final form, then to show it to Mr. Anderson.

Yesterday I dragged poor Sr. out to Wakayama with my huge quilt that was at the Suemasas'. The streetcars were awfully crowded and I felt sorry for him, doing so much for me. Before that, I suggested me getting a jeep and driving out to Wakayama, and he exploded over that, saying that I was going to run off with a driver again. When I only wanted to prevent him from going through all that work for me. Anyway, what a load off my mind!

It was a balmy autumn day, and me thought of the olden days of yore. Yes, I remember, Kay, and with the same sentiments over the sunny days when we first tasted freedom. Weren't they wonderful days? At least, we can treasure those wonderful memories which grow sweeter as the years go by, like the hymn.

Kay, my dear, I was thinking that even if I hate to leave you behind, I will be so glad to get out of this doggoned country. I look at the stupid people on the street and am glad that I will not have to see them much longer. And I visit my relatives, and the Suemasas, and am glad that soon I will no longer have to bow and utter polite stammerings which are merely form with no meaning whatsoever. I'll be good and glad to get out of here, and now I marvel that I even considered staying here any longer than necessary. You hurry up and leave this place, too. The sooner we get out of here, the better. Although Miye says I'll find America changed, I don't care. Any place could be better than here.

And I want to get Sr. out of here, too. I told him that you sent him your love, and he said that he wants more directly. He said something different, but I do not remember. Doggone those brats around me—wish they would let me alone. I can't concentrate when they are around with their typical Jap curiosity.

Yesterday when I went through Osaka, the subways had that same old stench. Isn't it awful, how these Japs use the subways for latrines? UGH—how barbaric. And Sr. said that the Osaka subway used to be beautiful. It's so much fun to speak to him in Spanish. You really don't need much of a vocabulary to talk about everyday things. From Osaka to Wakayama we went on the GI car, and a bunch of Nisei girls and officers [boarded] on the way. They had a lot of beer with them—eight or nine cases. Sr. said they were going on a weekend party, and the beer and girls were the supplies. But I was thinking, how tragic that these Nisei girls want to go out and have fun like that. If they were in the States, they would never go out on parties with them, and all this "friendship" is temporary. And these Nisei girls think they are something. O, did I tell you that Carol's boyfriend DIDN'T come back to her, as he promised? Dirty stinker!

Babs' Gomis is now in Los Angeles. She goes out to Saturday night dances with the others, but I don't know if she has any boyfriends. Sr. said that Gomis never did promise her anything, so he is not to blame. I don't know who's to blame, but I can't help but feel sorry for Babs. He surely was a handsome guy.

Now that I've started writing, and that the curious boys have left, I feel like writing. Haven't been in [a] writing mood since the opening of the library. Now it is running pretty smoothly, and I have a wonderful girl here—Ueda-san—who is enthusiastic about it and very competent and reliable. She is a godsend.

Father Dunn is so wonderful! He really is kind-hearted. Last Saturday when I went up to see him, during the course of the conversation he said that he would rather go hungry for a week than see me go without a meal. That really touched me. He does exaggerate, but he means much of what he says. Everybody in Corps thinks a lot of him, I am sure. It is so wonderful to walk around the building and to see how people greet him with a smile and with respect. Just as they should to a good father. I hope I can keep in touch with him as long as he lives. One of my very permanent friends. It was so funny—he told Chaplain Ogborne that he didn't want to see my face again, so I immediately went into his office to see what was up. He comes out with, "Anyone who would write to *Stars and Stripes* is no friend of mine!" He has me scared at times, until I find out that he is joking. May he get his reward in heaven.

Haven't been going to church ever since I've had to work Sundays at the library. Dearest, I don't think I'll go up to Tokyo at all until [it's] time for me to go home. I really don't care such an awful lot about seeing the people I OUGHT to see, so I think I'll let it go till the last.

Have an hour more, so I guess I'll type up a bit.

Kyoto, October 28, 1946

Dearest Miye,

Today I received three letters, including one from you, and did I feel popular! I showed Sr. some parts of your letter, like the part where you said he could have the pick of any college, and that you were curious to see him, but that he would think you a "stupid dope," and he surely smiled sweetly when he saw that. I know you'd like him a lot. Although Kay says that she gets bored with his talk, I find him very interesting. I guess it's because Kay is a talker, while I am more of a listener. But you are both, so I know you'd like him. And I've talked about you so much, and have your picture up in my "rogue's gallery," so that he practically knows you.

Wonder if I've told you about how Sr. went to Wakayama with me to return my quilt? He certainly was kind to do it for me, for it took a whole day, practically, and it is so unpleasant to go in those crowded streetcars. I had wanted to make a round of my pap's relatives in Wakayama before I left, but seeing the streetcars so crowded, I have just about given up the idea. It ain't worth it. There's no one I really care about, anyhow, except my aged aunt. The others starved me, and I still can't forget it.

I hear that the cost of living in the US is so high that I am rather afraid of going back. I'd better get me [a] job right away. You know, it was so kind of you, and just like you to tell me that I could use your 300 or so dollars that you have.

I feel pretty good nowadays, since I am going home. And all these girls compliment me on my letters that I sent in to the papers. I feel like I am getting some belated recognition. And this morning, Father Dunn says, "What's that guy (Mr. Anderson) going to do when you leave? He won't have anyone to write beautiful articles in the *Nippon Times* anymore." Then Chaplain Ogborne adds, when he gets back to the States and picks up a book that I wrote, he is going to say, "I once knew that girl." All of which is very flattering, but very good for my morale.

Tonight my Uneno-san is coming. She says she is very busy now since two of her pupils are going to be baptized next month. And this morning, at breakfast, Sr. was saying that he has studied and knows that the Protestants were just as intolerant and inhuman in their persecution as the Catholics. Especially the Spanish inquisition—there are many Protestant cases to equal that. Maybe so. I haven't really read up much on such things.

Kyoto, October 31, 1946

Dearest Miye,

Doggone it, the next boat is on November 8, and I won't be on it! O, for once in my life, I do wish that I had money. If I did, I could be on that boat, headed for home. Here, I'd been trying for three days, and had phoned up for no less than thirty times to the US Maritime Commission in Yokohama, but I could not get them. Then, finally, this morning, one operator had the kindness to tell me that the number had been changed. Then I was able to get them right away. They informed me that my brother had not paid yet, and that the boat for November 8 was all filled up, and that they didn't know when the next boat was leaving. Boy, what a letdown! But then, they said it would take three weeks at least for my brother to pay and so I guess the outlook isn't so bad, since it's only two weeks since I first went to see about it. If I don't get home by Christmas, I'm going to swim home!

Hope there's a letter for me from you today. It's past ten in the morning now, so I guess I'll go and see. I've been working on this slang book of ours. I want to get it done before I leave the country. Really, there's a lot of work connected with it. But I enjoy doing it. And I was thinking, why don't I continue with it—even after I get back to the States? And I could publish a book back there. It won't be as easy as here, since there are so many things being published, and lots of people can write much better than I. While over here, there isn't much competition. Kay said we could get it published anytime now, only the price would be at least twenty yen. Whew! That's a lot! You see, the paper is so expensive here. Kay suggested me sending paper from the States after I got there, but I don't know if that is possible. What to do? I want to get it off my mind, though. However, at such a high price, I'm quite certain that it would not sell much. Or would it? I don't know. I know that I wouldn't pay any twenty yen for a little booklet like ours.

It's getting quite cold over here. And we have no heat in our library. Mr. Anderson promised me that here we would have heat just like in the Headquarters building, but that ALSO proved to be another vain promise. But, by golly, I am not going to freeze this winter, too. I'll strike and refuse to come to the library. I have a desk in the Daiken Building in their office, and I could do my work there.

We're going to have a Halloween party at the Station Hotel tonight. I'm not so keen on it—I'd rather sleep. Think I'll go down for refreshments, then come up to my room. I know what I could do—sort out the letters that have accumulated. Seems like I don't have any time at all to call my own, and that makes me sore.

Hate to give you another one-page letter, but I'm doing it.

Kyoto, November 2, 1946

Dearest Miye,

I love you, and am so happy when I think that I can actually see you soon. Your most interesting, as usual, letter came yesterday, and I was so pleased over it that I read Sr. parts of it. I am so proud of myself the way you praise me up and down. I don't care what the others say, but when you say something nice, I just beam all over.

Caught a cold, and had the awfullest headache yesterday, so stayed at home and slept all afternoon. When I got up for supper, my head did ache and I was so sleepy that I didn't go to Catholic prayers as I'd told Cecilia I would. And I had her tell Uneno-san not to come for English lessons. I tried to sleep after that, but I couldn't. Began thinking of how I was soon to leave, and couldn't lie still. So I packed up a box of my junk to send home, then felt better. I want to send everything possible home so that I won't have to lug it around. Want to take only the necessities.

Did I tell you that I heard from Teruko? She is sad that I am leaving. She wouldn't tell me what happened, but said that she would like to see me. But then, she is with her husband, so I guess it isn't too serious. But still, my heart bleeds for her.

I'm so glad that you are taking care of yourself with all the liver, spinach and calcium pills for Little Mary. She must grow up big and strong like me. I can't imagine you big with child. And how will I recognize Nick when I reach San Francisco? O, gosh, when I think of getting back there, I get so excited I don't know what to do.

Just had to answer a phone. These Japanese do have the longest way of [talking but never getting] to the point. When you are in a hurry, it certainly is despairing.

November 5. I forgot completely about your letter until last night. Haven't had time to write to you at all. O, for more time! There are so many things I want to do and ought to do, and no time to do it. There is no one in the library to really administer things. And now they want to get out the circulating collection to all the prefectures. We are going to get more help, but those who come can barely read English, and they cannot judge what books are good to send out, or how to manage the library and the store room. What helpless people the Japanese are! They cannot think for themselves. These people who work here are very willing to help, but they cannot do anything for themselves. I must watch them and tell them what to do.

Also, I want to get letters written, I want to get that slang book off my mind, I must spend so much time with Sr., and I want to go sightseeing. Besides, I must teach my Uneno-san two times a week. I think I'll cut it down to one time a week. I just don't have time for more, and it makes me very angry when I have no time. Besides, I must get my full quota of sleep or I am very cross. So what a fix I am in.

Anyway, I'll just disregard everything else and write to you. But after I get through complaining, I have nothing to write. Wonder if I told you that I'll probably leave in December? Doggone it, I'll have to phone up to Yokohama every few days about that, and that takes so much time, too. No, I can't sit and concentrate upon writing to you. Every little thing that I must do comes up and I begin thinking about it. This morning I got some boxes of my junk sent off to Boston. I like to travel as light as possible. And I got your china set packed up so that I can take it with me. And I should buy some souvenirs, but have not the money. O, bother—there are so many darn things on my mind that I am going to go nuts.

Little Boy Blue came to see me on Sat. night. He phoned up to my room around 9:15 while Sr. was there, and Sr. got awfully angry, saying that that is no time for a boy to call up a decent girl. But his getting angry doesn't bother me anymore. It's his nature, and it blows over in a couple of hours. But he said that I would have to be back by 9:30, so I was not able to talk to Little Boy Blue as I wanted. He is so sweet, such an idealist, and so lost that my heart goes out to him in maternal pride.

Guess I'd better quit and let Ueda-san use the typewriter. Gee, am I sore because I don't have the time I want and need! Last night I went to the tailor's to have my coat fitted. It is quite nice. Had a blanket dyed, and also some material I had dyed that my Blanche sent. Got a letter from her yesterday. She is such a sweet kid. When I think of meeting all the people I used to know, I get kind of afraid because I am such a country hick still.

Just think, Miye, it won't be long now! O, I'm so happy that I'll be able to see you soon!

Kyoto, November 5, 1946

Dearest Kay,

Phoned up Yokohama today, and who should be there but Misa-chan. And she told me that there is such a long waiting list that I wouldn't be able to get on the boat until next year. Well, well. Anyway, I was glad that I found out something definite. What I hate is all the uncertainty they make us suffer. Now, why couldn't the people I phoned up before have given me such simple information? So I don't have to hurry up so much about the book after all. It makes me feel better, for I hate to be rushed as much as you do.

Anyway, I have some of that list for you that Little Boy Blue brought to me. Wish I could work on the index while I am in the mood, but I'm just too darned busy. Guess I'll have to spend another Christmas and New Year's over here, but I don't mind too much since I am in the library. Sr. will be glad to hear it, and I hope you will too. I'll get to see you yet for quite a while.

It's so wonderful—we have two more people working in the library, and two GI replacements in the CIE who are now working in the library. What a relief to get this much-needed personnel! And it's good to have GIs around, for they can get lots done that we foreign nationals and Japanese cannot.

Just wrote to your mother this morning, too. Should have waited till this afternoon and then let her know that I won't leave until next year. I'll write her a card.

Did I tell you that I am having a coat made from a dyed blanket? Went to the tailor's to have it tried on, and it is quite nice. I need a coat very badly.

So I'll write again later. Haven't been hearing from you, so I guess you are in Chiba.[151] Hope you are enjoying yourself.

Kyoto, November 10, 1946

Dearest Miye,

It was certainly good to hear from you on Saturday! I was beginning to feel quite forlorn without any mail at all for about a week. But on Saturday, not only do I hear from you, but also from my mom and Blanche, too. It was a happy day for me!

Miye, I can't get over the marvel of your transformation from tomboy to such a conscientious housewife. It is really amazing how proud you are of your newly painted kitchen and bathroom. And you knitting, and taking lessons in nutrition! Love does work wonders, and Nick is a lucky man! But I'm awfully happy to hear you with your domestic problems and all. And it really does not surprise me, for you are very adaptable anyhow. Little Mary—suppose she turns out to be a boy like the people's upstairs? O, well, you can try again if it is a boy the first time. She ought to be strong and healthy after the attention you are giving to your diet!

I read *A Bell for Adano*[152] as you advised me to. And I did enjoy it immensely. Yes, from what I have seen of the occupation in Japan, that story could be true. Except of course, it might be a little exaggerated. But isn't that Major Jappolo (or however you spell it) wonderful? I just love people like that who fight for the right, and love to see others happy. I'd like to read more of his stories. When I had the book, Hauchecorne saw it and said that he met John Hersey in Tokyo, and that he writes for *Life*. That Hauchecorne gets around, and knows all the writers and artists and Bohemians who come near here.

Today I packed up a parcel to send to you. O, you know what, Sr. got the cutest little white baby dresses for your Little Mary. One is flannel and the other is cotton. I don't know where he ever hunted those rare things down—you can't just go out and buy them. He had to go way over to Osaka to get them, and was so happy when he showed them to me. He said he'd write "From the permanently *onaka-okii hito* [big-bellied person] to the tempo-

151. A city in Chiba Prefecture, about 21 miles southeast of Tokyo.
152. A novel about village life in occupied Italy by John Hersey (1914–93).

rarily *onaka-okii hito*" on it. Isn't that cute? But he is angry with me today, and has gone home. So I got the notion to pack up the things and get them sent off before Little Mary gets too big to wear them. Also, I sent some old sheets of mine, which aren't really sheets, but they were given to me, and I didn't know what to do with them, now that we have our sheets furnished by the hotel, so I thought you might find a use for them. And please tell me if you care for the books I sent, for if you do, I can send you more. But if you don't like them, I won't send you anymore. I like them because they are so handy to carry around. Besides, those are about the only books we can get now.

Kyoto, November 11, 1946

Dearest Miye,

I forgot to tell you before—I heard from Pete Okada![153] You see, a woman who works with him in the Osaka CI&E came to the library with a note from Pete for me. He expects his mother and wife to come in December. I told this woman about the magazines we want to circulate to the schools, and she said that she ought to talk Pete into coming to the library to see about it. I hope he does come, for I am very anxious to see him.

Surely got a lot done this weekend. Got my letters for over a month sorted out, parcels made to send back to the States, and to some relatives in Japan, cleaned out my junk, scrubbed my bathroom with the cleanser Blanche sent me, wrote lots of Japanese duty letters. The only things left for me to do now are to write my English duty letters, to iron, and to darn socks. Sr. is angry with me, so I have a lot of time to myself. I am stubborn, and I will not give in first!

Yesterday I re-read *The Call of the Wild* and enjoyed it. Now I am on *Benjamin Franklin* by Carl Van Doren. Have you ever read it? I am only on the first chapters, and they are nearly the same as his autobiography. I do like old Ben, though. These pocket editions are easy to read in bed, for they are so light that your arm doesn't get tired from holding them. For a change, I am craving reading material, and I am lucky that I have access to a lot of books, even if they are the Armed Service Editions. There are quite a few good books among them.

Remember Shiojima-sensei who used to be in Los Angeles, the teacher and photographer? I got a letter from him today, and was I happy! He is in Tokyo now, and he invited me to stay at his place if I should ever go to Tokyo. He wrote me out a map of his place, put kana along the hard kanji, and in all, was very thoughtful. He's really one swell man, and his wife is equally

153. An acquaintance from the Holiness church in Los Angeles.

nice. They are among the few whose actions and hospitality to me didn't change after fortune turned against me, and I'll surely remember them. Now I feel like going to Tokyo, for I'll have a place to stay where I won't have to "enryo." Maybe I'll go next week, if my brother comes through with my passage money. I'll get my passport, make reservations, visit all the people I want to, and get a lot of things off my mind. I want to see Kay, too.

I hate to admit it, but I do miss Sr. But I'll still be stubborn tonight! It's after nine, so I'll go quietly to bed. If I don't have enough resolution to write some duty letters. I love to write to you, but it is so hard to write to others!

Kyoto, November 14, 1946

Dear Kay,

Let me tell you about my encounter with the RTO. Where shall I start? Well, those passive girls who work there informed me that foreign nationals could not have sleepers anymore. SO I up and phoned the RTO and asked them. They said no. Then I said how about American citizens? They said, "what is your racial origin?" I said Japanese. They said such people were not allowed. So I got all mad and went down to the RTO. First I asked the dumb GI at the window about the sleepers, and if American citizens of Japanese racial extraction could not use the sleepers, and he says no. I forgot—over the phone I asked what orders those were, and they said [Military Regulations, Standing] Orders No. 315. So I asked, first of all at the window to see that circular. Then while he was hunting for it, I pounced on the GI sitting close by, and out came my questions. I said how about GIs—Nisei. He said it's according to those who sign up for them. I said how about ex-GIs, Nisei who have civilian jobs—are they prohibited? He began a long statement about people having to sign up for those sleepers, and a lot of hooey. By that time, the circular was found, and who but the captain came with it, along with around three or four GIs. I wanted to see the circular. Lo and behold it saith "Japanese and German nationals." Was I glad! For I knew I was right. And I told the captain I was an American, and pulled out my identification card to prove it. (By the way, that's very important—get one if at all possible.) He kept saying that we are not American citizens, and I said O so calmly that if we weren't American citizens, then what does that card mean. Finally, he had to admit that I was, but he lamely put in that I must have competent travel orders. Boy, what a victory for our side! When I told Sr. about it, he was so proud of me, and shook both my hands! He loves things like that.

Kyoto, November 26, 1946

Dearest Kay,

I thought I wrote to you last night, but now I don't seem to have it, so I'll start all over. First of all, let me say that I am going to make a carbon copy of this for you and send it off again because I can't bear to think of the buttinskys getting into it and delaying what I want you to know.

O, this whole business [of the library] is making me sick. They can't procure the thing [the building] until the fifteenth of December. And that furniture store that said we could have bookshelves within ten days goes back on its word like a typical Jap, so we can't get them until after the fifth. Mr. Weil is supposed to make out the list of books and mags to go to the schools, and he has been on it for a couple of weeks but no action. Woe is me. I am slowly discovering that it is not only the Japanese Krueger Foundation which cannot be depended upon, but the whole blamed army. Now I know how that librarian of CI&E library in Tokyo felt when he told me that he is tied up with things he wants to do, but can't because they must go through channels, and the higher-ups don't give a hang what happens. Well, I'll be glad when I'm not working for the army. But I guess it's that way no matter where you work, if you are working for someone else.

Sr. is so romantic and kind now that I feel funny. He is sad because I am going to fly away. I keep telling him he ought to get out of this country. He can leave, too. If he only had a job in America as a professor, he would come. So I'm going to get him over if it's the last thing I do.

I read a book, *The Postman Rings Twice*,[154] [the other day] and found lots of slang in there. I'll get you a copy.

At last I am beginning to feel a little normal. Now my shots are over with. And I suppose I have told you many times, but I'm definitely leaving December 29. Sr. said I should stay longer, but he thought it over and said if I should stay longer, they would probably put up all kinds of rules and regulations making it harder for us to get back. You know how it is—they are loose at first and then they tighten up.

Kyoto, November 26, 1946

Dearest Miye,

At long last, I have what I've been wanting for a long time—a typewriter and time to spend with you leisurely. First of all, let me tell you that I'm so sorry, so sorry, that I have been neglecting you. I really had you in my

154. A 1946 novel by James M. Cain (1892–1977). The correct title is *The Postman Always Rings Twice.*

thoughts all the time, but have been so harried that my head has been spinning.

But today, I am taking it easy. I am pretty disgusted with the whole works. And this morning I heard that Gen. Eichelburger put out an order prohibiting the procuring of anything for a month. Which means that I'll be on my way before we can procure this building. O, well, I don't care too much, for now I feel like much of the responsibility for this thing has fallen off my shoulders. Ever since Mr. Weil put his thumb into this pie, I've kind of let it go. And this morning when I asked Mr. Weil about sending out those books, he said that he would do it today if possible. But here it is nearly the end of the day, and as usual, he has not gotten it done. Another thing to complain about—he said that he would be over to the library this afternoon to look over the books. So I was all a-dither, for I had planned to cut and go to Uneno-san's farewell party for Father Gefell. Now I didn't know what to do. I didn't want to miss out on her party, for I knew she would be terribly disappointed, and also, I knew I would be in a fix if Mr. Weil came and found me gone. I was all worried about it when I was waiting for the bus, when along came Uneno-san, and she said that I ought to go to her party, and leave word at the library that in case Mr. Weil came, they should call her house. That was an ideal solution. So I had my cake and ate it too. And after all that anxiety, Mr. Weil didn't show up after all, the dear man.

The party was very nice. The girls had on beautiful kimonos. We had a tea ceremony in their little tea house at first, and how my legs ached![155] It was all impressive and nice, but frankly, I was glad when it was over with. Then the girls gave a marionette show. It was cleverly done. Have you heard of the story, *The Old Man with the Wen*? They did that, taking it from an English translation. But they had to put it all into dialogue, and I helped them with the pronunciation and the wording. They put in original touches of Japanese that Father Gefell knows, such as "*dozo*, *arigato*, *sayonara*, *hatchikai*,"[156] and also [American] terms like "Okay" and "Hubba hubba." So it was very funny and well done. I enjoyed it immensely.

And it was such a relief that Mr. Weil didn't show up at the library! So I came back, and started writing letters. I got a letter off to Elma. Thanks for her address. Also I wrote to Father Dunn, God bless him! Now I have my duty letters off, so I'm giving myself a treat and blabbing off to you.

Did I tell you that Little Boy Blue came on Sunday? He is really such a sweet idealist, and a wonderful friend. He said that he would miss me sorely.

155. It is obligatory to sit on one's legs throughout the formal tea ceremony. For the uninitiated visitor, this can be a painful ordeal.

156. "Please," "thank you," "good-bye," and "eighth floor" (where the Chaplains' section was).

And he does say some of the cleverest things—I wish I could remember them all. What he said touched me, though—that he would lose a dear friend who could not be replaced. Yes, I have very few friends, but the few friends I am lucky to have are true and tried.

Sr. also looks so sad because I am going to leave him. Now he doesn't have his fits of anger at all. Well, I hope he's learned a lesson. My gosh, I don't see how I stood his getting angry like he did. I think that is why people are not really kind to him—it's because he scares them off by becoming all [inflamed] or excited. While as for me, he did scare me and repel me at first by his fits, but after I found out that they are so transient, and mean nothing at all, I could look on coolly in a nonki way. Because he is really wonderful at heart. And if it's the last thing I do, I'm going to get him a job in the US teaching, and get him out of this country where no one appreciates him. But he's awfully thoughtful and kind now. I hate to leave him, in a way. Yes, it's only he and Kay I am sorry to leave. As for the others, I don't give a hang.

My whole horizon has brightened up. Now a new life will start out for me. I'm afraid I'll be sadly disillusioned after a while, but right now, the illusions are so delicious!

It's nearly 4:30. Guess I'd better close up the library for the days are getting short. As Kay said, maybe it's better I'll be leaving the library, for it will be hard for me to be bossed around by two Americans, after having built it up from nothing, and doing as I pleased.

What a relief to get all my shots over with, too. I've sent off nearly everything I am going to send. I'll have your box of china that Sr. gave you, and three suitcases to take with me only.

Sent in my request for travel orders today. Am keeping my fingers crossed, for I must go to Tokyo Saturday and put the final touches on my getting back. There are lots of people who want to go back, and all kinds of people go *before* the Nisei—who are American citizens. Sr. said, too, that pretty soon they might start making all kinds of regulations restricting our getting back to the States, so it's best to go while the going is good. Your advice was sound, after all. Now when I look back, I wonder how I could have been such a fool as to even think of staying here longer than I have to. I want Kay to get out as soon as she graduates, too. America might be changed, but I think it could never be as bad as Japan.

So I'll be leaving you. I don't get any mail nowadays at all. You're the only faithful one. I guess the others are busy, too, so I can't complain.

You know, Miye, Kay and I have gotten the brightest idea! I'm so happy every time I think of it. Well, you know, the army censors our letters inter-island (Jap mail). It delays our letters for weeks, which is very trying for us. So one time when I got a letter with the censored tape over one end, I merely pasted a piece of paper over the envelope and sent it back, with Kay's address. In that way, the censors will think that letter has been censored and will leave their dirty fingers off it. We've sent one envelope back and forth about three times now, and it's still going. She tears off my paper with her address on it, and puts on another paper with my address. In that way we get letters to each other within two or three days, and it's really wonderful. Guess we've outsmarted those stupid censors! We've got two envelopes like that, so we get our mail quite regularly now. And they used to love to censor our mail. Guess it's because we put what we think in them.

Kyoto, November 28, 1946

Dearest Miye,

I certainly love holidays! The only trouble with them is that we don't have enough of them. Today is Thanksgiving. This morning I worked on that slang, and then went to get a permanent. We have a barber shop and beauty shop for our own use, so it is wonderful—no waiting at all. And it is right in this hotel, too.

Only three more weeks! Only one more month and I'll be seeing you! I can hardly believe it is true. I got my travel orders yesterday, and I'm all set to go tomorrow night. I'm going to spend just one day in Tokyo, because I get so tired out, and don't get over it for days and days afterwards. If I come home Sunday morning, maybe I can sleep all day and recuperate. Only Pete O. said he might come over Sunday, so that is all the more reason to come home.

Sr. didn't come home last night. You know, many times he has to teach in Osaka until late so that he comes around ten. Then he comes to my room, and we have tea and whatever we happen to have around. I must have my full quota of sleep, so I often go to bed around eight or nine, then get up around ten and then go to bed after he leaves. My mother, who told me never to have a man in the same room with me, would be shocked if she saw me now. But Sr. surely is honorable, and he's never said things like he did once upon a time. He certainly is wonderful, and so refreshing after the sex-minded Japanese and the nearly equally sex-minded GIs.

What I started to tell you was that last night I was all tired out, and took a bath, washed my hair, and went to bed early. But I guess it's just a force of habit, I got up around eleven and had to have some tea. And Sr. didn't come home last night. I surely missed him. I discovered he didn't come home last night because I phoned him up this morning early. It's taking me the longest time to get to what I want to tell you. All this is merely the background for what I want to pour forth on you. You see, it suddenly struck me how truthful was what Kay said, namely, that there is such a great difference between those who work for the army and those who don't. I went to see Miss Clapp, the American teacher at Doshisha University yesterday. She is an American citizen, just recently come from the States. But she and her friend, Miss Hibbard, have to use the international post office; thus they can send and receive only cards. And it takes one month for anything to get to them.

In contrast, look at these dependents over here. They surely live "the life of Riley" over here. They moved into the very best houses in Kyoto—houses of millionaires. Lots of servants they have for next to nothing. They get fresh food and the choice of whatever is at the PX. There used to be an ex-GI living here with his Russian wife. Cecilia said she goes to see them, now in their new home. They have FOUR servants—a cook, a maid, one houseboy, one man to take care of the furnace. The young bride is so bored with all that time on her hands. This surely isn't very educational for her to become used to, then have to get along like an American housewife later.

The other day when I was waiting for the army bus to come around, three buses for the dependents came while I was waiting, mind you. And not one of them had a soul on it. I've yet to see anyone on one of those buses. Yet, they are running so frequently. Remember, this in Japan where private autos are almost nonexistent among the Japanese, and here gasoline is a very rare item. And the Japanese have to wait literally hours for the streetcars. While we, civilian employees of the army, and GIs who can't get other means of transportation, have to ride these buses. Which we have to wait fifteen minutes or more for.

But the other day when I went to the Imperial University, I could see how life for the students was—how it contrasted with ours. There is a serious shortage of electricity in Japan now, so that only important factories get electricity all the time. But anything connected with the army always has electricity. At the Imperial University, those students were not able to conduct experiments in physics and chemistry because they stop the electricity. And look how the Headquarters building is always brightly lit up at night—when no one is there. And further, look how those tennis courts, where no one ever plays, are brightly lit up night after night for the convenience of the army. It must take a tremendous lot of electricity to light up those courts every night. And no electricity for the poor students to even do any experiments.

Miss Clapp was saying that she was dreading the electricity strike since they do all their cooking by electricity. And they get gas only one hour a day. And she is a wonderful Christian woman who loves the Japanese people. If anyone should get any privileges, it should be she. But no, she isn't connected with the army, so she has a hard time. There ain't no justice around here. And again I repeat: I'm glad I'm getting out of here.

It's nice and sunny today. Sr. had to teach this morning, but this afternoon ought to be free. Hope we can go someplace. Yesterday, from the street the palace grounds looked so beautiful with those majestic gingko trees with their dark brown branches and trunks contrasting with the bright yellow leaves. It really took my breath away with all its grand beauty. I'd like to see all the grounds.

Miss Clapp said the strike has been delaying the mail. I hope I get some of the things I should be getting. Emma said she sent some things, and I want to get them before I leave.

I must go down for lunch. We're going to have Thanksgiving dinner at night now. Lots of foreign nationals kicked, so we have much better food now.

Kyoto, December 3, 1946

Dear Miye,

When you receive this letter you'd better not write to me anymore since I am sure to be on the boat by around the 20th. So I think I'll quit work around the 18th and go up to Yokohama. Gee, Miye, I'm so thrilled to think that I'll actually see you soon.

Now I don't have time to write at all. I just didn't want to neglect you too much. Went up to Yokohama last Saturday. And came home that night. O, a big happening. Pete Okada came over Sunday. Sr. was madder than a nest of hornets because I wasn't going to spend the Sunday with him, but it was worth it. Good old Pete! He's surely grown up. And I see how much older he is. So I am older too, although I don't realize it. He surely has a fine choice of words. I think he will make a wonderful leader of Nisei. He came over in the morning, then had lunch at our hotel. We gabbed the whole afternoon, then visited the Nishi Honganji, where he took some pictures. He has a lot of good sense, and I'm sure he is doing a lot of good over here. I only wish I'd gotten in touch with him sooner. And just when his wife and mother reach here, I think I'll be gone.

Hope Sr. does come to America too. Kay is coming the early part of next year. I think the sooner he gets out of this country, the better.

I'll write again when I have a little more time. Guess I'd better go back to the office now.

Kyoto, December 4, 1946

Dearest Kay,

Today I felt like an ambassador of goodwill when I went to the Daimaru Dept. store and talked to the salesgirls about America. It was mostly questions from them, and me trying to struggle with the answers. But it was rather satisfactory, after all.

Went to see Miss Clapp, and she said she would give me letters to people she knows in Boston, and they could advise me what to do. That's something to rely upon. And I'll get letters from Mr. Anderson. Another thing—he said I would have to go up to Tokyo to meet the next librarian, so I might be up again after all. After I come back, I feel lousy for the next 3 or 4 days, but after that, I get an itching foot again.

Incorrigible.

Ain't that impressive, that million-dollar word?

Tomorrow I must participate in some discussion about the new Kyoto Joshi Dai they are going to set up. O, you know what—that Kinoshit in person came today! Said she saw about me in the papers. And she gave me some sweet potatoes, which I gave to the people working in the library. God, her talking reminded me of the awful time I spent in fear and trembling of her, and I never want to see her again! She is staying in that house in Kyoto. I never told her I was going back to the U.S. Boy, it would be fun to sling some final mud on her, but she isn't worth the time it would take to do it.

Kyoto, December 12, 1946

Dearest Miye,

Mr. Weil is dead. Why do such things happen? He left us so carefree and nonchalantly. He was flying to Kyushu when the plane crashed. We just heard the shocking news yesterday. What a pity. He was a fine young man. Even if I wrote a lot against him, I know that down at heart he was a splendid man. That threw a blanket of gloom over our whole office. Good thing he wasn't married, for his wife would be awfully broken up.

I am feeling way down in the dumps this morning. I have failed. You see, Kay and I went to see Miss Clapp yesterday, and had the liveliest conversation with her and two American teachers at the Army School. The two women left before we did, and when we were together with Miss Clapp, she confided that they didn't have much wood. I said that there are many old boxes and pieces of left-over wood at Daiken, so I'd try to get her some. So this morning I asked the Japanese man who is in charge of the laborers, and he said he couldn't [give us any], but if Mr. Anderson asked Capt. Sawbridge, the Headquarters Commandant, he could give us some. So I asked Mr. Anderson, and he said that they were not supposed to have anything to do with the missionaries, they had come over with the understanding that they would live off the land, and there was nothing that he could do. That left me flat. And poor Miss Clapp and Miss Hibbard have to be in a cold building all day; to have to come home [then] to no fireplace is awful. They said that the wood at Daiken goes to the dependents. Ugh, those dependents are swimming in plenty. And the laborers at Daiken used to take home that wood, and I betcha they still do. Well, I haven't given up, yet.

Wow, is it cold today! It is cold and cloudy and dreary. I'm certainly glad I'm getting out of here. They are getting stricter and stricter in everything. When the army first came in, we could get supplies and stuff very freely if we wanted. And look at them now, even particular about the old wood they throw away.

It's like a dream that I can actually go back home! It's really too good to be true, and I'm afraid something will come along and knock all my pretty plans to pieces. Right now, I am planning to go to my sister Emma's (the one who was in Honolulu) place in Monterey for a week or so, and also I want to see you in Richmond, in an interesting condition, as the saying goes. Then I want to go to my brother George's in Chicago. I'll leave them before my welcome wears too thin, and then back to my aged parents. I don't know exactly what I will do, but I am thinking of going back to school. Maybe Boston University if I can make it. I like this library work so much that I am thinking of taking a course in library [science], which will take me three years more. But what do I care? I want to take life easy, and this working doesn't coincide with my idea of what life should be. Just so I have enough to get along, I don't care what happens.

And Teruko gave me the sweetest kimono! And the best letter! I'm going to translate it one of these days. Funny, though, she says the same thing as you—it won't matter if I go to America, for our souls can communicate. Isn't that wonderful?[157]

157. This is the last of Mary's letters from Japan. She set sail for home on January 1, 1947.

Epilogue

Epilogue

In closing her "Dear Kay" term paper, Mary wrote, "One chapter of my life has ended. The one thing I have gained from being in Japan is that I have the confidence to face anything. Come what may, I will survive. Also, I realize the value of friends and family. My true friends never left me, no matter what. These relationships are the most precious thing in the world, and far outweigh any material possessions."

Returning to the United States and reuniting with her friends and family was a joyous occasion for Mary. However, rebuilding a life after long years of separation and hardship was neither a simple nor an easy task. At the end of the war, Mary's once close community of family and friends were, like so many other Nikkei families, scattered all over the country. Miye returned to California to her husband. George and his family stayed in the Chicago area. Emma moved to Hawaii, where her husband, Hilo, resumed his duties as a Methodist minister. Mary's parents stayed in Boston, where her father, then sixty-eight, found work as a custodian at the Boston Center for Adult Education. After graduating from South Dakota Wesleyan, Blanche joined the elder Kimotos in Boston and enrolled in graduate school at Boston University.

After a joyful reunion with Miye in California, Mary took the train to join her parents and youngest sister in Boston. She immediately found work as a cook at the Milton Academy, an exclusive private school outside of Boston. Although she had completed the program of study at Joshi Dai, Japanese women's colleges did not at that time issue university degrees, so Mary enrolled in Boston University in order to get her diploma.

While in Boston, Mary met and fell in love with Yoneo Paul Tomita. Ironically, Paul had been a political science student from Japan who, like Mary, had been stranded when the two countries went to war. During the war years, he had managed to work in an Episcopalian monastery. When peace came, Paul tried to get a job with the State Department so he could return to Japan to participate in its democratization. However, as a Japanese national ineligible for American citizenship, he was warned that there was no guarantee that he would ever be able to return to the United States. Although she agonized over the decision, Mary understandably found it impossible to return to Japan under that condition.

Paul and Mary got married in 1948 and moved to Oakland, California, where Paul became a gardener, an all too familiar experience for many well-educated minority men in those days. Despite their poverty, Paul insisted that Mary attend the University of California to pursue her dream of a doctorate in Far Eastern history. But the arrival of two babies and financial strains forced Mary to give up and opt instead for Master's degrees in Oriental languages and U.S. history. Then, in order to find employment, she took courses to get teaching and librarianship certificates. With those credentials Mary worked for many years as a school librarian while raising a family.

Mary and Kay's book of American slang never did get published. Finding a Japanese publisher was a full-time job, and Mary and Kay both had another priority: getting back to the United States. Kay was able to return to the United States in late 1947 and settled in Los Angeles. Although they continued to correspond for a time, Mary's romance with Paul, their marriage, and the first hectic years of raising a family and working took their toll. Mary and Kay eventually lost touch with each other.

Although Mary did fulfill her promise to write on behalf of Sr. in search of a teaching position in the United States, she lost contact with him soon after she settled in Boston. Recently, through the Spanish embassy, Mary was able to contact him and discovered that he had married a Japanese woman and has two children and two grandchildren. He lives in the same house in Nara. Mary lost touch with Dr. Simms and others of her close friends during the occupation days.

Ironically, Mary did somewhat better when it came to keeping up with some of her Japanese friends. As Mary reported in her letters, the Nagatas' son Yoshiya died in the war. But Iza-chan survived and went on to invent a revolutionary method of producing capacitors, eventually turning a garage operation into two large factories. Two of his four children, Midori and Ken, came to the United States to study; both stayed with Mary during their student years. His daughter Midori married and settled in the United States. Miyoko, Iza-chan's sister, faithfully sends Mary a present each Christmas.

Among Mary's Tokyo Joshi Dai classmates, Odashima Teruko is now a widow living in the Tokyo area. Mary's trips to Japan have been the occasion for several happy reunions with these and other classmates. On her last visit, Mary went to the Joshi Dai campus with Teruko and visited their old teacher, Mrs. Kitamura.

One of Mary's former roommates in Tokyo, Yamada Masako, died of pleurisy during the war, but Mary stays in touch with the others, Youkiye Yamada (Crider) and Clara Iwamoto (Seko). Natsuko Kitagawa, a classmate at Waseda International Institute, lived in Honolulu until she passed away in 1994. Mary's two students in the prewar years, the Shiojima sisters, Yoshiko and Kiyoko, continue to be good friends. Mary also remains close to Tomi-san, with whom she has stayed on each of her six trips back to Japan.

As for Mary's siblings, Emma lives in Honolulu, where her husband, Hilo, was a pastor for several churches before becoming Chaplain for the University of Hawaii. He died in 1982. Emma became a librarian and is now retired. Their one daughter, Emma Lee Yu, lives in New York City. George is retired and lives in El Cerrito, California. His wife, Betty, died in 1991. Their daughter, Diana, lives in Paris. Fred Suzukawa, Betty's brother, spent a career in the army and is now retired. Mary's youngest sister, Blanche, is a child psychiatrist in Michigan and has three children and a grandchild.

Mary's parents stayed on in Boston until her father died in 1953. Her mother came to live with Mary and Paul until her death in 1968. Two years later Paul Tomita died suddenly, felled by a heart attack. Mary was devastated. A further tragedy followed in 1988, when her elder son committed suicide. To her great regret, Mary had not known that he suffered from schizophrenia. Toyoji, her other son, a musician and landscape contractor, is married and lives in an adjoining unit of her home.

After Nick Nishita finished his graduate degree in soil science at Berkeley, he and Miye moved to Los Angeles. Nick became a researcher at UCLA, and Miye went to work as a hospital laboratory technician. The Nishitas had four children. Their daughter, Mary's namesake, received a doctorate in education from UCLA, taught school, and now resides in Hawaii. Miye and Mary remained the closest of friends through the years. After a long and valiant fight against cancer, Miye died in 1991, shortly after this project was begun. Mary remains active in church and community affairs.

Index

Index

In this index an "f" after a number indicates a separate reference on the next page, and an "ff" indicates separate references on the next two pages. A continuous discussion over two or more pages is indicated by a span of page numbers, e.g., "pp. 57–58." *Passim* is used for a cluster of references in close but not continuous sequence.

Library of Congress Cataloging-in-Publication Data

Tomita, Mary Kimoto.
Dear Miye: letters home from Japan, 1939–1946 / Mary Kimoto Tomita ; edited with an introduction and notes by Robert G. Lee.
p. cm.—(Asian America)
Includes index.
ISBN 0-8047-2419-9 (cl.) : ISBN 0-8047-2967-0 (pbk.)
1. Tomita, Mary Kimoto—Correspondence. 2. Japanese Americans—Correspondence. 3. Japanese Americans—Japan—Correspondence. 4. World War, 1939–1945—Japanese Americans. I. Lee, Robert G. II. Title. III. Series.
E184.J3T65 1995
940.53'1503956073—dc20 94-24110 CIP

⊗This book is printed on acid-free, recycled paper. It has been typeset in 10½/12½ Adobe Minion by Tseng Information Systems.

Original printing 1995

Last figure below indicates year of this printing:

04 03 02